Trusts and Estates 2019/20

Trusts and Estates 2019/20

Iris Wünschmann-Lyall MA (Cantab) TEP

and

Chris Erwood CTA ATT TEP

Based upon the original work by Matthew Hutton MA (Oxon) CTA (Fellow) AIIT TEP

Series General Editor: Mark McLaughlin CTA (Fellow) ATT (Fellow) TEP

Bloomsbury Professional

LONDON • DUBLIN • EDINBURGH • NEW YORK • NEW DELHI • SYDNEY

Bloomsbury Professional
Bloomsbury Publishing Plc

41–43 Boltro Road, Haywards Heath, RH16 1BJ, UK

BLOOMSBURY and the Diana logo are trademarks of Bloomsbury Publishing Plc

Reprinted 2019

British Library Cataloguing-in-Publication Data

A catalogue record for this book is available from the British Library.

ISBN: 978-1-52650-998-7

Typeset by Evolution Design & Digital Ltd (Kent)
Printed and bound by CPI Group (UK) Ltd, Croydon, CR0 4YY

To find out more about our authors and books visit www.bloomsburyprofessional.com. Here you will find extracts, author information, details of forthcoming events and the option to sign up for our newsletters

Preface

This is the fourteenth year this book has been published as part of the Core Tax Annuals series from Bloomsbury Professional, comprising a set of six titles which deal with the principal taxes. The rationale behind the Tax Annuals series is to develop a user-friendly practical theme, so as to provide for accountants, lawyers and other professional advisers (and, indeed, for taxpayers themselves) a core set of tax annuals from which they can easily find effective guidance on the mainstream areas of UK tax law.

As in previous editions, this book aims to illustrate with examples and tables the primary points of legislation and practice. Although packed full of relevant data, a book of this length can essentially do no more than address the day-to day-fundamentals of the tax system as it relates to trusts and deceased estates. However, it does introduce the reader to some of the more complex aspects of the UK tax system routinely met in practice and aims to provide useful guidance and commentary. The introduction on page 1 explains how the book is structured, dealing in turn with the tax aspects of:

- starting a trust;
- running a trust;
- ending a trust;
- disabled trusts; and
- deceased estates.

The taxation of trusts and estates, whilst it remains a complex and misunderstood area, has not changed significantly in the last two years but successive legislation has impacted directly on the relevant property trust regime affecting the calculation of the ten-year and hence exit charges. The government's original consultation process on *Inheritance Tax: Simplifying charges on trusts* ran its course and many of the earlier proposals (ie settlement nil rate band) were quietly dropped to be replaced by targeted anti-avoidance measures, such as anti-fragmentation of nil rate band for the popular pilot trust. A further consultation on how to make the taxation of trusts simpler, fairer and more transparent was launched in November 2018 and closed on 28 February 2019 with the final report expected in due course.

The government's focus continues to favour the introduction of penal anti-avoidance provisions in relation to offshore taxation and increased penalties as evidenced by *Finance (No 2) Act 2017, Finance Act 2018* and *Finance Act 2019*. This book also considers compliance issues and in particular sets out the stringent penalty regime introduced by *Finance Act 2007*.

We would like to extend our special thanks to Matthew Hutton, the original author of the much earlier editions of this book. The broad structure of that original edition is largely unchanged but over the years the depth and breadth of content and incorporation of pertinent examples has expanded considerably to reflect the major legislative changes.

Chris Erwood
Iris Wünschmann-Lyall
June 2019

Contents

Table of Examples

[*All references are to paragraph number*]

Chapter 10 Deceased estates: practical IHT considerations

Chapter 11 Deceased estates: income tax and CGT

Chapter 12 Deceased estates: post-death re-arrangements

Table of statutes

[All references are to paragraph numbers]

Table of statutory instruments and other guidance

[All references are to paragraph numbers]

Table of cases

[*All references are to paragraph numbers*]

Abbreviations and references

Abbreviations

The following abbreviations are used in this book.

A&M	accumulation and maintenance
AIM	Alternative Investment Market
App	Appendix
APR	agricultural property relief
BPR	business property relief
CA	Court of Appeal
CGT	capital gains tax
ChD	Chancery Division
Col	column
CTT	capital transfer tax
DLA	disability living allowance
DTR	double taxation relief
EIS	Enterprise Investment Scheme
ESC	Extra-statutory Concession
FA	Finance Act
FOTRA	free of tax to residents abroad
GAAR	general anti-abuse rule
HL	House of Lords
HM	Her Majesty's
HMRC	Her Majesty's Revenue and Customs
ICTA 1988	Income and Corporation Taxes Act 1988
IHT	inheritance tax
IHTA 1984	Inheritance Tax Act 1984
IHTM	HMRC Inheritance Tax Manual
IPDI	immediate post-death interest
IRPR	Inland Revenue Press Release
ITA 2007	Income Tax Act 2007
ITTOIA 2005	Income Tax (Trading and Other Income) Act 2005
NI	National Insurance
NRB	nil rate band
OEIC	open-ended investment company
para	paragraph
PET	potentially exempt transfer

PIP	personal independent payment
PPR	principal private residence
PR	personal representative
Pt	Part
QB	Queen's Bench Division
RAT	rate applicable to trusts
s	section
Sch	Schedule
SDLT	stamp duty land tax
SDRT	stamp duty reserve tax
SEIS	seed enterprise investment scheme
SI	Statutory Instrument
SP	Inland Revenue Statement of Practice
SpC	Special Commissioners
SRT	Statutory residence test
TCGA 1992	Taxation of Chargeable Gains Act 1992
TMA 1970	Taxes Management Act 1970
TNRB	transferable nil rate band
TSEM	HMRC Trusts, Settlements and Estates Manual
TSI	transitional serial interest

References

AC	Law Reports, Appeal Cases
All ER	All England Law Reports
STC	Simon's Tax Cases
STC (SCD)	Simon's Tax Cases, Special Commissioners' Decisions
STI	Simon's Tax Intelligence
TC	Official Reports of Tax Cases

NB: The masculine gender, wherever it appears, includes the feminine.

Chapter 1

Introduction

1.1 This book is a quick reference guide for trustees, personal representatives and their professional advisers to the tax aspects of dealing with trusts and deceased estates, specifically in satisfying their various compliance responsibilities to HMRC. To this end, the book adopts a compliance-based approach, though within its pages are numerous suggestions both for mitigating tax liabilities and for simplifying the administration involved in trusts and deceased estates. The book deals only with UK-resident trusts. The taxes covered are income tax, capital gains tax, inheritance tax and stamp duties (including stamp duty on shares and stamp duty land tax on land).

This book is designed specifically for ease of use, enabling the reader to find the information required quickly and without having to wade through a mass of detail, which may be irrelevant to him. It is not (and cannot be) a complete guide to the tax aspects of UK resident trusts and deceased estates, however.

The introductory chapter discusses the concept of a trust and distinguishes trusts from estates. **Chapters 2** to **8** deal with trusts: specifically the tax implications of starting, running and then bringing them to an end. **Chapters 9** to **13** of the book are concerned with deceased estates, including a discussion of the penalty regime in **Chapter 9**.

Reference is made throughout the book to various HMRC forms, which can be accessed from HMRC's website at www.gov.uk.

Compliance responsibilities within HMRC can be summarised as follows. Income tax and capital gains tax are dealt with by HMRC Trusts (formerly IR Trusts), based at Nottingham, Edinburgh and Belfast. Income tax and capital gains tax in deceased estates are generally handled by the tax district that dealt with the affairs of the deceased when he was alive. Only in a complex estate will compliance be dealt with by a specialist division of HMRC Trusts in Cardiff. See Chapters 4, 6 and 9 for details of the compliance responsibilities of trustees and personal representatives.

A brief word about tax years used in this book. The tax rates, allowances and exemptions mentioned are generally those for 2019/20, unless mentioned otherwise.

A consultation exercise was launched by HMRC in December 2003 on the modernisation and simplification of the income and capital gains taxation of trusts. From tax year 2004/05 the rate of income tax and capital gains tax paid by trustees was aligned with the marginal rate of individuals, with income tax of discretionary and accumulation trusts payable at 32.5% for dividends and otherwise 40%: rising to 42.5% and 50% respectively from 2010/11. The punitive income tax rates for discretionary and accumulation trusts have been reduced to 37.5% for dividends and 45% for all other income from 6 April 2013. Further changes were introduced in *Finance Act 2016* and a new basic tax rate for dividends of 7.5% with a higher trust tax rate for dividends of 38.1% was introduced from 6 April 2016. These rates are subject to the proviso that the first £1,000 of income in any tax year attracts the tax rate which normally would apply to this income source, for example 7.5% to dividends and the standard rate of 20% to all other income.

A reform of capital gains tax took effect for 2008/09, introducing a uniform rate of tax of 18% for all taxpayers, including trustees. This generous rate was increased to 28% for gains realised by trustees and personal representatives of deceased persons on or after 23 June 2010. From 6 April 2016 this was reduced to 20% with an additional 8% rate for gains on disposals of residential property which do not benefit from principal private residence relief. Indexation allowance and taper relief have been abolished and entrepreneurs' relief (see **5.32–5.34**) has been introduced. The above said, however, the most significant tax reform within the context of this book remains the 'alignment' of the inheritance tax regime for trusts which took effect from 2006/07 (see, generally, **Chapter 6**).

A Consultation was launched by the Office of Tax Simplification in April 2018 on the simplification of inheritance tax. Their first report was published in November 2018. The overall aim of this review was to identify areas with unnecessary complexity and to work with HMRC on administrative changes to simplify the administration of estates.

The Chancellor announced in the Autumn 2017 Budget that in 2018 the government would publish a consultation on how to make the taxation of trusts simpler, fairer and more transparent. This Consultation was launched in November 2018 and closed on 28 February 2019. The final report has not yet been published at the date of publication and the government will consult on proposed specific reforms in due course.

Chapter 2

Background

SIGNPOSTS

- **What is a trust** – Trustees hold the legal ownership of property for the benefit of the beneficiaries. A trustee is liable for 'breach of trust' if he does not follow the terms of the trust deed (see **2.1–2.4**).
- **'Components' of a trust** – A trust will have a settlor, trustees, a trust fund, a trust period and beneficiaries. All these are defined within the trust deed (see **2.5**).
- **Different types of trust** – The type of trust and its taxation consequences depend on the terms of the trust deed. *FA 2006* radically changed the tax treatment for the different types of trust (see **2.6–2.11**).
- **Trusts distinguished from estates** – Trusts can be made during lifetime, or arise under a will or on intestacy. Sometimes there is an overlap, when a trust is established while the administration period continues (see **2.16–2.18**).
- **Tax treatment** – The income tax and inheritance tax rates depend on the type of trust. Tax rates during the administration period of an estate are different from tax rates applying to trusts. Capital gains tax is charged at 20% from 6 April 2016 with an additional rate of 8% for disposals of residential property which do not benefit from private residence relief (see **2.19**).

WHAT IS A TRUST?

Types of ownership

2.1 A trust or settlement is a long-established creature of the English legal system. Ownership of property may be divided into two categories; legal and beneficial (or equitable). A trust makes use of this distinction by giving to trustees the legal ownership of property, to hold that property for the enjoyment of the various beneficiaries. Legal ownership implies the registration of property, eg land or company shares, so that HM Land Registry or the Registrar of Companies would consider the trustees to be the owners of the trust property (and would not be concerned with the trusts of the particular settlement). Note that a 'settlement' can be wider than a trust for tax purposes; for example, a joint bank account which is funded by a gift will be a settlement in certain circumstances.

The law was examined in *Wagstaff v Revenue and Customs Commissioners* [2014] UKFTT 43 (TC). The three certainties to establish a trust: certainty of intention, subject matter and objects were referred to by the Tribunal and need to be present to establish a valid trust.

The beneficiaries

2.2 All the persons who may benefit under the trust should be described in the trust deed, either by name or by reference to a class. For example, beneficiaries can be defined as 'the children of the settlor and their descendants', or they can be individually named.

Some settlements include powers to add or remove beneficiaries.

Trustee powers

2.3 A person who, typically with others, owns property as a trustee is treated in relation to the trust quite separately from his own or beneficial property, both under the general law and for tax purposes. Being a trustee implies a power, and indeed duty, to manage the trust property for the benefit of the beneficiaries. These powers of management may be found under the general law, eg the *Trustee Act 1925*, the *Trustee Investments Act 1961* and, most recently, the *Trustee Act 2000*, all as amplified or extended by the provisions of the trust deed.

Focus

- Trustees cannot just 'sit on the property'. It is important to convene annual trustees' meetings, at which the investments and the needs of the beneficiaries are considered.
- Records of any decisions and discussions should be kept.

The duty of care to be exercised by trustees can be found in *Trustee Act 2000. Section 1* states:

> '(1) Whenever the duty under this subsection applies to a trustee, he must exercise such care and skill as is reasonable in the circumstances, having regard in particular–

(a) to any special knowledge or experience that he has or holds himself out as having, and

(b) if he acts as trustee in the course of a business or profession, to any special knowledge or experience that it is reasonable to expect of a person acting in the course of that kind of business or profession.'

The statutory duty can be excluded by contrary express indication in the trust deed – see also STEP Standard Provisions.

Trustees' decisions

2.4 Ideally a trust will have at least two trustees (and, in relation to land, under English law there must be at least two). Trustees must generally act unanimously, though the trust deed may give power to act by a majority. Generally, the terms of the deed should be followed strictly; otherwise, the trustees may be personally liable for 'breach of trust'.

Sometimes a trustee may also be a beneficiary, though in that event the trustee must be very careful about exercising trust powers for his own benefit; typically the trust deed will require him not to be involved in any decisions that benefit him. The same could apply also where a trustee (not being a beneficiary) can benefit in relation to trust property, for example where the trust fund includes shares in a private company and the trustee also owns shares himself.

A standard legal definition of a trust

2.5

> 'A trust is an equitable obligation, binding a person (called a trustee) to deal with property (called trust property) owned by him or a separate fund, distinct from his own private property for the benefit of persons (called beneficiaries or, in old cases, cestuis que trust), of whom he may himself be one and any one of whom may enforce the obligation: any act or neglect on the part of a trustee which is not authorised or excused by the terms of the trust instrument, or by law, is called a breach of trust.' (Underhill and Hayton, *Law of Trusts and Trustees*, 17th edn, p 2)

A trust (or settlement) will have:

- A **settlor**, which is the person who makes the settlement. Ideally, each settlement will have only one settlor, though some might have husband and wife as joint settlors. Any person who adds property to a settlement by a gift will be a settlor in relation to that settlement (which may involve anti-avoidance rules for the various taxes, discussed at **4.24–4.31** for income tax, **5.21–5.22** for capital gains tax – albeit repealed from 2008/09

– and **6.18–6.23** for inheritance tax). *FA 2006*, in introducing generally conformed definitions for both income tax and capital gains tax purposes, specifically defines the term 'settlor' for these two taxes. Regulations made pursuant to *FA 2005, s 103* ensure that for all tax and other legal purposes members of a registered civil partnership are treated as a married couple. It may be that, after 4 December 2005, the members of a registered civil partnership together make a settlement, though as with husband and wife it is considered preferable for each settlor to have their own settlement.

- A **trust deed**, setting out the terms of the trust, including identification of the beneficiaries.
- **Trustees**, who manage the trust property and accept responsibility for the trust.
- The **trust fund**, which may consist of an initial nominal sum, eg £10 followed by a transfer of the substantive trust property; alternatively, the substantive trust property may be transferred to the trustees at outset. Other property may be transferred in future.
- A **trust period** (except for charitable trusts) within which the trust must come to an end: see **8.1–8.3**. This is likely to be 80 years for trusts created prior to 6 April 2010, and, following the *Perpetuities and Accumulations Act 2009*, 125 years for trusts created after 5 April 2010. Ideally, the trust deed will specify the 'default beneficiaries' who will enjoy such capital as may remain at the end of the trust period.
- A **governing law**, assumed in this book to be the law of England and Wales (Scottish law rules, in particular, being different).

Focus

Sometimes, the person named as settlor in a trust deed may not be the settlor for tax purposes. This can arise when funds are added to the trust by a person other than the settlor named in the trust deed.

DIFFERENT TYPES OF TRUST

Discretionary trusts

2.6 A discretionary trust gives to the trustees a discretion as to how to pay the income between a class of income beneficiaries. Alternatively, the trust deed may allow the trustees, instead of paying out income for a particular tax year, to 'accumulate' that income. Such power of accumulation may operate only within a particular period of time, for example 21 years from the date of the trust deed. This statutory restriction has been removed by the *Perpetuities* *and Accumulations Act 2009* for trusts created after 5 April 2010: see **Chapter 8** for the impact on existing trusts. Accumulations of income are added to capital, though the trust deed may allow past accumulations to be paid out as income of the current year.

Discretion over capital is different; the capital beneficiaries may be different to the income beneficiaries.

Accumulation and maintenance ('A&M') – before 22 March 2006

2.7 The A&M is a special type of discretionary trust, broadly for the benefit of children under the age of 25 or, from 6 April 2008, 18. For income tax and capital gains tax purposes, it is treated exactly like a discretionary (or 'relevant property') trust until either a beneficiary has a right to the income or becomes absolutely entitled at age 18.

The inheritance tax treatment, following *FA 2006*, is complex. A&M trusts, where all the beneficiaries had an interest in possession on 21 March 2006, or where the beneficiaries become entitled at age 18, do not suffer the special exit and ten-yearly charges imposed under the discretionary regime (see **6.32–6.45**). To qualify for this special inheritance tax treatment (see **6.47–6.53**), two sets of conditions must be satisfied (under *IHTA 1984, s 71*):

- there must be no interest in possession (that is, right to income) in the settlement; the income must be accumulated insofar as it is not applied for maintenance, education or benefit of the beneficiaries;
- one or more beneficiaries will become entitled to income or capital before reaching a specified age not exceeding 25 years or, from 6 April 2008, 18; and
- broadly, no more than 25 years have elapsed since the creation of the settlement or all the beneficiaries have a common parent or grandparent.

A&M trusts which were in existence on 21 March 2006, but where one or more beneficiaries did not have an interest in possession on that date, and where the beneficiaries did not become entitled to both income and capital at age 18, will suffer exit charges and potentially ten-yearly charges. The calculation of these charges is complex and depends on whether the settlement is now classified as an 'age 18 to 25' trust (see **6.54**) or is subject to the relevant property regime (see **6.32–6.45**).

Following *FA 2006*, no new A&M trusts can be created after 21 March 2006. Transitional rules apply, until 5 April 2008, to A&M trusts in being at 22 March 2006: see **6.51–6.53**. While the transitional period came to an end at midnight on 5 April 2008, the traditional beneficial treatment of A&M trusts for IHT purposes continues after that date, provided that the beneficiaries become absolutely entitled to capital at age 18.

Strictly speaking, the expression 'A&M trusts' is something of a misnomer, albeit in widespread use. This is because it was never the case that a trust was within the A&M regime, rather that, from time to time, capital held on the trusts of a particular settlement might have been within the regime, whether in whole or in part, subject to satisfying the above two conditions. Increasingly, however, the protection of the A&M regime is being consigned to history.

Bereaved minor trusts and 'age 18 to 25' trusts

2.8 Bereaved minor trusts ('BMTs') and 'age 18 to 25' trusts were introduced by *FA 2006* to replace A&M settlements; however, both these types of trusts are far more restrictive in their application than A&M settlements. The provisions governing the trusts can be found in *IHTA 1984, ss 71A–71D*.

2.9 Following *IHTA 1984, s 71A*, BMTs can only arise on the death of a parent. They can be established following the terms of the will of a deceased parent, following the Criminal Injuries Compensation Scheme, or held on statutory trusts following intestacy. A bereaved minor must become entitled to the trust property at age 18.

For income tax and capital gains tax, BMTs are taxed like discretionary trusts. *IHTA 1984, s 71B* provides that BMTs are not subject to exit charges or ten-year anniversary for IHT, provided that the conditions of *IHTA 1984, s 71A* are complied with.

2.10 Similar to BMTs, an 'age 18 to 25' trust can only arise on the death of a parent or legal guardian (see *IHTA 1984, s 71D*). An 'age 18 to 25' trust can only be created either under the will of a deceased parent or under the Criminal Injuries Compensation Scheme. In addition, such trust must satisfy the following conditions:

- a beneficiary must become absolutely entitled to the trust property, its income and any accumulated income at the age of 25; and
- for as long as the beneficiary is under the age of 25, the settled property must be applied for his benefit; and
- he must be entitled to all the income arising on the settled property, or no such income may be applied for the benefit of another person.

For income tax and capital gains tax, 'age 18 to 25' trusts are taxed like discretionary trusts. *IHTA 1984, s 71F* provides that 'age 18 to 25' trusts are subject to the IHT relevant property regime, except that the time for calculating exit charges only runs from the beneficiary's eighteenth birthday. This has the effect that there will not be any ten-year anniversary charges, and the maximum rate of an exit charge will be 4.2% when a beneficiary becomes absolutely entitled to trust property at the age of 25 (see **6.54**).

Life interest trusts

2.11 An interest in possession trust has one or more fixed interests in income. The right to income may be for the life of the beneficiary (called the life tenant), or it may come to an end at an earlier stage, for example on his marriage or remarriage, or indeed it may be for a fixed period. It may also be 'defeasible' – that is the trustees can exercise a power (called a power of appointment) diverting the income to another beneficiary.

What happens on the death of a life tenant or earlier termination of the life interest will depend on the trust deed. There could, for example, be successive life interests to his children or they might benefit outright at, say, age 25. For more detailed discussion, see **6.55–6.64**.

Following *FA 2006*, most interest in possession trusts created on or after 22 March 2006 will, for IHT purposes, be treated in the same way as discretionary trusts (being 'non-estate' interests in possessions): see **6.61–6.64**. Exceptions to this principle are 'transitional serial interests' (see **6.60**), trusts for a disabled person (see **2.13**) and 'immediate post-death interests' arising under a will (see **6.63–6.64**).

To qualify as an immediate post- death interest ('IPDI') following *IHTA 1984, s 49A,* certain conditions must be satisfied:

- the IPDI must be effected by will or on intestacy;
- the life tenant must have become beneficially entitled to the interest in possession on the death of the testator or intestate; and
- it is not a bereaved minor trust or disabled trust.

Examples of different types of trust

2.12

Example 2.1—Discretionary trust

Albert made a trust on 1 January 2011 for the benefit of his four children: Charles, Debbie, Edward and Fiona, and their spouses and children. The trustees are Albert, his wife Betty and their family solicitor. Income and capital may be divided between any of the beneficiaries as the trustees decide. At the end of the 125-year trust period the capital, if any remains, is to be divided equally between Charles, Debbie, Edward and Fiona (or their respective estates in the event that they have died). As the trust was established after 5 April 2010 there is no 21-year restriction on income accumulations.

Example 2.2—Accumulation and maintenance trust

Jack and Jill together made a settlement on 1 January 1999 to benefit their three grandchildren: Alice, who was born on 1 March 1979; Belinda, who was born on 5 June 1982; and Celia who was born on 15 July 1990. The grandchildren become entitled to income in their *pro rata* share of the settlement on reaching the age of 25. Capital is to be held for their children, ie the great-grandchildren of the settlors, on attaining the age of 25.

Alice became entitled to her one-third share of the income of the settlement on 1 March 2004, which was before 22 March 2006, when the *FA 2006* rules were introduced. Her share in the settlement therefore is not subject to the relevant property regime and will escape any exit and ten-yearly IHT charges.

It was open to the trustees to continue the benefit of the A&M regime beyond 5 April 2008, by changing the terms of the trusts so that capital vests absolutely in Jack's and Jill's grandchildren at age 18; however, after taking advice, they decided that they did not want the grandchildren to become entitled to money at such a young age. Therefore the capital then in the settlement will have entered the 'relevant property' regime on 6 April 2008 (see **6.47–6.53** and, specifically, Examples 6.15, 6.16 and 6.17). Belinda's and Celia's respective shares will be subject to ongoing IHT exit and ten-yearly charges.

Example 2.3—Bereaved minor trust

Geoff, Susan's father, died intestate in August 2018. Susan was only five years old. Following the intestacy rules, Patricia, Geoff's wife, inherited all the personal possessions, received a statutory legacy of £250,000 and half the remainder. The other half will be held on trust for Susan absolutely, contingent on attaining the age of 18. Susan's trust fund will be taxed as a discretionary trust for income tax and capital gains tax, but will not be subject to the relevant property regime for IHT.

Example 2.4—Age 18-to-25 trust

Caroline died in October 2018. Following provisions in her will, her estate is left to her children, Andrew and Eva, in equal shares absolutely upon attaining the age of 25 years. Andrew is 19 years old and Eva is just about to turn 18. The income and capital gains will be taxed like a discretionary trust. The trust will not be subject to ten-year anniversary charges, but the trustees will have to pay an exit charge for IHT when either child becomes absolutely entitled to the trust property at age 25. The exit charges will only ever be a maximum of 4.2% above the then nil rate band for IHT.

Example 2.5—Interest in possession (or life interest) trust

Alistair's father made a settlement for him on his 21st birthday on 1 January 2006, transferring 200 acres of farmland and a farmhouse to the trustees. Alistair is entitled to the income from the trust fund, though the trustees have power to appoint the income away from him. They also may advance capital to him at their discretion. On termination of the interest in possession, the income of the trust is to be held for such of Alistair's children, if any, surviving on his death in equal shares (or, if none, for Alistair's brother Ben absolutely). The terms of the trust provides that, if Alistair leaves children, they become entitled to the capital at age 25.

Note that the traditional IHT treatment of a life interest trust under which the capital is deemed to be owned absolutely by the beneficiary, as an 'estate' life interest (see **6.55**) applies only in general terms where, as here, the trust was made before 22 March 2006 or where there is an 'immediate post-death interest' under a will trust: see **6.63**. If Alistair's father had made the trust for his son on 1 January 2007, the capital would have fallen into the relevant property regime, albeit possibly not so material in this case insofar as 100% agricultural property relief applies.

Some other types of trust

Charitable trusts

2.13 Income and capital must be applied exclusively for 'charitable purposes'. A charitable trust will normally continue in perpetuity, that is, it is not required to come to an end after any particular time.

Charities are subject to specific rules in respect of income tax and corporation tax. The former are contained in *ITA 2007, Pt 10* and the latter in *CTA 2010, Pt 11*. The general rule is this: income arising to a charity will be exempt from tax, provided that it is spent or accumulated for charitable purposes. The income does not have to be spent in the year of receipt, nor does the spending have to be for income-type purposes. It would, therefore, be quite reasonable for governors of a school to save up for a few years to fund extra classrooms; the income they receive ultimately to be spent on the classrooms is exempt (as, indeed, is the income arising from investment of that income).

A gain that arises on disposing of an asset to a charity is tax free (see **3.30**). Similarly, there is a complete exemption from CGT for all chargeable gains made by the charity, provided that the proceeds are spent or accumulated for charitable purposes (*TCGA 1992, s 256*).

Gifts to a charity, whether made during lifetime or on death, are completely free from IHT (*IHTA 1984, s 23*). Exemption does depend on the charity existing permanently for charitable purposes; a 'time charity' (that is, one where the charitable status might come to an end after, say, ten years) does not have the same blanket exemption (*IHTA 1984, s 69*). Similarly, if there is a possibility of a benefit to the settlor, anti-avoidance provisions come into play.

A transfer out of a discretionary settlement to a charity is exempt, ie the normal 'exit' charge (see **6.36–6.38**) is precluded.

The *Finance Act 2012* introduces a reduced rate of IHT of 36%, if 10% or more of a deceased's estate (after deducting IHT exemptions, reliefs and the nil rate band) is left to charity. This reduced rate applies where death occurs on or after 6 April 2012 (see **10.79**)

An interesting question arises where a person who has inherited money under a deceased estate varies his entitlement within two years after the death in favour of a charity (see **12.1–12.4**). Provided the statutory requirements are met, then, so far as the deceased estate is concerned, the benefit of the charities exemption from IHT is available.

However, for income tax purposes the gift is treated as having been made by the individual beneficiary. Why should he not get the benefit of Gift Aid relief? In *St Dunstans v Major* [1997] STC (SCD) 212, a case decided by the Special Commissioners in 1997, it was held, broadly speaking, that one could not get both IHT exemption and Gift Aid relief. This was on the footing that the IHT saving was a 'benefit', which denied Gift Aid relief. However, if the IHT saving goes not to the original beneficiary but to some other person or charity, the decision in *St Dunstans v Major* should not apply.

Example 2.6—Post-death Gift Aid double dip precluded – albeit with limitations

The deceased left an estate of £500,000 to his wife in 2017/18. This is all spouse exempt. One year after he died, his widow varied the will by making a gift of £175,000 to the daughter and £150,000 to the son. This used the nil rate band of the deceased, the appropriate procedures were followed and no IHT was chargeable on the gift treated as made by the deceased.

The son then made a gift of £10,000 net to the Red Cross. This is treated as a gross gift of £12,500, ie enabling the Red Cross to recover tax of £2,500, plus the transitional supplement of £320. Is the son, being a higher rate taxpayer, able to get higher rate relief on the gross payment? *St Dunstans v Major* seems to present no problem because there is no IHT saving to anybody, whether to the son or anybody else. Assuming no further variation is made, of the £325,000 passed away by the widow, only £315,000 was retained by the children, with £10,000 applied for charitable purposes. In this case, however, no IHT saving is made, other than the usual one that the gift by the son would not be a chargeable transfer for IHT if he were to die within seven years.

The same would apply if the husband's will had left express legacies of £175,000 to the daughter and £150,000 to the son, ie there had been no variation by the widow and the son simply varied £10,000 of his entitlement in favour of the Red Cross. This is because the whole gift is within the nil rate band and there is therefore no room for the charities exemption to apply. If, by contrast, the gift to the son had been £175,000 (out of a total chargeable transfer of £350,000), the question would depend on where the IHT saving went; if, under the terms of the will, the son had to bear any tax chargeable on his gift, he would have benefited and *St Dunstans v Major* would apply, denying Gift Aid relief.

If, on the other hand, as is more usual, the IHT liability was borne by residue, the beneficiary of the charitable gift would have been the mother and not the son, and therefore *St Dunstans v Major* would not apply and Gift Aid would be available.

The acquisition of shares by a charity (ie 'a body of persons established for charitable purposes only') is expressly exempt from stamp duty (*FA 1982, s 129*). This exemption depends on a compliance process known as 'adjudication', ie the document of transfer must be submitted to HMRC Stamp Taxes for confirmation. Note that this exemption for tax covers only transfers to a charity and not transfers by a charity. However, it is likely that in the latter case no stamp duty will be charged because where shares are transferred to a beneficiary a transfer may be certified as exempt under Category L of the *Stamp Duty (Exempt Instruments) Regulations 1987.*

The purchase of land by a charity is expressly exempt from SDLT, subject to satisfying certain conditions (*FA 2003, Sch 8*)

Disabled trusts

2.14 This is, traditionally, a discretionary trust which exists for the benefit of a disabled person. While discretionary, it is treated for IHT as an interest in possession trust even though there may be power to accumulate income (*IHTA 1984, s 89*), if certain conditions are satisfied. *Finance Act 2006* introduced *IHTA 1984, s 89 A,* which allowed self-settlement, and *IHTA 1984, s 89B,* which brought in the option of a life interest version of a disabled trust.

For disabled trusts created prior to 8 April 2013, which were not subject to subsequent amendments, the condition is that not less than half of the fund is applied during the beneficiary's lifetime for his benefit.

Following changes introduced in *FA 2013* the condition for trusts created on or after 8 April 2013 is that any of the settled property or income which is applied during the disabled person's lifetime is applied for his benefit with the proviso that this requirement is not treated as breached if the trustees have powers allowing them to apply income and/or capital other than for the disabled person's benefit up to an 'annual limit', being the lower of £3,000 and 3% of the maximum value of the settled property during that period.

FA 2006 extended the definition of 'disabled person's trust', so that included within the meaning of 'disabled person's interest' are the cases where: (a) there is an express interest in possession for a disabled person; and (b) a person makes a settlement on himself (whether discretionary or interest in possession in form) in reasonable expectation of disability (*IHTA 1984, ss 89A* and *89B*).

Note that, rather unfairly, it is not possible to make a qualifying disabled trust in expectation of the disability of another person. The provisions for disabled trusts are, together with 'transitional serial interests' (see **6.60**), the exception to the principle that a non-charitable settlement made on or after 22 March 2006 will necessarily fall within the relevant property regime. To secure the favoured IHT treatment, one of the four sets of conditions must be satisfied at the outset; it is not sufficient if, not applying immediately, they come to be satisfied at some stage thereafter.

In light of the *Welfare Reform Act 2012*, *FA 2013* has amended the definition of a 'disabled person', and the capital and income rules are harmonised across the various taxes (IHT, CGT and income tax) for vulnerable beneficiaries.

Finance Act 2014 extends the CGT uplift on death provisions so that they will apply to a vulnerable beneficiary where such beneficiary dies on or after 5 December 2013.

For a detailed analysis see **Chapter 7**

Protective trusts

2.15 This is an interest in possession trust, which will come to an end either if the life tenant (called the principal beneficiary) becomes bankrupt or if he takes any steps to sell or alienate his interest under the settlement. In that case, the trust becomes discretionary (*Trustee Act 1925, s 33*).

Bare trusts

2.16 While there is legal ownership of the trust fund by the trustees, the beneficiaries are absolutely entitled or would be so entitled but for being under the age of majority of 18 (or some other incapacity). Here, for all income tax,

CGT and IHT purposes, there is a 'see through' analysis and the beneficiaries are treated as the taxpayers.

TRUSTS DISTINGUISHED FROM ESTATES

2.17 The main distinction is, obviously, that a trust is made by someone in their lifetime, whereas a deceased estate arises only on death. However, a trust can arise either under a will or indeed under an intestacy, if the beneficiaries are not entitled to both income and capital. An intestacy happens where, or to the extent that, a person dies without having made a will, in which case there are statutory rules that determine who becomes entitled to what and when. It, therefore, becomes important to be able to determine at what point the administration of a deceased estate comes to an end and the ensuing will trust begins. Very often the same individuals may be both personal representatives (PRs) of the estate and trustees of the will trust, though the tax rules can be different, as illustrated at **2.20**.

Deceased estates will vary considerably in their flexibility. A very simple case might be this: a husband dies owning all his property (comprising just say the family home, personal effects and bank accounts) jointly with his wife as 'joint tenants'. Here, there is a special rule whereby, on the death of a joint tenant, his interest passes automatically by operation of law to the surviving joint tenant(s). There would be no estate administration at all, nor indeed a continuing will trust. At the other end of the scale, the will itself might provide for quite complicated trusts.

Estate administration

2.18 Quite apart from the terms of the trust, the nature of the assets owned by the deceased may mean that quite a few years are taken in completing the administration of the estate. For example, where there are large numbers of assets, it may be difficult to ascertain these assets and to agree their value with HMRC.

The general rule is that, once the PRs have paid out any legacies, have 'ascertained' the residue (ie what is left after paying the legacies and any liabilities of the estate) and have paid off or quantified all tax due, the administration is complete. In practice, this will happen when the estate accounts have been drawn up and signed by the beneficiaries. Before that, the PRs may make interim distributions of capital to the beneficiaries entitled.

Rights of beneficiaries

2.19 In a deceased estate, no beneficiary has a right to any particular asset (even if the asset is the subject of a specific gift in the will to the beneficiary), until such time as the PRs choose to release that asset from the estate. All that the beneficiary has, meanwhile, is what is called a '*chose* in action', that is, a right to have the estate properly administered and, in course of time, his entitlement paid over. Therefore, for CGT, if the PRs sell a particular asset, which the will has 'earmarked' for one beneficiary, the disposal is that of the PRs.

Income tax

2.20 The rates of tax, for trustees and personal representatives, are as follows:

For tax year 2018/19

	Trusts	Estates
Discretionary and accumulation	38.1%/45%	7.5%/20%
Life interest	7.5%/20%	7.5%/20%

For tax year 2019/20

	Trusts	Estates
Discretionary and accumulation	38.1%/45%	7.5%/20%
Life interest	7.5%/20%	7.5%/20%

The basis of tax, for beneficiaries, is as follows:

	Trusts	Estates
Discretionary and accumulation	Receipts basis	Receipts basis
Life interest	Arising (or 'see through') basis	Receipts basis

Capital gains tax

2.21 For tax year 2018/19

	Trusts	Estates
Rate of tax	20% with an additional 8% surcharge for gains on residential property which does not benefit from private residence relief	20% with an additional 8% surcharge for gains on residential property which does not benefit from private residence relief
Annual exemption	£5,850 (subject to reduction: see **5.36–5.39**)	£11,700 in year of death and two following tax years

For tax year 2019/20

	Trusts	Estates
Rate of tax	20% with an additional 8% charge for gains on residential property which does not benefit from private residence relief	20% with an additional 8% charge for gains on residential property which does not benefit from private residence relief
Annual exemption	£6,000 (subject to reduction: see **5.36–5.39**)	£12,000 in year of death and two following tax years

Inheritance tax

2.22

	Trusts	Estates
Discretionary – or 'relevant property'	Exit and ten-year charges	No implications. Will trust succeeding estate administration deemed to commence at date of death
Accumulation and maintenance regime (trusts made before 22 March 2006)	No implications, up to 6 April 2008: continues thereafter only if absolute right to capital at age 18	No implications. Will trust succeeding estate administration deemed to commence at date of death

	Trusts	Estates
Bereaved minor trust	No implications	No implications. Will trust succeeding estate administration deemed to commence at date of death
'Age 18 to 25' trusts and old-style A&M trusts converted to comply	Exit charges but no ten-year charges	No implications. Will trust succeeding estate administration deemed to commence at date of death
Life interest	Where 'estate' life interest, charge on death of beneficiary (subject to quick succession relief). If 'non-estate' life interest and made on or after 22 March 2006, relevant property treatment applies, unless a transitional serial interest or a disabled trust	Where 'estate' life interest, charge on death of beneficiary (subject to quick succession relief). No charge on death if a 'non-estate' life interest (eg created by a life-time transfer made on or after 22 March 2006, other than for a disabled person)

Chapter 3

Starting a trust

SIGNPOSTS

- **Settlement** – Be aware that, apart from the specific anti-avoidance rules, the statute does not define the term 'settlement'. The former term is widely drawn to capture most arrangements (see **3.4**).
- **Tax trigger** – Whilst the mere act of creation of the trust may not in itself be a chargeable event, the transfer of assets into a trust structure may be a chargeable event for both CGT and IHT purposes, and may involve different transfer values (see **3.2**, **3.5** and **3.16**).
- ***FA 2006* impact** – The trust reforms introduced in *FA 2006* have had a significant impact for IHT purposes, with a knock-on effect for CGT, in relation to the creation of a lifetime interest in possession trust (see **3.11**, **3.16** and **3.26**).
- **Compliance** – It is of critical importance to understand the initial and ongoing compliance requirements relating to the creation of a fresh trust, even where a tax liability is not in point (see **3.6**, **3.8–3.10**, **3.18** and **3.23**).

CGT DISPOSAL

3.1 Setting up a trust will involve a settlor parting with property by way of transfer into that trust, as a trust cannot exist without assets. Initially, this may be only a nominal sum, such as £10 or £100, with the transfer of what might be called the 'substantive trust fund' following shortly thereafter. Alternatively, the substantive trust fund may be transferred in at the outset. Subsequent transfers of property into the trust may be made by the original settlor (or, indeed, anyone else), but such later additions will not always be the recommended route from a tax perspective.

A gift is a disposal

3.2 Any such transfers of property to the trust will be a disposal for CGT purposes unless the assets are otherwise exempt from CGT, eg sterling cash (though not foreign currency). Alternatively, the transfer, when taking other disposals into account, may be within the settlor's annual exemption, viz £12,000 for the tax year 2019/20 otherwise, a chargeable gain may arise. For years prior to 2016/17, CGT was charged at a flat rate of 18% (for a basic rate taxpayer) or 28% (for a higher rate taxpayer, estates and trusts) but *FA 2016* introduced reduced CGT rates (applicable to trust, estates and individuals) effective from 6 April 2016. Thereafter the CGT rate payable on most gains realised by trustees is reduced to 20%. However, gains on the disposal of interests in UK residential properties (to the extent the private residence relief exemption is neither available in part or in full) and gains arising in respect of carried interest (as defined) continue to attract an additional 8% premium rebasing the rate to 28%. Irrespective of the CGT rate it may be possible to defer recognition of the CGT liability by electing for 'hold-over' relief (see **3.5–3.7**).

Losses

Focus

Be aware of the circumstances in which CGT losses realised on asset transfer into trust are ring-fenced from general use.

3.3 The action of the settlor in transferring assets into a trust might not give rise to a gain, but rather to a loss (ie where the market value of the asset at the date of transfer is less than the settlor's CGT base cost). Losses are generally deductible from other gains to arrive at the net taxable gains for the year. However, *TCGA 1992, s 18(3)* contains a special anti-avoidance rule which comes into play where the transferor is 'connected' with the transferee – for this purpose, a settlor is connected with the trustees of the settlement. In such case, the loss realised by the settlor on transfer of assets into trust cannot be offset against the settlor's general gains but is ring-fenced and carried forward to be used only against a gain arising on a subsequent transfer of chargeable assets by the settlor into that same trust.

Example 3.1—Alistair's interest in possession trust

Alistair's father, Jack, is a farmer. On 1 January 2016, Jack created a trust for his adult son and settled 200 acres of farmland which he had acquired in 2005 at £3,250 per acre resulting in a total CGT base cost of £650,000. He also settled the farmhouse which he had acquired two years earlier, albeit carrying no gain on disposal. On 1 January 2016, the land was worth only £3,000 per acre, a total of £600,000, resulting in a loss to Jack as settlor of £50,000 (£600,000 - £650,000). However, this loss cannot be set against Jack's general gains and may only be used to offset a gain arising on a future disposal by him to the same trust.

On 1 May 2019, Jack settled further assets into the same trust comprising cash of £100,000, together with a cottage worth £90,000 subject to an assured tenancy. The gift of the cottage triggered a gain of £30,000, of which £12,000 is covered by Jack's annual exemption for 2019/20 and the balance of £18,000 covered by the brought-forward 'connected party' loss. The remainder of that loss, £32,000 (£50,000 - £18,000) is carried forward and as before is restricted for use against any future gains realised by Jack on any future gift of a chargeable asset into the same trust.

Statutory definitions for income tax and CGT

3.4

- With effect from 2006/07, the statutory rules define the expressions 'settled property' and 'settlor' in the same terms both for income tax (*ITA 2007, ss 466–473*) and for CGT purposes (*TCGA 1992, ss 68A, 68B* and *68C*).
- There is no general definition of 'settlement' (except for anti-avoidance purposes: see below). The CGT definition of 'settled property' (in *TCGA 1992, s 68*) is broadly any property held in trust other than assets held by someone as nominee or bare trustee for another person; as from 2006/07 this definition is also applied for income tax purposes (*ITA 2007, s 466*).
- The expression 'settlement' is defined for anti-avoidance income tax purposes to include 'any disposition, trust, covenant, agreement, arrangement or transfer of assets' and 'settlor' in relation to a settlement means 'any person by whom the settlement was made' (*ITTOIA 2005, s 620(1)*).
- The rules relating to anti-avoidance take (a) property comprised in a settlement as including any property originating from that settlor and (b) income arising under the settlement only as income originating from that settlor (*ITTOIA 2005, s 644(3)*).
- Interestingly, although for CGT purposes the expression 'settlement' in *TCGA 1992* is given the income tax definition, this is only for certain offshore trust purposes. Otherwise, there is no CGT definition of settlement. The anti-avoidance settlor interest rule in *TCGA 1992, s 77* simply ensured that in the spirit of income tax, gains were assessed on the settlor only in relation to property originating from that person (whether directly or indirectly): see **5.21–5.22**; however, this 'look through' CGT treatment only applied up to and including 2007/08 and was repealed

from 2008/09 et seq. It remains to be seen whether the current 2019/20 tiered rates of 20%/28% for trusts versus 10%/20%/28% for individuals will pave the way for a return to the pre-2008/09 position.

CGT HOLD-OVER RELIEF

Two categories

3.5 Hold-over avoids recognition of the gain arising to the settlor, by corresponding adjustment of the base cost of the asset in the hands of the trustees – this has the effect of potentially increasing the gain realised on later sale by the trustees on the assumption that the asset will increase or at the very least remain at the same value at date of transfer into Trust. Holdover relief falls into two categories:

- *TCGA 1992, s 260* for (broadly) transfers that are treated as immediately chargeable for IHT purposes, typically transfers into a discretionary trust and most lifetime trusts created post March 2006 (eg those now within the relevant property regime). This is available even if the transfer is within the settlor's nil rate of £325,000 for 2019/20, thus occasioning no positive charge to IHT; or
- *TCGA 1992, s 165*, which is defined not in terms of the type of transfer but by reference to the type of asset concerned, viz a business asset: this will include, for example, an asset used in the settlor's profession or trade, shares in an unquoted trading company and property that qualifies as 'agricultural property' for purposes of agricultural property relief from IHT.

In a situation where both sections apply, eg a gift of shares in a private trading company to a discretionary trust (or other relevant property trust), *s 260* relief takes priority (*TCGA 1992, s 165(3)(d)*). The significance of this is that *s 260* relief does not suffer from various restrictions that apply to exclude part of the gain from *s 165* relief, eg where the asset has not been used for business purposes throughout the settlor's period of ownership.

Note that, from 10 December 2003, a hold-over claim (whether under *TCGA 1992, s 260* or *165*) may not be made for a transfer to a trust which is or within six years of the end of the year in which the transfer is made, becomes settlor-interested (*TCGA 1992, ss 169B* and *169C*). From 2006/07, the term 'settlor-interested' is extended to include parental settlements, namely where under the provisions of the trust a minor unmarried child of the settlor can benefit.

The claim

3.6 Hold-over relief must be expressly claimed on help sheet HS 295, except to the extent the underlying gain arises on initial transfer by the settlor into the trust where the consent of the trustees is not required such that the claim may be made in the body of the settlor's self-assessment return. The old and more generous time period (of five years and ten months) for making a claim was shortened to four years from the end of the relevant tax year with effect from 1 April 2010 (*FA 2008, s 118* and *Sch 29, para 12*; *Finance Act 2008 Schedule 39 (Appointed Day, Transitional Provisions and Savings) Order 2009, SI 2009/403*). Help sheet HS 295 requires the settlor to specify under which legislative section the hold-over claim is made (ie *TCGA 1992, s 165* or *s 260*). For a valid hold-over claim, the settlor need not compute nor seek HMRC agreement to the gain that is held over, nor indeed necessarily obtain a professional valuation of the asset nor seek HMRC agreement to the same at that time, although there is some wisdom in doing so. He must simply confirm on help sheet HS 295 that a gain would occur (Statement of Practice SP8/92).

The effect

3.7 The practical effect of hold-over relief is twofold.

First, it dis-applies immediate recognition of a gain arising to the transferor which would otherwise be charged for a basic rate taxpayer at 10% (or at 18% if attributable to UK residential property) or for a higher rate taxpayer at 20% (or at 28% if attributable to UK residential property) subject to any applicable reliefs.

Secondly, it treats the transferee, in this case the trustees, as acquiring the asset at the acquisition cost of the settlor or later March 1982 value (or, for a transfer prior to 6 April 2008, the original acquisition cost increased by any indexation allowance accrued to April 1998 when indexation allowance was repealed for individuals and trustees).

It is important to be aware that if a gain was held over into a trust that was a pre-22 March 2006 qualifying interest in possession (ie a business asset under *TCGA 1992, s 165*), the held-over gain is extinguished but crystallised on the death of the life tenant who held that qualifying interest. Even so, it may be possible to hold over the gain once more at that point.

Example 3.2—Albert's discretionary trust

On 31 May 2019, Albert transfers to the trustees quoted shares that have a market value of £280,000 – there are 15 individual holdings which in total result in a gain arising to Albert of £100,000. He uses his annual exemption for 2019/20 to cover the combined gain of £11,800 on two of the holdings leaving a chargeable gain of £88,200 on the remaining 13 holdings (all of which produce gains of more than £200 so cannot use the remainder of the unused annual exemption) which he elects to hold over under *s 260*. His self-assessment return for the year notes the disposals and the holdover election. The trustees are therefore treated as having acquired the two shareholdings, for which the gain is recognised, at market value but the remaining 13 holdings subject to the hold over election are treated as acquired by the trustees at Albert's base cost.

Example 3.3— Arthur's interest in possession trust

On 1 March 2006 (and thus before the introduction of the *FA 2006* trust reforms), Arthur created a qualifying interest in possession trust in favour of his three nieces. He transferred to the trustees, shares in a private company valued at £100,000 but with a base cost to Arthur of £1,000. The company was, and still is, a qualifying unquoted trading company, and therefore the initial gain of £99,000 (£100,000 - £1,000) was eligible for hold-over relief under *s 165*. Arthur had made use of his annual exemption for 2005/06 against various disposals on the stock market and wanted to hold over the whole of the gain on making the settlement. He did this in his self-assessment for the year.

Should one of the life tenant nieces die, the held-over gain that arose on the shares transferred into the trust will come into charge at that point.

COMPLIANCE: TRUST REGISTER

3.8 There are currently three specialist trust districts within HMRC: Edinburgh, Nottingham and Truro.

The 1990 change in practice

3.9 Prior to 1990, it was the accepted practice when creating a new trust to send a copy of the trust deed to HMRC who would provide a ruling on the tax treatment of the trust based on its classification (eg discretionary). That practice was often useful in ensuring HMRC confirmation that the tax treatment desired by the draftsman had, in fact, been achieved, eg that the settlor and spouse had effectively been excluded from benefit so that the settlor-interested anti-avoidance rules would not apply (see **4.24–4.29** and **5.21–5.22**). Now, with an established self-assessment process which places the onus on the taxpayer to 'get it right', this useful practice has been withdrawn.

HMRC requirements

3.10 Prior to April 2017, there was a requirement that the creation of an income/gains producing trust (to include the creation under will upon the testator's death but excluding a bare trust) be notified to HMRC. This prompted the allocation of a unique SA tax reference leading to the requirement to file annual self-assessment trust returns. The detail of that notification to HMRC was set out in form 41G (Trust) albeit such form was not required by statute and the information could be supplied in some other format.

It was a good discipline for either the solicitor draftsman of the settlement, or the tax professional who acts for the family, to submit form 41G (Trust) within a month or two after the settlement creation to ensure that notification to HMRC was not forgotten.

However, this practice changed in 2017/18 when in order to comply with the UK's obligations under the EU Fourth Anti-Money Laundering Directive (4AMLD), HMRC announced in January 2017 the intention to introduce an online system to create, record and manage a more formal trusts register (TRS). Form 41G was withdrawn with effect from April 2017 and after a delayed start the online facility, which provides a single point of access to both register and update records online, was rolled out on 10 July 2017. The registration process is mandatory and applies to all UK express trusts and to non-UK trusts which receive income from a UK source or have UK assets on which they are liable to pay income tax, CGT, inheritance tax, stamp duty land tax or stamp duty reserve tax (bare trusts are excluded).

The TRS requires more information about the trust and its beneficiaries than HMRC obtained under the old 41G notification system. Trustees are required to provide information on the identities of the settlors, other trustees, beneficiaries, all other natural or legal persons exercising effective control over the trust, and all other persons identified in a document or instrument relating to the trust, including a letter or memorandum of wishes. For individuals, the details to be supplied include name and address and, if that address is not in the UK, the passport number or identification card number, the date of birth and the national insurance number and unique taxpayer reference, if any. If a trust has a class of beneficiaries, not all of whom have been determined, then trustees will simply need to provide a description of the class of persons who are entitled to benefit from the trust, rather than individual names and addresses.

Trustees are also required to provide general information concerning the trust. These include its name, the date on which it was established, a statement of accounts describing the assets identifying the value of each category of the trust assets (including the address of any property held by the trust), the country where it is resident for tax purposes, the place where it is administered and a contact address. Trustees also need to provide the name of any advisers who are being paid to provide legal, financial, tax or other advice to the trustees.

Given the frustrating teething problems associated with the creation of the register, HMRC had little choice but to make a number of extensions to the original optimistic registration deadline for notification of both new and existing trusts with a final deadline fixed at 5 March 2018. Thereafter, unless it can be demonstrated that the trustees have taken reasonable steps to so register, late registration penalties will be levied as follows:

- £100 for registering up to three months after the deadline;
- £200 for registering between three and six months after the deadline; and
- £300 or 5% of the total tax liability in the relevant year (whichever is higher) for registering more than six months after the deadline.

New trusts which have a first time TRS registration obligation in respect of a liability arising for 2017/18 et seq will need to be registered by 5 October following the end of the tax year in which that liability arose if a penalty is to be avoided.

To validate TRS compliance, a tick box is included on the trust self-assessment Return (SA900) to confirm the trust register has been checked and updated. There is also an annual requirement on or before 31 January each year to notify any changes that have occurred in the previous tax year or to confirm that there have been no changes but this excludes the need to notify a change in the value of trust assets.

As at time of writing, there is still no online facility to notify HMRC of any change to the submitted TRS information and as such the penalties for contravention of this online requirement remain suspended. However, HMRC confirmed that this project, which involves switching to a new system (a 'micro service') intended to be more intuitive, easier to navigate and with several advantages over the current 'iForm' service, is now underway. HMRC propose to roll out the new service at the start of the summer of 2019 and functionality will be expanded gradually in a series of deployments, which will include the ability to update details. HMRC have advised that until such time as the facility is available, Q20 (amendments to the TRS) of the SA trust return should be left blank and the data should instead be provided to HMRC in written format.

Failure to register under TRS will incur not only penalties but may also possibly lead to 'naming and shaming' of those involved. Breaches can also be a criminal offence with a maximum prison sentence of two years.

On 5 July 2018, HMRC:

- updated its guidance on records to be kept which also contains a list of UK law enforcement authorities that can request information about the beneficial owners of such trusts (see tinyurl.com/yaro44yd); and
- updated its TRS guidance to show the types of trusts that must be registered (see https://www.gov.uk/guidance/register-your-clients-trust).

The fifth version of the EU-wide Money Laundering Directive (5MLD), which entered into force at EU-level on 10 July 2018, amends the Fourth Money Laundering Directive (4MLD) which created the requirement for the Trust Register. 5MLD is intended to further increase the transparency of trusts (and other legal arrangements with similar structures) and requires the UK (and other Member States to extend registration of beneficial ownership of trusts to all UK resident express trusts and that own UK real estate or that have a business relationship with an entity obliged to carry out customer (anti money laundering) due diligence, such as a bank, estate agent or accountant. 5MLD also requires Member States to share data from the register under certain defined circumstances, in particular as part of the customer due diligence requirements mentioned above.

The UK (and other Member States) have 18 months from 10 July 2018 to integrate the 5MLD into domestic law (thus by 10 January 2020), with a further two months to implement the trust registration requirements (thus by 10 March 2020). A consultation on how the UK will implement 5MLD is expected shortly with draft secondary legislation expected in summer 2019.

INHERITANCE TAX

Potentially exempt transfers

3.11 Just as for CGT purposes where the gift into trust involves a disposal there may also be IHT implications by reason of the transfer of value. IHT is both a gifts tax and an estate duty. That said, however, lifetime gifts into an interest in qualifying possession trust made before 22 March 2006 were treated as 'potentially exempt transfers' (PETs), which became fully exempt from IHT by reason of the donor surviving the transfer by at least seven years.

A transfer of value is, broadly, a disposition which causes the value of the donor's estate to reduce as a consequence of that transfer (*IHTA 1984, s 3*). Since 22 March 2006, the PET qualification has a much reduced application as it is now largely restricted to a transfer of value (which is not an exempt transfer) made by an individual either to another individual or to the trustees of a disabled trust (*IHTA 1984, s 3A*); although it may also be in point on lifetime termination of a pre-22 March 2006 qualifying interest in possession whereupon the trust comes to an end (see **6.2** and **6.55**). A PET is assumed to be exempt unless the donor dies within seven years of gift such that its PET status fails; thus no notice for IHT needs to be given of exempt transfers or PETs when first made irrespective of amount.

A gift to an interest in possession trust (life interest trust) or to an A&M trust before 22 March 2006 was also a PET. A lifetime gift to a life interest trust on or after 22 March 2006 (even where for the benefit of the settlor or his spouse) is now an immediately chargeable transfer (see **3.16–3.19**) unless it is a qualifying trust for a disabled person. Furthermore, the tax favoured A&M regime can no longer apply to any lifetime transfer made on or after 22 March 2006.

A chargeable transfer is a transfer of value which is not wholly covered or partially franked by an exemption, eg the spouse exemption or the £3,000 annual exemption, and which is not afforded the 'wait and see' protection of a PET classification (*IHTA 1984, s 2*). A PET becomes a failed PET if the donor fails to survive the PET by seven years, and at that point it assumes the form of a chargeable lifetime transfer. Accordingly, a chargeable lifetime transfer will embrace any lifetime transfer of value, not otherwise exempt, that is not a PET.

Failed PETs

3.12 If the donor dies within seven years, the PET fails and becomes a chargeable lifetime transfer (*IHTA 1984, s 3A(4)*) prompting consideration of IHT implications which may arise through the administration of the estate. However, because the failed PET has now become a chargeable transfer, it will be necessary for the IHT account (Inheritance Tax Account IHT100), described at **3.19**, to be completed and submitted. If the amount of the transfer of value is within the nil rate band of the settlor, there will be no immediate implications of the gift (though it would have the effect of denying, to that extent, the nil rate band available to the estate).

Who bears the tax?

3.13 One important point to be considered where a lifetime gift is chargeable (either at time made or by reason of PET failure) is who bears the tax. The primary responsibility for bearing the tax on a failed PET will fall on the transferee (if an outright gift) or the trustees in whom the property is vested (*IHTA 1984, s 199(1)(b)* and *(c)*): this is confirmed in HMRC's Inheritance Tax Manual at IHTM30042. However, at IHTM14593, HMRC say that it is only if the transferor is *obliged* to pay the tax on a failed PET (which would in practice be paid by the personal representatives (PRs) of his estate) that he is treated as having made a further gift, which, therefore, needs to be grossed up in order to calculate the tax liability. The PRs of the transferor are secondarily liable subject to the limitations set out in *IHTA 1984, s 204(8)*, as confirmed by HMRC at IHTM30042 but IHTM30044 states that, in practice, PRs will be liable only in limited circumstances. By contrast, in the case of an immediately chargeable transfer, HMRC regard the settlor/transferor as primarily liable (*IHTA 1984, s 199(1)(a)*), and grossing up will apply if he pays the tax. Subject to the limitation in *IHTA 1984, s 204(6)* the trustees can also be liable under *IHTA 1984, s 199(1)(c)*, as confirmed at IHTM30062 (which contains a helpful table summarising HMRC's views on the order of liability).

Interest in possession trust

3.14 The gift by Arthur to the trustees (see **Example 3.3** at **3.7**) was a PET, though it would not have been if made on or after 22 March 2006. If he survived the gift by at least seven years, the transfer would become fully exempt. However, even if he should not so survive, the subject matter of the gift (in that case shares in an unquoted trading company) would attract business property relief (BPR) at 100% (assuming all conditions were met as at the point of death) and would reduce the chargeable transfer to nil, with no IHT implications. This assumes that Arthur had not 'reserved a benefit' in the gift (see **6.18–6.23**), though this is possibly academic in the event of 100% BPR continuing until his death and, importantly, that the negative 'clawback' conditions were satisfied (see **6.27**).

Life interest trust

3.15 See **Example 3.1 at 3.3**, where the property transferred by Jack, Alistair's father was (a) farmland worth £600,000 and (b) the main farmhouse worth on the open market £400,000 but with an 'agricultural value' of only £300,000. It was accepted that the house was 'agricultural property' attracting agricultural property relief (APR) given not on the market value but on the typically lower 'agricultural value': this requires the presumption that the property is subject to a perpetual covenant prohibiting non-agricultural use. See **10.59–10.64** for a more detailed discussion on APR.

Consider that Jack died five years after the gift, having reserved no benefit therein, and assume the law stays the same. The farmland attracted APR at 100%, reducing the chargeable transfer to nil. However, given the agricultural value restriction, the chargeable transfer of the house was £100,000 (£400,000 - APR £300,000). Jack had made no chargeable transfers within seven years before the gift to the trust, and therefore the £100,000 has first call on his nil rate band, with the effect, however, of denying the nil rate band to that extent against the death estate. The gift will be reported in the Inheritance Tax Account (IHT400) submitted by the PRs. Indeed, following *FA 1999* the PRs have a statutory duty to record details of all lifetime gifts made within seven years before death (*IHTA 1984, s 216(3)(b)*).

Chargeable transfers

> **Focus**
>
> The impact of *FA 2006* is to remove the favourable PET classification attaching to transfers into most lifetime trusts created post 21 March 2006.

> Despite the IHT downside, this can carry beneficial CGT treatment which should not be overlooked as part of an overall tax planning strategy.

3.16 The distinction between PETs and chargeable transfers was explained at **3.11**. Apart from PETs which become chargeable transfers by reason of the settlor's (donor's) death within seven years, the most common form of chargeable transfers before 22 March 2006 comprised gifts to a discretionary settlement. Post 21 March 2006, lifetime gifts to any form of settlement (called 'relevant property trusts' after the IHT regime which governs them), other than for a disabled person, are chargeable transfers. Such transfers have an advantage in enabling any gain on non-business assets to be 'held over' (subject to the restriction for settlor interest), thus 'deferring' recognition of the gain until ultimate disposal by the trustees (see **3.5–3.7**).

The IHT implications of the transfer into a relevant property trust will depend upon the amount of the chargeable transfer and the cumulative amount of all chargeable transfers made by the settlor in the previous seven years. If the aggregate of the value going into the trust plus gifts made by the settlor in the previous seven years does not exceed the upper limit of the nil rate band (£325,000 for 2019/20 and fixed at that level until 6 April 2021), the IHT charge is at 0%. To the extent that it exceeds the upper limit, the IHT charge is at 20% (or an equivalent of 25% if the tax is borne by the settlor – see **10.101** et seq); however, if the settlor dies within seven years, there will be a further 20% top up charge (subject to IHT taper relief) for the trustees to pay at that stage.

The annual exemption

3.17 In computing the chargeable transfer, exemptions such as the £3,000 annual exemption may be taken into account noting that any unused part of the annual exemption for the previous year may also be used (but only after the current exemption has been utilised). The annual exemption is applied against gifts in the strict time order in which they are made during the tax year (this allocation also applies to PETs). The general approach is that, if a person wishes to create both, say, a relevant property trust and a disabled trust (excluded from the relevant property regime) at about the same time, he should create the former at least a day before the latter. This has two beneficial effects:

- maximising the use of the annual exemption, which might otherwise be wasted against the initial PET creation of the disabled trust; and
- if he does die within seven years after making the disabled trust, its existence would not be taken into account in computing the IHT consequences attributable to the periodic/exit charge regime applied to the relevant property trust (see **6.32–6.38**).

Payment of tax and notification of transfer

3.18 The payment date for IHT due on a lifetime transfer (but not on death) into trust will be dependent on the date on which the transfer is made: where the transfer is made after 5 April but before 1 October in the tax year, the tax will fall due on the following 30 April (*IHTA 1984, s 226*), otherwise the tax will fall due for settlement six months from the end of the month in which the transfer is made. While the settlor is primarily liable for any tax due, it is better to have the tax paid by the trustees out of the transfer; payment by the settlor is treated as a further gift to the trust which would cause the grossing-up principles to apply and this in turn would increase the value of the settlement for later exit charge calculations for distributions made within the first ten years.

Even if IHT is not payable, notice of the transfer should be given within six months after the end of the month in which the gift was made (12 months for events occurring prior to 6 April 2014) unless the reporting exceptions apply. The *de minimis* provisions, absolving the settlor from having to give notice, were updated with effect from 6 April 2007 (*Inheritance Tax (Delivery of Accounts) (Excepted Transfers and Excepted Terminations) Regulations 2008, SI 2008/605*).

The Regulations provide that if only cash or quoted shares or securities have been transferred, no account is required if their value together with the total of the transferor's chargeable transfers in the previous seven years does not exceed the IHT threshold for the year of transfer (ie £325,000 for 2019/20). Otherwise, submission of an account may only be avoided where:

(a) the value of the chargeable transfer plus the transferor's chargeable transfers in the previous seven years does not exceed 80% of the IHT threshold (ie £260,000 for 2019/20); and

(b) the value of the transfer of value does not exceed the IHT threshold (£325,000 for 2019/20) less the total of chargeable transfers made by him in the previous seven years.

Note that, in the case of (b), the transferor cannot rely on the 100% reduction by agricultural or business property relief to avoid giving notice if the gross value of the transfer exceeds the threshold.

Form IHT100 and IHT100 series event forms

3.19 The following information is requested, to which notes in form IHT100 refer:

- Name, address and reference of the person dealing with the account.
- Date and type of transfer, ie whether in particular a PET chargeable on the transferor's death within seven years or a gift to a discretionary trust.

- Details of the transferor.
- Details of the transferees.
- Details of the transfer including:
  - any associated transfers;
  - the date and value of the gift;
  - deductions, eg liabilities;
  - reliefs and exemptions, eg the annual exemption or agricultural or business property relief;
  - details relating to agricultural and business and property relief (the so called 'clawback' rules), which must be satisfied in the event of the transferor's death within seven years: see **6.27**, **10.58** and **10.64**.
- Payment of tax: whether the tax is to be borne by the transferee, whether any tax is to be paid by instalments (see **10.94–10.97**) and whether any deductions are claimed.
- Whether the transferor has made any other transfers of value in the previous seven years.
- Declaration by the transferor.

Example 3.4— Albert's discretionary trust (2)

The gift of listed shares is valued at £280,000 (see **Example 3.2** at **3.7**) with the basis of that valuation (in a case of quoted shares) based on the lower of the average of recorded bargains or the 'quarter-up' rule. However, Albert may also deduct his unused IHT annual exemptions for 2019/20 and 2018/19, reducing the chargeable transfer to £274,000 (£280,000 – (£3,000+£3,000)). Such amount is within Albert's 2019/20 nil rate band of £325,000 and, having made no chargeable transfers in the seven preceding years, the de minimis provisions will apply such that he will not need to make a return on form IHT100.

STAMP DUTIES

3.20 Stamp duties are the oldest form of taxation in the UK, going back to 1694. A major reform occurred in 2003, with the introduction of a new tax (stamp duty land tax or SDLT) on transfers of UK land and the repeal of stamp duties on all other types of property except shares and marketable securities.

Prior to that, in 1996, stamp duty reserve tax (or SDRT) was introduced to impose a 0.5% charge (the same rate as stamp duty) on agreements to transfer marketable securities for a consideration: this applies largely to dealing through The Stock Exchange, being paperless and not otherwise caught by stamp duty insofar as it applies only to documents.

If trustees acquire shares or land, stamp duty (at 0.5%) and stamp duty land tax (at rates up to 12% properties purchased at a cost in excess of £1.5 million, effective from 6 April 2015 with an additional 3% levy for second residential properties imposed with effect from 6 April 2016) will apply as they do to purchasers in the ordinary course: see **13.1–13.5** for further details. It is more likely, however, that on starting a trust the settlor will give to the trustees, if not cash, either shares or land. In either case, there is no stamp duty or stamp duty land tax (SDLT) to pay.

To counter perceived abuse, *FA 2013* introduced legislation to impose a new higher rate of SDLT on the acquisition by 'non-natural' persons of high value residential property (annual tax on enveloped dwellings (ATED)). The rate, effective from 21 March 2012, is set at 15% and from 20 March 2014 applies where the chargeable consideration exceeds £500,000 (£2 million for the period to 19 March 2014). For this purpose, a 'non-natural' person will be defined to include companies, collective investment schemes and certain partnerships. In addition, *FA 2013* sets out the basis of an annual SDLT charge imposed on properties in such ownership effective from 1 April 2013.

Compliance

3.21 In the case of shares, the transfer document will be 'self-certified' with Category L under the *Stamp Duties (Exempt Instruments) Regulations 1987, SI 1987/516*, avoiding the fixed duty of £5 that would otherwise be chargeable, at least before 13 March 2008. For gifts of shares and securities made on or after 13 March 2008 the fixed £5 duty has been abolished (*FA 2008, s 99* and *Sch 22, para 10*).

In the case of land, the trustees will self-certify the transfer document as exempt under *FA 2003, Sch 3, para 1* and will complete a self-certification form SDLT 60. Each of these documents is then used as appropriate to trigger re-registration, whether in the books of the company or at one of the UK land registries. There is now no need to complete form SDLT 60 for land transactions occurring on or after 12 March 2008 (*FA 2008, s 94* and *Sch 30*); now it is the Land Registry transfer form TR1 which is used to procure re-registration.

Only a 'pure' gift will attract the exemption. There is a trap where land is charged with a liability, typically a mortgage, and the transferee (in this case the trustees) accepts liability for the mortgage: the amount of the mortgage constitutes consideration paid by them. (The same principle applies to shares, though it would be extremely unusual for shares to be so charged.) If the amount of the mortgage does not exceed £125,000 for residential property (£125,000 before 2 September 2008 and after 31 December 2009) or £150,000 for non-residential property, there will still be no positive SDLT liability. However (assuming the mortgage is £1,000 or more, or, from 12 March 2008, £40,000 or more) the document cannot be self-certified and the trustees must, within 30 days of the gift, complete form SDLT1 and send it to the Stamp Office at Netherton, from whom they will receive HMRC Certificate SDLT5, which is sent to the Land Registry to procure registration.

From 3 December 2014, the old system of SDLT (not ATED) applied to residential properties which operated on a single rate basis determined with reference to value, was replaced with a five-tiered rate table (the single rate system continues to apply to commercial properties) resulting in maximum charge of 12% for properties valued in excess of £1.5 million but with an additional 3% levy imposed for the purchase of a second residential property introduced with effect from 6 April 2016.

Example 3.5— Arthur's interest in possession trust (2)

Arthur made a gift of unlisted shares to the trustees of his interest in possession trust on 1 March 2006 (see **Example 3.3** at **3.7**). The stock transfer forms will have been certified, typically by Arthur, as exempt from stamp duty under Category L of the *1987 Regulations*. The trustees will send these certified forms to the registrars of the respective companies to procure re-registration of the trustees as owners of the shares.

Example 3.6— Alistair's interest in possession trust (2)

Consider that the land given by Jack, Alistair's father, to the life interest trust established for his son on 1 January 2016 had been burdened by a mortgage of £140,000 (which would have reduced the transfer of value for IHT purposes). The trustees assume direct liability to the mortgage lender for payment of interest and repayment of capital and as a consequence the £140,000 is treated as consideration paid by the trustees for the land. However, being within the nil rate threshold for non-residential property of £150,000, no SDLT is payable, although, in order to avoid penalties (see **Chapter 7**), the trustees must get in to the Stamp Office at Netherton form SDLT1 duly completed no more than 30 days after the transaction. Had the mortgage been £175,000, SDLT of £1,750 would have been payable and a cheque for this amount should accompany form SDLT1.

ISSUES TO CONSIDER

Non-tax issues

3.22 Putting assets into trust should not be dictated solely by tax, although it should be done in a tax-efficient manner. Consider the following advantages:

- protection;
- control; and
- flexibility.

Protection

3.23 While the beneficiaries have the right to ensure that the trustees act properly in administering the trust, no beneficiary has a right to any asset in the trust, except to the extent that the trust deed so provides or the trustees so decide. That is, where the trust deed gives a right to income (but, while the trustees have a power to advance capital), there is no right to capital and as such there is no asset owned by the beneficiary that can be taken into account by a court in insolvency or matrimonial proceedings. Equally, there is no asset that a beneficiary who is inclined towards profligacy can sell. The beneficiary may have a right to income during his lifetime, although the trustees may be able to deprive him of that right at any time.

Control

3.24 It is generally, though not invariably, tax-inefficient if the settlor or spouse is a beneficiary (see **4.24–4.29** and **4.44–4.53** for income tax, **5.21–5.22** for CGT (for 2007/08 and earlier) and **6.18–6.23** for IHT). It is important to note the CGT disadvantage of a trust being settlor-interested, whereby a hold-over relief election on the transfer of assets into trust is denied (see **3.5**, last paragraph) effective from 10 December 2003. However, there is nothing to prevent the settlor and spouse from being trustees, thus enabling them to maintain a degree of '*control*' over the trust asset, which may be useful where it is shares in a family company or a share in the family farm. That said, they must remember to administer the trust property for the beneficiaries and thus avoid HMRC attacking the arrangement as a sham trust.

Settlor and spouse trustees should be aware and recognise that conflicts of interest could arise. Consider the position where shares in a family company are put into the trust: it might be in the interests of the beneficiaries that the trustees accept an offer for purchase, whereas, in relation to a residual holding retained by the settlor, the latter may wish, for sentimental reasons, to reject the offer. It is always sensible for there to be at least one other trustee apart from the settlor or the settlor and spouse, if only 'to see fair play' and, indeed, to provide a continuing trustee should the settlor and spouse die unexpectedly.

Flexibility

3.25 A person may wish, for estate planning reasons, to make an effective gift of an asset and hence remove it from his estate, but they may be unsure as to whom, among a number of children, the asset should ultimately go. Prior to 22 March 2006, an immediate IHT liability could be avoided through creation of an A&M trust (if the children were under the age of 25), and since then, through creation of a discretionary trust where either the value is within the nil rate band or in excess of the nil rate band but where business or agricultural assets are involved thereby providing access to APR or BPR. Alternatively, there could be a trust divided into life interests among the siblings, with the trustees having an overriding power of appointment but since 22 March 2006, any such transfer into a lifetime trust (with the exception of a disabled trust), whatever its terms, will be an immediately chargeable transfer. This means that, to the extent that the value settled exceeds the settlor's nil rate band, IHT at 20% (or 25% if the settlor meets the IHT entry charge) will be payable on that excess (to rise to 40%, subject to IHT taper relief, should the settlor die within seven years).

Tax efficiency

3.26 It is always sensible for those advising on a trust to have in mind the way that the trust fits into the overall family tax planning and to ensure that it is tax efficient. The following are merely some 'pointers':

- Unless there are particular reasons for wanting to include the settlor or spouse, ensure that they are irrevocably excluded. This will mean that the trust income is not assessed on the settlor and that, for IHT purposes, the settlor is treated as effectively alienated from the assets previously within his estate. However, one reason for perhaps including the settlor and/or spouse as beneficiaries while accepting the IHT downside might be with a view to securing CGT efficiency. For example, inclusion of the settlor or spouse may be desirable to secure CGT principal private residence relief for a house held by the trustees (see **5.25**), while accepting the consequential disadvantage for any residential property owned directly by the settlor and/or spouse (except within the last 18 months of ownership for periods up to 5 April 2019 and reduced to nine months thereafter under provisions contained in *Finance Act 2019* during which it is possible to have principal private residence relief running on two properties concurrently, through use of the election procedure).

- Decide what type of trust is appropriate to the circumstances, noting that it is no longer possible to recreate the pre 22 March 2006 A&M trust scenario with its favourable tax benefits. Where there are a large number of beneficiaries, and irrespective of whether or not they are closely related, it may be appropriate to consider a discretionary trust. However, it should be borne in mind that, if the chargeable value of assets transferred into the newly created trust exceeds the settlor's nil rate band, there will be IHT to pay at 20% of the excess (or effective 25% rate if the settlor meets the IHT entry charge) with a further 20% top-up should the settlor die within seven years. If the property is earmarked for just one beneficiary, or a limited number of beneficiaries, a life interest trust may be more appropriate. However, post 21 March 2006, such a gift to a life interest trust is an immediately chargeable transfer and thus, in order to avoid an immediate IHT liability at 20% (or 25% if met by the settlor) the chargeable value should be confined to within the settlor's available nil rate band. There may be income tax advantages of having a life interest rather than a discretionary structure, where there is one or just a few principal beneficiaries.

- *Dividend income.* Up to 5 April 2016, the earlier reform of dividend taxation introduced on 6 April 1999 meant that for those trusts without the benefit of a brought-forward tax pool when an income distribution was made out of a dividend source at the trustees' discretion, this would translate into an effective tax rate of 50.5% (55% for 2012/13) (see **Example 4.26** at **4.110**). The increased trust dividend rate of 38.1% introduced with effect from 6 April 2016, coupled with the withdrawal of the notional tax credit, has altered the position but even so the rate for a life interest trust would be only 7.5%, albeit further tax may be payable in the hands of the life tenant should they be a higher rate or super rate taxpayer. Alternative forms of investment in eg instruments paying interest or commercial property paying land do not carry this disadvantage.

- *CGT.* There is no tax distinction between types of trust in the rate payable by the trustees, which, subject to the annual exemption, is for 2019/20 fixed at 28% for UK residential property/carried interest gains and 20% for all other gains (28% for 22 June 2010 to 5 April 2016). Consider the CGT implications on creation. Will it be possible to hold over the gains (see **3.5–3.7**)? Bear in mind that a gain held over will crystallise on the death of a pre 22 March 2006 life tenant or later qualifying transitional serial interest (TSI): see **6.58**.

- *Type of return.* Trustees have to consider what type of investment return is more appropriate, given the current 2019/20 income tax rate of 45% applied to non-dividend income and 38.1% for dividend income received by either a discretionary or accumulation trust or 20% applied to non-dividend income and 7.5% to dividend income received by a life interest trust. The only limitation is that up to the first £1,000 of income received by a discretionary or accumulation trust (which also applies to interest under the accrued income scheme received by an interest in possession trust which is otherwise taxable at 45%) is taxed at the standard 20% rate (or the 7.5% dividend ordinary rate). By contrast, irrespective of the trust type capital gains over and above the annual exemption are taxed at 20% or 28% dependent on the gain type.

- *Compliance.* Do not forget the need to register the trust through the online portal (see **3.8–3.10**). Furthermore, for IHT purposes, the chargeable transfer upon creation or later of a relevant property trust must be reported to HMRC by submission of IHT100 (and accompanying IHT100 event form) unless the excepted transfer regulations apply (see **3.16–3.19**).
- *Agricultural or business property.* If such property is transferred into trust, ensure that the reliefs anticipated are in fact available and be aware of the need for the relief to continue to be available if the settlor dies within seven years: the 'clawback' rules, summarised at **6.27**.

CHARITABLE TRUSTS

3.27 This book does not deal with public charitable trusts and only private charitable trusts in passing. These are registered under *Charities Act 1993, s 3* – before *Charities Act 2006* took effect in 2008. A detailed form is available from the Charity Commissioners to be filled in and supplied, with a copy of the draft trust deed, to confirm whether the trust will be treated as charitable. To fall within the definition of charity, the objects of the trust should be (now, under *Charities Act 2006, s 2(2)*):

- the prevention or relief of poverty;
- the advancement of education;
- the advancement of religion;
- the advancement of health or the saving of lives;
- the advancement of citizenship or community development;
- the advancement of the arts, culture, heritage or science;
- the advancement of amateur sports;
- the advancement of human rights, conflict resolution or reconciliation or the promotion of religious or racial harmony or equality and diversity;
- the advancement of environmental protection or improvement;
- the relief of those in need by reason of youth, age, ill health, disability, financial hardship or other disadvantage;
- the advancement of animal welfare;

- the promotion of the efficiency of the armed forces of the Crown, or of the efficiency of the police, fire and rescue services or ambulance services; or
- any other purposes recognised as charitable purposes under existing charity law or analogous to or within the spirit of those purposes or the purposes listed above.

These 13 'charitable descriptions of purposes' constitute broadly the first three historic heads of charity set out below, plus those purposes within the fourth head which the courts have accepted as 'charitable':

- the relief of poverty;
- the advancement of religion;
- education; or
- other purposes beneficial to the community.

It is important to note that in the recent case of *Routier and anor v HMRC* [2014] EWHC 3010 it was held that irrespective of the charitable qualification of the trust object, in order for the disposition into trust to access IHT exemption the charitable purpose must be governed by UK law.

Family charitable trust versus CAF account

3.28 An individual can set up their own account within the Charities Aid Foundation (CAF), such that payments to the account will attract Gift Aid relief and, through a personal chequebook, donations may be made by the individual from time to time as they wish. However, a small administrative charge will be made by the CAF and cheques may be written only in favour of registered charities or other recognised charitable bodies, eg churches. The advantage, therefore, of a personal trust, although involving some complexity in terms of establishment and perhaps administration, is that, provided the trustees are satisfied that income and capital are applied for charitable purposes, they need not necessarily find their way to a registered charity.

Tax advantages summarised

3.29 The operation of Gift Aid relief and the detailed tax exemptions for charities are outside the scope of this work and thus are only mentioned in passing. The following tax exemptions are available on setting up a charity:

- *Income tax*: Gift Aid is given to cash gifts. Relief is also available for listed shares and units in authorised unit trusts, as well as (by *FA 2002*) freehold or leasehold interests in UK land.

- *CGT*: A disposal of a chargeable asset to a charity is exempt (*TCGA 1992, s 257*).
- *IHT*: Gifts and legacies to charities are exempt transfers (*IHTA 1984, s 23*). Similarly, there is an exemption for transfers out of a relevant property trust to charities. Note, however, that, where there is a possibility of a benefit to the settlor, there are anti-avoidance provisions for IHT.
- *Stamp duties*: Transfers of shares to a charity are exempt from stamp duty subject to 'adjudication' by HMRC Stamp Taxes. Despite that exemption, however, most transfers to any type of trust (including charitable trusts) will be gifts, which may simply be self-certified as exempt (under Category L of the *Stamp Duty (Exempt Instruments) Regulations 1987*). Following the introduction of the present regime for land on 1 December 2003, gifts of real property can be self-certified as exempt from stamp duty land tax (*FA 2003, Sch 3, para 1*), although there is no longer the requirement for self-certification on form SDLT 60 for transfers on or after 12 March 2008. There is a specific exemption from stamp duty land tax for gifts of land to charities (*FA 2003, Sch 8*) and (by *FA 2004*) to charitable trusts.

Example 3.7—Zebedee's charitable trust

Zebedee has a personal interest in certain orphanages being run in Russia. As well as committing himself to those orphanages in terms of time, he wishes to provide for them financially out of a substantial share portfolio, which he has recently inherited from his father. He therefore decides to set up the Russian Orphanage Trust with £100,000.

A draft of the trust deed will have to be supplied for prior approval by the Charity Commission, which may take two to three months, under cover of their standard form, which will ask detailed questions about the charity, its proposed method of operation, the trustees etc.

Out of his share portfolio, it would be sensible for Zebedee to select shares that carry the greater gain, since there will be no CGT on transferring the shares to the charity. Nor will there be any IHT implications. The gift may be certified category L for stamp duty.

Being listed shares, income tax relief will be available on the gift. That is, Zebedee's taxable income will be reduced by the market value of the shares given to the trust. He will also benefit from the CGT relief.

Chapter 4

Running a trust: income tax

SIGNPOSTS

- **Residence** – The correct determination of the residence status of a trust is critical when quantifying the extent of its income tax liability and thus this must not be overlooked in the tax planning process (see **4.4**).
- **Settlor interest** – Beware of the scope and impact of the penal anti-avoidance rules which can create a complex compliance and distortive tax position (see **4.25**, **4.29** and **4.31**).
- **Pre-owned asset tax** – Although not commonly seen in practice, its harsh financial impact clearly demands that its early stage identification is paramount (see **4.44**, **4.48** and **4.52**).
- **Trustee expenses** – A clear understanding is required of the treatment of trustee expenses and in particular their interaction with income in both determining tax liability for the trust and the beneficiary (see **4.117**, **4.120** and **4.121**).

RESIDENCE

Residence and domicile explained

4.1 The general liability to UK income tax (and CGT) is determined by residence. The principal hallmark of residence is its determination by reference to physical presence in the UK during the UK tax year. Residence should be distinguished from domicile, which is broadly the country or jurisdiction which a person considers to be his permanent home – domicile is not relevant to trustees, though residence is. A person can be resident (though not domiciled) in more than one country during a tax year (though most non-UK countries will tend to use the calendar year as the measure of liability). In that case, a double tax treaty may apply to determine in which country a person should be treated as primarily resident for a particular period/tax year.

Personal residence

4.2 Generally, for periods up to and including 5 April 2013, a person was treated as UK tax resident in a tax year if:

- he was physically present in the UK for more than 183 days during that tax year; or
- he spent 91 days or more on average per tax year in the UK over a four-year period; the latter was also called 'ordinary residence', which had the meaning of habitual residence (although he may also be UK resident in certain circumstances if he spent less than 91 days in the UK during a tax year).

It is important to note that, while the first bullet point reflects the statutory rule, the second bullet point reflected then HMRC practice (based on case law), as described in their explanatory booklet HMRC6. The latter replaced IR20 and applied to residence determination with effect from 6 April 2009 – it was updated in February 2010 to apply for the position prior to 6 April 2011 and again in December 2010 to apply for the position from 6 April 2011. *FA 2008, s 24* introduced, for the purposes of the statutory rule, a provision that (except for qualifying transit passengers) it is physical presence in the UK at midnight which will constitute a day's presence in the UK. HMRC have said that they will apply this rule also to the non-statutory test.

UK residence extends liability to income tax on worldwide income (subject to a limitation for the remittance basis user where non-UK domicile status applies). Non-UK residence limits that liability to income arising from within the UK.

The post 5 April 2013 position is now determined by *FA 2013,* which sets out the statutory residence test (SRT). Despite the complexities of the rules, in conjunction with HMRC guidance issued in May 2013 and September 2013, RDR3 Guide released in December 2013 and updated on 8 June 2016, and the latest update to RDR1 on 19 July 2018, the SRT has removed many of the inconsistencies which arose out of the non-statute interpretation. The SRT is not covered in any depth in this book and readers are referred to *Income Tax 2019/20* (Bloomsbury Professional) and *Capital Gains Tax 2019/20* (Bloomsbury Professional) for more detail on this complex subject.

HMRC and Treasury review of individual residence and domicile

Focus

The first step towards a statutory residence test (first mooted as long ago as 1998) was set out in the HMRC consultative document issued on 17 June

2011; legislation is now included within the *FA 2013* which places the rules squarely within the ambit of the statute with effect from 6 April 2013.

4.3 A background paper was published in April 2003 to consider the possibility of modernising the then rules, which had been developed over the past 200 years. Specific statutory changes made by *FA 2008* are noted at **4.2**. While there were official indications in 2008 that an overall statutory test of residence might be introduced in future, the then existing rules remained rather unsatisfactorily a mixed one of statute, case law and HMRC practice (*FA 2008* also introduced a fresh code of taxation for UK resident but non-UK domiciliaries, which is outside the scope of this book: see *Booth & Schwarz: Residence, Domicile and UK Taxation* (20th Edn), (Bloomsbury Professional)). On 17 June 2011, HMRC published their long-awaited consultation document as part of the step process towards introduction of a statutory residence test (SRT) and the proposed framework pivoted on a three-part determinative basis which specifically linked physical presence with quality of lifestyle. Progress remained slow with the delivery of the HMRC summary of responses to their June 2011 publication together with an outline of the proposed draft legislation belatedly issued in June 2012. In December 2012, HMRC published a detailed Guidance Note (HMRC 'What's New?' dated 18 December 2012) setting out the scope of the new rules, now included in the *FA 2013* and effective from 6 April 2013. Further HMRC guidance can be found on the HMRC website (see HMRC 'What's New?' dated May 2013 and supplemented by further HMRC guidance notes released in September 2013 and December 2013).

On 31 January 2018, the existing HMRC guidance set out in RDR1 was updated and expanded to incorporate the *F(No2)A 2017* provisions regarding the deemed domicile rules which took effect from 6 April 2017. Further updated guidance on residence, domicile and the remittance basis contained in the section is in 'Section 5 How does domicile affect your UK Income Tax and Capital Gains Tax liability?' which was issued on 19 July 2018.

Trustee residence

4.4 As has been explained at **2.1–2.4** both general and tax liabilities of a person as trustee are quite distinct from liabilities which he may have in his personal capacity. The residence of trustees is determined as a body, though any individual trustee will be personally liable for the tax. If all the trustees are personally resident in the UK, then as a body they are treated as UK resident. If all the trustees are personally resident outside the UK, then as a body they are treated as non-UK resident. If there is a mix of resident and non-resident trustees, the treatment of the trustees as a body will be determined with reference to the residence (ordinary residence prior to 6 April 2013), and domicile status of the settlor until 'he ceases to be a settlor'. If the settlor was resident (and prior to 6 April 2013 ordinarily resident) or domiciled in the UK at any point from the date of the settlement until that time, and at least one trustee is UK resident, then as a body the trustees are all treated as resident. If the settlor was not resident, (and prior to 6 April 2013 ordinarily resident) or domiciled in the UK, from the date of the settlement until that time, then as a body the trustees are all treated as non-UK resident. A person ceases to be a settlor when no property of which he is the settlor is comprised in the settlement (and that might occur after his death), provided that there is no undertaking to provide property to the settlement in future and there is no reciprocal arrangement with another person to give property to the settlement (*ITA 2007, ss 467–476*).

Note that the rules for residence for CGT purposes were revised and aligned with the income tax treatment with effect from 6 April 2007: see **5.8–5.10**.

Example 4.1—The Bertie discretionary trust

The trustees of the Bertie Discretionary trust are Bertie, Betty and their family solicitor who are all personally resident in the UK. The trustees as a body are, therefore, UK resident.

Example 4.2—The Harry/Hector discretionary trusts

Grant is a wealthy Texan and has two sons, Harry and Hector. Harry has an English wife and has made his family home in London. Hector, on the other hand, lives in Texas and works in the family business.

In 2010, Harry and Hector each made a discretionary trust. The trustees of Harry's trust are Grant, Harry and a friend of the family now living and working in France. The trustees of Hector's trust are Grant, Hector and his brother Harry.

Each trust has 'mixed resident' trustees, containing at least one who is, and at least one who is not, personally resident in the UK (as determined under the post-5 April 2013 statute rules). Thus, the residence determination of the trustees as a body is made by reference to the status of the settlor.

Harry's trust is treated as UK resident, because Harry the settlor is UK resident (even if he may not have acquired a UK domicile).

Hector's trust, on the other hand, is non-UK resident because the settlor Hector is not resident, or domiciled in the UK: therefore, the one UK-resident trustee is treated for this purpose as being a non-UK resident.

THE BASIS OF INCOME TAXATION

4.5 Income tax is, generally, chargeable on income. 'Generally' because certain capital receipts are treated for income tax purposes as if they were income, even though in law they may retain their capital character; for example, see below.

Some capital receipts treated as income

4.6

- Where a shareholder in a company sells his shares back to the company, the proceeds of sale in his hands may be treated either as income or as capital according to defined statutory rules. Where it is the trustees who sell the shares, the proceeds are generally treated as income (even though the proceeds may be treated as capital under trust law) unless *CTA 2010, s 1033* applies. From 6 April 2010 to 5 April 2013, the effective tax rate on net dividend income arising within a discretionary trust was 36.11% and, from 6 April 2013 to 5 April 2016, the effective rate was reduced to 30.56%: accordingly, for 2015/2016 a cash dividend of £90 would be grossed up to £100 by the non-repayable notional tax credit. The 2015/2016 trust rate for qualifying distributions was 37.5% (42.5% for the period 6 April 2010 to 5 April 2013 inclusive) which, after the notional 10% tax credit, left a residual liability of 27.5% – expressed as a percentage of the net cash dividend of £90, this was 30.56%. The position is now altered for 2016/2017 onwards following the withdrawal of the notional 10% dividend tax credit and the increase in the dividend tax rate to 38.1%.

- Chargeable event gains (onshore and offshore policies).

- Capital receipts from the sale of land can, in certain circumstances, be subject to income tax if the land was acquired or developed with a view to realising a gain (*ITA 2007, Pt 13, Ch 3*).

- Where a person grants, for a premium, a lease of no longer than 50 years, part of that premium (calculated on a formula basis) is assessed to income tax (*ITTOIA 2005, s 277*).

- More generally, there is a body of statutory rules designed to prevent a taxpayer from turning income into capital for tax purposes – 'the transactions in securities' regime now found in *ITA 2007, Pt 13, Ch 1*.

Oddly enough, the Acts themselves do not define income, other than stating that it is charged under specific provisions of *ITEPA 2003* or *ITTOIA 2005*.

Different types of income

4.7 In identifying the income of a trust for a particular tax year, it is essential to be clear under which charging provision the income falls, especially since there are different rules for losses. For the purposes of this book, the charging provisions may be found in the following parts of *ITTOIA 2005*:

- Part 2 – Trading income;
- Part 3 – Property income;
- Part 4 – Savings and investment income;
- Part 5 – Chapter 5, dealing with amounts treated as the income of the settlor of a settlement;
- Part 8 – Foreign income: special rules; and
- Part 9 – Partnerships.

ITA 2007, Pt 9 contains special rules about settlements and trustees and, in particular, the provisions for discretionary and accumulation settlements.

COMPLIANCE IN SUMMARY

4.8 Under the self-assessment system trustees must make a return to HMRC of the trust's annual liabilities for income tax and CGT.

Notifying the liability to tax

> **Focus**
>
> Be aware of the automatic and stand-alone late filing penalty (introduced with effect from 2010/11) – this will be triggered irrespective of the extent (if any) of the trust liability to tax on its income and/or gains.

4.9 Trustees who first become liable to income tax or CGT must normally notify HMRC no later than the 5 October following the end of the relevant tax year, unless they have already received a notice to file a return from HMRC (*TMA 1970, s 7(1)*). See **3.11** which discusses the online trust register (TRS) introduced with effect from 2017/18 and **4.11** below.

Generally speaking, each first-named trustee will receive from HMRC, within a week or two after the end of the tax year, the self-assessment form SA900 (see **4.54–4.62**) or more commonly a notice to file if previously filed online (as is more likely the case). It will be the responsibility of the trustee or their appointed adviser to complete any necessary supplementary pages (see **4.66–4.86**) in respect of income that is not covered on the main SA900. There are two options for calculating the tax: (i) if the return is completed and submitted to HMRC on or before 31 October, HMRC will calculate the tax due; or (ii) otherwise, the tax must be calculated by the trustees. The SA900 must be submitted either on or before the 31 October if in hardcopy paper format else on or before the 31 January following the end of the tax year if in electronic format. For returns prior to 2009/10, even if that return was delivered after the due date, provided all tax due was paid on or before the due date, the late filing penalty was mitigated to nil. For returns for 2010/11 and later, the late filing penalty applies regardless of whether the tax is timely paid, or indeed irrespective of whether a tax liability exists at all.

HMRC belatedly recognised that the combined effect of the 2016/17 introduction of the revised dividend rates with its removal of the notional dividend tax credit and the cessation of tax withholding at source for most interest receipts would have caused a substantial increase in the number of trusts that should register under self-assessment. Following representations from the various professional bodies, HMRC announced as an interim measure for 2016/17 that trustees would not need to register under self-assessment to report savings interest income alone if the income tax liability concerned was under £100 in total provided that the trust has no other income. HMRC confirmed that this relaxation in reporting requirements also applies for 2017/18 and in the HMRC Trusts and Estates Newsletter dated December 2017, this has been further extended to 2018/19 but, as at time of writing, there is no indication that HMRC will extend beyond this.

The modified reporting relaxation does not apply to discretionary or accumulation trusts with savings income in excess of the standard rate band.

Paying the tax

4.10 Income tax is normally collected in two equal annual instalments where the payment on account conditions are satisfied, the first on 31 January during the tax year, and the second on 31 July following the end of the tax year. To the extent that these two 'payments on account' are insufficient, a 'balancing payment' is due on 31 January after the end of the tax year, ie together with the first payment on account for the following year if due.

Where such payments on account exceed the total tax due, a repayment is due from HMRC. Interest on the tax payment will be paid by HMRC if repayment is made after 31 January following the tax year.

The first tax year

4.11 The past advantage of following the then form 41G (Trust) procedure when a trust was first created was that this generated automatic issue of the annual returns – the 41G process has now been withdrawn from April 2017 following the rollout of the online trust register (see **3.10**). The payment on account system does not operate until one year's liability has been determined. Therefore, for the first tax year, the liability will fall due on 31 January following the end of that tax year. If, for any reason, HMRC have not been notified of the existence of the trust and there is a trust tax liability for the year that is not notified to HMRC before 6 October after the end of the tax year, a penalty will apply.

Example 4.3—Existing trust: the Brown trust

The Brown Trust was created on 1 January 2015 and form 41G (Trust) was submitted at that time. Income was received in 2014/15 and subsequent tax years and on 6 April 2019 Bob as the first-named trustee received the 2018/19 trust self-assessment return for completion. The 2018/19 payments on account were made on 31 January 2019 and 31 July 2019, each based on 50% of the tax liability for the previous 2017/18 tax year. A balancing payment of any additional tax due for 2018/19 should be made on or before 31 January 2020 (together with any CGT for 2018/19). Assuming that Bob decides to complete the trust self-assessment return himself and to work out the tax, the trust return must be delivered on or before 31 January 2020 if submitted online or by 31 October 2019 if in paper form.

Example 4.4—New settlement: the Scarlett trust

Scarlett established a new family trust on 31 December 2018 but, as at 31 August 2019, neither she nor the trustees had informed HMRC through the TRS of its existence. Trust income arose between 1 January and 5 April 2019; thus, to avoid a penalty, the trustees need to give notice to HMRC by completing the Trust Online Register by 5 October 2019. The 2018/19 liability will fall due for settlement on 31 January 2020 and the trustees should also submit the trust self-assessment return by that date (assuming that the form is issued by HMRC before 1 November 2019). The trustees will not be liable to a penalty for notifying HMRC after 5 October 2019, so long as any tax liability is paid by 31 January 2020 (*TMA 1970, s 7(8)*), if they file their return in paper form on or before 31 October 2019 or electronically on or before 31 January 2020 – or, if later, within three months after the form is issued by HMRC (*TMA 1970, s 8A(1D), (1E)*). But see also the last sentence of **4.9** above.

Appeals, enquiries and discoveries

4.12 Appeals may be made against various HMRC notices or assessments. There is a strict time limit of 30 days following the issue of HMRC's notice or assessment.

The self-assessment regime enables HMRC to 'enquire' into a tax return. Notification of commencement of an enquiry must be made within 12 months after the actual date of submission of the return (unless the return was submitted late, when the 'enquiry window' closes 12 months after the end of the calendar quarter in which the return was actually submitted). If the enquiry results in HMRC concluding that the trustees have under-declared their tax, HMRC will amend the self-assessment, giving rise to the additional tax liability that the trustees must pay.

For a 'discovery assessment', there must have been fraud or negligence by the trustees or an agent (or at the end of the enquiry window HMRC cannot have been reasonably expected to be aware that too little tax has been charged, on the basis of the information supplied to HMRC). Apart from the 'discovery' mechanism, HMRC cannot later challenge a return if they do not raise an enquiry within the specified time limit. In the (non-trust) case of *J Hicks* (TC6301) it was established that for the issue of a discovery assessment to be valid, HMRC must show the tax insufficiency attributable to lack of full disclosure in the return directly arose from the taxpayer's failure to take reasonable care. The thorny question of acceptable time limits within which HMRC must raise a discovery assessment was heavily debated in the case of *Clive Beagles v HMRC* [2018] UKUT 380. The Tribunal found in favour of the taxpayer concluding that a discovery must retain its 'newness' thereby requiring HMRC to issue assessments within an acceptable timeframe.

THE INTEREST AND PENALTY REGIME

4.13 It has always been important, and all the more so under the self-assessment regime, for a taxpayer to make timely payment to HMRC of any tax due. Any unpaid tax will carry interest from the due date until payment. If tax has been overpaid, a (non-taxable) repayment supplement is due. The rates of interest on unpaid and overpaid tax vary from time to time, with changes in the bank base rate and are published by press release; see **4.17–4.18**.

Interest will therefore be due (inter alia) on:

- late paid payments on account due on 31 January and 31 July;
- late payments of balancing payments of income tax and CGT on 31 January after the end of the tax year;
- tax payable on HMRC's amendment to a self-assessment; and
- surcharges or penalties (after 30 days have passed).

Surcharges

4.14 Where the trustees fail to pay income tax or CGT due 28 days or more after the due date, a surcharge of 5% of the unpaid tax becomes payable. If the liability remains unpaid six months after the due date, the surcharge is doubled to 10% and, if still unpaid 12 months later, the surcharge is increased to 15% (*TMA 1970, s 59C*).

Penalties

> **Focus**
>
> Be aware of *FA 2009* draconian late/non-filing penalties imposed with effect from April 2010.

4.15 A comprehensive penalty regime was introduced by *FA 2007, Sch 24,* as extended by *FA 2008, Sch 40* to apply across all the taxes including IHT and *FA 2009, s 106, Sch 55*. For income tax (and CGT), the regime first applies to self-assessment returns for 2008/09. The regime leaves in place the system of fixed penalties, which include:

- failure to make a return by the due date: £100;
- continuing failure to make a return: £10 per day, up to a maximum of 90 days;
- failure to produce documents: £50;
- failure to keep and preserve records: £3,000.

(*TMA 1970, ss 93, 97AA, 98*)

The regime applies where:

(a) the taxpayer gives inaccurate information to HMRC, whether carelessly or deliberately; or

(b) the taxpayer fails to inform HMRC within 30 days of an assessment that the assessment is too low.

A failure within (b) carries a maximum penalty of 30% of the 'potential lost revenue'. The maximum penalties for (a) are: 30% for a careless inaccuracy; 70% for a deliberate but not concealed inaccuracy; and 100% for a deliberate and concealed inaccuracy. The previous system of mitigation of penalties has been replaced by a statutory regime for a reduction for disclosure, depending on whether a disclosure is prompted by HMRC or is unprompted (viz made at a time when the taxpayer has no reason to believe that HMRC have discovered or are about to discover the inaccuracy). A 30% penalty can be reduced to zero if disclosure is unprompted or 15% if prompted. A 70% penalty can be reduced to 20% if disclosure is unprompted or 35% if prompted; and a 100% penalty can be reduced to 30% if disclosure is unprompted or 50% if prompted. HMRC can also reduce a penalty if they think it right to do so because of special circumstances.

A penalty introduced in 2008 applies where a taxpayer gives inaccurate information to HMRC and that inaccuracy is attributable to a third party deliberately supplying false information to the taxpayer or to the third party deliberately withholding information from the taxpayer, with the intention that the relevant document contains the inaccuracy (*FA 2008, Sch 40, para 3*). This penalty is chargeable on the third party (whether or not the taxpayer is liable to a penalty) with a maximum of 100% of the potential lost revenue.

Additional penalty regimes have been introduced by *FA 2009*: under *Sch 55* for failure to make returns etc, and under *Sch 56* for failure to make payments on time. These draconian provisions took effect on 1 April 2010 and are as follows:

1 day late:	A fixed penalty of £100
3 months late:	Additional £10 for each following day, up to a maximum of £900
6 months late:	Additional £300 or 5% of the tax due, if higher
12 months late:	Additional £300 or 5% of the tax due, if higher. In serious cases of late submission, the penalty may be set at 100% of the tax due

The taxpayer account

4.16 Each taxpayer has an 'account' with HMRC, which will have a running balance of tax due together with interest (or perhaps repayments due with repayment supplement). The 'official rate' of interest was reduced from 3% to 2.50% for 2017/18 but the 'official rate' of interest for 2018/19 has not yet been announced but is likely to remain at 2.50%.

The interest rate on unpaid tax was increased from 3% (effective from 21 November 2017) to 3.25% with effect from 21 August 2018. The interest rate on overpaid tax remains as 0.5%.

Interest rates: recent changes

Underpaid tax

4.17

From	6 September 2006	to	5 August 2007	7.5%
From	6 August 2007	to	5 January 2008	8.5%
From	6 January 2008	to	5 November 2008	7.5%
From	6 November 2008	to	5 December 2008	6.5%
From	6 December 2008	to	5 January 2009	5.5%
From	6 January 2009	to	26 January 2009	4.5%
From	27 January 2009	to	23 March 2009	3.5%
From	24 March 2009	to	28 September 2009	2.5%
From	29 September 2009	to	22 August 2016	3.0%
From	23 August 2016	to	20 November 2017	2.75%
From	21 November 2017	to	20 August 2018	3.0%
From	21 August 2018			3.25%

Overpaid tax

4.18

From	6 September 2006	to	5 August 2007	3.0%
From	6 August 2007	to	5 January 2008	4.0%
From	6 January 2008	to	5 November 2008	3.0%
From	6 November 2008	to	5 December 2008	2.25%
From	6 December 2008	to	5 January 2009	1.5%
From	6 January 2009	to	26 January 2009	0.75%
From	27 January 2009	to	28 September 2009	0%
From	29 September 2009			0.5%

Example 4.5—The Black discretionary trust

The net income tax liability of the trust for 2017/18 was £5,000 with 2018/19 payments on account of £2,500 due on each of 31 January 2019 and 31 July 2019. On each of those dates, they actually paid only £2,000 but planned to pay the outstanding £1,000, together with the £2,375 balancing payment due (the total liability for 2018/19 is £7,375) on 31 January 2020.

Interest will be calculated as follows (assuming no further changes in rates):

	Tax	*Period*	*Rate*	*Interest*
	underpaid			
From 1.2.19 to 31.7.19	£500	182 days	3.25%	£8.10
From 1.8.19 to 31.1.20	£1,000	184 days	3.25%	£16.38
Total interest due				£24.48

ABSOLUTE ENTITLEMENT TO INCOME

4.19 A settlement in which the beneficiary has an interest in possession (whether such interest was in existence before or on/after 22 March 2006) means that the beneficiary is entitled to the income as it arises. The trustees may deduct proper income expenses (see **4.117–4.119**) before the income is distributed but, otherwise, the income is that of the beneficiary. Distinguish this from a situation where the trustees have a discretionary power over income or power to withhold income: this is not an interest in possession settlement (see **4.32–4.34**). There may be some monetary receipts of the trust that are treated as capital under trust law but are nonetheless treated as income for tax purposes, eg premiums received under leases granted for less than 50 years (see **4.6**) – such receipts do not become income of the life tenant (*ITTOIA 2005, Pt 3, Ch 4*) simply by reason of their income tax treatment rather their classification is determined under trust law, ie policy (chargeable event) gains taxed as income but properly treated at trust capital.

The life tenant's income

Focus

The transparent nature of the life interest trust is mirrored in the treatment of the trust income in the hands of the beneficiary; thus, trust income is taxed on the beneficiary on an arising basis, irrespective of date of onward distribution to that beneficiary.

4.20 Although the life tenant may not physically receive the income until after the end of a tax year, it is still treated as his income for that tax year in which it arose to the trust, and it is the rate of tax in force for that year which determines, firstly, how much tax the trustees should withhold on account of lower rate or basic rate tax (now impacted by the withdrawal of the notional dividend tax credit and withholding on most savings income with effect from 6 April 2016) and, secondly, the liability of the beneficiary to higher rate tax, if any. After making a payment to the beneficiary, the trustees must also complete a tax voucher (R185) showing the tax at the dividend, savings or basic rate, and the net sum to which the beneficiary is entitled.

For 2015/16 there was a 0% starting rate applicable to individuals (but not trusts) but restricted to savings income within the band of £5,000 (but subject to the level of earnings), and both the savings rate and basic rate were set at 20%.

For 2016/17 et seq the 0% savings band available to individuals alone is withdrawn and replaced with a tax free £1,000 savings allowance for basic rate taxpayers or a lower £500 allowance for higher rate taxpayers. Neither of the tax free allowances are available to a trust (bare trust excepted). Similarly, from 2016/17 and 2017/18 there was a newly created tax free dividend allowance of £5,000 which is reduced to £2,000 for 2018/19 et seq but again this is restricted to individual taxpayers (irrespective of whether basic, higher or super rate) and thus not available to trusts (bare trust excepted) –

this works in tandem with the 2016/17 et seq withdrawal of the 10% notional dividend credit and introduction of the fresh dividend rates of 7.5% (basic rate taxpayer/non-discretionary or accumulation trust), 32.5% (higher rate taxpayer) and 38.1% (super rate taxpayer/discretionary or accumulation trust). From a trust perspective, the combination of these changes coupled with the 2016/17 et seq withdrawal of the requirement to deduct tax at source from interest paid by most financial institutions/deposit takers has encouraged most trusts to mandate the trust income to the life tenant in order to avoid the compliance issues of filing trust returns and settling the tax due on now untaxed income receipts but see **4.9** above for relaxation in the filing rules for 2017/18 and 2018/19.

The *F(No 2)A 2017* has introduced a fresh £1,000 trading and property tax allowance; effective from 6 April 2017 but this is not extended to trusts (bare trust excepted).

Exempt income

4.21 This transparent (or 'see through') analysis will apply also to income that is exempt in the hands of the beneficiary, eg interest free of tax to residents abroad (FOTRA) government securities payable to a non-UK resident life tenant. In such cases, the trustees will arrange to receive the interest gross, and they will pay this to the non-UK resident beneficiary without requirement to withhold or account for any tax thereon.

Annuity income

4.22 A trust term may provide for the payment of an annuity, eg £1,000 per annum. For the trustees this will be a 'charge on income', or if income is insufficient, on capital. The trustees must deduct tax to the extent that the annuity is paid out of income. Where the income is paid out of a non-dividend source, there is no problem, since the trustees are chargeable to 20% on the income and will deduct tax at 20% on paying the annuity. However, where for years up to 2015/16, the income was paid out of a dividend source, the trustees were only given credit for the 10% non-repayable notional tax credit, so there was a further 10% liability to be deducted from the gross annuity prior to payment. For 2016/17 et seq following the withdrawal of the notional tax credit, the tax shortfall due by the trustees will total the full 20%.

Rights to occupy property

4.23 A trust might give to a life tenant the right to occupy a property, but currently for UK trusts there is no assessment of notional income.

Example 4.6—Interest in possession settlement pre 6 April 2016

The trust income for 2015/16 comprised £2,700 of dividends carrying a non-repayable 10% tax credit of £300 plus rental income of £5,000 (net of allowable expenses). The dividends were mandated directly to the life tenant, but the rental income was paid into a trustee account from which all rental expenses were paid. Net payments of rental income were then made to the life tenant after the end of the tax year.

Accordingly, in 2015/16 the life tenant received dividends totalling £2,700 and, on 1 June 2016, the trustees paid him a cheque for £4,000 together with form R185. This showed trust income for 2015/16 as follows:

- Net rental income of £4,000 and a 20% tax credit of £1,000.

It should be noted that as the dividend income is mandated to the life tenant, there is no requirement to report that income on the Trust return nor report that dividend income on form R185. The trustees will have to complete the Land and Property Supplementary Pages SA 903 (see **4.74–4.77**), because it is they and not the life tenant who manage the property, and will account for basic rate tax on the net income.

Because no part of the trust income is subject to the trustees' discretion, question 13 on p 7 of form SA900 does not apply.

Example 4.7—Interest in possession settlement post 5 April 2016

The trust income for 2018/19 comprised £2,700 of gross dividends plus rental income of £5,000 (net of allowable expenses). The dividends were mandated directly to the life tenant, but the rental income was paid into a trustee account from which all rental expenses are paid. Net payments of rental income were then made to the life tenant after the end of the tax year.

Accordingly, in 2018/19 the life tenant received dividends totalling £2,700 and, on 1 June 2019, the trustees paid him a cheque for £4,000 together with form R185. This showed trust income for 2018/19 as follows:

- Net rental income of £4,000 and a 20% tax credit of £1,000.

As before, since the dividend income was mandated to the life tenant, there was no requirement to report the income on form R185. However, the withdrawal of the notional tax credit and levy of a positive individual dividend tax rate of 7.5% or 32.5% or 38.1% (dependent on the life tenant's personal tax position) means it is the life tenant who was now responsible for settling the tax due on that mandated dividend income source. The trustees will have to complete the Land and Property Supplementary

Pages SA 903 (see **4.74–4.77**), because it was they and not the life tenant who managed the property, and must account for basic rate tax on the net income.

Because no part of the trust income is subject to the trustees' discretion, question 13 on p 7 of form SA900 does not apply.

SETTLOR-INTERESTED TRUSTS

4.24 Income tax, CGT (prior to 2008/09) and IHT contain rules to ensure that tax cannot be avoided by placing assets into a trust from which the settlor or (apart from IHT) his spouse can benefit. The rules for income tax go back over many years and were significantly less complex in 1995.

Income taxed on the settlor

4.25 As a general principle, the anti-avoidance rules apply to treat the income (or gain prior to 6 April 2008) as that of the settlor for tax purposes. There is one principal rule in *ITTOIA 2005, s 624*: income of a trust is treated as belonging to the settlor, unless it derived from property in which he has no interest. A settlor is treated as having an interest in property if that property (or any property derived from it) *could* be applied for his benefit or for the benefit of his spouse or civil partner – see the examples below. Note that, for this purpose, 'spouse' does not include widow or widower; similarly, if a civil partner can only benefit after the death of the settlor there is no liability on the settlor during his lifetime provided the settlor is excluded from benefit. Note also that a settlement by one spouse/civil partner for the other is caught if the gift does not carry the right to the whole of the income or if the gift is property which really amounts to a right to income (*ITTOIA 2005, s 625*).

The income tax impact of the settlor-interested trust was addressed in the case of *Rogge, Kent and others v HMRC* [2012] UKFTT 49 (TC). The First-tier Tribunal held that the settlor of a settlor-interested trust was liable to income tax on all trust income, even where that trust income stemmed from payments originally made by the settlor to the trust.

Any income tax that a settlor pays on trust income as a consequence of the settlor-interested rules, but which is not actually paid to him, can be recovered from the trustees, ie the settlor is not left 'out of pocket'. By the same token, any refund or reduction in personal liability received as a consequence of assessment on the settlor properly belongs to the trust and must be repaid by the settlor to the trustees – that repayment is not treated as an addition to the trust by the settlor. Of course, if the income is actually paid to the settlor, it will be treated as his anyway and then he cannot recover from the trustees the tax on that income. *ITTOIA 2005, s 646* (amended to have effect for years commencing 6 April 2010 onwards) enables the settlor to require HMRC to issue a certificate showing the amount of repayment due in respect of their income where the settlor has difficulty in working out the position. An illustration of the calculation is set out in HMRC Trusts, Settlements and Estates Manual at TSEM4550.

Where there is a discretionary trust and the settlor is a basic rate taxpayer, it may be beneficial (in the long run) for the trust to be settlor-interested in so far as income is concerned. This is because, although the additional rate bringing the trustees' liability up to 45% for non-dividend income (50% for 2010/11 to 2012/13) or 38.1% for dividend income (37.5% for 2014/15 and 2015/16, 42.5% for 2010/11 to 2012/13) will apply, the settlor will be able to recover the tax, albeit to pass back to the trust, and there will be a saving of some 25% (30% for 2010/11 to 2012/13) in tax or, if dividend income, 30.6% (27.5% for 2013/14 to 2015/16, 32.5% for 2010/11 to 2012/13) (see **4.32**).

Capital sums

4.26 There are further anti-avoidance rules which deal with capital sums (*ITTOIA 2005, ss 633–643*). These potentially penal rules are typically aimed at discretionary settlements from which the settlor or spouse is excluded from benefit but from which the settlor receives a capital sum (also see **4.30** regarding similar treatment for parental settlements). This is not common in practice, although it could arise in a situation where the trustees borrow money from the settlor or spouse and subsequently repay the loan (or vice versa). If there is undistributed income in the trust, the loan repayment is assessed on the settlor to the extent that it falls within that undistributed income available for that tax year or the following ten years and irrespective of the character of that income. *ITTOIA 2005, s 640* in effect gives the settlor credit for the tax paid by the trustees, which is likely to remove much if not all of the sting of this rule. However, there may be an issue to the extent that the income concerned is dividend income on which the discretionary trustees will have suffered tax at 38.1% (37.5% for 2013/14 to 2015/16, 42.5% for 2010/11 to 2012/13) but the settlor's liability is (for 2013/14 onwards) set at 40% or 45% by reason of the loss of trust income character.

Treatment of income

Two examples from the courts

4.27 A case illustrating the rule was *Young v Pearce; Young v Scrutton* [1996] STC 743. Two husbands ran a profitable company and between them owned all the shares. There was a reorganisation of the share capital as a result of which new preference shares were issued to the two wives – such shares entitled them to 30% of the profits of the company but virtually nothing else. The court held that this was a statutory settlement and that, as a consequence, the husbands remained liable on the income from the preference shares. Interestingly, had the shares given to the wives been, say, a separate class of non-voting ordinary shares with rights to capital on a winding up, the appeals of the taxpayers should have succeeded.

4.28 In *Jones v Garnett* [2007] STC 1536, Geoff Jones was the sole director of a company in which each of he and his wife, Diana, owned one of two issued shares (having subscribed for cash). Diana Jones performed secretarial and administrative duties for a wage, but the fee earning work was all done by Geoff. Geoff drew a salary set at a lower level than would have been commanded by an independent director performing the same duties. Overturning both the Special Commissioners and the High Court, the Court of Appeal held that there was no 'arrangement' to be caught as a statutory settlement. While there might have been an expectation that surplus income would arise in the company, which could be distributed both to Geoff and to Diana Jones, there was no guarantee that that would be so. The unanimous decision of the House of Lords dismissing HMRC's appeal was issued on 25 July 2007. Agreeing with HMRC, the House of Lords held that there had been a statutory settlement (within what is now *ITTOIA 2005, s 625*) in Geoff giving the opportunity to his wife Diana to subscribe for a share at par, with the expectation of future profit. Geoff Jones' appeal, therefore, from the Court of Appeal on that point failed. However, the House of Lords went on to find, dismissing the appeal by HMRC that the 'outright gift' exception for transfers between spouses (now *ITTOIA 2005, s 626*) would apply in this case. Although Diana had subscribed for her share herself, the element of 'bounty' contributed by her husband meant that there had been a gift. In the words of Lord Hope of Craighead:

> 'an arrangement by which one spouse uses a private company as a tax-efficient vehicle for distributing to the other's income which its business generates is likely to constitute a "settlement" on the other spouse … but so long as the shares from which that income arises are ordinary shares, and not shares carrying contractual rights which are restricted wholly or substantial to a right to income, the settlement will fall within the exception'.

4.29 A day after the judgment was delivered, a Ministerial Statement was issued by the Exchequer Secretary stating that legislation would be introduced in due course to ensure that there is greater clarity in the law on the tax treatment of 'income splitting'. The Government took the view that individuals involved in such arrangements should pay tax on what is in substance their own income. Of course, such legislation would apply only for the future and not for the past. Following the Pre-Budget Report on 9 October 2007, a consultative document outlining the scope of intended legislation was issued, but this was roundly criticised by the professional bodies, and it was later announced that the proposed 'income-shifting' legislation would be deferred until 2009. The

Pre-Budget Report dated 24 November 2008 stated that, 'given the current economic challenges', income-shifting legislation would not be brought forward at *FA 2009* and, to date, no such legislation has been put in place; however, the issue remains very much under review such that complacency should not be assumed.

Example 4.8—Settlor-interested discretionary trust

Algernon had made a discretionary trust on 1 January 2001 and, whilst the trust deed excluded Algernon from benefit under the settlement, it did not exclude his wife during Algernon's lifetime. Consequently, this is a settlor-interested trust and the trust income is treated as that of Algernon for income tax purposes, irrespective of the person to whom it is actually paid. Had the trust deed excluded his wife from benefit during Algernon's lifetime (but not necessarily on Algernon's death) the settlor-interested rules would not have come into operation.

Algernon is an additional rate taxpayer, and the gross trust income for 2018/19 is £10,000, of which £9,500 is dividends and £500 is gross interest. Ignoring trustees' management expenses, the trust will be liable to tax as follows:

2018/19		£
Interest	500	
Standard rate band (to cover)	(500) @ 20%	100.00
Balance	Nil	
Dividends	9,500	
Standard rate band (balance)	(500) @ 7.5%	37.50
Balance	9,000 @ 38.1%	3,429.00
Total liability before payments on account		3,566.50

Algernon will be required to include the following trust income in his personal return:

	Gross Income	Tax credit
	£	£
Interest (gross)	500.00	
Tax credit		100.00
Dividends (gross)	9,500.00	
Tax credit		3,466.50

TRUSTS FOR SETTLOR'S MINOR CHILDREN (PARENTAL SETTLEMENTS)

The general principle

4.30 Anti – avoidance measures operate to ensure that a settlor cannot escape an income tax liability by having income, from a settlement or bare trust he has made, paid or redirected to his minor unmarried children. Any such income is assessed on the parent settlor, subject to a *de minimis* limit of £100 per child, per parent, per annum (*ITTOIA 2005, ss 629–632*). Note that, once the threshold has been exceeded, the whole of the income is taxable on the parent.

Retained income

> **Focus**
>
> Income from capital added post 8 March 1999 to pre-existing settlements will still trigger the anti-avoidance rules, such that the parent settlor will be subject to tax on the income whether or not the income is paid out by the trustees.

4.31 Before *FA 1999*, the tax impact could be avoided by retaining income within the trust until the child became 18, in other words the tax liability of the parent settlor was restricted to the level of income paid out. The *FA 1999* rules continue to apply to income from capital originally transferred to settlements made before 9 March 1999.

To avoid the *FA 1999* tax charge on the parent settlor, it remains essential that the income concerned is subject to the discretionary or accumulation regime, ie it is not the income of the child either by reason of bare trust or more unusually by virtue of an interest in possession through exclusion of *Trustee Act 1925, s 31*. However, where *s 31* is not so excluded income would not be paid out to the child, as the child could not give a good 'receipt' for the income until reaching the age of 18. The income would thus be retained by the trustees in a separate account, but for income tax purposes it would be that of the child and, therefore, could benefit from the child's personal allowance, lower and basic rates of income tax.

For bare trusts or interest in possession trusts made on or after 9 March 1999 and for income from capital added on or after that date to pre-existing settlements, the anti-avoidance rules apply whether or not the income is paid out until such time as the child reaches age 18.

Example 4.9—Parental settlement

On 1 January 2015, Cathy and Tim created a discretionary settlement for the benefit of their three minor children Lucy, Chris and Will.

Of the trust fund, Tim, an additional rate taxpayer, contributed £125,000 and Cathy, a basic rate taxpayer, contributed £125,000. The 2018/19 trust income comprised interest income of £3,000, applied by the trustees in that year for the benefit of Lucy, who had her 11th birthday on 1 January 2019.

The full amount of the trust income is assessed on the parent settlors for 2018/19 , with £1,500 (50%) treated as Tim's income and £1,500 (50%) treated as Cathy's income. Each settlor has a right of recovery from the settlement for any additional personal tax liability due on the trust income. The trustees will be liable for 20% on the first £1,000 tranche of trust income (sheltered by the standard rate band), with the balance liable at the 45% rate. Tim will have a small personal liability based on his share of the income sheltered by the standard rate band which has borne tax at 20% (eg £500 @ (45 – 20)% = £125) and he may recover this from the trustees. In contrast, Cathy may seek a repayment of tax of her share of the income in excess of the standard rate band which has borne 25% tax (eg £1,000 @ (45 – 20)% = £250) and she must account for this to the trustees.

POWER TO ACCUMULATE OR A DISCRETION OVER INCOME: TAX RATES

4.32 From 6 April 2016, the rate of tax payable by trustees of a settlement on income in excess of the standard rate band (see **4.35**), where the income can be accumulated or the income is subject to the discretionary trust regime, is 38.1% for dividend income (37.5% for 2013/14 to 2015/16, 42.5% for 2010/11 to 2012/13) and 45% for all other income (50% for 2010/11 to 2012/13) (see **4.34**). As from 2006/07, the rate applicable to trusts is payable even on the income of settlor-interested trusts (see **4.26–4.29**); the settlor is credited with the tax paid by the trustees, although he must account to the trustees for the benefit but also retains the right of recovery in the event of any shortfall (*ITTOIA 2005, s 646(5)*).

This mechanism arises under *ITA 2007, Pt 9, Ch 3*. (There is a quite separate procedure under *ITA 2007, Pt 9, Ch 3*, which arises where payments are made by trustees to the beneficiary; see **4.41–4.43**.)

Permitted accumulation periods

4.33 A settlement where there is a power to accumulate income is treated for income tax purposes in the same way as a discretionary trust. Very often, a discretionary trust will itself contain a power to accumulate. A power to accumulate in an otherwise interest in possession trust would prevent it from being interest in possession and would bring it within the discretionary and accumulation regime. Prior to the introduction of the *Perpetuities and Accumulations Act 2009* and excluding charitable trusts, the trustees could only accumulate income over the following periods:

- 21 years from the date of the settlement;
- during the infancy of a beneficiary; or
- during the lifetime of a person in being at the date of the settlement, eg the settlor or spouse.

Following enactment of the *Perpetuities and Accumulations Act 2009*, there is no longer a statutory time restriction on trustees' power to accumulate income (subject always to the provisions of the trust deed): see **9.1** for the impact on existing trusts.

Different types of income

4.34 Trustees may receive income falling into different categories:

- For years prior to 6 April 2016, a dividend of £90 carried a non-repayable tax credit of £10 which resulted in gross income of £100. That pre 6 April 2016 dividend income receipt by the discretionary or accumulation trustees was subject to tax at the then trust dividend rate of 37.5% (42.5% for 2010/11 to 2012/13), of which 10% was met by the tax credit, to leave a further 27.5% of the gross to be paid by the trustees. From 2008/09, that tax credit was extended to dividends from qualifying non-UK companies, where the trust shareholding was less than 10% (which limit was removed from 2009/10 by *FA 2009, Sch 19*, subject to qualifying conditions). With effect from 6 April 2016, the dividend rate no longer carries a non-repayable 10% tax credit and the rate for dividends not falling within the standard rate band is rebased to 38.1% – dividends falling within the standard rate band attract tax at a rate of 7.5%. It should be noted that the dividend allowance available to basic rate and higher rate individual taxpayers is not extended to trusts (bare trusts excepted).
- For years prior to 6 April 2016 most interest income was received net of 20% tax (the basic rate) deducted at source. Here, out of gross income of £100 the discretionary or accumulation trustees received £80 and had to pay HMRC a further £25 to meet the total tax liability of 45% (50% for 2010/11 to 2012/13). From 6 April 2016, savings interest income is paid

gross without any tax deduction at source thereby increasing the tax liability due by the trust on 31 January 2017 et seq (but see **4.9** for a relaxation of the reporting rules for 2016/17, 2017/18 and 2018/19). It should be noted that the interest allowance available to basic rate and higher rate individual taxpayers is not extended to trusts (bare trusts excepted).

- Income received gross, eg rental income. Here, the trustees must pay 45% (50% for 2010/11 to 2012/13).

Example 4.10—Furniss discretionary trust

The trustees of the Furniss received the following income in the year ended 5 April 2019:

Dividend income (gross)	£15,000
REIT income	£1,000
Less tax deducted at source	(£200)
Net	£800
Rental income (gross)	£10,000

The tax liability will be as follows:

	Rate computation	*Tax/Credit*	*Trustees' tax liability*
Dividend income £15,000	Dividend trust rate @ 38.1%		£5,715.00
REIT income £1,000	@ 20%	£200 less tax deducted at source £200	£0.00
Rental income £10,000	@ 45%		£4,500.00
Total			£10,215.00

THE STANDARD RATE BAND

4.35 A *de minimis* rule applying from 2005/06 was one of only two changes to the trust regime to be enacted by *FA 2005* (the other being a special regime for trusts with vulnerable beneficiaries – see **4.37–4.40**). This *de minimis* rule applies where a trust is subject to the special rates, ie is discretionary or accumulation in character (see **4.32–4.34**). The special rates of tax applicable to such trusts are 38.1% (37.5% for 2013/14 to 2015/16, 42.5% for 2010/11 to 2012/13) for dividend income and otherwise 45% (50% for 2010/11 to 2012/13). In 2005/06, the first £500 of taxable income was charged at the basic rate (then 22%), the lower rate (20%) or the dividend ordinary rate (10%), as appropriate to the type of income concerned. From 2006/07 onwards, the standard rate band has been increased to £1,000 but this is further sub-divided between all the non-exempt settlements made by the same settlor (and irrespective of whether those settlements produce income), up to a maximum of five; that is, the standard rate band cannot be less than £200. The standard rate band is allocated first to basic rate income, then savings income and lastly dividend income. Deductible trust management expenses (see **4.117–4.119**) must be deducted before arriving at the amount falling within the lower rate band.

Distributions of income

4.36 Where trustees exercise their discretion to distribute income (see **4.41**), the trustees must account for the tax due thereon, although such tax may be franked by qualifying (real) tax already borne on trust income. Added to those types is tax payable at the lower rates under this rule. Amendments have been made to the existing legislation to ensure that this benefit cannot be obtained twice, ie under the rules as well as under the previous regime.

Example 4.11—Effect of trust management expenses

In 2018/19, a discretionary trust received net REIT income of £1,750 which has suffered 20% tax deducted at source. The trustees incurred qualifying management expenses of £150. The computation is as follows:

REIT income (net)	£1,750
Less management expenses	(£150)
Adjusted net interest	£1,600
Tax credit at 20% on gross equivalent (A)	400
Adjusted gross	2,000
Tax thereon:	
£1,000 @ 20% (standard rate band)	£200
£1000 @ 45%	£450
Gross liability	650
Less tax credit (A)	(£400)
Further tax payable by the trustees	£250

Following the 2016/17 change to treatment of dividend income with the withdrawal of the notional 10% tax credit, the full 7.5%/38.1% real tax paid by the trust enters the tax pool.

TRUSTS FOR VULNERABLE BENEFICIARIES

4.37 This subject is covered in more detail in Chapter 7 and the following is a mere summary of the rules, introduced by *FA 2005* and applicable from 2004/05. They enable a discretionary or accumulation trust, which would otherwise be taxed at the rate applicable to trusts, to be taxed instead according to the personal financial circumstances of one or more beneficiaries, provided they are qualifying 'vulnerable persons'.

The term 'vulnerable persons' is defined as 'disabled persons' and 'relevant minors':

- Disabled persons are those falling within the IHT definition in *IHTA 1984, s 74(4)*.
- A 'relevant minor' is simply a person under 18 with at least one parent having died.

The trust must be a 'qualifying trust' as defined. In the case of a disabled person that means that where any trust property is applied for the benefit of a beneficiary it must be applied for the benefit of that disabled person subject to a de minimis (see below). In the case of a relevant minor, a qualifying trust may be either a trust arising by statute on intestacy or a will trust (or one established under the Criminal Injuries Compensation Scheme), which ensures that the minor receives capital and income and accumulations absolutely at age 18.

The outcome of a consultation on the definition of vulnerable beneficiary trusts and harmonisation of the income tax, CGT and IHT conditions to reduce the complexities is reflected in measures contained within *FA 2013* and effective from 6 April 2013 in respect of trusts created on or after 8 April 2013. The legislation aligned the qualification with the introduction of the personal independent payment (PIP) benefit, which replaced the former disability living allowance (DLA) benefit and introduced a modification to the application of income and capital for non-vulnerable beneficiary benefit restricted to the lesser of £3,000 or 3% of the settled fund per annum. Importantly, *FA 2013* also removed the former disregard rule concerning provisions which grant powers of advancement to include the statutory power under *Trustee Act 1925, s 32*.

FA 2014 contained further measures which expand the range of trusts qualifying for the special income (and CGT/IHT) treatment and enable the CGT uplift to apply on the death of the vulnerable beneficiary.

Electing for special treatment

4.38 The election must be made on or before 12 months after the 31 January following the end of the tax year to which it will first apply. Interestingly, the election itself is a gateway that merely permits access to the relief, with the latter in turn claimed on an annual basis. Once the election is in place, the claim for its application can most easily be made by checking Box 8.18 and 10B of the trust return. Therefore, to adopt the regime for 2018/19, the election must be made on or before 31 January 2021. The election alone must be made both by the trustees and the vulnerable person – or someone on his behalf. HMRC specify what must be contained in the election, which is irrevocable. The election automatically ceases to have effect when (i) the person ceases to be vulnerable, or (ii) the trust is no longer qualifying or comes to an end, in which event the trustees must inform HMRC within 90 days.

Special treatments

4.39 The rule is intended to make the vulnerable person's personal allowances and both the savings and basic rate available to the trustees when calculating the liability on trust income. As explained above, this treatment may be claimed each tax year and it does not apply where the trust is settlor-interested such that the income is already taxed on the settlor (see **4.26–4.29**). *FA 2005* provides a series of steps to calculate what is known as the 'vulnerable person's liability' and then to ascertain the reduction in the income tax liability of the trustees (*FA 2005, ss 23–45* and *Sch 1*). Note that, if the election is made for this special treatment, and income is distributed onward to the beneficiary by the trustees, the regime for discretionary payments under *ITA 2007, Pt 9, Ch 7* continues to apply (see **4.41–4.43**). For relief once claimed applies equally for CGT purposes but the applicable provisions vary as to whether the vulnerable person is UK resident or non-UK resident. Here, of course, the relief could prove beneficial, given the disparity in the CGT rate applied to the trust and the perhaps basic rate beneficiary.

For an illustration of the impact of the election on the income of a vulnerable beneficiary trust see **7.11**.

Administration

4.40 HMRC are empowered to confirm that the beneficiary is, indeed, vulnerable and that the settlement is a qualifying trust, subject to giving a minimum of 60 days' notice. If HMRC find that the statutory requirements are not met (or that since the effective date of the election there has been an event that terminates the validity of the election), they can give notice that the election never had or has ceased to have effect.

DISCRETIONARY PAYMENTS

4.41 A special charging regime operates under *ITA 2007, Pt 9, Ch 7* where trustees make payments of income in exercise of their discretion. By definition, the regime cannot apply to accumulations of income, which are generally added to capital net of the 45% charge for non-dividend income (50% for 2010/11 to 2012/13) or 38.1% charge for dividend income (37.5% for 2013/14 to 2015/16). That said, however, a trust deed may empower trustees to make payments out of accumulated income as if this were income of the current year. In that case, the distribution regime will apply.

Income distributions made to the trust beneficiary are deemed to be made net of 45% (50% for 2010/11 to 2012/13) tax at source irrespective of the income type supporting the payment, eg a net payment of £4,400 is equivalent to a gross payment of £8,000 less a £3,600 tax credit.

Liability of the beneficiary

4.42 Any payment made to a discretionary beneficiary is treated as made net of 45% (50% for 2010/11 to 2012/13) tax, with the latter funded by real tax borne by the trustees and paid over to HMRC. Such tax is to be treated as real tax in the hands of the beneficiary, such that the latter may then recover all or part of the tax (unless he is a super rate taxpayer).

The tax pool

4.43 However, on the occasion of income distribution to the beneficiary, this does not simply mean that the trustees must pay a further 45% (50% for 2010/11 to 2012/13), because that charge can be franked by the real tax the trustees have already paid (known as the 'tax pool'). The initial change in dividend taxation from 6 April 1999 made a significant difference for the period 1999/2000 to 2015/16 insofar as the notional tax credit on dividends could not enter the tax pool, although the additional 27.5% of the prevailing 37.5% dividend rate in force for 2013/14 to 2015/16 (32.5% for 2010/11 to 2012/13) did enter the tax pool. The combination of the higher tax credits for the three years to 5 April 2013 added to the lower pre-6 April 2010 franking credits (built up at the lower rates for dividends at 22.5% net of the 10% notional credit) added to the similar taxation of non-dividend income demanded greater account be taken of the available tax pool credit when considering an income distribution for 2013/14 to 2015/16. Tax pools in hand at the end of 1998/99 could never be augmented (except in relation to non-dividend income) and thus would simply be run down through distributions of income over the years.

The introduction of the 38.1% dividend rate and withdrawal of the notional 10% tax credit effective from 6 April 2016 has a real impact on the tax pool and the ability to fund income distributions out of post-tax income but see commentary at **4.36** above.

It should be noted that tax paid on income used to meet trustee management expenses cannot enter the tax pool.

Example 4.12— Furniss discretionary trust (2)

Consider **Example 4.10**. In 2018/19, the trustees have gross dividend income of £15,000, net REIT income of £800 and gross rental income of £10,000 and have had to pay additional tax of £10,215 under *ITA 2007, s 479* leaving them with net income of £15,585 ((£15,000 + £10,000 + £800) – (£5,715 + £4,500)). However, disregarding the interest and rental income, they cannot simply distribute that amount to the beneficiaries. The reason for this is explained by the following table:

Trust income net of tax liability		15,585
Less net distribution to beneficiaries		(15,585)
Net distribution grossed up at 45%	28,336	
Tax thereon at 45%	12,751	
Covered by real tax paid by trustees	(£10,415)*	
Remaining liability of trustees on distribution		(£2,336)
Shortfall in trust income to meet tax liability on distribution		2,336
Gross income of beneficiaries		£28,336
Tax thereon @ 45%		(£12,751)
Net income of beneficiaries		£15,585

**£200 + £10,215*

THE PRE-OWNED ASSETS REGIME

Summary

4.44 This charge to income tax applies from 2005/06 (*FA 2004, Sch 15*). The charge is applied to the value of the benefit of enjoying 'pre-owned assets' at any time from 6 April 2006 onwards. These generally are assets that were previously owned by the taxpayer and that have been disposed of in whole or in part since 18 March 1986. According to the then Finance Bill 2004 Standing Committee Report, the declared target of this charge is: '…the range of schemes that allow wealthy taxpayers to give their assets away, or achieve the appearance of doing so, and so benefit from the inheritance tax exemption for lifetime gifts, while in reality retaining continuing enjoyment of and access to those assets, much as before'.

In broad terms, the aim of the pre-owned asset tax (POAT) regime is to create an adverse income tax consequence for arrangements which have, according to the courts, successfully evaded the reservation of benefit regime for IHT (see **6.18–6.23**) while enabling the taxpayer to continue to enjoy some benefit for the asset which he has given away. This is the point of the transitional provisions described at **4.51**: HMRC intend that a person should 'pay' for the continuing enjoyment of an asset which has been given away, whether in the form of the reservation of benefit code, under which he is treated as continuing to be beneficially entitled, or, if not, under the POAT regime.

Separate rules apply to:

- land;
- chattels; and
- intangible property comprised in a settlement where the settlor retains an interest.

Land

4.45 There is an income tax charge where a taxpayer occupies any land, whether alone or with others, and either the disposal condition or the contribution condition is met (*FA 2004, Sch 15, paras 3–5*):

(i) The disposal condition is that the taxpayer has, since 17 March 1986, disposed of all or part of his interest in the land other than by an excluded transaction.

(ii) The contribution condition is that, at any time since 17 March 1986, he has directly or indirectly provided (other than by an excluded transaction) any of the consideration given by someone else for the acquisition of an interest in the land.

HMRC substantially revised their initial POAT Guidance notes on the interpretation of 'occupation' (last updated on 29 February 2012) and the revised material was inserted into the Inheritance Tax Manual at IHTM44000–IHTM44116. HMRC persist in their consideration that the meaning of the word is 'to be taken quite widely', but now accept that 'occupy' for this purpose does require (or, at the least, imply) a degree of control such that a casual visitor will not be penalised.

Where the regime applies, it is the 'appropriate rental value' that is charged to income tax, less any payments made in pursuance of a legal obligation. That rental value equates broadly to the rent payable on a landlord's repairing lease.

Chattels

4.46 Principles similar to the above apply for chattels (*FA 2004, Sch 15, paras 6–7*) except that:

- instead of occupation, the test is possession or use of a chattel; and
- instead of the appropriate rental value, the charge is on the appropriate amount, which is the official rate of interest at the beginning of the relevant tax year, thus 2.50% for 2017/18 et seq, 3% for 2016/17 and 2015/16 and 3.25% for 2014/2015 (4% for 2010/11 to 2013/14 inclusive, 6.25% for 2008/09, and 4.75% for 2009/10). Note: the official rate of interest for 2018/19 has yet to be announced but is likely to remain at 2.50%.

Intangible property comprised in a settlement where the settlor retains an interest

4.47 Here the charge is based not on the enjoyment of benefits but rather on the satisfaction of a set of circumstances (with no let-out for any payments made by the chargeable person): *FA 2004, Sch 15, para 8*. The set of circumstances is:

- under the settlement, any of the income arising would be taxed on the settlor (see **4.26–4.29**);
- any such income would be treated as so taxable, disregarding benefits received by his spouse; and
- that property includes any 'relevant property', viz intangible property which is or represents a property settled by or added to the settlement by the chargeable person after 17 March 2006.

Intangible property would include cash and investments (though not land or chattels). The purpose of this charge is to catch certain (though by no means all) IHT avoidance schemes based on the use of trusts. The tax is charged at the official rate of interest in force (see **4.46**) at the beginning of the relevant tax year.

Exclusions

4.48 These are defined separately for the disposal and contribution conditions respectively (and, in any case, apply only to land or chattels). Broadly speaking, these embrace the following (*FA 2004, Sch 15, para 10*):

- there was a disposal of the individual's whole interest in the property except for any right expressly reserved by him, whether by an arm's-length transaction with an unconnected person or by a transaction that might be expected to be made at arm's length between unconnected persons;
- regulations made in March 2005 added an exemption for certain part disposals; significantly, where made 'inter family' after 6 March 2005, the exemption will not apply if the consideration takes the form of cash or marketable securities;
- the transfer of a property to his spouse (or former spouse under a court order);
- a disposal to a life interest trust in which his spouse or (under a court order) former spouse continues to have an interest in possession (except on the death of the beneficiary);
- the disposal was one within the exemption from IHT for dispositions for the maintenance of the family;
- the disposal is an outright gift to an individual, which is wholly exempt from inheritance tax under either the annual exemption or the small gifts exemption.

An important additional exclusion, in the case of the contribution condition, is where the contribution consisted of an outright gift of money made at least seven years before the occupation of the 'relevant property' begins.

The exemptions

4.49 Again, the drafting is complex, but the exemptions (which apply to all three categories within the regime) are (*FA 2004, Sch 15, para 11*):

- the taxpayer's estate for IHT purposes includes the relevant property (or property which derives its value from the relevant property);
- the property would be treated as part of the taxpayer's estate as property subject to a reservation of benefit (see **6.18–6.23**);
- the property would be subject to a reservation of benefit apart from certain prescribed exemptions, eg gifts to charities;
- the relevant property would be treated as a gift with reservation but for the exception for co-ownership arrangements under IHT, ie insofar as the

chargeable person has given part of their interest to someone with whom they share occupation; and

- the relevant property would fall to be a gift with reservation of benefit but for an exemption which either (a) requires payment of full consideration in either money or money's worth or (b) allows occupation as a result of a change in circumstances, which was unforeseen when the gift was made, the donor cannot maintain himself through old age, infirmity or otherwise and the occupation represents a reasonable provision by the relative donee for the donor's care and maintenance.

De minimis exemption

4.50 There is a very small *de minimis* exemption where the aggregate of the amounts otherwise chargeable under the regime do not exceed £5,000 (*FA 2004, Sch 15, para 13*); this amount has not altered since the introduction of POAT. If the benefit does exceed this level then the whole benefit is taxable and not just the excess.

A person who disposed of property received under a will or intestacy by an IHT protected variation (see **13.1–13.4**) is not caught by the regime (*FA 2004, Sch 15, para 17*).

Transitional provisions

4.51 A person who is caught by the regime can make an irrevocable election to opt (back) into the reservation of benefit regime (*FA 2004, Sch 15, paras 20–22*) but note that this does not work in reverse in that it is not possible to elect out of the IHT reservation code into POAT. The effect of the election is that the property concerned is treated as part of the person's estate on death with a liability for IHT falling back on the donee. The election must be made before the 31 January following the end of the tax year in which the regime first applies, thus initially this was thought to be 31 January 2007. *FA 2007, s 66* gives HMRC discretion to accept a late election and this has indeed been applied on a sensible basis in practice.

Scope

4.52 Although the regime is specifically targeted at schemes made with a view to avoiding the reservation of benefit regime, whether in relation to houses, land, chattels or insurance policies, the breadth of the rules will mean that many 'innocent' arrangements will also be caught. Ideally, a careful review should have been made of all action taken since 18 March 1986 that might produce an income tax charge under the regime, to decide what should be done in vulnerable cases, viz whether:

- to pay the income tax charge;
- to pay to the donee such an amount each year as will escape the charge;
- to bring the benefit to an end (most probably as a deemed potentially exempt transfer for IHT purposes: see **6.18–6.24**); or
- to opt into the reservation of benefit regime, with an IHT liability for the donee following the donor's death.

Application

4.53 The POAT regime is far from straightforward, despite publication by HMRC in March 2005 of Guidance Notes, which have been, and continue to be, updated (see **4.45**). For those cases that might be caught by the rules, there is no real alternative to a careful professional analysis of whether the arrangements adopted are in fact caught and, if so, prompting consideration of what action if any should now be taken.

Example 4.13—Richard: Home loan scheme

On 1 July 2001, Richard, acting on advice from his solicitors, entered into a 'home loan' scheme. Under the terms of the scheme, he sold his home to a newly created qualifying life interest trust established for himself, of which the trustees were himself, his wife Marion and his solicitor. The market value purchase price of £750,000 was satisfied by an IOU from the trustees to Richard, though that IOU was not secured on the house. Richard then settled the IOU on a second qualifying life interest trust (from which he and Marion were irrevocably excluded) established for his three children. The intention was that, once seven years had expired from the gift of the IOU that value would fall out of Richard's estate for IHT purposes such that, on his later death, only the house value in excess of £750,000 would attract IHT. At the time of Richard's later death, the house was worth £1 million.

Assume that the arrangement has since 2005/06 been caught by the pre-owned assets (POAT) regime. Richard has a choice between, broadly, (i) paying income (POAT charge) tax year by year, so long as he continues to occupy the house, on the appropriate rental value of £750,000 worth of the house, and (ii) unscrambling the scheme (whether by virtue of powers in the settlements or by opting into the reservation of benefit regime). Either way, there is no simple solution, and each choice and its tax impact must be considered in the round. What is of paramount importance is that the problem is identified and dealt with in advance of Richard's death.

Example 4.14—Rosemary: chattels

On 1 April 1989, Rosemary, a widow, gave to her two adult children chattels with a combined value of £300,000. No single chattel was worth more than £6,000, and so no CGT was payable by reason of the favourable chattels relief rule. Rosemary made an agreement with each of her children that she would continue to keep the chattels at her home and pay the insurance, together with an arm's-length fee (negotiated independently by valuers acting for each side) equal to 1% of the chattels' capital value. This fee, on which the children pay income tax as an income receipt, is renegotiated every three years.

More than seven years have elapsed since the time of the gift, such that the initial PET is now IHT exempt. Nor is it considered that there is any reservation of benefit for IHT purposes (see **6.18–6.23**) because full consideration was paid and continues to be paid by Rosemary for her continuing enjoyment of the chattels. Equally, it is now argued, and accepted in principle by HMRC, that, if the amount paid by Rosemary does constitute full consideration, there will be no POAT issues. Although, in the early days, HMRC were prepared to challenge such an argument, it would appear that, certainly since 2007, HMRC have relaxed their stance and indeed are known to have accepted the argument following death in a few specific cases. Nevertheless, it should be noted that HMRC have not formally confirmed this view and, indeed, in their pre-owned assets guidance at www.hmrc.gov.uk/poa/poa_guidance2.htm#21, it states: 'Note that the charge is computed differently from land and while any rental payments made to the owner will reduce the amount on which he is chargeable [viz based on the official rate], the fact that he pays a market rent for their use does not prevent an income tax charge arising'.

Example 4.15—Rodney: settled intangible property

On 1 June 2002, Rodney entered into an '*Eversden*' IHT planning arrangement (see *IRC v Eversden* [2003] STC 822, CA) for his grandchildren based on an insurance policy issued by a major life company. This arrangement (no longer possible under *FA 2003*) required Rodney to make a settlement of the policy on a life interest trust for his wife, Tania, with power for the trustees to bring Tania's interest to an end in favour of trusts for a variety of family beneficiaries (including Rodney). The trustees duly took this action within six months and the policy is now held in trust for Rodney's eight grandchildren. But there is always the possibility of the trustees exercising their powers to pay all or part of the capital back to Rodney.

The arrangement is caught by the POAT rule. Accordingly, the 'official rate' (see **4.46**) applied to the value of the policy at the beginning of each tax year (£1 million as at 6 April 2018) will be assessed on him for income tax purposes. That is, as a super rate taxpayer, he will suffer £11,250 income tax (45% of (£1million @ 2.50%)) for 2018/19. It would be possible to avoid the charge for the future, if Rodney were irrevocably to give up his interest under the trust, perhaps keeping his wife Tania as a beneficiary. That would put paid to the pre-owned assets charge.

SELF-ASSESSMENT FORM SA900 (2018/19)

4.54 Since the introduction of self-assessment in 1996/97, the self-assessment compliance returns and related literature have been subject to continuous revision, based in no small part upon comments made by practitioners. The basic trust and estate form SA900, which contains 12 pages for 2018/19, has seen little real change over the years.

Basic details (2018/19 trust return)

4.55 Page 1 gives at the top a tax reference (the trust UTR), a date (eg 6 April 2019), the addressee, viz the first-named trustee or personal representative, the name of the trust and the trust district and telephone number. Page 2 carries 2 steps with multiple check boxes.

Step 1: What type of trust

4.56 Step 1 enables the trustee to go directly to question 17 on page 10, that is to confirm details of the trustee, if:

- the trust is a bare trust and the beneficiary has an immediate and absolute right to both capital and income; or
- the addressee is a PR and (broadly) no gross income has been received (see **12.1–12.5**); or
- the trust is interest in possession (irrespective of whether a qualifying interest or not) and no tax liability arises to the trust, eg because all income has been received net of tax, or because all the income has been mandated to the beneficiaries and the trust has not made any chargeable disposals.

Step 2: Supplementary pages

4.57 Step 2 directs the taxpayer to questions 1–7 and 23 to confirm whether any of the following supplementary pages need to be completed and returned:

- trade;
- partnership;
- land and property;
- foreign;
- capital gains;
- non-residence;
- charities.

In the case of estates, there is an additional form (estate pension charges etc), though not relevant to trusts.

Any supplementary pages should be completed before going to questions 8 to 21.

Rate of tax

4.58 Question 8 lists a variety of questions to include whether the trust is settlor interested or if a vulnerable beneficiary election applies. Importantly, it asks for the capacity in which the return is being completed, eg if a trustee, whether the trust is liable to income tax, at either/both the trust rate (45% for 2018/19) or the dividend trust rate (38.1% for 2018/19) on any part of the income.

On page 3, step 3 confirms that blue or black ink (if completed in paper format) must be used to complete the return and that pence should not be included. Income and gains are rounded down to the nearest pound and tax credits and tax deductions are rounded up.

Details of other income

4.59 Question 9 on pages 4 to 5 asks for details of any other income not already included on the supplementary pages, eg interest, dividends, gains on UK life insurance policies, life annuities and other income which must then be listed in the appropriate boxes.

On page 6, question 10B asks whether the trustees wish to claim any reliefs. Question 10B asks whether the trustees want to claim special income tax treatment where a valid vulnerable beneficiary election has effect (see **4.37–4.40**). Question 10C relates to employee benefit trusts. Question 11 asks whether any annual payments were made out of capital or out of income not brought into charge to income tax (in which case the trustees must account to HMRC for the tax deducted). Question 12 asks whether any assets or funds have been put into the settlement during the year covered by the tax return eg 2018/19 and requests details of the same to include value.

Types and rates of income, trustee expenses

4.60 On page 7, question 13 is appropriate only to discretionary or accumulation trusts. Question 13 asks whether any part of the trust income is not liable to tax at the rate applicable to trusts or the dividend trust rate. The function of this page is to separate out income that belongs to a life tenant, and income that is subject to the trustees' discretion and in each case to identify the trust management expenses. Question 13A also makes reference to the brought-forward tax pool balance applicable to that element of the trust which is not settlor interested, where there is a mixed trust fund.

Payments of income or capital

4.61 On page 8, question 14 asks discretionary trustees whether discretionary payments of income have been made to beneficiaries and question 15 asks whether any capital payments have been made to or for minor unmarried children of the settlor during his lifetime. Question 15A asks whether there were any capital transactions between the trustees and the settlors.

Final questions

4.62 Question 16 on page 9 addresses trusts that are, or at some time have been, non-UK resident, or have received any capital from another, non-UK resident, trust. If the answer is yes, HMRC want to know whether the trustees have made any capital payments to, or provided any benefits for, the beneficiaries. This question is designed to apply special anti-avoidance tax rules which are beyond the scope of this book.

On page 10, question 17 asks the trustees whether they want to calculate the tax and question 18 whether they want to claim a repayment of tax.

On page 11, questions 19 and 20 has been adapted to refer to the online trusts register launched in July 2017. There is no longer a requirement to provide details of the trustees' representatives/agent but rather the request is for a contact number and confirmation that the trusts register has been updated for any changes.

Question 21 is for other information: for example, the date on which the trust or the administration period of an estate came to an end (Box 21.2) or where the administration period has come to an end and there is a continuing trust (Box 21.3) or where the trust has come to an end in the year (Box 21.4). Box 21.5 admits the possibility of provisional figures only being available and it is important that this box is checked where appropriate. Box 21.6 refers to rare refunds received from various government departments. Boxes 21.7 and 21.8 refer to disclosure of tax avoidance schemes specified by statute (especially under *FA 2006* for direct taxes), in which case a scheme reference number must be given and the tax year specified in which the expected advantage arises. Boxes 21.9 and 21.10 refer to the capital allowance/balancing charge secure under the Business Premises Renovation Scheme. Finally, Box 21.11 is the infamous 'white space' which must be used for the provision of additional information.

On page 12, Question 22 is the statutory declaration that the information given is correct and complete to the best of the trustee's knowledge and belief.

REVENUE GUIDES (2018/19)

Trust and Estate Tax Return Guide: SA950

4.63 Form SA950 is 'essential reading' for trustees. As stated on page 1 this guide has step-by-step instructions to help you fill in the trusts and estates tax return. The notes are numbered to match the boxes in the tax return. Further help is offered by telephoning either the relevant HMRC office or the helpline.

Successive tax years have seen improvements to the drafting of the tax return guide, which for 2018/19 runs to 28 pages.

The guide starts with a step-by-step explanation of the tax return, including a helpful flow chart on pages 6 and 7. Each of the supplementary pages is summarised on pages 8 to 9 and the balance of the guide contains a detailed commentary on the relevant boxes, including a summary of the relevant law. For 2018/19 there are eight supplementary pages, seven of which are discussed below from **4.66** to **4.86**. The supplementary form SA908 on estate pension charges etc is not considered in this book.

Discretionary payments: income or capital?

4.64 For example, question 14 asks whether discretionary payments of income have been made to beneficiaries. The general rule (though not necessarily so) is that what is capital (under trust law) in the hands of the trustees will be capital for the beneficiary and similarly with income. The guidance notes state helpfully on page 23 (Boxes 14.1 to 14.14) that:

- payments out of trust income are always the income of the beneficiaries;
- payments out of trust capital including out of accumulated income or deemed income are not usually regarded as the income of a beneficiary irrespective of the purpose for which they're made;
- exceptionally, payments out of capital are treated as the income of the beneficiary where, by the terms of the trust instrument, payments out of capital must be made, or may be made, in order to supplement income. For example, the trustees may use or have to use capital to make income up to a fixed amount or a certain defined level; and
- payment is regarded as taking place when a beneficiary is legally entitled to ask for money to be paid over, for example, when it becomes irrevocably their property following the trustees' resolution to allocate or appropriate it to them.

Example 4.16— Tom: discretionary payments

The trustees make regular payments from the trust capital to fund part of the school fees of one of the beneficiaries, Tom – this is an income purpose but even so it will not convert such payments into Tom's income. The only exception in the school fee trust type case noted by the guide is where, say, the trustees are to pay Tom income of £5,000 per annum, they only have £3,000 of income to this end and have to resort to capital for the remaining £2,000. In that case, the £2,000 will be treated as Tom's income.

Trust and Estate Tax Calculation Guide: SA951 (2018/19)

4.65 Form SA951 is obviously for use only where the trustees (or personal representatives) or their advisers compute the tax and not where the tax return is submitted to HMRC on or before 31 October, in which case HMRC will calculate the tax. Incidentally, if the return is delivered after that date, HMRC will still calculate the tax but do not guarantee to do so by 31 January; if any tax due is not paid by that date, there would be interest implications.

The calculation is split into eight stages, of which stages 3 and 8 will apply only to discretionary and accumulation trusts:

- Stage 1 applies to all the income and deductions the trustees have included in their tax return and sorts them into the trust and estate tax return categories which will be taxed later in the process. All trustees and personal representatives should complete stage 1.
- Stage 2 is for personal representatives only.

- Stage 3 is for trustees who are taxable at the trust rate or the dividend trust rate. Certain types of income and deemed income are chargeable at the trust rate or the dividend trust rate whether or not the trustees are normally taxable at the basic/savings/dividend ordinary rate. These types of income include accrued income charges, income from deeply discounted securities, gilt strips, offshore income gains, income from companies purchasing their own shares and gains on life insurance policies, life annuities and capital redemption policies. If, apart from these types of income, the trustees are taxable at the basic/savings/dividend ordinary rate only, or the trustees are the trustee of an unauthorised unit trust, which is generally taxable at the basic rate only, the trustees should complete stage 4. These stages will charge the income listed above at the correct rates. Stage 3 is to be completed by the trustees who are chargeable to the trust rate or dividend trust rate, on any income other than that listed above.
- Stage 4 is for trustees of an unauthorised unit trust.
- Stage 5 is for other trustees, not taxable at the trust rate or the dividend trust rate.
- Stage 6 brings in all the tax the trustees have already deducted from income (so the trustees will need the tax return and any supplementary pages again), and works out any non-payable tax credits.
- Stage 7 makes adjustments to the tax calculated in earlier sections and adds in capital gains tax. The final box of stage 6, box T6.26 gives the figure for box 17.1 in the trust and estate tax return.
- Stage 8 works out what the trustees have to pay HMRC by 31 January 2020, or what HMRC have to pay the trustees, and checks if the trustees will have to make 2019/20 payments on account.
- Stage 9 is for trustees who make discretionary payments to beneficiaries.

SUPPLEMENTARY PAGES (2018/19)

Trade

Form SA901

4.66 Like all supplementary pages, form SA901 carries its own set of notes, SA901 (Notes). The main tax return consists of pages TT1 to TT4 and Notes TTN1 to TTN8. Trustees who carry on a trade, whether as sole traders or in partnership, are like any other taxpayer. They will need either the accounts for the business covering the basis period for tax year 2018/19, eg the year ended 31 March 2019 or, if there are no accounts, the relevant books and records.

How long must I keep records?

4.67 Page TTN1 warns that records of all business transactions must be kept until at least 31 January 2025, in case they have to be produced for HMRC.

Profit and loss

4.68 Page TT1 asks for details of the business, capital allowances and balancing charges and income and expenses. Only if the annual turnover is £30,000 or more, should the more detailed description of income, expenses and necessary tax adjustments on page TT2 be completed. When the annual turnover is less than £30,000, Boxes 1.24, 1.25 and 1.26 on page TT1 should be completed with turnover, expenses and net profit. In all cases, page TT3 requests the adjustments required to arrive at the taxable profit or loss.

Having said that, it seems to be the current experience that small businesses with an annual turnover of less than £30,000 are more likely to be targeted for an enquiry. That likelihood could perhaps be reduced by including full figures in the SA901.

Balance sheet

4.69 Page TT4 asks for a summary of the balance sheet. These details do not have to be completed if there is no balance sheet (or if the turnover was less than £30,000, though see the warning in the preceding paragraph). Box 1.116 is the 'white space' for additional information.

None of the supplementary pages need in themselves to be signed. However, as they form part of the main tax return, the information in them is therefore covered by the declaration on the tax return.

Example 4.17—Trading trust

The Graham Discretionary Trust owns a small garage in the village. The accounts for the year ended 31 March 2019 indicate a turnover of £50,000. Form SA901 must be completed in full. The business details will give the business name and description, its address and the dates of the accounting period.

Capital allowances are shown as follows:

- £2,000 as a writing-down allowance on a truck not used for private motoring; and
- £2,000 on other plant and machinery.

The turnover exceeds £30,000 and therefore page TT2 must be completed. The business being registered for VAT, it must be stated that the figures exclude VAT as well as stating the turnover.

Summary details of income and expenses produce gross income of £50,000 and total expenses of £35,000, a net profit of £15,000. This is reduced for tax purposes by the capital allowances to £11,000. No adjustments are required on page TT3 (eg brought-forward losses) and the total taxable profits are shown as Box 1.92.

A summary balance sheet is included on page TT4.

Partnership

Form SA902 (2018/19)

4.70 Again, form SA902 comes with SA902 (Notes). It is common for trustees to trade in a partnership.

The partnership tax return

4.71 The main partnership tax return will be made by the 'representative partner'. This will include a summary of the share of profits, losses or income allocated to each of the partners during the relevant period. This summary is called the 'partnership statement' and the information on it will be used to complete the trust and estate partnership page. Most partnerships will issue a short or abridged version of the partnership statement, which will show trading income (or loss) and interest received less tax deducted. The 'full' version covers all the possible types of partnership income. If the trustees belong to more than one partnership, they will receive separate partnership statements and should complete a set of the relevant trust and estate partnership pages for each business.

Form SA902 asks for the partnership reference number, the partnership trade and whether commencement or cessation of the partnership happened during 2018/19. Under the share of the partnership's trading or professional income the basis period is given, together with the partner's share of the profit or loss for tax purposes. Adjustments are made for 'overlap profit' (which occurs when there is an overlapping of basis periods, so that the same profits are taxable in two different tax years). Overlap relief exists to relieve the profits in a later tax year, so that over the life of the business, tax is paid by the trust or estate on no more profits than are earned. There is then in the case of farm or market gardening trades an adjustment for farmer's averaging and, where a loss arises, the treatment of the loss. Total taxable profits are mentioned at Box 2.22 for entry in the main return.

Trading trustees

4.72 A partner or a sole trader is personally responsible for the debts and liabilities of the business, even to the extent of his own personal assets. While no protection is available for a sole trader, it may be possible within a partnership to get limited liability under the *Limited Partnerships Act 1907* (or even, more recently, under the *Limited Liability Partnerships Act 2000*, when the whole partnership has limited liability).

The *1907 Act* assumes there is at least one 'general partner' who will have unlimited liability. The partnership needs to be registered. A limited partner may not participate in the management of the firm but will have his, its or their liability limited to the capital subscribed. All the capital tax reliefs available to traders may be enjoyed by members of a limited liability partnership, eg agricultural or business property relief from IHT and roll-over relief from CGT.

Record keeping

4.73 As with sole traders, record keeping must be taken seriously, with records used to make the partnership tax return 2018/19 kept until at least 31 January 2025. In the absence of fraud or negligence and assuming the return was submitted on or before 31 October 2019 if in paper form, or 31 January 2020 if submitted electronically, HMRC will have up to 12 months from the date on which the return was delivered to decide whether to make an enquiry.

Land and property (UK property)

Form SA903 (2018/19)

4.74 The relative notes, SA903 (Notes), consist of eight pages. The form should be completed if the trust (or estate) has:

- rental income or other receipts from UK land and property;
- premiums arising from UK leases of less than 50 years;
- furnished holiday lettings in the UK; or
- a 'reverse premium' (viz where the trustees enter into a lease with a landlord and receive a payment as an inducement from the landlord to take up the lease. That payment will be taxable on the trustees as income of a property business).

Form SA903 itself runs to only two pages. Page TL1 deals with furnished holiday lettings in the UK (see **4.77**). That is, if the trust has rental income, which does not derive from furnished holiday lets, the trustees need complete only page TL2. If the trust does have income from furnished holiday lets, then having completed page TL1, the total is carried forward to the top of page TL2 at Box 3.19 to which are added rents and other income, chargeable premiums and reverse premiums. There follow summary details of expenses to give net profit and then the tax adjustment.

In terms of the details on page TL2, the notes at TLN5 confirm that if the gross property income is less than £15,000 per annum, the expenses do not have to be listed separately and the total figure can be entered at Box 3.29. Of course, it may be that trust accounts have been prepared which show the expenses.

Deductible expenses

4.75 The notes are helpful in summarising the types of expenditure that are allowable for tax purposes and those that are not.

On tax adjustments, in prior years there was a blanket 10% allowance of gross rents for 'wear and tear' which could be used as an alternative to a deduction for the specific cost or replacements 'renewals basis'. Both the 'wear and tear' allowance and renewals basis were withdrawn with effect from 6 April 2016; thereafter a deduction for relevant expenditure is secured by means of capital allowances.

Furnished holiday lettings

4.76 In the past, income from furnished holiday lets was generally treated as trading income, with more favourable treatment given for income tax and CGT, but this treatment was repealed with effect from 6 April 2010. From 2010/11, such activity still constitutes a business for income tax and CGT purposes, but restrictions are now imposed with regard to the offset of losses for income tax. To qualify, the property must be (*ITTOIA 2005, ss 323–326*):

- furnished and let on a commercial basis with a view to profits;
- available for holiday lettings to the public on a commercial basis for 210 days or more during the year;
- actually let commercially as holiday accommodation for at least 105 days during the year; and
- not occupied continuously for more than 31 days by the same person for at least seven months during the year.

For 2009/10, this deemed trading treatment is applied to property anywhere in the EEA.

'Whose property business?'

4.77 Trustees might own property but have delegated its management to a beneficiary under *Law of Property Act 1925, s 29(1)*. In such a case, it will usually be the beneficiary rather than the trustees who is regarded as carrying on the rental business and all the income and expenses should be included in the beneficiary's return. This could be helpful if the beneficiary owns other property beneficially, which he lets, as all the income will be added together as a single property business. If one property gives rise to a loss, and the other to a profit, the loss can be offset against the profit in computing the total tax position.

Example 4.18— Bertie's trust: property income

Bertie's trust owns a cottage, which is let furnished. The rent is £5,000 per annum and the total expenses amount to £1,500 with capital allowances due of £500. Box 3.20 shows gross income of £5,000. Because this is less than £15,000, the expenses do not have to be detailed (although the receipts etc should be kept to answer any HMRC enquiry), and the total of the expenses should be put at Box 3.30. Capital allowances of £500 can be claimed at Box 3.33 with the adjusted profit at Box 3.39 of £3,000.

Foreign

Form SA904 (2018/19)

4.78 Form SA904 (Notes) accompanies the five-page SA904.

Basis of taxation

4.79 Given that the trustees are UK resident, any income from abroad is taxed as it arises, regardless of whether the trustees bring that income to the UK. The only exception is in a case of 'unremittable' income, for example on account of exchange controls, in which case a claim can be made that it should not be taxed in the current year, ie until such year as it is remitted to the UK (*ITTOIA 2005, s 842*).

To calculate the UK tax liability, the conversion rate of foreign currency is that in force when the income arose, ie not necessarily the rate at the end of the tax year.

Treatment of foreign tax

4.80 Foreign income will typically be subject to tax in the country where it arises. The trustees have a choice between setting the foreign tax paid against the UK tax liability (which will generally be more favourable) and simply treating the foreign tax as an expense by deducting it from the income received in the UK, to arrive at the taxable amount. The former is called 'tax credit relief'.

The UK has negotiated double tax agreements (DTAs) with large numbers of foreign countries, which seek to restrict the impact of double taxation in both the UK and other relevant countries. Under such agreements, there is a reduction in the amount of foreign tax withholding that can be applied against the foreign income source, and hence a reduction in the tax credit available for relief against UK tax. Pages TFN 20 to 24 show, in each case, the rate of withholding tax applied under the DTA with that foreign country in the case of dividend interest, royalty and management/technical fees. The DTA will provide a maximum percentage of tax credit relief and, if the actual foreign tax paid exceeds this sum, a refund of that excess might be claimed direct from the overseas tax authorities, subject to time limits etc.

Pages TFN 16 to 19 constitute a working sheet for calculating tax credit relief where the UK trust or estate is *not* liable to pay tax at the rate applicable to trusts. Special instructions are given for calculating tax credit relief where the trust is liable to pay tax at the rate applicable to trusts.

Different types of income

4.81 The obvious types of foreign income that might arise are:

- foreign savings;
- income from land and property abroad; and
- other overseas income, eg income from foreign trusts.

Of these the first, foreign savings, is the most likely. Where, as in the usual case, the income is taxed on the arising basis, the details are given on page TF1.

Example 4.19—Foreign tax credit relief

The income of the discretionary trust comprises overseas interest of £3,000 (from which foreign tax of 15% (£450) has been withheld) and rental income from a foreign property of £10,000 (on which foreign tax at a rate of 60% (£6,000) has been paid). No other deductions are due and the whole of the income is liable to UK tax at 45%. There is no DTA with the overseas country which would otherwise restrict the allowable tax credit.

The property income has been subjected to foreign tax at a rate in excess of 45%, and so tax credit relief is restricted as follows:

	UK tax at 45%	*Tax credit relief allowed*
Interest £3,000	£1,350	£450
Property £10,000	£4,500	(Max) £4,500
	£5,850	£4,950

The balance of the foreign tax paid on the property income (£6,000 – £4,500 = £1,500) is not available to credit against the UK tax on the interest income, nor can it be repaid or carried forward or back.

Non-residence, etc

Form SA906 (2018/19)

4.82 The general assumption in this book is that the trust or deceased estate is UK resident. If this is so, there is no need for supplemental page SA906. There may, however, be cases where the page is relevant.

The preliminary questions on form SA906 request confirmation as to:

- whether the trustees or personal representatives are as a whole resident or non-resident in the UK for income tax and separately for CGT purposes;
- whether they are resident in a country other than the UK under a double taxation agreement at the same time as being UK resident; and
- in the case of a deceased estate, whether the deceased was non-UK domiciled at the date of death.

Information is then requested if the trustees or PRs claim to be non-resident in the UK for income tax and, separately, CGT purposes, in particular as to whether, when claiming to be non-UK resident for 2018/19, they were UK resident for 2017/18.

An annual status

4.83 Generally speaking, residence or non-UK residence is a state that exists throughout the year. Although there are concessions for recognition of split year residence for income tax the general rule is that a person is UK resident if resident in the UK for any part of the tax year.

Page TNR2 of SA906 requests certain information if the trustees or personal representatives claim to be dual resident.

A non-UK resident trust: income tax consequences

4.84 The trustees will be liable to income tax on UK source income, for example:

- dividends from UK companies, which since 6 April 2016 no longer carry the 10% non-repayable tax credit;
- interest on income from bank deposits, etc, which since 6 April 2016 no longer carries a 20% withholding at source; and
- gross income received from rents as a property business.

Discretionary or accumulation trusts will be subject to income tax at 38.1% on UK dividend income (37.5% for 2015/16) and 45% for all other UK source income (50% for 2012/13), notwithstanding that they are non-UK resident. It would obviously be advisable for such trusts not to own UK property.

Anti-avoidance regime for settlors and beneficiaries

4.85 There is a complex set of provisions in *ITA 2007, Pt 13, Ch 2* comprising the separate transferor and benefits charges. The first of these generally catches the settlor of the trust (as the 'transferor') and the second the beneficiary (as the recipient of a 'benefit' from a trust). The regime applies where a transfer of assets has been made and as a consequence of which income becomes payable to persons resident or domiciled outside the UK and:

- in the case of the transferor charge, the settlor who is resident in the UK has 'power to enjoy' the income of the non-UK resident person, in this case trustees, or receives a capital sum from the trustees. Where this applies, the income is treated as that of the settlor;
- under the benefits charge, a beneficiary resident in the UK receives a benefit from the trustees and there is in the trust either for that or preceding tax years 'relevant income', viz income out of which a benefit can be paid.

Both charging regimes have a limitation in that, where the settlor or beneficiary is domiciled outside the UK and the income arises but remains outside the UK or the benefit is enjoyed outside the UK, the elective remittance basis may apply (subject to a claim) to relieve any charge to tax.

Both regimes have also historically had the benefit of a 'purpose test' (before 2007/08, in *ICTA 1988, s 741*), ie they will not apply if it can be shown that:

- tax avoidance was not a purpose of the transfer in the first place; or
- the transfer was a *bona fide* commercial transaction and was not designed to avoid a tax liability.

With effect from 5 December 2005, the 'purpose test' was tightened up through what is now to be found in *ITA 2007, ss 736–742* and in an acquiescent nod to the EU, a modification of EU defence was introduced within *ITA 2007, s 742A,* effective from 6 April 2012. A person will now only escape liability under either regime if he satisfies HMRC that either Condition A or Condition B is met:

- Condition A is that it would be reasonable to draw the conclusion, from all the circumstances of the case, that the purpose of avoiding liability to taxation was not the purpose, or one of the purposes, for which the relevant transactions or any of them were effected;
- Condition B is that:
  - all the relevant transactions were genuine commercial transactions, and
  - it would be reasonable to draw the conclusion, from all the circumstances of the case, that any one or more of those transactions was not more than incidentally designed for the purpose of avoiding liability to taxation.

Further provisions fill out this exemption and, in particular, deal with cases where there are transactions both before and on or after 5 December 2005.

Charities

Form SA907 (2018/19)

4.86 Supplemental form SA907 is different from the other forms insofar as it constitutes a claim to exemption from tax and requires signature.

Separate references must be stated for HMRC charity repayment reference and the Charity Commission registration number (or, in Scotland, the Scottish charity number).

Form SA907 envisages that the claim to exemption may be for part rather than all of the charity's income and gains, though usually it would be for all. It must be confirmed that all income and gains claimed to be exempt have been, or will be, applied for charitable purposes.

Information must be returned either for the year ended 5 April 2019 or for a period ending in that tax year. Accounts should be enclosed.

Repayments may have already been claimed on form R68, although further repayments may be due.

The form asks for a summary of the heads of income on which exemption is claimed, for expenses as included in the charity accounts and summary of assets.

Example 4.20—Charity income and gains

The Russian Orphanage Trust established by Zebedee (see Example 3.7 at **3.30**) should submit each year:

- form SA900; and
- supplementary page SA907.

The income of the trust comprises principally of dividends but also of a small amount of REIT income which has suffered 20% tax at source.

The dividends will be received gross with no further liability due but the tax deducted from the REIT income can be reclaimed.

Any gains made by the trustees on selling shares will be free from CGT.

The trustees are well able to certify that all income and gains have been, or will be, applied for charitable purposes.

INTEREST (2018/19)

Different types of income

4.87 Question 9 on pages 4 and 5 of the trust and estate tax return asks, 'Did the trust or estate receive any other income not already included on the supplementary pages?' A look at pages 5 to 8 of the trust and estate tax calculation guide will show a distinction between:

- income other than savings or dividend type income (carried through from the supplementary pages, viz, trade, partnership, land and property, foreign income and other income);
- savings type income; 20%; and
- dividend type income; 7.5%.

Deemed income will include proceeds of a company purchase of own shares unless *CTA 2010, s 1033* applies.

Income carried over from any of the supplementary pages will feature in the first column. The next four columns respond to question 9 of the main tax return.

Savings type income

4.88 The heading 'savings type income' responds to the main subheading, interest, on page 3 of the tax return. Since 6 April 2016 most deposit and other savings interest will have been received gross and that interest (from UK banks, building societies and deposit takers) is entered in Box 9.1. Interest that has been received net of tax should be entered at Boxes 9.2 to 9.4:

- the net amount received;
- the amount of tax deducted; and
- the gross amount of interest before deduction of tax.

Gross or net receipt

4.89 Most interest earned post-5 April 2016 will no longer be received net after deduction of tax at 20% (the 'lower' savings rate) but rather received gross as was always the case for interest from the National Savings Bank (recognised at Box 9.8). It was recognised that this absence of tax deduction at source would have the effect of increasing the trust end of year liability as well as bringing more trusts within the scope of self-assessment – the latter was a concern with HMRC alert to the potential increase in workload following the increase in self-assessment registration. Accordingly, HMRC confirmed that for 2016/17, 2017/18 and 2018/19 those trusts not registered under SA and in receipt of interest income only where the tax liability thereon does not exceed £100 have no SA reporting requirement.

Types of interest

4.90

- Interest from UK banks, building societies and deposit takers:
  - paid gross; or
  - paid net after deduction of tax.
- Interest on certificates of tax deposits where applied in payment of a tax liability.
- Interest on government stocks.
- Interest on other loan stocks.
- The interest element within purchased life annuities.
- Interest distributions from UK authorised unit trusts and open-ended investment companies (note, not dividends).
- National Savings (other than First Option and Fixed Rate Savings Bonds) – paid gross.
- National Savings First Option and Fixed Rate Savings Bonds.
- Other income from UK savings and investments (except dividends).

Tax vouchers

4.91 A payment of interest will usually be accompanied by a tax voucher, issued by the borrowing institution. Note the position with accumulation units or shares in UK authorised unit trusts and open-ended investment companies, when the interest distribution is automatically reinvested in the unit trust or open-ended investment company. The gross interest, tax deducted and net interest distribution invested must still be returned and income tax paid.

By contrast, any amount shown on the tax voucher as 'equalisation' is not subject to income tax being a repayment of capital. When CGT is calculated, the amount of equalisation should be deducted from the cost of the units or shares purchased during the year.

Calculation of tax deduction where not shown on the voucher

4.92 Suppose the statement reveals interest paid of £80 after tax:

Tax deducted = After tax amount × 25%: £80 × 25% = £20.

Suppose the statement shows interest of £100 before tax:

Tax deducted = Before tax amount × 20%: £100 × 20% = £20.

ACCRUED INCOME SCHEME (2018/19)

4.93 Interest-bearing securities such as government loan stock (or gilts) will be acquired (or sold) either 'ex-dividend' (or 'ex-div') or 'cum-dividend' (or 'cum-div'). A purchase ex-div means that the next interest payment belongs to the seller; whereas a purchase cum-div will entitle the purchaser to the next interest payment. The fact that a security may be ex-div or cum-div will be reflected in the price.

The aim behind this scheme is to ensure that each person pays income tax on the interest on securities, which accrues during his period of legal ownership. Tax is, therefore, charged on an accruals basis and by reference to legal rather than beneficial ownership (*ITA 2007, Pt 12*).

Trust law/tax law difference

4.94 For trust law, the purchase price of a security cum-div is paid out of capital and the proceeds of sale will be a capital receipt. For tax law, the accrued income scheme seeks to identify the element of income arising in a purchase or sale and to subject that income to income tax.

Scope of the scheme

Focus

The £5,000 holding exemption providing exclusion from the accrued income scheme for individuals and personal representatives is not extended to trustees (with the exception of trusts for the disabled).

4.95 The accrued income scheme includes all interest-bearing securities including permanent interest-bearing shares in a building society, government loan stock and company loan stock, though not including shares in a company or National Savings Certificates (*ITA 2007, s 619*).

There is a *de minimis* exemption from the scheme if the nominal value of all the accrued income securities held by an individual, or by trustees of a disabled trust, or by personal representatives, did not exceed £5,000 throughout that year and the preceding year (*ITA 2007, s 639*). However, there is no such general exemption for trustees.

How the scheme works

4.96 When trustees purchase interest-bearing securities cum-interest, they are treated as purchasing the interest that had accrued by the settlement date of the transfer. The accrued interest is called the 'rebate' amount. Note that a gift to trustees carries the same consequence. Similarly, when the trustees sell cum-interest, they are treated as having received the accrued interest as income, known as the 'accrued amount', which is assessable on the trustees and is shown on the stockbroker's contract note (*ITA 2007, ss 628–635*).

Relief is given for the rebate amount either against the next interest received from that security or against the accrued interest on sale, whichever comes first. The relief can be given in a different year of assessment from that in which the purchase is made.

Each security must be dealt with separately. The total of all the chargeable amounts should be entered by personal representatives in Box 9.14, but by trustees in Box 9.38.

Example 4.21—Accrued income scheme: purchase of stock

24 May 2018: Trustees buy £20,000 of 2.5% Treasury Stock 2021

Accrued interest therein is £106.85 (8 March 2018 to 24 May 2018)

7 September 2018: Interest payment

Interest paid gross	£250.00
Relief for accrued interest in the purchase	(£106.85)
Income for tax purposes	£143.15

Example 4.22—Accrued income scheme: sale of stock

24 May 2018: Trustees buy (as in Example 4.21)

24 June 2018: Sale of stock

Accrued interest:

On sale	106 days	£145.20
On purchase	78 days	(£106.85)
Assessable (as miscellaneous income)		£38.35

Example 4.23—Life tenant entitled to income

The whole of the interest received belongs to the beneficiary. There are two views:

- Method 1: In Example 4.21, the beneficiary receives the income plus the tax recovery;
- Method 2: Alternatively, if the trustees must pay tax on the accrued income out of capital, which is the case for trust law, they should retain the recovery on a rebate amount.

HMRC do not mind which method is used, as in either case the statutory income is £143.15 gross.

The trustees receive:

Gross interest	£250
Less tax	(£50)
Net	£200

Recovery of tax on rebate amount:

£143.15 @ 20% = 28.63.

- Method 1: If the beneficiary receives the tax recovery as well as the interest, he has £228.63.
- Method 2: If the trustees withhold the recovery, the beneficiary has £200.

DIVIDENDS (2018/19)

4.97 The system of dividend taxation changed with effect from 6 April 1999 (tax year 1999/2000). This book does not deal with the 'old system'.

The non-repayable tax credit

4.98 For years prior to 6 April 2016, a dividend from a UK company carried a 10% notional tax non-repayable credit, available for offset against the trust's liability to tax (*ITTOIA 2005, s 397*). The same principle applied to 'other qualifying distributions' from UK companies, which were not dividends and qualifying foreign dividends (with effect from 2008/09). Similarly, with dividend distributions from UK-authorised unit trusts and open-ended investment companies, shown separately on page 4 of the tax return.

Post-5 April 2016, UK dividend income paid is treated as gross income which no longer carries the notional 10% credit. Such income received by the discretionary or accumulation trustees attracts tax at 7.5% to the extent the dividend income is sheltered within the standard rate band and 38.1% on any excess. Such income received by the interest in possession trustees attracts tax at 7.5%.

Example 4.24—Trustees self-assessing dividend income

In 2018/19, the trustees receive dividends from UK companies totalling £4,500 and dividends totalling £1,000 from UK Unit trusts.

The amounts are entered as follows:

Box	
9.10	£4,500
9.11	£1,000

SCRIP (OR STOCK) DIVIDENDS (2018/19)

4.99 A company may choose to pay a dividend, not in cash but in the form of shares in itself. This assumes that the company has the power to do so in its articles of association. A company was more likely to pay a scrip dividend before the dividend regime changed on 6 April 1999. This was because, before then, a cash dividend carried an obligation for the company to make a payment of 'advance corporation tax' (ACT) to HMRC, which did not apply to scrip dividends. There was, therefore, a possible cash flow advantage to the company, especially in circumstances where it did not have a liability to mainstream corporation tax against which the ACT could be offset. Now, however, the old disadvantage for the company continues, that is in watering down its equity, and therefore such a dividend might be expected to be relatively uncommon.

Trustees

4.100 Trustees of discretionary or accumulation trusts are treated as having received the 'cash equivalent of the share capital', which is either the amount of a cash alternative or the market value of the shares received (*ITTOIA 2005, ss 410(3), 411(2)* and *412*). As noted at **4.98** the treatment of dividend income changed with effect from 6 April 2016 and the changes carry across to the treatment of scrip dividends.

Trustees of life interest trusts are treated as though the appropriate amount in cash was received by the individual life tenant (*ITTOIA 2005, s 410(2)*) and must still account for the 7.5% tax thereon. The life tenant beneficiary will receive a credit for that tax payment but must meet any additional tax liability (32.5% or 38.1% dependent on their circumstances). There is a further problem, however, in that as a matter of trust law, the stock dividend may be received by the trustees as capital, although of course the life tenant is entitled to income. This is a problem that arises especially with 'enhanced' stock dividends where the value of the stock may be say, 50% higher than a cash alternative: the problem is illustrated in Example 4.30 at **4.116**. The easiest solution with an ordinary stock dividend would, no doubt, be for the trustees simply to treat the life tenant as receiving the stock with no further tax liability for the trustees and any additional tax depending upon the personal circumstances of the beneficiary.

Personal representatives

4.101 A stock dividend received by the PRs is treated as forming part of the aggregate estate income (*ITTOIA 2005, s 413(4)(a)*). They will have a requirement to account for the 7.5% tax due thereon.

Example 4.25—Pre-sale dividends

Pre-sale dividends have been used for some time to extract value from a company in a tax efficient way in order to reduce the shareholder's liability to CGT. To do so, however, the company must have sufficient distributable profit or reserves: if not, a stock dividend can provide a useful solution.

Sarah, a higher rate taxpayer, had acquired for £100,000 all the shares in a trading company, for which she had received an offer of £500,000 in 2007/08. She is a super rate taxpayer and, ignoring the annual exemption, her liability to CGT would be £160,000 ((500,000 – 100,000) @ 40%). The company had no distributable reserves. The company decided, instead of a dividend, to issue new shares on the basis of four for one.

Under the old taper regime, for CGT purposes the original shares were treated separately from the new shares. 20% of the proceeds of sale, that is £100,000, would be attributed to the original shares, with no chargeable gain.

The remaining £400,000 would be treated as given for the new shares. This would have attracted income tax rather than CGT. As the sale of the company followed immediately after the issue of the stock dividend, the stock dividend would be valued on the basis of the sale consideration, ie £400,000. Income tax on this amount would be charged at 22.5% (ie the dividend upper rate after the tax credit), viz £90,000.

The saving to Sarah was £70,000 (£160,000 – £90,000).

Had this happened in 2018/19 (long after the end of the taper relief regime) with the reduction in the CGT rate to 20% and tailored share identification rules, the comparison would be rather different: the CGT payable (ignoring the annual exemption), in the absence of a stock dividend, would be £80,000 – or even £40,000 if Sarah was entitled to entrepreneurs' relief. In this way, the CGT analysis would present a more favourable picture than the income tax position.

LIFE INSURANCE POLICIES, ETC (2018/19)

Non-qualifying policies and chargeable events

4.102 There is a general exemption from CGT on qualifying life insurance policies (*TCGA 1992, s 210(2)*). However, there is a very complex set of provisions in the income tax legislation, which charge to income tax certain gains on non-qualifying policies (*ITTOIA 2005, Pt 4, Ch 9*). Details here are requested on page 5 of form SA900. Where the gain is paid gross (offshore), the amount is entered in Box 9.14; where net (onshore), the gain is put in 9.16, with the tax deducted in Box 9.15.

Cases where income tax arises are called 'chargeable events', and the relevant insurance company will be able to advise whether the particular policy is exempt from tax or whether the gain triggers income tax. Very often, the insurance company will already have informed HMRC of the event and the gain.

Where the chargeable event is the death of the policyholder, the income will usually be that of the individual for the year in which he died, and therefore is properly entered in form SA900. In very rare circumstances, a gain will be taxed on the personal representatives, but only to the extent that tax at the basic rate has *not* been deducted.

If the person who made the policy has written the benefits in trust, any gain will usually be treated as his *unless* he was non-UK resident or had died in the year before the year in which the chargeable event occurred (*ITTOIA 2005, ss 465, 467*). If, therefore, he had died on 1 January 2018 before the chargeable event in 2018/19, the gain will be taxed on the trustees at 45% for that 2018/19 year.

In the March 2016 Budget, the government announced its intention to change the tax rules for calculating chargeable event gains on part surrenders and part assignments for value under life assurance policies following the inequitable outcome of the *Lobler* case. HMRC opened a consultation, which ran from 20 April to 13 July 2016 inviting views on three options for change designed to ensure disproportionate gains, which did not reflect the economic reality of the situation, should no longer arise for both new and existing policyholders albeit the concept of the familiar 5% tax-deferred allowances would be retained. These options were:

- taxing the economic gain – this option would retain the current 5% tax-deferred allowances but would bring into charge a proportionate fraction of any underlying economic gain whenever an amount in excess of 5% was withdrawn;
- the 100% allowance – under this option no gain would arise until all of the premium(s) paid have been withdrawn, after which all withdrawals would be taxed in full, effectively changing the current cumulative annual 5% tax-deferred allowances into a lifetime 100% tax-deferred allowance. This is the simplest of the three options; and
- deferral of excessive gains – this more complicated option would maintain the current method for calculating gains but would limit the amount of gain that could be brought into charge on a part surrender (or part assignment for value) to a pre-determined amount of the premium (eg a cumulative 3% for each year since the policy commenced), holding the remaining gain over until the next part surrender or part assignment when the process would begin again until final surrender when all deferred gains would be brought into charge.

Surprisingly, and despite the strong concerns expressed in the consultation process, it has been confirmed that no new legislation will be introduced to give effect to any of the above options. Instead *FA 2017* set out an alternative and far less satisfactorily remedy that will allow the policy holders who have inadvertently triggered 'a wholly disproportionate gain' to apply to HMRC to have their gain recalculated on a 'just and reasonable' basis.

Other income

4.103 Specifically mentioned at Box 9.26 of page 5 is proceeds received from a company when it purchases its own shares. The general tax rule is that the cash received by the shareholder is treated as income, unless (in prescribed circumstances) the shareholder qualifies for capital investment. The company will usually get confirmation from HMRC in advance whether income or capital investment applies.

However (since 1997), where the shareholders are trustees, the proceeds will be taxed at the dividend trust rate of 38.1% (37.5% for 2015/16) without any in built tax credit. Interestingly, the SA900 includes Box 9.25 headed tax credit which would imply that an entry is required. However, page 19 of the HMRC guidance makes it clear that no entry should be made in this Box.

Qualifying policies

4.104

- Whole of life policies (whether single life or joint lives and survivor).

- Term assurance.
- Endowment policies for at least ten years (or the earlier death of the life assured). No capital payment must be made other than on whole or partial surrender of the policy. Premiums must be payable at least annually.

Non-qualifying policies

4.105

- Single premium bonds.
- Term assurance of less than ten years unless the surrender value does not exceed the premiums paid.
- Certain unit-linked whole of life policies.

Chargeable events on non-qualifying policies

4.106 These include (under *ITTOIA 2005, s 484*):

- Death of the life assured.
- Maturity of the policy.
- Surrender in whole of the policy rights.
- Assignment for money or money's worth of the rights under the policy.

DISCRETIONARY PAYMENTS OF INCOME (2018/19)

4.107 Question 14 on page 8 of the tax return asks, 'Have discretionary payments of income been made to beneficiaries?' Seven boxes are provided to give the names of the beneficiaries and the amount of the payment (which will always reflect the actual payment made). Further, a box must be ticked if the beneficiary was a minor and unmarried child of the settlor who was alive when the payment was made; this is because the income will be taxed on the settlor (see **4.30–4.31**).

The purpose of this question is to ensure that payments of income are made subject to the deduction of tax at 45% for 2018/19 (50% for 2012/13) (see **4.41–4.43**). This is a requirement of *ITA 2007, Pt 9, Ch 7.* If the trustees have paid income tax in the past, which has not already been utilised against earlier income distributions to beneficiaries, this will provide a 'tax pool' which can be used to 'frank' the tax due on distributions. Hence, Box 14.15 asks for details of any amount of an unused tax pool brought forward from 2017/18.

The tax pool

4.108 The tax pool is of use only insofar as the trust continues within the discretionary or accumulation regime: see **4.111** for an example. Hence, it is very important to ensure that the tax pool is 'stripped' in the years before, for example, an A&M settlement ceases to be within the accumulation phase. Interestingly, if there are several beneficiaries of an A&M trust, and one of them attains 25, this does not in itself reduce the tax pool. The regime will apply if:

- a payment is made by the trustees in an exercise of discretion; and
- the sum is income of the beneficiary for tax purposes.

Income or capital

4.109 Decided cases have addressed the situation (and possible argument by HMRC) that a payment of capital by the trustees might constitute income in the hands of the beneficiary. However, HMRC at present apply a relatively relaxed practice – see **4.64**.

The tax voucher

4.110 After making a payment to the beneficiary, the trustees must also complete a tax voucher (R185 (Trust Income)), showing the gross income, the amount of tax deducted and paid to HMRC and the net sum to which the beneficiary is entitled.

Example 4.26—Trustees' tax liability on distributing income

Ignoring the impact of the standard rate band for ease of explanation, assume the trustees have post-tax dividend income of £619.00, having paid tax of £381.00 representing the 38.1% dividend trust rate (£1,000 @ 38.1%) and make an income distribution of £550. The whole of that tax paid by the trustees can be used to 'frank' the tax under *ITA 2007, s 466* for which they must account on making the distribution:

Net income of trust		£619.00
Section 496 liability on net payment of £550 to beneficiary	£450.00	
Met by trustees' tax payment above	(£381.00)	
Remaining liability of trustees		(£69.00)

Available for distribution to beneficiary	£550.00
Section 496 liability	£450.00
Gross income of beneficiary	£1,000.00
Tax thereon @ 45% (met by trustees)	(£450.00)
Net income of beneficiary	£550.00

The point therefore is that, in the absence of a brought forward tax pool to frank the tax shortfall on distribution of £69.00, a super rate taxpayer will receive only £550.00 cash out of an original dividend received by the trustees of £1,000, an effective rate of tax of 45%.

Operation of the tax pool

4.111

Example 4.27—Tax pool illustration

Consider that the trustees have undistributed cash income of £6,050 brought forward from 2017/18 and a 2018/19 tax pool balance (to include £5,000 brought forward from 2017/18) of £6,200. If, in 2018/19, they distribute all of the 2017/18 net cash to the beneficiary, the latter's position would be as follows:

Gross (£6,050 × 100/55)	£11,000
Tax @ 45%	(£4,950)
Net	£6,050
Form R185 (Trust Income) given to the beneficiary would record:	
Net	£6,050
Tax	£4,950

In the absence of any other transactions, the tax pool would be:

Brought forward/current	£6,200
Used 2018/19	(£4,950)
Balance carried forward	£1,250

LOSSES (2018/19)

4.112 A trading loss (but not a loss from furnished holiday lettings, with effect from 2010/11) will arise in a particular year where the allowable expenses exceed the taxable income. The loss may be set against general income of that or the preceding tax year and, to the extent unused, may be carried forward against future profits from that trade (*ITA 2007, s 64*).

A property business loss can be carried forward for use only against future property business profits (*ITA 2007, s 118*).

Trust management expenses may exceed the income in that year and this will trigger a loss.

Some, though not all, of the losses may be set against certain types of income from other transactions in the category of 'other income' of which the gross amount is shown in Box 9.34. In the absence of such income, losses can be carried forward to be set against similar income in future years. Losses cannot be set against annual payments.

4.113 Trading losses in 2018/19 may be:

- offset against other income for 2018/19;
- carried back and offset against other income for 2017/18;
- carried back and (to the extent that they are related to losses incurred in a new trade) offset against other income for 2015/16 and later years; or
- carried forward against future profits from that trade.

There are provisions that restrict losses from farming or market gardening where more than five years of consecutive loss have occurred (subject to concessionary relief, such as in the circumstances of foot and mouth).

Page TT2 asks for details of any share of investment income arising for the partnership and share of losses on partnership investments. Box 2.25 is the 'white space'.

Example 4.28—Partnership losses

Adam has transferred a one-third share in his family farm into a new discretionary settlement. The partnership capital is £330,000. The partnership is a limited partnership under the *Limited Partnerships Act 1907*. Adam is the general partner, with a two-thirds share of the income and capital, and the trustees, a limited partner, with one-third. For the year ended 31 March 2019, there is a loss of £15,000.

Form SA902 is completed showing the trustees' share of the loss of £5,000 in Box 2.7. The whole of the loss is shown in Box 2.15 as offset against other income for 2018/19.

INTEREST PAYMENTS BY TRUSTEES (2018/19)

Deductible interest

4.114 The tax system gives relief for interest paid by trustees in certain circumstances, eg:

- interest on money borrowed for use as capital in a trade (*ITTOIA 2005, ss 29* and *52*); and
- interest on a loan to purchase property let within a property business (*ITTOIA 2005, s 272(1)*).

All the above will be recognised as deductions in computing the profits of the trade, partnership or property business as the case may be.

There are other statutory reliefs for payments of interest, given generally to 'a person' under *ITA 2007, s 383*, which of course includes trustees as well as an individual. However, most of the specific provisions in that part of *ITA 2007* are, perhaps somewhat curiously, restricted to individuals, for example the relief under *ss 398* and *399* on interest paid on a loan to invest in a partnership. That said, it is possible that HMRC have not challenged some claims to interest relief by trustees which are not allowed by the legislation. HMRC have confirmed that the statutory distinction in treatment as between individuals and trustees is correct.

Non-deductible interest

4.115 Certain types of interest are not allowable, eg interest on overdue tax.

Question 10A on page 6 of the trust and estate return is phrased 'do you want to claim any reliefs or have you made any annual payments?' These might be:

- Interest (or alternative finance payments) eligible for relief on qualifying loans, of which the only one mentioned is a loan to pay IHT. This relief is given *only* to personal representatives to pay IHT before a grant of probate in respect of personal property, ie not including tax on land. Relief is given solely on interest paid for one year. If the interest cannot be relieved in the year of payment it can be carried back to the previous year and then forward to subsequent years of assessment (*ITA 2007, ss 403–405*).
- Other charges, viz annuities and other annual payments. Here the trustees must deduct basic rate tax and account to the beneficiary for the net amount as recorded on a tax deduction certificate. The assumption is that the trustees have, in the relevant tax year, taxable income equal at least to the amount of the gross annuity. If not, and there is a shortfall, the trustees are taxable on it, ie they will find themselves out of pocket, which they may have to make good by resorting to capital.

Example 4.29—Annuity

The trustees have gross income of £10,000 made up as follows:

	Net	*Tax*	*Gross*
Dividend income			£1,000
REIT income	£3,200	£800	£4,000
Rental income			£5,000

The trust deed requires the trustees to pay a gross annuity of £3,600. Tax on this is £720. They have sufficient income to pay the annuity out of income and thus fill in the return as follows:

Box					
10.2A	£2,880	10.3A	£720	10.4A	£3,600

ANNUAL PAYMENTS OUT OF CAPITAL (2018/19)

Duty to withhold tax

4.116 Question 11 also embraces annual payments out of income not brought into charge to income tax. On making the annual payment, the trustees must withhold tax at the basic rate for 2018/19 (20%) which they hand to HMRC, paying over to the beneficiary the balance only. The beneficiary also receives a tax deduction certificate and may be able to reclaim the tax or, if a higher rate taxpayer, will have to pay a further 20% on the gross amount.

If the trustees do not have income, or sufficient income, to make the payment, it will be made out of capital, and the trustees must account for the tax due to HMRC.

Examples might be:

- an annuity paid out of capital; or
- as mentioned in the return guide notes, enhanced scrip dividends received by the trustees against which they have made compensatory payments out of capital to beneficiaries. As explained in **4.99–4.101**, the trustees must determine, as a matter of trust law, whether the enhanced scrip dividend is received as trust income or as trust capital. Here they face a conundrum, as illustrated below.

Example 4.30—Enhanced stock dividend

The trustees receive an enhanced stock dividend worth £150, which has a 'cash alternative' of £100. This belongs to the capital of the trust. The trustees decide to compensate the life tenant for loss of the cash alternative income and, following the case of *Re Malam, Malam v Hitchens* [1894] 3 Ch 578, they pay the life tenant the value of that cash alternative, namely £100 gross or, after deduction of 20% tax, £80.

According to HMRC, the trustees make an annual payment from which they must deduct basic rate tax. As a matter of trust law they must balance the interests of income and capital beneficiaries. With a net amount of £100 and grossing up at 20%, the gross income becomes £125. However, that might prejudice the capital beneficiaries and/or require the trustees to sell some of the shares.

Therefore, they might deduct the basic rate tax from the cash equivalent and distribute the balance. However, no tax credit is due and a life tenant who is a super rate taxpayer, would therefore be worse off as a result. That is, the beneficiary is marginally worse off with the stock dividend alternative when compared to the cash dividend.

	Cash dividend	*Re Malam analysis*
Beneficiary's cash receipt	£100.00	£80.00
Less higher rate tax: 38.1% of £100	(38.10)	
Less 20% higher rate tax on £100 gross		(£20.00)
Beneficiary's net cash receipt	£61.90	£60.00

Given also the professional costs of dealing with usually relatively small amounts, plus the CGT implications of selling the stock, etc it is likely (as explained in **4.99–4.101**) to be better to take the cash alternative. Happily, such situations are comparatively rare.

TRUST MANAGEMENT EXPENSES

Trust and tax law

Focus

Revenue and Customs Commissioners v Trustees of the Peter Clay Discretionary Trust [2008] EWCA Civ 1441 provides solid guidance when considering the deductibility of trustees' management expenses.

4.117 While the distinction between income and capital will generally be the same for tax law as it is for trust law, this will not always be the case; for example, some capital receipts for trust law purposes are subject to income tax (generally for anti-avoidance reasons). This parallel is true with expenses, in that, while a particular expense may be properly deductible against trust income, it will not necessarily be deductible for tax purposes.

An expense may be deducted from trust income if:

- under trust law it is properly chargeable against income, eg management expenses of a property within a property business; and
- it is actually paid out of income for the year.

In *Bosanquet v Allan; Carver v Duncan* [1985] AC 1082, the House of Lords held that, in the absence of special provisions in the trust deed, premiums on life assurance policies were chargeable to capital not to income. A well-drawn trust deed will allow trustees to set such premiums, however, either against income or against capital. Legal expenses or fees paid to other professional advisers, which are not directly referable to the income, should be charged to capital.

Following a review of the tax implications of management expenses, HMRC issued on 2 February 2006 a final version of their guidance paper first released in draft in September 2004. Detailed attention should be given to these expressed principles, with any deviation clearly noted in the 'white space' in the self-assessment return. Following the House of Lords decision in *Carver v Duncan,* HMRC expressed the view that an expense, even if recurrent, which is incurred for the benefit of the whole trust fund, should be charged to capital. There is only limited scope for apportionment, in the case of some accountancy and audit fees. The main disagreement with the professional bodies is the trustees' annual management fee, which HMRC claim is to be charged wholly to capital.

4.118 The test case on trust management expenses was finally decided by the Court of Appeal on 19 December 2008 and the basis continues to remain accepted practice. There were five categories of disputed fees: the accountancy fees, the custodian fees, the trustee management fees, the bank charges and the investment managers' fees. Following the decisions of the Special Commissioner and the High Court (largely in favour of the taxpayers and HMRC, respectively), it had been agreed between the parties and the Court of Appeal held that a proper apportionment between income and capital was permitted for all of the bank charges, custodian fees and the professional fees for accountancy and administration.

4.119 That left the substantive issue of the deductibility of the fees paid to both the executive and the non-executive trustees. Here the Court of Appeal ruled in favour in principle of the taxpayer trustees (*Revenue and Customs Commissioners v Trustees of the Peter Clay Discretionary Trust* [2008] EWCA Civ 1441). The Special Commissioners had erred in law in ruling in favour of an attribution between income and capital in respect of the trust management fees on 'the general principle of fairness'. This approach was not permissible in the light of the House of Lords decision in *Carver v Duncan*. However, in finding for an apportionment for the fees charged by the executive trustee, the Court of Appeal went on to say that, if professional fees incurred by the trustees for accountancy services could properly be apportioned on a time basis between income and capital, it was impossible to see why the fees charged by the executive trustee should not also be capable of apportionment. Indeed, there was no reason in principle why the, much smaller, fixed, fees of the non-executive trustees could not also be apportioned insofar as it could be estimated, if not ascertained, what part of their time was devoted to income matters. Finally, as to the investment management fees, those were chargeable against capital as determined by the Special Commissioners; only (which was not the case here) could expenses incurred before the trustees had made the decision to accumulate income be charged against income. The decision is now final.

Trust management expenses

Life interest trusts

4.120 Subject to specific deductions in calculating taxable income, eg for trade or property business purposes, trust management expenses allocable to income are deducted from the life tenant's net share of income, which is then grossed up to produce the statutory taxable income.

Discretionary or accumulation trusts

4.121 Trust management expenses may be deducted from, and hence used to shelter, the income otherwise taxed at the rate applicable to trusts or at the dividend trust rate. However, such expenses are not a 'pound for pound' offset, and thus cannot be deducted in calculating the income taxed only at the 7.5% dividend rate for 2018/19 (10% pre 6 April 2016) or the 20% basic rate (for 2009/10 and later).

Expenses are deducted against income in strict order:

- UK dividend or scrip dividends, (which prior to 6 April 2016 carried a non-repayable10% tax credit);
- foreign dividends (which prior to 6 April 2016, a claim is made for the non-repayable tax credit under *ITTOIA 2005, s 397A)*; and
- 20% rate income.

Two useful examples are given on pages 21 and 22 of the SA900 Guide on which the following examples are based.

Example 4.31—Allowable expenses: HMRC's Example A (updated)

In 2018/19, £1,000 from which tax of £200 has been deducted. A total of £500 of income is allocated for specific purposes and the trust has allowable trustee management expenses of £500. Only one-half of the trust income is taxable at the rate applicable to trusts. The tax calculation is as follows:

		Rent	*Interest*
		£	*£*
Income (gross)		4,000	1,000
minus income allocated for specific purposes (apportioned at a ratio of 4:1)		(400)	(100)
		3,600	900
minus income not taxable at the rate applicable to trusts		(1,800)	(450)
		1,800	450
Expenses	500		
minus apportioned to income allocated for specific purposes (500 × 500/5,000)	(50)		
	450		
minus apportioned to income not taxable at the rate applicable to trusts (500 × 2,250/5,000)	(225)		
Net balance allowable against income taxable at the rate applicable to trusts	225		
Gross equivalent (225 × 100/80)			(281)
Amount taxable at rate applicable to trusts		**1,800**	**169**

Example 4.32—Allowable expenses: HMRC's Example B (updated)

Boris is the trustee of an Interest on possession trust. In 2018/19 the trust received rental income of £1,500 and REIT income of £1,000 from which basic rate tax of £200 has been deducted and incurred allowable trustees' management expenses of £250.

	Rent	*Interest*
	£	*£*
Trust gross income	1,500	1,000
Tax due by trust	(300)	(200)
Net income	1,200	800

The trust will receive credit for the tax deducted at source from the REIT income (£200), so the trust will have to pay £300 in tax.

The life tenant's income for tax purposes will be:

	Rent	*Interest*
Net income (as above)	1,200	800
minus Management expenses		(250)
Adjusted net income	1,200	550
Tax credit	300	137
Adjusted gross (net × 100/80)	£1,500	£687

CAPITAL PAYMENTS (2018/19)

4.122 Questions 15 and 15A require details of two types of capital payment made by the trustees:

- payments to settlor's children; and
- capital transactions between the trustees and the settlors.

Payments to settlor's children

4.123 These are capital payments to, or for the benefit of, minor unmarried children of the settlor during the settlor's lifetime.

Such payments will include the transfer of assets as well as cash. This is relevant in the context of *ITTOIA 2005, ss 629* to *632* (see **4.30–4.31**). The rule cannot be avoided by the trustees purporting to distribute capital when there remains within the trust a balance of undistributed income, which might otherwise escape assessment on the settlor. Of course, if all the income has been distributed and assessed on the settlor, there will be no further income tax implications for the trustees making such capital payments.

Example 4.33—Parental income

The trustees of a post-9 March 1999 parental settlement have undistributed income from 2016/17 of £2,500 and a further £5,000 of income for the 2018/19 year to date. On 31 March 2019, they advance £10,000 of capital to a minor beneficiary. The amount of £7,500, equal to the undistributed income of 2017/18 and 2018/19, is assessed on the settlor parent for 2018/19 under *ITTOIA 2005, s 629*.

Capital transactions between the trustees and the settlors

4.124 This refers to the anti-avoidance provision in *ITTOIA 2005, ss 633–642*. The anti-avoidance rules for settlements have traditionally attacked situations where the trustees have retained undistributed income in the trust that HMRC perceive is being used for the benefit of the settlor. The particular mischief in question is where the trustees lend money to the settlor, or repay money to the settlor that the settlor has previously lent to the trust. Payments to the settlor's spouse are similarly caught, as are payments to a third party at the direction of the settlor, or payments that may be applied for the settlor's benefit. The capital sum might be paid directly or through a company connected with the settlor.

Answers to this question might trigger situations where these rules might be in point. This could have the result that, for up to a period of ten years, any undistributed income would be assessed on the settlor up to the amount of the capital payment.

Example 4.34—Repayment of loan to settlor

(Based on a 1964 House of Lords decision *De Vigier v IRC* [1964] 1 WLR 1073.)

The trustees wanted to take up a rights issue on shares that the trust owned. To fund the purchase, they borrowed money from the wife of the settlor but repaid the money within the year. However, the trustees had undistributed income and thus the settlor was assessed up to the amount of the loan. The amount of the loan repayment was liable to assessment on the settlor to the extent that it fell within the income available up to the end of that tax year or the following ten years.

The tax is charged on the relevant amount, grossed up at 45% but carries a 45% tax credit. In this way, for 2018/19, £11,000 net is grossed up to £20,000, producing a tax liability of £9,000 for a super rate taxpayer. Interestingly, in this instance the settlor has no right of reimbursement from the trustees (as he has elsewhere in the settlement code). However, set against the tax chargeable on the settlor is 'the deductible amount' computed under *ITTOIA 2005, s 640*. This is expressed as the lowest of three amounts and has the effect (in particular) that tax paid by the trustees on the grossed-up income available during the tax year in question such as corresponds to the sum assessed on the settlor constitutes the deductible amount. This effectively avoids double taxation and so, in circumstances where, as at present, the special rates for trustees and the marginal rate for individuals are the same, the settlor effectively suffers no penalty.

CALCULATION OF TAX (2018/19)

4.125 The trustee who has managed to wade through the tax return to question 17, and is then faced with the question 'Do you want to calculate the tax?' may be forgiven for answering, 'No' with no little gusto.

If he wants HMRC to calculate the tax for 2018/19, he must ensure that the completed form is with HMRC on or before 31 October 2019. This will give HMRC time to calculate the income tax and CGT due, after taking into account the instalments paid on 1 January and 31 July 2019, and to tell the trustees before 31 January 2020 how much they have to pay.

If the trustees want HMRC to calculate the tax, but get the form in after 31 October, HMRC will still do so, but with no guarantee that they will meet the 31 January deadline. In this case, the trustees have satisfied their statutory obligation to make the return; however, if they wish to avoid paying interest on tax, they should estimate the amount due and pay it on or before 31 January 2020. That said, see **4.9** and **4.127**.

If, on the other hand, the trustees do want to calculate the tax, they should make use of form SA951, the 2018/19 Trust and Estate Tax Calculation Guide (see **4.65**), in which event HMRC will have the opportunity to amend the trustees' self-assessment.

Repayments due

4.126 If it transpires (or there is a possibility) that the trust has paid too much tax, the 'Yes' box, question 18 must be ticked. If not, any amount owed will be set against the next tax bill (which will normally happen if the amount is small, eg below £10). A repayment made on or before 31 January 2019 will not carry interest from HMRC. If paid thereafter, repayment supplement (which is non-taxable) will be due; see **4.18** for the rates (currently nil).

Tax year 2018/19: relevant dates and time limits

4.127

First payment on account	31 January 2019
Second payment on account	31 July 2019
Notification of liability to tax, if no return received	5 October 2019
Deadline for submission of tax return if HMRC are to calculate the tax liability	31 October 2019

Tax return to be submitted by and tax paid by*	31 January 2020
Tax enquiry window (return submitted on 31 January 2020)**	31 January 2021
Business records to be retained until	31 January 2025

* 31 October 2019 is the due date for submission of paper returns (and 31 January 2020 for online returns). But a penalty will be levied for late submission of a paper return if it is filed, whether or not all tax due is paid, on or before 31 January 2020.

* If a return is submitted before 31 January 2020, the enquiry window closes 12 months following submission of the return. If later than 31 January 2020, the window closes 12 months after the month end of the quarter in which the return was submitted.

Chapter 5

Running a trust: capital gains tax

SIGNPOSTS

- **Basics** – Revisit the mechanics for determining the chargeable gain – base cost, substitute proceeds, relieving provisions, deferral reliefs (see **5.1–5.5** and **5.18**).
- **Foreign aspects** – The foreign dimension must be considered as part of the overall tax strategy (see **5.8**, **5.10–5.11** and **5.59–5.61**).
- **Anti-avoidance** – Critical to the process is the recognition and cost of the anti-avoidance measures, particularly in relation to settlor-interested trusts (see **5.9**, **5.15**, **5.21–5.22**, and **5.46–5.50**).

THE REGIME IN SUMMARY

Actual and deemed disposals

5.1 CGT is payable on actual disposals, which includes a disposal by way of gift (*TCGA 1992, s 1*). CGT may also be charged on deemed disposals, eg where within a qualifying life interest trust (which does not fall within the relevant property regime by reason of creation on death or after 22 March 2006 or valid TSI), the life tenant dies or where, within any type of trust, one or more beneficiaries becomes absolutely entitled to the property against the trustees. This situation is discussed in more detail in **8.5–8.11**.

Disposal proceeds

5.2 The gain has to be calculated. In simple terms, the gain is the sale proceeds (net of costs of sale) less the cost of acquisition (increased by incidental costs of acquisition and valid improvement costs). In the case of a gift, the market value at the date of the gift is substituted for the absent sale proceeds. The same 'market value' rule applies where the trustees make a disposal, even by way of sale, to a 'connected person', eg the settlor or anyone related to him.

Deductions

5.3 Base cost: This is its acquisition costs unless the asset was acquired before 31 March 1982, when the cost basis is rebased to its value at 31 March 1982.

Also allowed as deductions from the gain are the professional and other incidental costs of acquiring (but not if March 1982 value used) and disposing of the asset.

Until April 1998, an allowance was given for the effect of inflation, namely the 'indexation allowance'. However, the indexation allowance was 'frozen' at that date from which point the relief was, in general terms, replaced by taper relief. No indexation allowance or, indeed, taper relief is given for disposals on or after 6 April 2008.

There are various other reliefs that are dealt with in the course of this book and these are listed at **5.4** below.

Finally, after the application of any reliefs and losses (see **5.13–5.15**), a deduction is allowed for the annual exemption (see **5.37–5.40**) which, for 2019/20, will vary in amount between £6,000 and (because of the rules described at **5.38–5.39**) £1,200.

The standard rate of CGT payable by trustees from 23 June 2010 to 5 April 2016 was 28% (18% between 6 April 2009 and 22 June 2010, and 40% in 2007/08) but *FA 2016* introduced reduced CGT rates (applicable to trust, estates and individuals) effective from 6 April 2016. The rate of CGT payable on most gains realised by trustees is now reduced to 20% (from 28%). However, gains on the disposal of interests in UK residential properties that do not qualify for private residence relief and gains arising in respect of carried interest (as defined) continue to attract an 8% premium at 28%.

Various reliefs

5.4

- Principal private residence relief (see **5.25–5.27**): In parallel to the relief given to individuals, trustees making a gain on the disposal of a house that has been used as the only or main residence of a beneficiary who occupies under the terms of the trust, may have the gain wholly or partly relieved – access to this relief is preserved under the CGT charge on the disposal by non-residents (to include trusts) of UK residential property, which came into effect on 6 April 2015. Legislation in *FA 2004* introduced with effect from 10 December 2003, prevents the combination of deferral by hold-over of the gain arising on the gift of a residence into a relevant property trust (namely a trust subject to the IHT regime of 10-year anniversary and exit charges) and principal private residence relief for the trustees (or beneficiary if in their ownership) on ultimate sale by them (see **5.27** and Example 5.9). Note: *FA 2019* has reduced the non-occupation ownership from 18 months to 9 months with effect from 6 April 2019.

- Entrepreneurs' relief (see **5.32–5.34**): Introduced from 2008/09 to mitigate the effect of the withdrawal of business assets taper relief. To a large extent, this represents a return to the old retirement relief which came to an end on 6 April 2003 (not considered in this book although, for a description, see **5.34–5.36** of the 2007/08 edition) and is confined to truly business assets.
- Taper relief: Introduced in 1998 but withdrawn from 6 April 2008. It was designed to relieve the impact of CGT according to the length of time the particular asset had been owned, with very significant favour being given to business assets.
- Roll-over relief (see **5.28–5.31**): This is a specific relief given to trustees who trade, whether as a body or in partnership, by way of deferral of a gain realised on the sale of one business asset into the acquisition cost of another.
- Enterprise Investment Scheme (EIS): Allows trustees to defer a gain realised on any asset by making an investment in a qualifying EIS company (see **5.23–5.24**).
- Hold-over relief: The trustees of certain trusts may defer recognition of CGT which would otherwise trigger when they advance certain assets to a beneficiary. The in-built gain is deducted from the market value base cost to arrive at the adjusted base cost and hence may serve to increase the net gain when the beneficiary comes to sell the asset or in other prescribed clawback situations.

FA 2016 introduced a new CGT relief for investment in qualifying shares made by a 'qualifying person'. The relief, which is in addition to entrepreneur relief, provides for a reduced 10% tax rate on the disposal of gains (up to £10 million) realised on qualifying shares in a trading company, or a company that is the holding company of a trading group. The 'investors' relief' can apply only to gains on shares subscribed for by the trust (as well as an individual or their spouse or civil partner) where at least one of the beneficiaries is an eligible beneficiary as defined in respect of the disposal, namely:

- Immediately before the disposal the individual has an interest in possession (whether or not a qualifying interest as defined for IHT purposes) and that interest was held for a minimum three years prior to disposal.
- At no time was that individual a 'relevant employee' in respect of the company in which the trust holds shares.

- At time of claim for relief the individual elected to be treated as an eligible beneficiary in respect of the disposal.

DEFERRED CONSIDERATION

5.5 CGT is triggered by a disposal or deemed disposal. The date of the disposal for CGT purposes is the date on which the binding contract of sale is made (even if the sale is 'completed' in a subsequent tax year) (*TCGA 1992, s 28(1)*). A disposal requires the passing of beneficial interest and this will not occur if the contract is not completed (*Underwood v HMRC* [2008] EWCA Civ 1423).

If the contract is conditional, the date of disposal occurs on the date the contract becomes unconditional, eg the date on which the condition is satisfied (*TCGA 1992, s 28(2)*).

Instalment reliefs

5.6 The CGT falls due on 31 January following the end of the tax year in which the disposal takes place (but see *FA 2019* commentary below re gains on residential properties effective April 2020). The fact that the sale proceeds might not be paid for some time makes no difference. That said, however, there is a relief (historically called 'hardship' relief) which can apply where the whole or part of the proceeds is receivable by instalments over a period exceeding 18 months, beginning no earlier than the date of the disposal (*TCGA 1992, s 280*). In such a case, the taxpayer can ask for instalment relief and may agree with HMRC a plan for payment of the tax over a period not exceeding eight years but ending no later than the date of the last instalment. Importantly, there is no longer any need to satisfy HMRC that payment in one sum would cause undue hardship. In practice, HMRC will agree a payment plan that ensures the taxpayer does not have to pay in tax more than 50% of the proceeds actually received.

Importantly and often overlooked, CGT may also be paid by equal annual instalments over a 10-year period where the disposal was a gift (*TCGA 1992, s 281*): see **5.53** for details.

The outcome of the HMRC consultation in 2018 is now reflected in *FA 2019* which contains provisions, effective from April 2020, requiring the submission of a property return and imposition of a payment on account to be made within 30 days of the disposal of residential property. The measures, which also extend to the disposal of overseas properties, only apply where there is CGT at stake and thus do not apply to the disposal of the family home where the gain is wholly covered by principle private residence relief.

Contingent consideration

5.7 The vendor of a business may agree with the buyer that the price paid is, in part, determined by the future results of the business over, say, the next three years. This is colloquially known as an 'earn out'. Whilst part of the price may be paid shortly after the contract, it will not be known for another three years or so, as illustrated in the following example, whether any further element will become known and payable. This is a so-called *Marren v Ingles* situation, named after the House of Lords case ([1980] 1 WLR 983) of the same name. This established the principle that some valuation has to be placed on the future right, and that valuation is deemed to be part of the price received on sale. Three years later, when that right is quantified, there is a further disposal, which may itself give rise to a gain or a loss.

Example 5.1—Completion in a later tax year

The trustees enter into a binding contract to sell Blackacre on 31 March 2019, with the contract being completed on 30 April 2019. For CGT purposes the disposal falls into the tax year 2018/19.

Example 5.2—Instalment payment

The trustees have agreed to sell Blackacre for £100,000, payable in four equal annual instalments. The first instalment is due 30 days after the contract and the next three instalments on each anniversary of the contract. It would be open to the trustees to apply to HMRC for instalment relief.

Example 5.3—Earn-out provision

The trustees sell a business for £500,000 plus 10% of the profits shown by audited accounts over the next three years, payable nine months after the year-end in three years' time. The right to receive the further profits is quantified at £50,000. The immediate sale proceeds are therefore £550,000 (£500,000 + £50,000). In three years and nine months' time, the amount actually payable is £75,000. Therefore, a further gain of £25,000 (£75,000 – £50,000) arises at that time.

If, for disposals on or after 10 April 2003, a loss arises on realising the further right, that loss can (subject to conditions) be set off against the original gain (*TCGA 1992, s 279A*).

TRUST RESIDENCE

> **Focus**
>
> The protective 'isolation' clause for the professional trustee was withdrawn from 6 April 2008 onwards, and thus inclusion of a UK professional as a member of the trustee body can cause a trust to become UK resident.

5.8 Prior to 6 April 2007, separate residence tests applied for CGT and income tax (see **4.1–4.4**), and the CGT test at that time did not look through to the individual trustees, but rather presumed trustees (as a body of persons) to be resident and ordinarily resident in the UK, unless:

- the general administration of trusts was ordinarily carried on outside the UK; and
- the trustees, or a majority of them, were not resident or (prior to 6 April 2013) ordinarily resident in the UK (*TCGA 1992, s 69(1)*).

Prior to 6 April 2007, there was also a further provision which effectively 'isolated' the UK professional trustee when determining the residence status of the trust. This allowed a professional trustee, even though resident in the UK, eg a London solicitor, to be treated as non-UK resident if the settlor was not domiciled and/or resident in the UK. In such a case, all or the majority of the trustees were treated as non-UK resident and the general administration of the trust was treated as carried on outside the UK (even if, as a matter of fact, it was carried on in London).

The rules for residence were revised from 2007/08 (*TCGA 1992, s 69*). The income tax test now described in **4.1–4.4** applies also for CGT purposes, and the favourable rule for UK professional trustees described above has been repealed. However, professional body response to the current HMRC trust consultation launched in November 2018 has universally called for a reconsideration of this rule.

Anti-avoidance

The settlor and capital payments charges

5.9 The advantage of a trust being resident outside the UK is that, apart from anti-avoidance rules (see **5.59–5.61** and the 2015/16 introduction of the non-resident CGT (NRCGT) charge restricted to disposals of UK residential property – see *Capital Gains Tax 2019/20* (Bloomsbury Professional)), and assuming the trustees do not realise gains from UK assets used in a UK business, the trustees do not have a liability to CGT. This is the case even in relation to the disposal of assets situated in the UK (with exception for the NRCGT charge levied on the disposal of UK residential property in foreign ownership). In the 1980s and1990s, this ostensibly favourable position led to a considerable number of UK-resident domiciliaries establishing offshore trusts. The ideal asset to put into such a trust would be one showing no current gain but with a significant prospect of a substantial future gain, eg subscription shares in a private trading company. The intention would be that the trustees would sell the asset in due course, realise a significant gain and then use it in such a way as to benefit the beneficiary and his family but without advancing capital to him. It was in response to such situations that substantive anti-avoidance legislation was enacted in 1991, 1998 and 2000. The capital payments charge was further refined in 2008/09, following the changes to taxation made for UK-resident non-UK domiciled beneficiaries generally by *FA 2008*: see **5.60–5.62** for more detail.

The use of double tax treaties

5.10 Most recently, in the light of attempts to exploit the application of specific double tax treaties to procure a UK CGT advantage, *F(No 2)A 2005, s 33* prevents the use of a double tax treaty to argue that trustees are not UK resident in a particular year of disposal, with effect from 16 March 2005. It appears from the High Court decision in *Smallwood v HMRC* [2009] STC 1222, found in favour of the taxpayer, that such legislation was indeed necessary.

This same theme was echoed in the more recent case, in which the *Smallwood* case was cited, of *R Lee; N Bunter (TC5757)*. The taxpayers used the 'round the world scheme' to mitigate the trust CGT liability by exploiting the double tax treaty between the UK and Mauritius. The main issue centred on the place of effective management of the trust, which the Tribunal determined rested in the place where those most important decisions were taken and not, as argued, where the relevant share sale documentation was executed. It was determined 'the shots were called in the UK'.

Example 5.4—Trust residence

The Harry Trust is UK resident, and is therefore taxed on its worldwide gains as they arise.

The Hector Trust is non-UK resident. It was made by a person neither UK resident nor UK domiciled, who continues to be so, therefore, the settlor charge does not apply and no-one is taxed on the trustees' gains in the UK as they arise.

However, the capital payments charge (see **5.60–5.61**) will apply to the Hector Trust even though the trust was made by a non-UK domiciliary. As and when payments of capital are received by a UK-resident beneficiary, the 'trust gains' (or, from 2008/09, the so-called '*section 2(2)* amounts') (*TCGA 1992, s 87A*) of the settlement will be attributed to these payments insofar as they have not been previously attributed to other capital payments (including payments outside the capital payments charge made to a non-UK domiciled beneficiary). For capital payments received up to 2007/08, the charge applied only where the UK-resident beneficiary was also domiciled in the UK. From 2008/09, it matters not where the beneficiary is domiciled although, if outside the UK and the payment is received outside the UK, the elected remittance basis may apply (see, further, **5.61**).

EXPORTING THE RESIDENCE

5.11 It is unlikely, in the context of the present legislative climate, that trustees of a UK trust or indeed the family behind the trust will consider making the trust non-UK resident. If they do, however:

- there must be power in the trust for a successor body of non-UK resident trustees to be appointed;
- that new body would be appointed as trustees and the existing UK trustees would retire in the normal way. It is essential that the new trustees are properly appointed, viz under *Trustee Act 1925, s 37,* that they comprise at least two persons or a trust corporation. In the case of *Jasmine Trustees Ltd v Wells & Hind* [2007] WTLR 489, only one individual and a non-trust corporation company were appointed (at a time when two individuals were required), so the new (non-UK) trustees were not validly appointed and the former undischarged trustees remained liable for CGT on disposals in the interim;
- that act of appointment of non-UK resident trustees (affording the trust non residence status) would cause a deemed disposal and re-acquisition by the UK resident trustees of the assets in the trust at that time (*TCGA 1992, s 80*). Any resulting CGT would be a liability of the retiring UK trustees (and they should therefore retain sufficient funds to pay the tax as well as to satisfy any other liabilities, eg professional costs). However, on 3 December 2016 the FTT applied to Court of Justice of the European Union (CJEU) for a preliminary ruling on whether the exit charge on trust migration is compatible with the freedom of establishment, freedom to provide services and free movement of capital under Articles 49,56 and 64 of the Treaty. The Advocate General opined that whilst such a charge did constitute a restriction on freedom it is justified on the ground of preserving the allocation of powers of taxation between Member States but it remains to be seen whether the CJEU will reach the same conclusion; and

- any gains held over assets transferred into a trust which within six tax years of the end of the year in which the originally held over gain occurred would become immediately assessable on the UK trustees and, if not paid within 12 months, on the settlor (*TCGA 1992, s 168*).

The fact that the trustees would become non-UK resident would open up the possibility of the settlor charge and/or the capital payments charge. However:

- the settlor charge would apply only in relation to any tax year if the settlor was during that tax year alive and both resident and domiciled in the UK (*TCGA 1992, s 86*); and
- the capital payments charge would apply only if capital payments were made to a beneficiary resident and domiciled in the UK or (from 2008/09) to a UK resident beneficiary wherever domiciled (see **5.60–5.61** for further detail).

Considerations of changing the governing law and also issues of future administration (including cost) should also be borne in mind.

Exporting a UK resident trust is not a step to be taken lightly. Certainly, since 1998, rather more non-UK resident trusts have been brought back to the UK than UK resident trusts exported. However, depending on the nature of the assets and indeed the circumstances of the principal family, eg if one or a number of beneficiaries were to become non-UK resident and domiciled, it might be a step worth taking.

Example 5.5—Exporting a trust

The Harry Trust has been UK resident for many years. Harry had married an English woman, their children were raised in the UK and he has now reached retirement age. All his children have left home and are living in various parts of the world, none of them are UK resident nor indeed intend to return to the UK. In May 2019, Harry and his wife decide to retire permanently to Switzerland.

The trust has not made huge gains over the years, though if certain investments recently made do 'come good', it might become quite valuable. Harry wishes to move the residence of the trust to a tax haven jurisdiction and his co-trustees are in agreement to do so. He is prepared to 'bite the bullet' by accepting the 20% tax charge on in-built gains (28% for gains on residential properties/carried interest) on exporting the trust.

The settlor CGT charge will have no application for the future as Harry, the settlor, will become resident and domiciled outside the UK. Nor indeed will the capital payments charge have any impact, as all the beneficiaries have long since abandoned their English domiciles of origin and have made their permanent homes, and tax residence, elsewhere.

TAXABLE GAINS AND ALLOWABLE LOSSES

5.12 In principle, a gain realised on the disposal of any asset (see Example 5.13 at **5.56** for the method of calculation) is chargeable. That said, there are certain exempt assets such as sterling cash and, indeed, certain exemptions such as principal private residence relief (see **5.25–5.27**).

Losses

> **Focus**
>
> Losses must be claimed and, for 2010/11 onwards, that claim must be made within four years from the end of the tax year of realisation.

5.13 A loss will be allowable if the disposal of that asset at a gain would have been taxable (*TCGA 1992, s 16*). Allowable losses realised in the same year as a chargeable gain *must* be deducted from those gains in computing the taxable amount for the year (even if the effect is to 'waste' the annual exemption). By contrast, losses in a given year which cannot be used, eg because there are no current year gains, may be carried forward to a later year. Such brought-forward losses need not 'waste' the annual exemption, and the trustees need only use so much of the losses as are necessary to bring the gains down to the annual exemption threshold. Any losses remaining can then be carried forward to later years without time limit.

Losses must be claimed, in principle by recording it in the capital gains self-assessment pages (see **5.55**), within the permitted timeframe. With effect from April 2010, the time limit was reduced to four years from the end of the tax year in which the losses are realised, following *FA 2008, Sch 39* from 1 April 2010 (*Finance Act 2008 Schedule 39 (Appointed Day, Transitional Provisions and Savings) Order 2009, SI 2009/403*).

5.14 Trustees, as also individuals and personal representatives, are potentially affected by an anti-avoidance rule introduced with effect from 6 December 2006 (*TCGA 1992, s 16A* inserted by *FA 2007, s 27(3)*). A loss is not an allowable loss if it accrues 'directly or indirectly in consequence of, or otherwise in connection with, any arrangements (which includes any agreement, understanding, scheme, transaction or series of transactions (whether or not legally enforceable)) and the main purpose, or one of the main purposes, of the arrangements is to secure a tax advantage'.

The expression 'tax advantage' is defined to mean: relief or increased relief from tax, repayment or increased repayment of tax, the avoidance or reduction of a charge to tax or an assessment to tax, or the avoidance of a possible assessment tax; and 'tax' means CGT, corporation tax or income tax.

HMRC published revised guidance on the rules on 19 July 2007, but it is not always easy to appreciate why one type of transaction is said to be unaffected whereas another not entirely dissimilar is caught. Careful study should be made of the various examples supplied. Extreme caution is required in both effecting and reporting any transaction which may be affected by the rule.

Connected party losses

> **Focus**
>
> Connected party losses, eg losses arising from transactions between connected parties (as defined), are ring-fenced and not available for general offset.

5.15 If the trustees realise a loss by making a disposal to a 'connected person', eg the settlor, or a relative of the settlor, they cannot offset that loss generally against other trust gains (*TCGA 1992, s 18(3)*). The loss must be carried forward for use only against a future gain that arises from the trustees disposing of another asset to that same connected person.

Shares: identification rules

Background

5.16 Generally speaking, each asset must be treated separately for CGT purposes. Up to April 1998, however, there was a 'pooling' system for shares. Under this, each block of shares of the same class in the same company, held in the same capacity (viz as trustees as opposed to personal ownership) was regarded as a single asset, which would increase with purchases and decrease with sales. Immediately before each transaction the appropriate amount of indexation allowance (for inflation) was added to the pool.

This system changed following introduction of the taper relief regime on 6 April 1998 (but later repealed on 5 April 2008). This regime, as its name indicated, pivoted on the ownership period and thus required the identification of each asset to which the appropriate taper percentage could then be applied. At the same time, the 'anti bed-and-breakfast' rule was introduced, whereby (broadly) share acquisitions are matched with identical shares in the same company disposed of within the previous 30 days. (This 30-day rule is disapplied where the person acquiring the shares is not UK resident: this is a measure introduced by *FA 2006, s 74* from 22 March 2006, following an avoidance technique successfully applied by taxpayer trustees in 2005 in the case of *Hicks v Davies* [2005] STC 850).

Shares disposed of between 1998/99 and 2007/08 were identified with acquisitions in the following order:

(i) shares acquired on the same day;

(ii) shares acquired within the 30 days following the date of sale;

(iii) shares acquired since 5 April 1998 on a LIFO basis;

(iv) pooled shares held at 5 April 1998; and

(v) pooled shares held at 31 March 1982.

Example 5.6—Share identification old rules (1998/99 to 2007/08)

The trustees own 1,000 shares in XYZ plc, which have been acquired at various times. They disposed of 500 shares on 1 February 2008 (and repurchased 50 shares nine days later). The shares sold are identified on a LIFO basis with the following purchases:

- 50 shares acquired on 10 February 2008 (point (ii) above);
- 300 shares acquired on 1 September 2004 (point (iii) above);
- 150 shares held in the pool at 5 April 1998 (point (iv) above).

Note: The balance of 500 pooled shares may in fact have had a greater base cost using indexation and re-basing at 31 March 1982 than in comparison with those that were sold in February 2008, and will have commanded a higher taper percentage by reason of longer ownership, but the trustees must still follow the strict identification rules.

2008/09 onwards

5.17 Following the reform of CGT from 2008/09 which repealed the taper relief regime, and in its place introduced a much less complex system, the rules for share identification returned broadly to the pooling system which prevailed up to 5 April 1998 (as described in the first paragraph at **5.16**). However, the matching rules described at (i) same day dealing and (ii) reacquisition within 30 days following date of sale at **5.16** continue to apply. On 16 February 2015, HMRC updated its CGT manual (see CG51500) to simplify existing guidance and reflect the repeal of obsolete provisions in relation to the precise identification of shares where the holding contained shares which disposal did not result in a chargeable gain, eg where a claim to deferral has been made under the Enterprise Investment Scheme.

BASE COSTS

5.18 To compute the gain, the base (or acquisition) cost of the asset is required. This will be the original cost of the asset or, if the asset was acquired by the trustees by way of a gift, the market value when the asset entered the settlement or, where hold-over relief has been employed, the adjusted value incorporating the held-over gain. If, however, the trustees have owned the relevant asset since before 31 March 1982, then for disposals made after 5 April 2008 the cost basis will be fixed at the 31 March 1982 value.

Fixing the base cost

5.19 Typically with trusts, the base cost of an asset may not have been formally agreed with HMRC. Property may have been put into a settlement, especially if a qualifying (ie pre March 2006/TSI) life interest or an A&M settlement, which was a PET for IHT and therefore was assumed to be exempt, or where the gain was held over for CGT (the hold-over of a gain does not require the formal agreement of valuation with HMRC; all that the relevant election (on help sheet HS295) requires is a statement that a gain does arise on disposal; see **3.5–3.7**).

Post-transaction valuation check

5.20 Consider the asset is now sold, perhaps relatively early in the tax year, say, on 1 May 2019. On the face of it, it will not be until after the following 5 April, when completing the trust self-assessment return, that the trustees will report the gain and will need to calculate the base cost in order to establish the gain (or loss) on which they must pay tax on the following 31 January. HMRC agreement of a gain reported in this way may take some time and, to provide a degree of certainty, HMRC introduced a post-transaction valuation check known as the CG 34 procedure. The aim of the CG 34 process is to advance the valuation process by entering into discussion with, in the case of land, the district valuer, or, in the case of shares, the shares valuation division, but only once the asset concerned has been sold or is the subject of a deemed disposal. The form requires the applicant trustees to supply a CGT computation based on the valuation figure that the trustees offer. They should provide any comparables and itemise any relief due or to be claimed. HMRC warn that any inaccuracy in the responses on form CG 34 may invalidate a valuation agreed on the basis of it. It is therefore a procedure to be adopted with care and presented on a robust basis.

Interestingly, the HMRC Trusts view is that under self-assessment the CG 34 procedure should be submitted in all cases where the base cost is uncertain and making the appropriate reference to the outcome of the CG34 process on the self-assessment return. The intention behind this is clear, namely to avoid or mitigate the possibility of a subsequent liability to interest or to penalties through upward adjustment of the 'disputed' value.

HMRC have updated both Form CG 34 and the guidance notes to its completion – the latter now emphasise that the form and the required support data must be received by HMRC at least two months before the due filing date. The form should be sent to:

HMRC

P and CGT Compliance

Newcastle

NE98 1ZZ

Example 5.7—Illustrative computation

On 1 August 2018, the trustees sold for £500,000 land that was transferred to the settlement just under four years ago and which, throughout the trust period of ownership, was used for farming. The value had been recently enhanced by a change in planning policy by the local authority which enabled the trustees to obtain planning permission for residential development. What, however, is the gain?

This is a discretionary trust and when four years ago the land was transferred into trust, it was so transferred under a hold-over election (*TCGA 1992 s 260*). The settlor himself had acquired the land on the death of his late wife (spouse exempt for IHT) six years ago. In his view the land was then worth £10,000 but likely this increased to, say, £25,000 when put into the settlement. That market value on transfer into the settlement is, of course, irrelevant for CGT purposes by reason of the hold-over relief claim, although it was material for IHT as having been a chargeable transfer, albeit within the nil rate band. It was in fact that value of £25,000, less the current and previous year's annual exemptions of £3,000, which the settlor returned on form IHT 100.

What matters now is an agreement of value on the death of the late wife which will in turn determine the base cost under the hold-over relief claim. The trustees would, of course, like this value to be as high as possible, in order to mitigate the gain, but there does not seem to be much prospect of that. They have, however, found a valuer who is prepared to value the land at £20,000 which, if accepted, would save CGT of £2,000 (20% of the additional £10,000).

The trustees proceed with the CG 34 procedure and compute the gain as follows:

Sale proceeds		£500,000
Market value on acquisition, say	£25,000	
Less settlor's base cost, say	(£20,000)	
Gain held over	£5,000	
Trust acquisition cost (MV)	£25,000	
Less held-over gain	(£5,000)	
Adjusted base cost		(£20,000)
Net gain		£480,000

Submission of form CG 34 invites the district valuer to agree the market value on acquisition.

SETTLOR-INTERESTED TRUSTS

Focus

Gains of a settlor-interested trust ceased to be assessed on the settlor from 2008/09.

5.21 These anti-avoidance rules follow the income tax regime discussed in **4.24–4.25**. The CGT rules were introduced in 1988 and, while originally there was a separate code, this has now been generally aligned with the income tax provisions, although the legislation is not exactly the same. Both sets of rules apply whenever the settlement was made.

For disposals before 6 April 2008, the settlor was treated by *TCGA 1992, s 77* as if the gains of the trustees were his gains in any situation where:

- trust property or 'derived property' will or may benefit the settlor or his spouse. The expression 'derived property' means income from the property or any other property directly or indirectly representing the proceeds of the sale of that property; or
- there is a benefit for the settlor or his spouse that is derived directly or indirectly from the settlement property or derived property.

The rules do not apply if the spouse can only benefit after the settlor has died.

Note that, while, from 2008/09, the gains of a settlor-interested trust are assessed on the trustees and no longer on the settlor, the concept of a 'settlor-interested trust' remains. It is material for purposes of hold-over relief: a gain arising on a transfer into a settlor-interested trust cannot be held over (see **3.5**).

The old rules (prior to 2008/09)

5.22 The effect of the rules up to and including 2007/08 was as follows:

- The net trust gains of the year, after deducting trustees' losses for that and earlier years, are treated as gains of the settlor.
- The annual exemption applicable is, of course, that of the settlor and not of the trustees.
- The relevant rate of tax depends on the settlor's other income and gains and could therefore be as high as 40%, or as low as 10% – as against the trustees' rate of 40%.
- Before *FA 2002* the settlor could not reduce trust gains assessed on him by use of personal losses. However, as from 2003/04, a settlor's personal losses in excess of personal gains can be offset against trust gains assessed on him. (Further, he had the right to elect for this treatment in any of tax years 2000/01, 2001/02 and 2002/03.)
- If a settlor-interested trust has unrelieved losses for a particular year, these cannot be transferred to the settlor for use against his personal gains, but must be carried forward to offset subsequent gains made by the trustees.
- The settlor can recover from the trustees the tax assessed on him, though not in compensation for the forced use of his annual exemption or losses against the trust gains.
- If a settlement has sub-settlements or separate funds, and the settlor or spouse can benefit under one but not under others, the whole of the trust gains will be assessed on him and not only those gains that are funds that are 'settlor-interested'. However, see **5.41–5.44** for the 'sub-fund' election from 2006/07.
- From 2006/07 a settlement will also be 'settlor-interested' if, during the tax year, any of the settlor's minor unmarried children, not in a civil partnership, can benefit (*TCGA 1992, s 77(2A)*, added by *FA 2006*).

ENTERPRISE INVESTMENT SCHEME (EIS)

5.23 In the context of 'sheltering' or deferring gains from CGT, other than on business assets, almost the only opportunity for trustees is presented by EIS.

The present regime dates from 1998 and derives from the old reinvestment relief regime.

EIS effectively contains two separate codes:

- Deferral of CGT; thus the gain that would otherwise trigger CGT is effectively 'rolled into' a qualifying subscription in EIS shares and 'comes home to roost' only when those EIS shares are sold.
- An exemption from both income tax and CGT in respect of the EIS shares, for which the rules are far more stringent, but which in any case is not available for trustees.

The regime for both deferral and exemption is extremely complex. The relevant company must carry on a qualifying trade and the shares subscribed should be newly issued. From 2006/07 to 2011/12, the assets of the company must not exceed £7 million before the issue of shares, and £8 million immediately afterwards (*ICTA 1988, s 293(6A)*, as amended by *FA 2006*); the *FA 2012* increased the asset value to £15 million with effect from 6 April 2012. The company must carry on a 'qualifying trade'; from which certain 'low-risk' activities are excluded, eg farming and market gardening, operating or managing hotels and nursing homes, among others.

For deferral, there is no limit on the proportion of the company owned (whereas, in the case of exemption for individuals, it must not exceed 30%, taking other associated shareholdings into account).

To defer a gain on an EIS investment, subscription must be made within 12 months before, or three years after, the disposal. However, it should be noted that, prior to implementation of the measures contained in the Finance Act 2015, since 22 June 2010 it was no longer possible for deferred gains to qualify for entrepreneurs' relief (this will only have potential consequences for the interest in possession trusts, since a discretionary trust will never qualify for entrepreneurs' relief – see **5.34**). *FA 2015* contains measures to preserve entrepreneurs' relief in respect of qualifying gains realised on or after 3 December 2014 deferred by later EIS investment.

An EIS claim is made by completing and submitting to HMRC form EIS 3 issued by the company. The claim must be made before 31 January following five years after the end of the tax year in which the gain arose.

Deferral relief into venture capital trusts (VCTs) or seed enterprise investment schemes (SEISs) is not available for trustees.

EIS for trustees

5.24 The relief is extended to the following trusts:

- Discretionary trust: all the beneficiaries must be individuals.

- Interest in possession trust (to include those created in the post-*FA 2006* trust era): relief is given if any of the beneficiaries are individuals, although if there are non-individual beneficiaries, pro rata relief is obtained according to the proportion of the individual interests in possession borne to all the interests in possession. While individuals include charities, interests in possession do not include interests for a fixed term.

Assuming the trustees have realised the gain, it is the trustees who must make the qualifying EIS investment.

Example 5.8—EIS relief

On 1 January 2020, the trustees sold shares realising a taxable gain of £10,500 against which they set the annual exemption of £6,000, leaving a gain of £4,500 in charge to tax. It is open to them to make a qualifying reinvestment under EIS of £4,500 at any time before 1 January 2023 The shares must be new shares in a qualifying trading company, and the trustees must ensure that the anti-avoidance rules do not claw back the relief.

The CGT on the disposal would normally have to be paid on 31 January 2021. The trustees can pay the tax, subsequently make the investment and claim a refund of tax plus repayment supplement.

FA 2015 has introduced provisions that with effect from 3 December 2014 ensure gains eligible for entrepreneurs' relief (see **5.34**) but deferred by means of EIS investment continue to benefit from the original entrepreneurs' relief when that deferred gain springs back into charge on later sale of the EIS shares.

PRINCIPAL PRIVATE RESIDENCE RELIEF

5.25 The legislation extends to trustees the familiar and valuable principal private residence (PPR) relief given to individuals. Although contained in just eight sections of the Act (*TCGA 1992, ss 222–226B*) the relief is extremely complex and, to be understood, must be read in the context of a number of decided cases and HMRC statements and concessions. The general principle for trustees under *TCGA 1992, s 225* is that:

- the trustees sell a dwelling-house (viz a house or flat);
- during all or part of their period of ownership, the dwelling-house has been occupied by a beneficiary as his only or main residence;
- the beneficiary has been entitled to occupy under the terms of the settlement;

- if the beneficiary has more than one residence, the trustees and the beneficiary jointly can elect that the trust property (or indeed the beneficially owned property) shall be treated as the main residence for purposes of the relief. Accordingly, it is not open for an individual for any period of time to be accruing relief on a property that he and/or his spouse owns and occupies at the same time as relief is being given on a property within a trust which he occupies. That said, the last nine months 'deemed occupation' rule effective from 6 April 2019 (which replaced the previous 18-month time limit and is discussed in more detail at **5.26**) can, in appropriate circumstances, give relief on two properties concurrently occupied by the same individual, which can operate where the one property is owned outright and the other is owned by trustees. Similarly, with the first 12 months rule of 'deemed occupation'.

One of the interesting factors about *IHTA 1984, s 225* is that there is no pro rata test. This means that, whether the trust is discretionary or interest in possession in form and whether there are a number of beneficiaries, occupation by just one of them will secure the relief for the whole of the gain arising on disposal.

There continues to be a noticeable increase in the number of HMRC enquiries into cases where the property disposed of had grounds in excess of the statutory 0.5 hectare (approximately 1.25 acres). HMRC have denied that they are deliberately spearheading a campaign to actively review PPR relief, but have reluctantly admitted that they are carrying out transactional checks identified using a computer program 'Connect' which cross-checks against the SDLT records. In March 2013, HMRC launched a property sales campaign aimed at taxpayers who have sold a residential property other than the main home (whether located in the UK or abroad) but have failed to disclose the transaction.

The Autumn Budget 2013 set out the widely predicted intention to introduce a CGT charge on future gains made by non-residents disposing of UK residential property. Following a lengthy consultation period this measure, known as NRCGT, was brought onto the statute book in *FA 2015* effective from 6 April 2015 but restricted to the measure of gain accruing from that date (for more detail see *Capital Gains Tax 2019/20* (Bloomsbury Professional)). By *FA 2019* and effective from 6 April 2019, the NRCGT charge has been extended to disposal of all UK real estate including bare land.

In the case of *Wagstaff & Wagstaff v HMRC* [2014] TC03183, the First-tier Tribunal (FTT) held that a property subject to formal agreement which allowed a relative to live there for life (or until remarriage) constituted a trust arrangement. Accordingly, the gain arising on the later sale of the property (during the lifetime of the relative in occupation) was deemed realised by the owners in their capacity as trustees and as such the gain was eligible for CGT principal private residence relief (PPR) on grounds that:

- The property was purchased by Mr Wagstaff's mother ('Mrs Wagstaff') in 1990 and was sold to the taxpayers at a market value in 1996.

- The property did not form part of the taxpayers' own property.
- The sale of the property was covered by an agreement ('the Agreement') between the parties, under which Mrs Wagstaff was entitled to live at the property at no cost for the rest of her life or until her remarriage, subject to a one-off payment of £5,000.
- In 2005, she had an accident and lived with the taxpayers until suitable long-term accommodation was found. During this time, the property was still available to her.
- In 2006, she agreed to move into a better house, in which she lived on the same terms as the Agreement.
- The property then remained empty until it was sold in 2007 (to a third party) with her full permission.

The FTT held that in acquiring the property on terms that included the Agreement, the taxpayers had taken on the role of trustees:

- Their interest in the property was 'settled property' and the Agreement created a trust – it was not relevant that the Agreement made no reference to a trust.
- The parties intended the Agreement to set out legal rights and obligations regulating their relationship during Mrs Wagstaff's lifetime: this was the only basis on which she was prepared to part with ownership of the property.
- Mrs Wagstaff had effectively placed herself in the hands of her son and daughter-in-law, but only if they accepted particular legal obligations towards her.
- Her position in connection with the property was to be secure against any eventuality and better protected if the taxpayers accepted obligations usually associated with a trust and the role of trustee, as set out in the Agreement.

It should be noted that had Mrs Wagstaff died before the property been sold the trust would have ceased to exist and no PPR would have applied on its later sale.

The period of ownership

5.26 There is an interesting statutory 'concession' in *TCGA 1992, s 223(1)*. For periods up to 5 April 2014 relief was given automatically for the last 36 months of ownership (assuming that the property was not then used for business purposes), even if the beneficiary was not in occupation during that period, provided that at some time the principal private residence relief applied, eg the property has been used as the main or principal residence of the beneficiary during the trust ownership. *FA 2014* reduced the 36-month grace period to 18 months with effect from 6 April 2014 and *FA 2019* reduced the period further to nine months with effect from 6 April 2020. However, interestingly, the former 36-month period continues to apply where the disposal is made by a disabled person (or their spouse/civil partner) or long-term resident (or their spouse/civil partner) in a care home but only provided there is no other interest in any other property (which includes an entitlement to occupy under the terms of a trust). Where contracts were exchanged before 6 April 2014, the 36-month grace period continued to apply provided that the sale completed before 6 April 2015.

Similarly, there is a non-statutory concession where, for the first 12 months of ownership (or sometimes longer, up to a further 12 months in extenuating circumstances), the beneficiary cannot live in the house, either because of essential renovations or because the house is being built or reconstructed (HMRC extra-statutory concession D49). There are also further concessions, which give certain permitted periods of absence, some of which were given statutory effect in 2009.

Anti-avoidance rule for hold-over relief

5.27 An anti-avoidance rule was introduced on 10 December 2003 (*TCGA 1992, s 226A*), to counter an arrangement that had become common (see paragraph 3 of Example 5.9), by combining hold-over relief and principal private residence relief. Now, broadly speaking, for transfers into a relevant property trust (to include discretionary trusts and most lifetime interest in possession trusts created post 21 March 2006) on or after 10 December 2003, a choice must be made between hold-over relief for the settlor on entry and principal private residence relief for the trustees or beneficiary on subsequent disposal. Under transitional rules, applicable where a property was already held in a trust as at 10 December 2003, a subsequent sale by the trustees or beneficiary can attract principal private residence relief but only available against the time apportioned gain attributable to the period up to 9 December 2003.

Example 5.9—'Washing the gain'—in the past

The settlor of a discretionary trust made on 1 January 1994 owns a second property (acquired in January 1993 for £75,000) which is used by the family as an occasional holiday home and this is now worth £400,000. The grandchildren beneficiaries of the discretionary trust are aged 25, 20 and 16.

The settlor could, say on 9 December 2002, have transferred to the trust the house then valued at £150,000 and hence within his unused IHT nil rate band of £250,000, holding over the gain under *TCGA 1992, s 260*.

The trustees would then be treated as acquiring the house at the settlor's original base cost of £75,000. The trustees would exercise their power in the trust deed to allow the eldest grandchild to occupy it as a residence from year to year, given that he also lives elsewhere (it is important that his occupation is more than occasional). The trustees and the beneficiary irrevocably elected within the two-year period that the trust property is treated as the beneficiary's main residence. The house would then be sold for say £225,000 one year later, on 9 December 2003, realising a gain of £150,000, all of which would be exempt under *s 225*.

If the house should instead be sold on 9 December 2019, the anti-avoidance rule described in **5.27** would come into operation. Only 1/17th of the gain would be exempt under *s 225* (9 December 2002 to 9 December 2003). The remaining 16/17th (10 December 2003 to 9 December 2019) would be taxable (and, specifically, could not benefit from the last 9 months of ownership rule described in **5.26**).

If, since 10 December 2003, such a settlor is considering CGT mitigation possibilities for the house, the combination of hold-over relief into a discretionary trust and principal private residence relief within the trust is no longer open to him.

Prior to 22 March 2006, it would have been possible to achieve much the same result through a combination of *TCGA 1992, s 165* hold-over (for business assets, including 'furnished holiday accommodation' and agricultural property at that time) and *s 225* relief. Consider the husband owned a holiday home, which he gave to his wife on a no-gain, no-loss basis under *TCGA 1992, s 58*, she would then let the property as qualifying furnished holiday accommodation (within the meaning of *ITTOIA 2005, s 322* and following) after which she would gift the property into an interest in possession trust for the grandchildren, excluding herself and her husband as beneficiaries. The gain on transfer into trust would be held over under *s 165*. The trustees would then allow one or more of the beneficiaries to occupy the property as their only or main residence pursuant to powers in the settlement and, on sale by the trustees, the whole of the gain would be 'washed out' under *s 225*.

Unfortunately, however, virtually any interest in possession settlement created on or after 22 March 2006 would fall within the relevant property regime of 10-year anniversary and exit charges and so any hold-over would be under *s 260* rather than under *s 165* (*TCGA 1992, s 165(3)(d)*), whilst the combination of *s 260* hold-over and *s 225* PPR relief for the trustees has been precluded since 10 December 2003. Only if, within such an example, the grandparents were prepared for the property to become owned outright by the grandchildren might the suggestion still be effective. *Section 165* hold-over would apply on the gift by the grandmother to the grandchildren, who would then occupy and sell with the benefit of relief under *s 223*. However, even this suggestion would not work following 5 April 2011, unless the grandmother is able to establish the existence of a trade under general income tax principles, in view of the reform to the deemed trading treatment of furnished holiday accommodation.

ROLL-OVER RELIEF

5.28 The colloquially known 'roll-over relief' is formally called 'relief on replacement of business assets' (*TCGA 1992, ss 151–158*) – it operates as a deferral mechanism not absolute relief and should not be confused with holdover relief. This allows a trader to defer CGT, triggered by a gain on a business asset, by reinvesting the proceeds into the acquisition of a new asset used for the business. Complete relief depends on the investment of the total sale proceeds (net of incidental costs) into the new asset, though partial relief may be claimed. A new asset must (subject to extension by HMRC) be acquired within 12 months before, or three years after, disposal of the old asset. Special rules apply where the new asset is a depreciating asset with a useful life of less than 60 years.

Trades: actual and deemed

5.29 The relief applies only to trades, ie not to property investment. However, certain non-trades, eg the occupation of woodlands on a commercial basis and furnished holiday lettings, are treated as qualifying trades for this purpose.

In *Maurice and Shirley Bell v HMRC* [2018] TC06575 taxpayers were unsuccessful in a claim to CGT roll over relief under TCGA 1992, s 152 on the disposal of a farmhouse constructed on their farmland for their son. The building was not used only for the trade

Qualifying classes of assets

5.30 The old and the new assets must fall within certain specified qualifying categories including land and buildings, goodwill and certain quotas, although the old and the new assets do not have to fall within the same category, nor do the trades have to be the same.

The claim

Focus

Roll-over relief is extended to trustees but, critically, will only be in point if the trade and the asset are both in trustee ownership.

5.31 The claim to relief may be made on a 'protective' basis, that is, even when the new asset has not been acquired, ie by stating an intention that the taxpayer will acquire the new asset within the qualifying time. When that time expires he can either confirm the claim on the basis that the new asset has been acquired, or simply withdraw it, in which case tax will fall due, plus interest in the normal way.

A trustee is a taxpayer like any other for the purposes of roll-over relief. The important thing is obviously that it must be the trustees that carry on the trade whether as sole traders or in partnership. For this purpose they could be limited partners. However, both the trade and asset must be in the same ownership to secure the relief.

Example 5.10—Deferring the tax bill

The trustees are partners in a limited farming partnership. They have a one-third share in the capital of the firm. Among the assets is a barn, which has, throughout its ownership, been used for storing farm machinery and farm stocks. The barn is on the edge of the village and the partners have obtained planning permission for residential conversion. The barn is sold for £200,000, realising a gain of £180,000. The trustees, together with the other partners, will therefore have to pay CGT on the gain.

However, in the following three years, the partnership spends £205,000:

- as to £100,000, to acquire a further 40 acres;
- as to £30,000, extending the grain store; and
- as to £65,000, buying milk quotas; plus
- £10,000 on professional fees and disbursements.

The whole of the gain can, therefore, effectively be rolled over, subject to a claim.

ENTREPRENEURS' RELIEF

5.32 To compensate traders for the repeal of business assets taper relief from 2008/09, *FA 2008, Sch 3* introduced entrepreneurs' relief (*TCGA 1992, ss 169H–169S*). In broad terms, this relief reintroduced the provisions of retirement relief (for a brief description of which, see the 2007/08 edition of this book at **5.32–5.34**). For the period 6 April 2008 to 22 June 2010, gains qualifying for entrepreneurs' relief were reduced by 4/9ths, and taxed at a uniform tax rate of 18% to produce an effective tax rate for entrepreneurs' relief of 10%. Post 22 June 2010, the eligible gains are simply taxed at a stand-alone rate of 10%.

The lifetime limit for entrepreneur gains has been subject to successive increases since its first introduction on 6 April 2008. The position is as follows:

2008/09 and 2009/10	£1 million
6 April 2010 to 22 June 2010	£2 million
23 June 2010 to 5 April 2011	£5 million
2011/12 onwards	£10 million

Conditions

5.33 The relief is available on the following disposals:

- all or part of a trading business carried on by an individual, whether alone or in partnership;
- a disposal of assets used for a business which has come to an end, within three years after cessation;
- a disposal of shares in or securities of a company where the individual was an officer or employee personally owned a minimum of 5% of the ordinary voting share capital of the company;
- under an 'associated disposal', where there is a material disposal of business assets (whether in a partnership or in shares of a company) as part of a withdrawal by the individual from participation in the business of the partnership or the company. *FA 2015* has narrowed eligibility for this class by introducing a minimum 5% test requiring a connected disposal of at least a 5% shareholding in the company, or a 5% share in the partnership assets.

Until 5 April 2019, it was only necessary to satisfy the conditions for a period of 12 months ending with the disposal (and, in certain cases, ending at a time which falls within three years after the disposal). However, *FA 2019* contains provisions which extend the qualifying period from 12 months to 24 months effective from 6 April 2019.

There is no minimum age or, indeed, minimum or maximum working time requirement for an officer or employee of a company.

Extension to trustees

Focus

Whilst entrepreneurs' relief is only available to individuals, trustees of an interest in possession trust (whether pre-/post-March 2006) may 'piggy back' on the qualification of the underlying life tenant to secure relief but only provided the latter agrees to transfer his entitlement to the trustees.

5.34 Whilst trustees are not eligible to claim entrepreneurs' relief in their own right, they may nonetheless 'piggy back' on the underlying beneficiary's qualification thus gains realised by trustees can potentially attract entrepreneurs' relief (*TCGA 1992, s 169J*). There must be an interest in possession (whether established pre or post *FA 2006* trust reform) in the whole of the settled property or in part which contains the settlement business assets of which the trustees dispose. Those assets may be either shares or securities of a company or assets used for purposes of a business (but subject to the minimum 5% disposal rule introduced in *FA 2015*). Critically, where the disposal is of shares of a company, it must be the 'personal company' of the qualifying beneficiary, thus he must be an officer or employee, own outright the 5% minimum voting shareholding and have met these conditions for the minimum 12 months at the disposal date – there is no minimum requirement or ownership period for the trustees' shareholding. Where it is a business of which the trustees dispose, the business must be carried on by the beneficiary, whether alone or in partnership. Otherwise, the rules applying to disposals by an individual are applied to trustees.

Section 169O contains further provisions in the case where more than one beneficiary has an interest in the relevant settled property. An apportionment is made by reference to the proportional entitlement of the qualifying beneficiary to the income of the relevant settled property. Where the relief is to be claimed by the trustees, *s 169M* provides that there is a joint claim by the trustees and the qualifying beneficiary, which ensures that his lifetime maximum of qualifying gains is not exceeded.

INVESTORS' RELIEF

5.35 This relief was introduced with effect from 6 April 2016 and whilst similar in application to entrepreneurs' relief, it remains totally separate to it.

Originally restricted to individuals, substantial amendments to *FA 2016* extended the provisions of this new relief to trustees of interest in possession trusts by 'piggybacking' on the underlying life tenant where the latter meets the conditions of an eligible beneficiary (as defined). Investors' relief applies only to gains on the disposal of qualifying shares where the first £10 million will be taxed at the 10% rate – identical to that applicable under the entrepreneurs' relief provisions. The latter £10 million threshold is that of the underlying life tenant and thus relief transferred and utilised by the trust will reduce the level available to the life tenant in their own right.

For these purposes a qualifying share owned by the trust is such where, at the relevant time:

- it was acquired by subscription (as opposed to being purchased);
- the trust held the share continuously for the period beginning with the issue of the share and ending immediately before the disposal;

- the share was issued on or after 17 March 2016;
- when the share was issued, none of the shares or securities of the issuing company were listed on a recognised stock exchange (see below);
- the share falls within the definition of an 'ordinary share' both at the time of its issue and at the time immediately before its disposal;
- the issuing company was a trading company or the holding company of a trading group when the share was issued and has been so throughout the share-holding period;
- neither the underlying life tenant nor a person connected with him has been an officer or employee of that company, or of a connected company, at any time in the share-holding period; and
- the period beginning with the date the share was issued to the trustees and ending with the date of disposal is at least three years for shares issued on or after 6 April 2016 (and slightly longer for those issued between 17 March 2016 and 5 April 2016).

See *Capital Gains Tax 2019/20* Chapter 17 (published by Bloomsbury Professional) for a more detailed discussion of the relief.

TAPER RELIEF (FOR DISPOSALS BEFORE 2008/09)

5.36 Taper relief was introduced for disposals on or after 6 April 1998 (*TCGA 1992, Sch A1*) and was withdrawn from 2008/09. Details of the relief can be found at **5.37** to **5.42** of the 2008/09 edition of this book. For greater detail, see the general guidance at www.hmrc.gov.uk/cgt/shares/taper-indexation.htm.

THE ANNUAL EXEMPTION

5.37 The annual exemption, ie within which gains will be tax free, is for most trusts increased to £6,000 for 2019/20 (£5,850 for 2018/19) representing one-half of the individual's exemption. The individual's exemption is available to the trustees of a settlement for certain disabled persons and where a valid vulnerable beneficiary election is in place.

The anti-fragmentation rule

5.38 An anti-avoidance rule operates in circumstances where the same settlor has made more than one 'qualifying settlement' since 6 June 1978. This is to prevent a person making a number of settlements, each benefiting from the current £6,000 annual exemption (2019/20). If there is more than one qualifying settlement in a group, the annual exemption is divided between them, up to a maximum of five. That is, the annual exemption for a trust for 2019/20 can never be less than £1,200 (£6,000/5, or £12,000/10).

'Qualifying settlement'

5.39 The expression 'qualifying settlement' does not include charitable trusts, or trust death benefits of registered pension schemes (which are among 'excluded settlements' defined in *TCGA 1992, Sch 1, para 2(7)(b)*). Otherwise, the expression includes almost every type of settlement, even settlements that do not realise a gain. This means that there could be a total of five qualifying settlements, only one of which is making a gain in the tax year, but it gets the benefit of an annual exemption of only £1,200 (2019/20) and £4,800 (£6,000 – £1,200) of annual exemption is wasted, forfeiting £960 ((£4,800 @ 20%) or £1,344 (£4,800 @ 28%) for gains on residential property/carried interest in tax potentially saved and now payable.

Beware

5.40 This rule needs to be observed very carefully, since under self-assessment it is up to the trustees to claim the right amount of annual exemption. If, for some years, they have always claimed the maximum exemption, but it is then established that they should have claimed only, say, the minimum amount, issues of interest and penalties will arise. The real problem is that it may be difficult for the trustees to discover the existence of qualifying settlements.

Example 5.11—Splitting the annual exemption

As well as an A&M trust for his grandchildren (which continues as such after 5 April 2008, albeit with the capital vesting age reduced to 18 to comply with the transitional relief provisions), the settlor has also made the following trusts:

- a discretionary settlement, in which his wife (but not the settlor) is a potential beneficiary;
- a £10 'pilot' discretionary settlement, in conjunction with his will. This is not uncommon, and will effectively serve to 'tip' a pot of money into the pre-existing discretionary trust (see **6.42**);
- a trust of a seven-year IHT protection policy, to guard against the possibility of IHT becoming payable within seven years after the making of a PET. This will be a qualifying policy only for such time as the seven-year period stays in being; and

- a small discretionary trust for his nephews and nieces, with the trust fund invested in a single premium investment bond.

There are, therefore, a total of five qualifying settlements, and the annual exemption for any of the trusts which makes a gain will be only £1,200 for 2019/20

THE SUB-FUND ELECTION

5.41 Where a single settlement has more than one 'sub-settlement' or 'sub-fund', even with separate trustees, the gains or losses on those sub-settlements or funds form part of the overall computation of chargeable gains, which is assessed on the trustees of the main settlement. In broad terms, *FA 2006* (found in *TCGA 1992, Sch 4ZA*) allows trustees of the 'principal settlement' to elect that a fund or other specified portion of the settlement shall be treated for CGT purposes as a separate settlement. The creation of a sub-fund will involve a disposal by the trustees of the principal settlement. The election cannot take effect on a date earlier than that on which it is made, thus it cannot be backdated.

Conditions

5.42 The four conditions are as follows:

- the principal settlement is not itself a sub-fund settlement;
- the sub-fund does not comprise the whole of the property in the principal settlement;
- there is no asset an interest in which is comprised both in the sub-fund settlement and the principal settlement; and
- no person is a beneficiary under both the sub-fund settlement and the principal settlement.

The four conditions must be satisfied when the election is made, and the last three conditions must be satisfied throughout the period from when the election is treated as taking effect and ending immediately before the election is made.

Procedure

5.43 HMRC have provided a form (SFE 1) for making a sub-fund election. No election may be made after the second 31 January after the year of assessment in which the effective date falls. The sub-fund election must contain certain declarations, statements and information and it may not be revoked.

Consequences of a sub-fund election

5.44 Following the disposal which the trustees of the principal settlement are treated as having made, the trustees of the sub-fund settlement are treated as having acquired the relevant property at the date of the election taking effect and for a consideration equal to the then market value of the relevant assets.

For income tax purposes, corresponding provisions were introduced by *FA 2006*, now found in *ITA 2007, s 477*.

Example 5.12—The London Trust: Sub-fund illustration

The London Discretionary Trust, created some ten years ago, comprises a wide portfolio of rented property, quoted investments and a variety of shareholdings in private trading companies. The beneficiaries are, in broad terms, the grandchildren and remoter issue of the settlor. For various administrative reasons, in 2019/20 the trustees want to hive off the shares in the private trading companies into a separate settlement run by separate trustees (though this is not necessary under the legislation).

So this they do, ensuring that the beneficiaries are restricted to the children of the settlor's elder daughter and that those beneficiaries cannot in future benefit under the principal settlement. Separate trustees are appointed. The trustees of the principal settlement are treated as making a disposal at that time. The deemed gain cannot, however, be held over by election by the trustees of the principal settlement under *TCGA 1992, s 260* because although that settlement is a discretionary or 'relevant property' trust (as, indeed, is the sub-fund settlement) this is not a chargeable event for IHT purposes since by virtue of *IHTA 1984, s 81* for IHT purposes alone the assets are deemed to remain in the original trust.

ANTI-AVOIDANCE RULES

5.45 Trusts have a venerable history and continue to be regarded with suspicion by HMRC. While this book is primarily centred on the tax aspects of trusts, some of the non-tax issues and advantages are nonetheless summarised in **3.23–3.27**.

Avoidance perceived by HMRC

5.46 The very flexibility of a trust (as opposed to a company) has meant that, over recent years, it has been used as a vehicle for tax planning. The most effective tax planning occurs where tax advantages are obtained within the context of overall family and/or commercial structuring. It is when tax saving becomes an end in itself and arrangements are made with no other purpose that the courts perceive taxpayers to have 'crossed over to the wrong side of the line' and will therefore try to redress the balance. This is the subject of numerous decided cases, which generally have prompted changes in the law.

A simple example of an anti-avoidance rule has been the settlor-interested trust regime (see **5.21–5.22**), which seeks to counteract any perceived advantage a person may secure by using the mechanism of a trust from which he or his spouse can benefit to trigger disposal. From 2004/05 to 2007/08, the CGT rate for all types of trust was 40%. From 2008/09 until 22 June 2010, the rate was 18%, and so it was no longer necessary to charge the gains of a settlor-interested trust on the settlor, as there was no perceived advantage gained. From 6 April 2016 et seq trust gains are taxed at 20% else 28% for gains on UK residential properties/carried interest (from 23 June 2010 to 5 April 2016 trust gain were taxed at a flat 28%) whereas gains in the hands of the basic rate taxpayer continued to attract the lower 10% rate and, as such, this may pave the way for a reintroduction of the old regime.

In the case of *Trustees of the Morrison 2002 Maintenance Trust and others v HMTC* [2016] UKFTT 2050, HMRC were successful in challenging the validity of a carefully constructed scheme involving the creation of an Irish trust to sell shares in a Scottish trust. The plan was defeated through detailed consideration and application of the Ramsay doctrine (*W T Ramsay v Inland Revenue Commissioners* (1982) 54 TC 101.

Tax mitigation, avoidance and evasion

5.47 Generally speaking, tax planning is permissible. The traditional distinction was between tax avoidance, which was permissible, and tax evasion, which involved a breach of the law (sometimes the criminal law). More recently (by way of summary categorisation only), tax avoidance has been divided into 'acceptable' tax mitigation and 'unacceptable' tax avoidance, which falls just short of evasion.

On 1 August 2006, a disclosure regime was introduced for direct taxes. Arrangements with a view to tax avoidance which fall within one of seven prescribed descriptions, subject to exemptions, must be notified to HMRC within five days, failing which a fine of £5,000 will be levied.

HMRC continue to monitor types of transaction (sometimes sold as packages) whereby they perceive that the 'spirit' of the legislation is being undermined.

Some of these 'tax avoidance schemes' have been legislated against specifically in *FA 2000*, which attacked two UK trust schemes, two non-UK trust schemes and one scheme that applies wherever the trustees are resident; see below for examples.

FA 2004 introduced wide-ranging anti-avoidance rules in relation to settlor-interested trusts. As from 10 December 2003, a gain arising on transfer into a settlor-interested trust cannot be deferred by hold-over relief (see **3.5–3.7**) and, also from 10 December 2003, the combination of hold-over relief on a gift into a relevant property trust and principal private residence relief for the trustees on a subsequent disposal is no longer possible (see **5.27**).

One of the most recent developments in this area is the introduction of the general anti-abuse rule (GAAR) which is seen as the government's formal approach to the risk management of tax avoidance intended to strengthen and provide HMRC with the necessary armoury to counter abusive avoidance. Announced in the 2012 Budget, with the provisions contained within the *FA 2013*, the GAAR applies across the range of taxes, to include CGT, and includes the unique feature in the form of an independent advisory panel. Initial guidance was contained in HMRC's 'What's New?' dated 28 March 2013 but this was comprehensively updated on 30 January 2015.The latter 'HMRC GAAR Guidance' is effective for transactions entered into on or after the publication date of 30 January 2015 but HMRC have advised that this publication merely clarifies the application of GAAR and as such there is no change in the law or HMRC's interpretation of it.

Continuing to levy pressure, *FA 2016* introduced a new and controversial power allowing HMRC to raise a CGT (and income tax) assessment, based on information held by HMRC in the absence of a submitted self-assessment return. This is bolstered by a new 60% penalty for cases successfully tackled under GAAR.

The following two arrangements were among five counteracted by *FA 2000,* whereas the third rule was introduced by *FA 2004*.

Disposal of interest in a settlor-interested trust

5.48 There has been a long-standing rule that no chargeable gain arises when a beneficiary disposes of his interest under a settlement (*TCGA 1992, s 76*). This must be an interest original to the settlement, and thus it will not protect a person who buys an interest in a settlement. It applies only to trusts which have always been UK resident.

Prior to 9 December 2003 (introduction of holdover relief denial to settlor interested trusts by virtue of *TCGA 1992,ss 168B and 169C*) a person might make a settlement in which he has an immediate life interest. He transfers to the trustees shares in a private trading company worth £1 million and holds over the gain so that the trustees are treated as acquiring the shares with a base cost of, say, £100. The settlor is entitled to the income from the trust fund for life and the trustees also have power to advance capital to him. Both the settlor and trustees are UK resident.

Before 21 March 2000 the settlor might sell his interest in the settlement for say, £950,000. This would have been tax free. The purchaser would 'step into his shoes' in being appointed as a beneficiary. The shares could be advanced out under hold-over election and, the institution being exempt, would escape CGT on ultimate disposal. This is no longer possible.

Restriction of losses

5.49 Prior to 2000/01 (see **5.22**: fourth bullet point under 'Effect of the rules') personal losses could not be offset against trust gains assessed on the settlor under the settlor-interested rules. Since 2003/04, but before 2008/09 (when the gains of settlor-interested trusts become assessed on the trustees), there is an automatic set-off.

Consider that an individual not connected with the trust owns shares in a private company 'pregnant with gain'. He acquires an interest in the settlement and is added to the settlement as a beneficiary. He advances the shares to the trust under hold-over election, the trustees sell the shares and offset the gain against their losses. The proceeds of the sale are advanced to the new beneficiary. Where this occurs on or after 21 March 2000, ie someone has acquired an interest in a trust for consideration, the trustees cannot use their own losses to offset gains on the assets transferred by that person into trust under hold-over election.

No hold-over on transfers to a settlor-interested trust

5.50 Transfers into trust under hold-over relief have in the past been used for three specific tax planning purposes:

- As a device to enable valuable non-business property to be passed down a generation without paying either IHT or CGT, under 'son of *Melville*' arrangements (see *Melville v IRC* [2002] 1 WLR 407) (see **6.22**);
- To mitigate the effect of the 'tainted taper' problem where an asset has changed its status from non-business to business; and
- In effectively 'doubling up' principal private residence relief for a second home as well as the individual's principal family home (see **5.25–5.27**).

Rules effective from 10 December 2003 put paid to all of the above and, specifically in relation to private residences, a further set of rules prevents the combination of hold-over relief and principal private residence relief to achieve the tax advantage illustrated in Example 5.9 at **5.27**.

TAX PLANNING SUMMARY

5.51 Any or all of the following possibilities should be considered as part of a tax planning routine:

- Annual exemption (see **5.37–5.40**): Do make use of it. Be aware of the circumstances where the anti-fragmentation rules apply and be sure to claim the right amount each year.
- Losses (see **5.13–5.15**): Remember that current year losses must be set against current year gains, even if the effect is to 'waste' the annual exemption. Brought-forward losses, on the other hand, can be used only as far as is necessary to reduce the gains down to the annual exemption threshold. Losses arising on a disposal to a connected person can be set off only against a gain arising to the same connected person. Do remember to claim losses as they occur.
- If multiple disposals are made during the tax year, consider within a month or so of the end of it, ie early March, whether further disposals should be made to use the annual exemption or whether instead it might be worth triggering losses in appropriate cases to relieve tax liabilities.
- Note that, from 2006/07, a settlement whose beneficiaries include the minor unmarried children of the settlor, not in a civil partnership, is now settlor-interested. This rule continues to be relevant where a person wants to give an asset standing at a gain to a trust, as he will not be able to hold over the gain (see **3.5**). Further, if, within broadly six years after the end of the tax year in which the gift is made, the trust becomes settlor-interested, any hold-over relief previously claimed (on a disposal since 10 December 2003) is clawed back. There is no *de minimis* or *pro rata* let-out.
- Where the trustees own a property that is, or might be, occupied by a beneficiary so that principal private residence relief applies (see **5.25–5.27**), do ensure that the relief is maximised, ie it should not be considered after the property is sold. Consider the use of timely principal private residence relief elections where the trustees own what is manifestly not the beneficiary's main home: the election must be made within two years after the property is occupied by that beneficiary and note that the relief must be claimed in the body of the trust return. Be aware of the anti-avoidance rules described in **5.27**.
- Base costs: Where, having sold an asset, the gain cannot be established because the base cost has never been agreed, consider the CG 34 procedure (see **5.18–5.20**) with a view to agreeing the figures well before the time comes to pay the tax.
- EIS: By all means consider a subscription in qualifying shares as a means of deferring tax, but do not let the 'tax tail wag the investment dog'. Never make an investment just because it is tax efficient – the full

investment may be lost (and the beneficiaries will be quick to react). Consider the loss of entrepreneurs' relief.

- Payment of tax (see **5.54**): Be clear on the amount of CGT that will have to be paid on 31 January following the end of the tax year and budget for it. If the consideration is payable by instalments, consider the possibility of arranging with the inspector a deferred tax payment plan (see **5.6**).

THE TRUST AND ESTATE TAX RETURN (2018/19)

5.52 The form for returning capital gains tax is supplementary page SA905 (to be included within the main trust and estate return): see **5.55–5.58**.

The only circumstances in which SA905 need not be completed are (for 2018/19):

- where the total chargeable gains were less than, or equal to, the annual exemption (see **5.37–5.40**); and
- where the assets (ignoring exempt assets) disposed of during the tax year realise net proceeds of less than or equal to £46,800 with such limit calculated as at four times the individual annual exemption (£11,700 for 2018/19).

That said, it is not a bad discipline to fill in the pages as part of the ongoing 'housekeeping' of the trust. In particular, it is important to use the form:

- to claim allowable losses which may be used in future; and
- to make other claims or elections that require reference to, and completion of, other HMRC forms, viz:
  - private residence relief: help sheet HS 283;
  - roll-over relief: help sheet HS 290;
  - entrepreneurs' relief: help sheet HS 275;
  - hold-over relief for gifts: help sheet HS 295;
  - EIS deferral relief: help sheet HS 297;
  - business transfer relief (where a business is transferred to a company in return for the issue of shares): column G on TC2;
  - unremittable gains (asset disposed of outside the UK where exchange controls or shortage of foreign currency make the gain unremittable): column G on TC2;
  - negligible value claims – see help sheet HS 286 and column G on TC2; or
  - relief for foreign tax paid: if tax credit relief has not been claimed, the foreign tax ranks as a deduction against the chargeable gain. If

tax credit relief is claimed, page TF3 on the trust and estates foreign pages should be completed and help sheet IR390 referred to.

Tax year 2018/19: a compliance summary

5.53

Date for return	31 January 2020 if delivered online (or 31 October 2019, if delivered in paper form and where HMRC are to calculate the tax)
Payment of tax	31 January 2020 (or three months after the issue of the self-assessment return if later than 31 October 2019), subject to payment by instalments (see **5.6**)*
Interest and penalties	As for income tax (see **4.15–4.19**).

* CGT on gifts of certain assets (broadly, those subject to instalment relief for IHT – see **11.93–11.96**) can on written election be paid by 10 equal yearly instalments (*TCGA 1992, s 281*). The first instalment is payable on the usual due date, with any subsequent instalments payable on the subsequent anniversaries. Unpaid instalments carry any interest calculated at the prevailing rate. The instalment option is available also where assets leave a settlement and the disposal does not qualify for hold-over relief.

COMPLIANCE

Supplementary pages: Capital gains (SA905) (2018/19)

5.54 The self-assessment of CGT operates in tandem with income tax (whereas compliance for IHT is entirely separate). The same tax district and reference deals both with income tax and CGT, whether for individuals or for trustees. SA905 is possibly the most complex of the supplemental pages but has the benefit of substantive notes running to 17 pages and including many worked examples for 2018/19.

Gains and losses

5.55 SA905 (2018/19) falls broadly into two parts – chargeable gains and allowable losses:

- The trustees must identify total chargeable gains (after any reliefs) and allowable losses for the year. These will be computed on pages TC2 and TC3 of SA905. From the net gains will be deducted the relative annual exemption, £5,850 for 2018/19 (but could be less – see **5.37–5.40**), to produce the taxable gains charged at either 28% (residential property gains) or 20% (all other gains).

- As to capital losses, losses for the current year *must* be deducted from current year gains. Brought-forward losses need be deducted only from current year gains to the extent that gains remain in charge over the annual exemption for the year. A loss arising on a transaction with a connected person (eg on a transfer from the settlor) can be offset only against gains made on disposals by the settlor to the trustees. Losses must be claimed – page TC1 enables notice to be given of a loss realised in tax year 2018/19 which has not been fully offset against current year gains and hence is available to be carried forward. Losses must be claimed within four years from the end of the year in which they arose.

CGT implications of events within the trust

5.56

- Death of a beneficiary with an interest in possession provided the trust is not within the relevant property regime for IHT purposes (see **9.10**).
- A person becomes absolutely entitled to trust property (see **9.10**).
- The trustees become non-UK resident (see **5.8–5.10**).

Example 5.13—Computation on property disposal (2018/19)

On 28 May 2018 the trustees sold for £150,000 a cottage which they purchased on 31 March 1982 for £40,000 (and which they had let on successive long tenancies). The CGT calculation is as follows:

Disposal proceeds		£150,000
Less base cost of acquisition (March 1982)	£40,000	
Less improvement costs (May 1998)	£10,000	
Less incidental acquisition costs	£1,000	
Less incidental disposal costs	£2,000	
Total costs		(£53,000)
Chargeable gain		£97,000
Less: annual exemption		(£5,850)
		£91,150
CGT payable at 28%		£25,522

Additions of capital (2018/19)

5.57 Question 12 on page 6 of form SA900 asks, 'Have any assets or funds been put into the trust during the year?' The essence of a settlement or trust is that funds are contributed by way of 'bounty' or free gift thus the commercial sale by the trustees of an asset included in the settlement would not be the target of this question. However, if that commercial sale was made at a profit, this would realise a gain for the trustees.

HMRC need to keep track of the funds subject to the settlement and therefore, if further assets are contributed, there must be given:

- the settlor's name and address;
- a description of the asset; and
- the value of the asset.

Avoid contributing to someone else's settlement

5.58 There is no reason in principle why one person cannot contribute assets to a settlement made by another. However, this is not generally a good idea, and it is best in practice to keep separate each settlement for assets contributed by a single settlor. The only exception could perhaps be joint husband and wife settlements, especially where the amounts contributed are the same, although, even then, there can be complications.

Such complications arise in particular with the anti-avoidance rules for settlor-interested trusts (see **4.26–4.29** for income tax, and **6.18–6.23** for the reservation of benefit rules for IHT). It is important to be able to identify which property was contributed by which settlor and, unless the funds are strictly segregated, when in time assets are sold and reinvested, this identification process becomes more and more difficult.

One perceived advantage of having a single settlement with more than one settlor might be a saving in administrative and compliance costs. However, these could soon be outweighed by the tax compilations. There is, further, a CGT advantage in having more than one settlement, as each settlement will have its own annual exemption (subject to 'anti-fragmentation' rules; see **5.38–5.39**).

Example 5.14—The Cathy and Tim A&M Trust

On 1 January 1999, Cathy and Tim each settled £125,000 into an old-style A&M settlement created in favour of their three minor children. As the trust was created before the anti-avoidance rules for parental income which came into effect on 9 March 1999, only actual income paid or applied for the benefit of any of Cathy's and Tim's children will be assessed *pro rata* on Cathy and Tim. Consider that some 20 years later in January 2019, Cathy inherits capital from her father's estate and wishes to add £100,000 of this to the A&M trust fund which is now worth £500,000. Cathy achieves this by way of a deed of variation which for IHT purposes recognises her late father as the settlor (see **12.1–12.5**), but for income tax and CGT purposes, Cathy is treated as the 'settlor'.

It is necessary to establish the income that accrues from the £100,000 addition and that which accrues to the original £250,000 settled since:

- As a post 8 March 1999 addition, the income arising therefrom will be assessed on Cathy, irrespective of whether or not that income is distributed; and
- for the purposes of the charge under *ITTOIA 2005, ss 629–632*, it must be clear which income is treated as attributable to Tim (a higher rate taxpayer) and which to Cathy (only a basic rate taxpayer).

The easiest solution would be to retain the £100,000 addition as a segregated fund. However, this might not be so easy (and may not be welcomed by the stockbroker/investment manager). Based on a new fund value of £600,000 (£500,000 plus Cathy addition of £100,000) a sensible working solution might simply be to divide the income into 12 parts each year, assess two of those parts on Cathy (representing the income derived from the added £100,000) and the remaining ten parts (representing the £500,000 value pre addition) equally on Tim and Cathy insofar as distributions are made to or for the benefit of the children.

Capital received from non-UK resident trusts

5.59 Question 16 on page 9 of form SA900 asks, 'Has the trust at any time been non-resident or received any capital from another trust which is, or at any time has been, non-resident? If "Yes", have the trustees made any capital payments to, or provided any benefits for, the beneficiaries?'

It is assumed in this book that the trust concerned has always been UK resident. What relevance, therefore, could there be if a non-UK resident trust has paid any capital to a UK trust? The answer lies in *TCGA 1992, s 87* and for that a brief discussion of the anti-avoidance rules for non-UK resident trusts is necessary.

In the case of *Bowring v HMRC* [2015] UKUT 550, the Upper Tribunal decided that capital payments made to UK beneficiaries of a UK trust that had in turn received funds from an offshore trust were free of the capital gains that had originated in the latter offshore trust. This overturned the decision of the

First- tier Tribunal that interpreted *TCGA 1992, s 97(5)* so widely as to apply to beneficiaries who received distributions from the UK trust and were subject to tax under s 87 and/or s 91 because they had received the capital payments indirectly from the offshore trust.

The CGT regime

5.60 The 'settlor charge' in *TCGA 1992, s 86* taxes a UK resident and UK domiciled settlor on gains made by non-UK resident trustees of certain settlements made by him.

Section 87 (the 'capital payments' charge) taxes UK resident and (but see below for 2008/09 et seq) domiciled beneficiaries on capital payments received by them to the extent of the 'trust gains' (or, since 2008/09, the '*section 2(2)* amounts') (*TCGA 1992, s 87A*) made by non-UK resident trustees (insofar as they have not already been attributed to 'capital payments'). From 2008/09, the capital payments charge applies even where the recipient UK resident beneficiary is domiciled outside the UK (although the trustees can, by election, ensure that trust gains that accrued before 6 April 2008 cannot be attributed to capital payments made to non-UK domiciled beneficiaries and, where the payment is received outside the UK, the elected remittance basis may apply).

Furthermore, the rules have applied since 1998/99 even if the settlor of the trust was, and remains, non-UK domiciled. Nor does the horror end there. In an effort to encourage prompt capital distribution, there can be a 'supplementary charge' levied on the beneficiary by reference to the time that has elapsed between making the trust gain and the onward capital distribution; such charge is calculated with reference to a maximum period of six years, increasing the amount of the tax charge by 10% per annum. That is, for 2017/18 et seq the beneficiary could be facing a tax charge of up to 32% (20% + ((10% of 20%) × 6)), compared to a 2015/16 charge of 44.4% (28% + (10% of 28%) × 6).

Scope of 'capital payment'

5.61 Most commonly, such capital payments charges might arise where the payment is made directly to the beneficiary from the non UK-resident trust. A Court of Appeal decision in *Billingham v Cooper* [2001] STC 1177 confirmed HMRC's view that for the purposes of the *s 87* charge the benefit of an interest-free loan is a capital payment (benefit). HMRC also take the view that rent-free enjoyment by a beneficiary of trust property is a capital payment (benefit).

If the question is answered affirmatively, the total capital payments or value of benefits provided must be given, together with their allocation between the beneficiaries, if more than one (whose names and addresses must be given).

Equally, if the trust has received capital from any other trust that may have been non-UK resident, the name of the trust, the address of the trustee, the date of the establishment and the value received must be given.

Example 5.15— The Hector Trust: Beneficial loan deemed a capital payment

The Hector Trust, being non-UK resident, makes a payment to the Albert discretionary settlement of £100,000. The Albert trustees lend £50,000 to a beneficiary on 6 October 2018, interest-free, repayable on demand.

The beneficiary is treated as having received a capital payment of the interest forgone on £50,000 for six months. At the beneficial loan rate of 2.50% (3.00 % for 2016/17) from 6 October 2018 to 5 April 2019, the capital payment is only £625, which would translate to £1,250 for the full year.

If, however, the other £50,000 were advanced to the beneficiary absolutely on 6 October 2018, the capital payment would become £50,000. The effective rate of tax in 2018/19 could be anything between 10% and 32%, depending on when the matched trust gains were realised by the Hector Trust – and this may not be easy to find out.

Chapter 6

Running a trust: inheritance tax

SIGNPOSTS

- ***FA 2006*** – Understand the full impact of the IHT changes and their impact on the pre- and post-*FA 2006* trust classifications (see **6.47** and **6.53–6.56**).
- **Transitional relief** – Understand the transitional rules, particularly in relation to the old-style A&M trust (see **6.51** and **6.59–6.60**).
- **Foreign dimension** – Be aware of the pitfalls, advantages and relevance of the foreign aspects (see **6.5–6.10**).
- **Compliance** – Review the regulatory requirements, and penalty and interest provisions (see **6.11–6.17**).
- **Domicile** – *FA 2017* has given effect to the sweeping changes to the domicile rules, which became operative from 6 April 2017. The deemed domicile period has reduced to 15 out of 20 years and it is now more difficult for former UK domiciled individuals to claim a non-UK domicile of choice on their return to the UK.

COMPLIANCE IN SUMMARY

6.1 The point was made in **Chapter 3** (see **3.12–3.17**) that the principal distinction before 22 March 2006 was between:

- a PET, viz principally a life interest trust and an accumulation and maintenance (A&M) trust; and
- a chargeable transfer, viz a discretionary trust.

As from 22 March 2006, however, the creation of any lifetime non-charitable trust (other than a qualifying trust for a disabled person – see **2.10**) is a chargeable transfer. Accordingly, for IHT purposes alone, what was (in editions of this book before 2006/07) referred to as the 'discretionary trust regime' is now called the 'relevant property regime'. It is necessary to remember that, for trusts created before 22 March 2006, however, the above PET/chargeable transfer distinction applied.

PETs – creation of a qualifying disabled trust or, before 22 March 2006 an interest in possession or Accumulation & Maintenance trust (A&M)

6.2 In terms of ongoing compliance requirements, no action is required where:

- In the case of a life interest trust, the beneficiary remains alive and no capital leaves the trust (other than by advance to the life tenant). As the life tenant is treated for IHT purposes as if owning the underlying trust assets, an advance of capital to him is simply awarding unfettered ownership of that property (*IHTA 1984, s 49(1)*). On the contrary, if the trustees exercise a power to transfer capital to any other individual (other than the life tenant's UK-domiciled spouse or civil partner, which will be covered by the spousal exemption), the life tenant will be treated as having made a PET himself, with no adverse IHT implications unless he dies within the following seven years.
- In the case of an A&M trust, the basic conditions are satisfied (see **6.47**) where (see the last sentence below) capital vests at or before age 18. Once, or to the extent that the qualifying A&M conditions cease to be satisfied, the settlement leaves the favoured A&M regime and will either become an interest in possession trust or the capital will be owned outright. The options applicable to old-style A&M trusts in being at 22 March 2006, during the transitional period which came to an end on 5 April 2008, are set out at **6.52**. Any capital still left in the trust at 6 April 2008 (but not subject to an interest in possession established before 22 March 2006) is thereafter subject to the relevant property regime (see **6.31–6.46**), *unless* the terms of the trust were changed (if necessary) before 6 April 2008 to ensure that future absolute capital entitlement arises at age 18 (akin to a post 21 March 2006 Bereaved Minors Trust (BMT)) or on or before age 25 (akin to a post 21 March 18/25 trust which, despite the potential for an exit charge, is technically outside the full relevant property regime).

If a qualifying life interest settlement (remember this is a pre-22 March 2006 trust or valid TSI or later Immediate Post Death Interest (IPDI)) comes to an end because of the life tenant's death, IHT will be calculated on the combined total of the free estate and the settled estate, with the trustees meeting the tax attributable to the trust out of the trust fund (see **11.75–11.77**). If the life interest comes to an end on the life tenant's death within seven years after the PET of a capital advanced to someone else, this now failed PET may well be within the life tenant's nil rate band such that no IHT liability arises. To the extent that the PET exceeds the life tenant's nil rate band, unusually the trustees will be primarily responsible for the tax, although the transferee of the capital and, indeed, the life tenant's personal representatives could also have a residual (secondary) liability (*IHTA 1984, s 201(1)*).

Chargeable transfers

6.3 With a discretionary trust/relevant property trust, on the other hand, not only might there have been IHT implications at the outset (see **3.17–3.20**), but there can also be implications thereafter, both as to giving notice to HMRC, and more importantly as to payment of tax during the lifetime of the trust. These are explained in more detail in **6.32–6.46**. All non-exempt transfers into lifetime trusts made on or after 22 March 2006 (except for a qualifying trust for a disabled person) will be chargeable transfers.

Example 6.1—Bertie's discretionary trust

Bertie's discretionary trust was made on 1 January 2008 at a time when the nil rate band was £300,000. The value of the assets given to the trust was £305,000 and there were no later additions. Bertie had not made any transfers of value in the seven years ending on 31 December 2007 and thus had available his annual exemptions for 2007/08 and 2006/07, resulting in a chargeable transfer into the discretionary trust of £299,000 (£305,000 – (£3,000 + £3,000)). This value fell within his unused nil rate band such that (assuming that Bertie did not make any later additions) there would be no exit charges on a capital distribution made within the first ten years. The level of the ten-year anniversary charge depends on the value of assets held in the trust at that time (viz, 1 January 2018).

Example 6.2—Accumulation and maintenance (A&M) trust

The Murray Settlement, which held shares in the family trading company, was a qualifying A&M trust created by Adrian and Belinda on 1 January 2001. As at 22 March 2006 no part of the trust fund was subject to an absolute interest or interest in possession and at least one beneficiary remained who has not yet become entitled to such an interest where such interest will occur on or before age 25. This is a pre-6 April 2010 trust with a 21-year period of accumulation, which in this case expires on 1 January 2022. At that point, Cerys and Tom, (aged five and two when the settlement was first made) must have become entitled to at least an interest in possession. Accumulation could continue in respect of the prospective share of a beneficiary still under the age of 18. Failing any, however, the A&M regime will end and an interest in possession will commence.

Of course, this is a classic case of a type of settlement which was adversely affected by the IHT regime for trusts that took effect on 22 March 2006. Unless the terms of the trust were changed before 6 April 2008 (see **6.52**) to provide that the capital vests outright in the children at age 25 at latest, the trust fund would have entered the 'relevant property' regime on 6 April 2008.

If the trust was changed before 6 April 2008 so that capital vests absolutely at age 25, the advantage secured is that although the special charging regime for 'age 18-to-25' trusts will apply to the presumptive share in capital while the relevant child is between the ages of 18 and 25, that special charging regime will not apply to any such share until the relevant child attains age 18.

If the trust was changed before 6 April 2008 so that capital vests absolutely at age 18, the trust fund will be exempt from any IHT exit or ten-year charge, as the beneficial A&M status will be preserved.

Example 6.3—Interest in possession trust

Alistair is the life tenant of an interest in possession trust created on 1 January 2006. During Alistair's lifetime, the trustees have the power to appoint income away from him. If they did this in favour of any individual by way of capital appointment or (before 6 October 2008) carving out a TSI with continuing trust interest (see **6.59**) or by creating a disabled person's interest (see **2.13**), this would have been treated as a PET made by Alistair himself, that is with no IHT implications if he survived for seven years. On the other hand, if the appointment had created any other type of settlement, this would be treated as a chargeable transfer by Alistair and could, depending upon the value involved and Alistair's own gifts history within the seven preceding years, have had positive IHT implications.

DOTAS and trusts

6.4 IHT was initially brought within DOTAS on 6 April 2011. Its application was then restricted to specific IHT avoidance involving the use of relevant property trusts where the main benefit was the avoidance or reduction of the IHT entry charge when property was first transferred in. Few disclosures had been made under this heading which HMRC felt to be too narrow of scope to capture the more sophisticated arrangements and as a consequence on 31 July 2014 HMRC published a consultation document setting out their proposals to broaden the DOTAS regime, which from an IHT and Trust perspective included:

- an expansion of the ambit to include any arrangements specifically designed to avoid or reduce an immediate charge to IHT (thus no longer confined to the IHT entry charge on trust creation);

- a requirement to disclose arrangements which, although not giving rise to an immediate IHT charge, are intended to reduce/avoid the IHT payable on death; and
- an extension to IHT of the general DOTAS notification triggers such as confidentiality and premium fees.

These proposals, which were contained in the 'Summary of Responses' published by HMRC in December 2014 have now been incorporated into *FA 2015*.

HMRC have indicated that the strengthening of the IHT DOTAS provisions are not intended to catch arrangements which involve the straightforward use of reliefs and exemptions, ie use of the spousal exemption.

On 2 September 2015 HMRC issued fresh Guidance Disclosure of Tax Avoidance Schemes bringing readers up to date with the changes introduced in *FA 2014* and *FA 2015*. The latter changes include:

- increased penalty for persons using schemes which do not comply with reporting requirements;
- protection of persons who voluntarily provide information about potential failures to comply with DOTAS;
- requirement for promotors to notify HMRC if their details or those of one of their schemes change;
- enabling HMRC to publish information about schemes and promotors that it receives under the DOTAS rules;
- giving HMRC powers to obtain details of users of undisclosed schemes from introducers; and
- creating a new power requiring additional information to be sent to clients.

Following responses made to the consultation on its proposed draft changes to the hallmark regulations which closed in September 2015, HMRC made a number of amendments, which changes became effective from 23 February 2016. More specifically, on 1 December 2017, HMRC published the response to its consultation of 'Tackling evasion: A requirement to notify HMRC of offshore structures' which has now been used to develop a revised draft to the current widely-drawn IHT hallmark contained within *F(No 2)A 2017* referred to as 'a requirement to correct'.

The thrust of the 'requirement to correct' (RTC) provisions was to encourage taxpayers to update their tax affairs on or before 30 September 2018, with the imposition of heavy penalties for those who failed to do so by the 2018 deadline. On 21 August 2018 HMRC updated its guidance on RTC: see tinyurl.com/ycpz671e.

The later 1 April 2018 introduction of the *Inheritance Tax Avoidance Schemes (Prescribed Descriptions) Regulations SI2017/1172* operates to significantly widen those IHT disclosure provisions. Accordingly, any arrangement which involves one or more contrived steps and the main purpose of which is the avoidance or reduction of IHT in prescribed circumstances will, unless covered by specific exemption, be subject to disclosure. The prescribed circumstances are:

- the entry into and other interim charges on trusts;
- charges on participators;
- avoidance of the reservation of benefits code where the transaction does not fall within the ambit of pre-owned asset tax provisions; and
- a reduction in a person's estate which does not result in a chargeable lifetime transfer or PET.

HMRC updated guidance is set out 'Disclosure of Tax Avoidance Schemes (DOTAS)': see tinyurl.com/yddjh-4na)

THE TERRITORIAL LIMITATION OF IHT

6.5 The basis of IHT differs from that of income tax and CGT. Income tax and CGT broadly catch the income and gains of persons (including the body of trustees) who are resident (and prior to 6 April 2013), ordinarily resident in the UK at some time during the tax year. An income tax liability also arises on the UK source income of a non-UK resident and a modified CGT charge (NRCGT) applies to gains realised on the disposal of UK residential property (extended from 6 April 2019 to include all UK land) by non-UK residents (to include trusts).

There is some limitation (the 'remittance basis'), in that non-UK source income and gains of persons resident but not domiciled in the UK may, subject to election, escape UK tax, insofar as the income or proceeds of sale are not directly or indirectly brought to this country. *FA 2008* introduced an annual income tax charge of £30,000 on persons aged 18 or over who have been UK resident in at least seven of the preceding nine years who elect to claim the remittance basis (subject to a *de minimis* of £2,000 for unremitted income and gains). Legislation in this area was extremely complex and HMRC, in recognising the concerns of professional advisers, sought to simplify the procedure of which the first adjustments were reflected in *FA 2013*. Subsequent Finance Acts have made various technical clarifications to the concept of remittance to raising the annual charge to £60,000 for 'long-term' residents (UK resident for at least all or part of 12 tax years out of the last 14 tax years) effective from 6 April 2012.

FA 2015 contained measures effective 6 April 2015 which extended the level of the charge as follows:

- to £60,000 for those who have been UK resident for 12 out of the last 14 years; and
- to £90,000 for those who have been UK resident for 17 out of the last 20 years.

The proposed imposition of a minimum of a three-year period covered by the remittance basis election first announced in the Finance (No 1) Bill 2015 has long since been dropped but the following two 'rules' intended to restrict persons from being able to claim non-UK domiciled status for an indefinite period of time remained on the HMRC agenda:

- a '15-year rule' – a deemed domicile rule for long-term resident non-UK domiciled persons (see **6.6**); and
- a 'returning UK domiciliary rule' (see **6.6**).

The reform of the regime for non-UK domiciled persons incorporating the above proposals is now reflected in *F(No 2)A 2017*, and affects those persons who are non-UK domiciled under general law – it extends beyond IHT to include income tax and CGT. As a consequence, the top tier £90,000 RBU charge has been withdrawn with effect from 6 April 2017.

Actual domicile

6.6 IHT is different from the other taxes, as its scope is defined on the basis of domicile – residence is broadly irrelevant. Each individual acquires at birth a domicile of origin, which mirrors the domicile of his father (or mother if illegitimate/posthumous), or he may have a domicile of dependency up to age 16, which will generally follow the adopted domicile of (typically) his father. In the case of an adopted child, HMRC guidance states that a new domicile of origin is regarded as having been acquired from the relevant adoptive parent, ie the domicile of his child's adoptive father or, if there is no adoptive father, his adoptive mother at the time of his adoption (RDRM22110).

A domicile of origin may be displaced by the later acquisition of an independent domicile of choice; but, if that domicile of choice is abandoned without a new domicile of choice being acquired, the domicile of origin will revive – in effect, a domicile of origin always waits in the wings. A person may be resident in more than one country during the tax year, but he can have only one domicile.

It was first announced in the summer 2015 Budget that those individuals with a quasi-domicile of origin in the UK (defined for this purpose as those born in the UK to a parent domiciled in the UK), but with a domicile of choice outside the UK, would nonetheless be treated as UK domiciled whilst they were resident in the UK. *F(No 2)A 2017* now contains measures which provide that such an individual will be taxed as a UK domiciliary on resumption of UK residence status, irrespective of their domicile status under general law. In addition, such returning UK domiciliaries will not benefit from any favourable tax treatment in respect of trusts (excluded property trusts) set up while not domiciled in the UK.

The returning UK domiciliary will be able to lose their UK tax domicile in the tax year after departure from the UK, but only if the following conditions are satisfied:

(a) they have not been resident in the UK for more than 15 tax years preceding the year concerned; and

(b) they have not acquired an actual UK domicile under general law during their return period to the UK.

HMRC's guidance indicates:

- If (a) above applies but not (b), the individual will be subject to the 'five-year rule' (see **1.11**), ie five years' non-UK residence will be required to lose their UK domicile.
- If (b) above applies but not (a), the individual will be subject to the 'three-year rule' (see **1.7**), ie the individual will remain UK domiciled for IHT purposes for three years after acquiring a foreign domicile of choice under general law.
- If both (a) and (b) apply, the individual will be subject to both the 'five-year rule' and 'three-year rule', and can only lose UK tax domicile on the later of those events.

Deemed domicile

6.7 There was a special 'deemed domicile' rule, for IHT purposes alone (*IHTA 1984, s 267*). Under this rule (but subject to the overriding provisions of any applicable double tax agreement), a person who was not domiciled in the UK under the general law was treated as nonetheless domiciled here for IHT purposes if:

- he had been resident in the UK for at least (thus, all or part-year residence will count) 17 out of the last 20 tax years, when the deemed domicile would arise at the beginning of the 17th year; or
- he had been legally (as opposed to deemed) domiciled in any part of the UK at any time during the previous three anniversary years preceding the chargeable event.

F(No 2)A2017 now replaces this '17 out of 20' rule with a '15 out of 20' rule (in *s 267(1)(b)*), which contain two conditions:

- The person was resident in the UK for at least 15 of the 20 tax years immediately preceding the relevant tax year.

- The person was resident for at least one of the four tax years ending with the relevant tax year.

Both conditions must be met for the person to be deemed domiciled in the UK under the '15 out of 20' rule. Thus an individual who has been UK resident for at least 15 out of the 20 tax years immediately preceding the relevant tax year, but who was not resident in the UK for any of the four tax years ending with the relevant tax year, would not be deemed domiciled under that rule.

It should be noted that the first of the above conditions in the '15 out of 20' rule would be satisfied if the person is UK resident for at least 15 of the 20 tax years *immediately preceding* the relevant tax year (see below). The 'relevant tax year' for these purposes is the tax year in which the 'relevant time' falls (ie the time at which the person's domicile status falls to be determined). By contrast, the '17 out of 20' rule refers to UK residence in not less than 17 out of the 20 tax years *ending* with the tax year in which the relevant time falls. Thus the '15 out of 20' rule has the intended effect that an individual's deemed UK domicile status can commence significantly sooner than under the '17 out of 20' rule it replaces.

The above change to the deemed UK domicile provisions applies to times after 5 April 2017, subject to certain exceptions. For example, those leaving the UK before 6 April 2017 would not be subject to the '15 out of 20 rule' if they were not UK resident for the relevant tax year and any tax year beginning after 5 April 2017 preceding the relevant tax year.

It is intended that the returning UK domiciliary will be able to lose their UK tax domicile in the tax year after departure from the UK, but only if the following conditions are satisfied:

(a) they have not spent more than 15 tax years in the UK; and

(b) they have not acquired an actual UK domicile under general law during their return period to the UK.

HMRC's guidance indicates:

- If (a) above applies but not (b), the individual will be subject to the 'five-year rule' ie five years' non-UK residence will be required to lose their UK domicile.

- If (b) above applies but not (a), the individual will be subject to the 'three-year rule', ie the individual will remain UK domiciled for IHT purposes for three years after acquiring a foreign domicile of choice under general law.

- If both (a) and (b) apply, the individual will be subject to both the 'five-year rule' and 'three-year rule' and can only lose UK tax domicile on the later of those events.

For more detail, please see Chapter 1 of *Inheritance Tax 2019/20* (Bloomsbury Professional).

Elective domicile

6.8 This new category was introduced with effect from 6 April 2013 and as its title indicates, it enables a UK resident but non-domiciled individual who has a UK domiciled spouse/civil partner (whether or not that spouse/civil partner is themself UK resident) to make an irrevocable election to be treated as domiciled in the UK for IHT purposes alone and thus secure access to the unlimited spousal exemption. Further detail is contained in *Inheritance Tax 2018/19* (Bloomsbury Professional).

The scope of IHT

6.9 Generally (subject to any overriding double tax treaty provisions and certain defined asset exceptions), IHT will apply to:

- the worldwide estate of a person with a factual, deemed or elective domicile in the UK; and
- the UK-situs estate of a person, not UK domiciled (under general law) and not deemed domiciled here, but subject to exceptions as provided for under statute, eg FOTRA securities.

Excluded property

6.10 IHT does not apply to excluded property, viz:

- property situated outside the UK if it is owned by a person domiciled outside the UK for all IHT purposes (*IHTA 1984, s 6(1)*);
- certain government securities (known as FOTRA, ie 'free of tax to residents abroad') owned either by non-UK domiciliaries or individuals not resident in the UK, or by the trustees of an interest in possession trust if the beneficiary is non-UK domiciled and there would be excluded property in relation to him. Similarly, with FOTRA securities owned by discretionary trustees and all possible beneficiaries falling into that category (*IHTA 1984, s 6(2)*);
- the reversionary interest of a settlement, ie the interest that comes into being when a qualifying interest in possession expires. This is the corollary of the rule that the life tenant is treated as beneficially entitled to the trust property, in a case where the relevant property regime does not apply. There are anti-avoidance exceptions which apply if it is the settlor

or spouse who owns the reversionary interest (*IHTA 1984, s 48(1)*) or where the interest has been purchased (*IHTA 1984, s 81A*); and

- property outside the UK owned by trustees (wherever resident) of a settlement made by someone domiciled outside the UK, even if the settlor has since become UK domiciled, provided (and to the extent) that there has been no purchase of an interest in the settled property on or after 5 December 2005 (*IHTA 1984, s 48(3)–(3C)*). However, note the impact of later funds added at a time when the settlor has become UK domiciled as clarified in the case of *Barclays Wealth Trustees (Jersey) Limited v* HMRC [2015] EWHC 2878 (Ch) which considered the position of a foreign domiciled settlor who created an excluded settlement but later became UK domiciled (actual or deemed) at a time when later funds were so added. The question was did those added funds also benefit from the excluded settlement status conferred when the original settlement was created? In a carefully worded judgment it was held that the position is tested at the time the addition is made such in this case subsequent additions to the settlement made at a time when the settlor was UK domiciled did not acquire the character of excluded property – see *Inheritance Tax 2019/20* (Bloomsbury Professional), Chapter 11 at 11.73. However, following the Budget 2018 announcement *FA 2019* contains measures which '… reflect HMRC's established position in relation to the [IHT] treatment of existing trusts'. The legislation makes clear beyond doubt that additions of assets made by UK domiciled (or deemed domiciled) individuals to trusts at a time when they are/were non-UK domiciled are not excluded property. This provision applies to IHT charges arising from the date of Royal Assent (12 February 2019) whether or not the additions were made prior to that date.

Prior to *F(No 2)A 2017*, a relevant property trust which comprised only excluded property was outside the scope of IHT and thus did not attract either exit of or ten-year anniversary charges. This was also the case if the trust was settlor interested since the excluded property rules took precedence over the gift with reservation rules. *F(No 2)A 2017* now includes measures which provide that from 6 April 2017 all UK residential property owned directly or indirectly by non-UK domiciliaries will be within the scope of IHT.

The new provisions have a direct impact on the traditional non-resident relevant property trust structure which owns shares in an underlying offshore company that in turn owns UK residential property – the value of the shares attributable to that UK property asset will fall within the scope of IHT and will potentially thereafter attract ten-year anniversary charges/exit charges for events taking place from 6 April 2017. Furthermore, the trust's indirect ownership of the UK residential property will deny the latter's access to excluded property status and where the settlor is a potential beneficiary of the trust, the protection previously afforded from attack under the gift with reservation rule (see above) will be withdrawn.

For established mixed use property, the element subject to IHT is determined on a pro rata basis. However, where the use of the UK property subsequently changes from residential to non-residential (or vice versa) the property is within the scope of IHT if it has been a residential property at any time within the two years immediately preceding the chargeable event. Other UK situs assets (ie non UK residential property etc.) owned directly or indirectly by offshore trusts created by non UK domiciliaries continues to remain outside the IHT net.

Anti-avoidance legislation, effective from 6 April 2012, has already been introduced to counter perceived abuse through elaborate structured arrangements intended to exploit the excluded estate provisions.

FA 2013 contains retrospective provisions to ensure that the trustees of a trust which comprises excluded property assets will no longer incur an exit charge when the trust switches from investing in UK assets to open-ended investment companies (OEICs) and authorised unit trusts (AUTs), nor will there be a requirement to file an IHT return in respect of such investment change.

PAYMENT OF TAX

6.11 While a trust continues during the life tenant's lifetime, there will be no IHT implications if it is a qualifying interest namely a pre-22 March 2006 life interest trust, qualifying TSI (see **6.60**) interest in possession, immediate post-death interest (see **6.63**) or qualifying A&M in character. Note that, even after 5 April 2008, a trust can be A&M in character if it meets the hallmarks of a bereaved minors trust (BMT) (see **6.52**). However, this will not be true of a relevant property trust (see **6.29–6.46**), when there may be:

- a charge on the first and each subsequent ten-year anniversary of making the settlement; and
- a charge on the exit from the trust of all or any part of the trust property.

In respect of either event, unless the excepted settlements provisions of *SI 2008/605* (see **3.19**) or *SI 2008/606* apply, the trustees must:

- submit an IHT return (form IHT100), called an 'account'; and
- pay any tax due.

On the assumption that notice of the settlement was given to HMRC on the original creation of the trust, HMRC will have knowledge of the settlement and the names and addresses of the trustees. However, in cases where HMRC suspect there may be a settlement but do not have the information, they have a statutory power to serve notice, whether on the trustees or anyone else, eg a bank or stockbroker. However, this is not an automatic process, and HMRC must first obtain the consent of a Special Commissioner to serve such a notice; but, once served, a response must be given within 30 days (*IHTA 1984, s 219*).

As to the liability to pay tax, whether on the ten-year anniversary or on exit, much will depend upon the character of the trust property. If it is illiquid, viz invested in land or shares with no income produced, the trustees may find themselves with practical financial constraints. Happily, there are provisions (see **11.93–11.97**) whereby any tax due in these circumstances may be paid by instalments, the first one falling due on the date when the whole of the tax should have been paid, and the other nine instalments following at annual intervals (*IHTA 1984, ss 227–229*).

Due dates

Delivery of account

6.12 *FA 2014* contains previously announced measures effective from 6 April 2014 to align the tax payment and filing dates for trusts to six months from the end of the month in which the chargeable event occurs. However, for events occurring prior to 6 April 2014 the position was as follows:

The account, where appropriate, must be delivered:

- within 12 months after the end of the month in which the occasion of charge took place; or
- if later, at the end of a three-month period beginning from the date on which the trustees become liable for tax (*IHTA 1984, s 216*).

Payment of tax

6.13 By contrast, for trust chargeable events occurring prior to 6 April 2014 the tax fell due in advance of the delivery of the account (*IHTA 1984, s 226*), viz:

- If the chargeable event takes place after 5 April but before 1 October – the tax was due on 30 April of the following year.
- If the chargeable event occurs after 30 September and before 6 April – the tax was due six months from the end of the month in which the event occurred.

See above for *FA 2014* measures effective from 6 April 2014 for the reporting of/and tax payment due in respect of chargeable events occurring on or after 6 April 2014.

THE INTEREST AND PENALTY REGIME

Interest

6.14 Not surprisingly, and in keeping with the position across the tax spectrum, IHT paid late attracts interest, which is not deductible for tax purposes (*IHTA 1984, s 233*): see **6.16** for the rates. Sometimes, of course, the value of the property attracting the tax may not be known, and therefore the tax itself is not known at the due date. In such cases, payment can be made on account or use made of the little known but useful certificates of tax deposit procedure. In either case, if the lodged payment proves excessive such that some repayment is due, that repayment itself will attract repayment supplement and will itself be tax exempt.

Penalties

6.15 A revised penalty regime for IHT took effect on 1 April 2009 and applies to deaths and other chargeable events occurring on or after that date (where the return is due to be filed on or after 1 April 2010). This is the impact of *FA 2008, Sch 40* extending to IHT, among other taxes, the regime introduced by *FA 2007, Sch 24*. Readers are referred to the discussion at **4.15** for a summary of the system, maximum penalties and the mechanism of statutory reductions for disclosure. While the regime looks considerably more 'fierce' than that which applied before, HMRC do say at question 32 of their frequently asked questions on the regime published on 19 March 2009:

> 'HMRC recognise that IHT applies to a single event and concepts such as reasonable care will be somewhat different under these circumstances than for taxes where people have to make returns more regularly. HMRC also recognise that the position of personal representatives is different from other individuals and trustees who may make a transfer that is liable to IHT'.

For the position on penalties in relation to deaths and other chargeable events before 1 April 2009, readers are referred to **6.13** of the 2008/09 edition of this book.

Separately, *FA 2009, Sch 56* introduced a system of penalties for failure to make timely payments. These take effect from a date to be appointed by Treasury order which, at the time of publication, remains unstated. In broad terms, failure to pay IHT by the filing date (in the case of death, 12 months after the end of the month of death) carries a penalty of 5% of the unpaid tax, with a further 5% due on tax remaining unpaid five months after the penalty date, and a further 5% on tax remaining unpaid 11 months after the penalty date. Special provisions apply to tax payable by instalments.

IHT receipts exceeded £5.2 billion in 2017/18 and it is predicted that by 2021 the receipts will increase to £6.2 billion. With this backdrop it is not surprising that HMRC are forging ahead with the penalty regime.

Interest rates over recent years

Underpaid and overpaid tax

6.16

6 September 2005–5 September 2006	3%
6 September 2006–5 August 2007	4%
6 August 2007–5 January 2008	5%
6 January 2008–5 November 2008	4%
6 November 2008–5 January 2009	3%
6 January 2009–26 January 2009	2%
21 January 2009–23 March 2009	1%
24 March 2009–28 September 2009	0%
29 September 2009–22 August 2016	3%
23 August 2016–20 November 2017	2.75%
21 November 2017–20 August 2018	3.0%
21 August 2018 et seq	3.25% (subject to a minimum of 0.5% on tax repayments)

Professional obligation to notify

6.17 There is a further onerous obligation which applies specifically to solicitors and other professional advisers (barristers specifically excluded). If a UK-domiciled settlor makes a settlement with non-UK resident trustees (or gives a professional person concerned with the making of a settlement cause to think that non-UK resident trustees will be appointed), there is a stand-alone obligation (ie whether or not requested by HMRC) for that professional person to give notice to HMRC within three months (*IHTA 1984, s 218*).

GIFTS WITH RESERVATION

6.18 The reservation of benefit rules were introduced for IHT in March 1986 (*FA 1986, s 102* and *Sch 20*) and apply to any type of gift, not just a gift into trust. However, in so far as gifts into trust are concerned, they broadly operate to mirror the equivalent of the settlor-interested rules for income tax (see **4.26–4.29**) and for CGT (see **5.21–5.22**). They are narrower in scope, however, in that:

- they do not apply to gifts made before 18 March 1986; and also
- settlements from which the settlor but not his spouse is excluded do not come within the ambit of the rules.

As a general approach, it is usually sensible that settlor and spouse are irrevocably excluded from benefit, although the income tax and CGT rules (nor, of course, the reservation of benefit rules) will not apply if there is a possibility of the widow or widower of the settlor benefiting after the settlor's death. That said, there could be examples where a settlor-included settlement may be useful, eg to secure the principal private residence relief for trusts.

F(No 2)A 2017 has now extended the scope of IHT to all UK residential property owned directly or indirectly by non-UK domiciliaries (see **6.9**) such that the reservation of benefit provisions will now be an issue where a non-UK domiciled individual has retained a benefit in UK residential property gifted to an offshore company. To soften the impact, the legislation contains somewhat complicated provisions which can afford such formerly excluded property trusts 'protective' status.

Effects

6.19

- If the reservation of benefit continues until the settlor's death, the subject-matter of the gift is treated *as if* still comprised in his estate at its then market value (*FA 1986, s 102(3)*). Any IHT due thereon is payable by the donee.
- If the reservation of benefit is released during the settlor's lifetime he is treated as having made a PET at that time of its then value (*FA 1986, s 102(4)*) but the annual exemption is not available for use in this situation. It follows that if that PET is made within the seven years before his death, it will become a failed PET and treated as a lifetime chargeable transfer of value like any other.

Double charges

6.20 There could, however, be double taxation, eg a gift to a relevant property trust from which the settlor is not excluded from benefit would be both a chargeable transfer at the time when made and an ongoing gift with reservation of benefit. The *IHT (Double Charges Relief) Regulations 1987* contain complex provisions whereby, broadly speaking, the IHT charge is calculated separately on the chargeable transfer and the reservation of benefit in isolation, and whichever produces the highest levy is adopted.

Anti-avoidance rules from 2005/06: the 'pre-owned assets' regime

6.21 Effective from 6 April 2005, *FA 2004, Sch 15* introduced a savage income tax charge on (broadly) IHT mitigation arrangements put in place on or after 18 March 1986 under which, in relation to all of land, chattels and certain settlor-interested trusts, an individual continues to enjoy or derive a benefit from asset that they have given away in circumstances which would otherwise sidestep the reservation of benefit rules contained within *FA 1986, s 102* and *Sch 20*. The income tax charge can be avoided by:

- paying an annual amount prescribed by the legislation;
- terminating the benefit before the beginning of any year post 5 April 2005 (though the charge remains in force for any preceding years from 2005/06); or
- making an irrevocable election to opt back into the reservation of benefit regime.

See **4.44–4.53**.

Releasing the reservation – concept of 'settlement power' blocks avoidance arrangement

6.22 In *Melville v IRC* [2002] 1 WLR 407, the Court of Appeal affirmed on 31 July 2001 the effectiveness of a scheme designed to make use of hold-over relief from CGT for non-business property worth more than the nil rate band.

Consider that a person owned an investment property valued at £1 million and standing at a large gain, which he wished to give to his children. If he made the gift to a discretionary trust or other relevant property trust he could elect to hold over the gain but the gift would still incur a 20% (25% if met by the settlor) IHT entry charge on the value in excess of the available nil rate band (bolstered by any unused annual exemption). If, however, he could reduce the transfer of value to an amount within his nil rate band, he could escape an immediate IHT charge and still qualify for hold-over relief to circumvent the CGT charge.

It was considered that the value could be depressed by reserving a right to require the trustees to return the assets to him before 90 days have elapsed. Remember that for IHT purposes the market value notion is effectively disapplied for lifetime gifts and instead the value of the transfer is based on the drop-in value of the donor's estate post-gift. He made the gift, held over the gain and, the existence of the right reduces the transfer of value well below £1 million. Once 90 days had expired, he released the benefit of that right which was treated as a PET and survived that PET by seven years such that it became fully exempt.

The Court of Appeal confirmed that the valuable right retained by the settlor in such a situation was 'property' to be taken into account in computing the amount of the transfer of value.

In response to the *Melville* decision, *FA 2002, s 119* introduced the concept of a 'settlement power', which does not constitute property for IHT purposes.

This specifically counters the effect of the *Melville* arrangement by ensuring that the transfer of value made by the settlor whilst still computed on the loss to the donor basis permits no account to be taken for the valuable right retained in the settlor's estate. Further anti-avoidance legislation has been enacted to counteract the so-called 'sons of *Melville*' (see **5.49**).

FA 2006 blocks gift with reservation avoidance device using life interest settlements

6.23 In recent years, a common spousal will structure operated to put the deceased's share of the family home into a qualifying interest in possession trust (IPDI) for the benefit of both the surviving spouse and the adult children. Whilst the children would typically not choose to live in the matrimonial home, they could do so nonetheless under the trust terms and, under the *IHTA 1984, s 49(1)* regime, their *pro rata* share of the house would be treated as comprised in their estates and not in that of the surviving parent. The proportion of the deceased's interest in the house that could be left within his nil rate band on life interest for the children, with balance for the surviving spouse, would depend on both the value of the house and the extent of chargeable transfers made in the seven years before death plus any other chargeable transfers under the will.

However, consider that the surviving spouse is left, say, a 50% life interest in the deceased's half share of the house. The trustees might, in exercise of their powers of appointment, reduce the surviving spouse's interest to 10% of that 50% trust interest and increase those of the children to 90% of that 50% trust interest. This would be treated as a PET made by the surviving spouse, ie no IHT consequence subject to survival for seven years; equally, there would be no gift with reservation because the transfer of value had been engineered by the trustees, not created by the beneficiary.

This effect is changed from 22 March 2006, to provide that, in such circumstances, it is treated as a gift by the beneficiary in which he reserves a benefit for so long as he continues to occupy the house rent-free or for less than full consideration (or enjoys a benefit from any other trust asset) (*FA 1986, s 102ZA*).

AGRICULTURAL AND BUSINESS PROPERTY RELIEF

6.24 Business property relief (BPR) and agricultural property relief (APR) are quite separate reliefs, although they operate in much the same way (*IHTA 1984, ss 103–114* for BPR, and *ss 115–124C* for APR). The relief is given at either 100% or 50% and serves to reduce the value of the chargeable transfer for IHT purposes. This could be:

- with a qualifying (ie pre-March 2006) interest in possession trust, on the death of the life tenant; or
- with a relevant property trust, either when the property enters the trust or on the ten-year anniversary, or when the property leaves the trust.

Business property relief (BPR)

6.25 BPR will apply when the trust owns (*inter alia*):

- a business or an interest in a partnership business (100% relief);
- unquoted shares in a trading company (100% relief);
- a controlling shareholding in a quoted company (50%); or
- fixed assets, premises or plant held outside the business carried on by the trustees in partnership or a business carried on by the life tenant (50% relief).

The above represents a broad summary of the six categories of 'relevant business property' defined at *IHTA 1984, s 105(1).*

From a trust perspective the chief and most accessible category of property qualifying for BPR, see *s 105(1)(bb),* is 'any unquoted shares in a company'. 'Unquoted' for this purpose has a defined meaning, see (*IHTA 1984, s 105(1ZA)*) and whilst in relation to UK companies this will usually mean not quoted on the full list of the London Stock Exchange (Alternative Investment Market (AIM) excluded) it will also require non listing on *any* recognised exchange. This has given rise to considerable investor interest in small companies in light of the trust reforms contained in *FA 2006* which now bring more trusts within the relevant property regime.

Income Tax Act 2007, s 1005 was amended with effect from 19 July 2007 so as to allow HMRC to regard as a 'recognised stock exchange' any investment exchange that the Financial Services Authority designates as a 'recognised investment exchange'. This power was exercised, for example, in relation to part, but not all, of the market formerly known as OFEX, then PLUS and now ISDX. The result is confusing: some shares on PLUS qualify for BPR, while others do not and as a consequence great care should be taken in this area.

Since 2013 alone, HMRC designated the following as recognised stock exchanges for IHT purposes, with the latest additions made on 8 October 2018:

- The Channel Islands Securities Exchange Authority (20 December 2013).
- GXG Main Quote (23 September 2013).
- Global Board of Trade (30 July 2013).

- GXG Official List (16 May 2013).
- ICAP Securities & Derivatives Exchange Ltd (25 April 2013).
- European Wholesale Securities Market (18 January 2013).
- National Stock Exchange of Australia Ltd (19 June 2014).
- Singapore Exchange Securities Trading Limited (7 October 2014).
- Singapore Exchange Derivatives Trading Limited (7 October 2014).
- Euronext London (4 February 2015)
- GSX Ltd (16 August 2016)
- Botswana Stock Exchange (8 October 2018)

Agricultural property relief (APR)

6.26 APR will apply to the agricultural value of agricultural land used for agricultural purpose and (subject to some restrictions), farmhouses, farm cottages and farm buildings (defined as qualifying 'agricultural property' at *IHTA 1984, s 115(2))*. Relief will be given at 100% if the trustees own and farm the land themselves or if they let the land on a farm business tenancy (FBT) subject to satisfaction of the ownership rules. The trustees will get only 50% relief if they let the land prior to 1 September 1995 and cannot recover vacant possession within 12 (or by concession 24) months.

Further details of APR and BPR may be found in **11.55–11.67** or, for a more detailed discussion, see *Agricultural, Business and Heritage Property Relief (7th edn) (Bloomsbury Professional)*.

The clawback rules

Focus

Beware the retrospective effect of the clawback rules in respect of a settlor's death within seven years of a BPR/APR asset transfer into trust.

6.27 There are 'clawback' rules, which need to be considered carefully when property is put into trust with the attached benefit of APR or BPR and the settlor dies within seven years. To avoid a retrospective withdrawal of valuable relief, it must be shown that the trustees continue to own the original (or qualifying replacement property) as at the date of the settlor's death and, importantly, that it continues to attract APR or BPR in their hands at that time (*IHTA 1984, ss 113–113B* for BPR, and *ss 124–124C* for APR).

Example 6.4—Jack's discretionary Trust: The 'clawback trap'

In October 2013, Jack, who farmed (as sole trader) an agricultural estate of 1,000 acres, gifted 200 acres plus two cottages (all of which had development potential) into a discretionary trust. The transfer attracted BPR (on the authority of the High Court decision in *HMRC v the Trustees of the Nelson Dance Family Settlements* [2009] EWHC 71 Ch 22). Jack, who was not a beneficiary of the trust, died in December 2019 and this caused the original grant of BPR to be revisited. At the time of his death, Jack was paying a rent to the trustees for the 200 acres and cottages which had not yet been sold. There is a clawback of BPR as the trustees (by whom the test for BPR is measured) were not involved in Jack's sole trade nor is APR in point as the trustees have failed to satisfy the seven-year test by reference to Jack's use of the land. This loss of relief will have a positive IHT effect insofar as the gross value of the assets settled exceeded Jack's nil rate band on death.

By contrast, had Jack taken the trustees into a (perhaps, limited) partnership and the trustees had contributed the 200 acres and cottages to the partnership, there would have been no clawback of relief.

The 'first ten years exit' trap

Focus

The benefit of BPR/APR is excluded in calculating the rate of the exit charge applicable to appointments of non APR/BPR assets during the first ten years.

6.28 There is a trap with relevant property trusts comprising agricultural or business property in relation to an exit in the first ten years where the assets leaving the confines of the trust do not themselves qualify for APR or BPR; this is explained at **6.37** and careful note should be taken.

'RELEVANT PROPERTY' TRUSTS

Estate duty

6.29 Under estate duty (which was replaced by capital transfer tax in 1975), it was possible for a discretionary trust to be a family's 'tax-free money box' insofar as gifts, taxation and death duties were concerned. This assumed that the trust was made at least seven years before the settlor's death as, if not, it would have come into charge for estate duty on that death.

The capital transfer tax (CTT) regime

6.30 1975 saw the introduction of a regime for discretionary settlements under CTT, which was thought to be excessively draconian (which in a sense it was, when compared with the previous regime). Since then, however, the regime has come to be seen as relatively benign if viewed in the broader context. It has to be said that much of the legislation is fairly complex; the spirit behind it, however, is as follows.

Taxing the trust

6.31

- The ten-year charge: the thinking behind the legislation is to treat each relevant property trust as a separate taxpayer and to subject it to IHT as if the property in the settlement had been the subject of a lifetime gift made every generation. The rate of IHT on death is 40%, whereas the rate on chargeable lifetime gifts (which the donor survives by more than seven years) is 20%. A generation is assumed to be 33⅓ years. HMRC want to collect the money rather more regularly than three times every 100 years, so the charge on property in the settlement is collected every ten years on the anniversary of the creation of the trust at a maximum rate of 6%, which equates to 20% every 33⅓ years. However, 6% is a maximum rate and, in very many cases, the effective rate will be much less than this, given the effect of the nil rate band. The method of calculation is explained in greater detail at **6.32–6.35**.
- The exit charge (see **6.36–6.38**): This is charged on the value of the property (cash or assets) leaving the trust between ten-year anniversaries. The exit charge cannot exceed 5.85% (6% × 39/40) but in practice is much less.

The settlor usually has a marked dislike of incurring a tax charge, such that the vast majority of relevant property settlements are created within the nil rate band with the result that the exit/ten-year charges may be very small or nothing at all – this favourable position looked to be scuppered by the initial HMRC proposals concerning the introduction of a single settlement rate, the details of which were set out in the trust simplification consultative document dated 6 June 2014 but this proposal has now been disregarded. However, it is affected by the anti-avoidance measures applicable to pilot trusts introduced in *F(No 2)A 2015* (see **6.32**). Prior to 22 March 2006, very often the main reason for using a discretionary in preference to any other type of settlement was the CGT advantage of hold-over relief. (However, note the rule effective from

10 December 2003, which prevents hold-over relief on a transfer to a settlor-interested settlement (see **3.5**).)

Example 6.5—Monty's Settlement: IHT impact of capital advance

Monty's Settlement, made on 1 January 2006 in favour of his grandchildren, was created with a value within his nil rate band. By the time of the first ten-year anniversary on 1 January 2016, the trust fund had, with successful investment management, grown to £800,000. A capital advance of £50,000 had been made on 1 January 2015 and the rate of tax charged on this exit was nil (see **6.37**).

However, on the first ten-year anniversary on 1 January 2016 there was a positive charge, as the value of the trust fund exceeded the then 2015/16 nil rate band (£325,000). The detailed calculation is shown in Example 6.6 at **6.35**.

Any exit of capital in the ten-year period immediately following that anniversary on 1 January 2016 will, for its exit rate, be related back to the rate established on that last ten-year anniversary but subject to possible adjustment for any increase in the nil rate band (see **6.38**).

THE TEN-YEAR CHARGE

6.32 The ten-year anniversary charge is the main IHT charge for 'relevant property' settlements. Its calculation, whilst not necessarily straightforward, has been seriously complicated by the March 2006 trust reforms, which brought previously favoured trusts within the relevant property regime. There is no doubt that the complexities of the charges triggered under the relevant property regime have been heightened by the *FA 2006* trust legislation. Responding to the concerns of professional advisers, it was announced in the March 2012 Budget that there would be a consultative process launched to explore possible options for simplifying the calculation of the IHT periodic and exit charges on trusts that hold or dispose of relevant property. HMRC subsequently published a consultation document on 13 July 2012 and the outcome of that consultation merited careful reading both then and now since it provided an insight into HMRC thinking. In essence, HMRC rejected calls to exclude the 'age 18-to-25' trusts, old-style A&M trusts, and post-March 2006 interest in possession trusts from the regime of periodic and interim IHT charges, but they did accept the need to:

- introduce a simplified method of calculating such charges;
- introduce clearer rules relating to accumulated income; and

- align IHT trust charge filing and payment dates.

On 31 May 2013, HMRC released a follow-up consultative document (see 'Inheritance tax: simplifying charges on trusts – the next stage') which provided more detail on the proposed method of reforms for the above three headings, namely:

(i) Ten-year charge:

- Dropping the seven-year settlor cumulative history.
- Ignoring non-relevant property.
- Dividing the nil rate band by the total number of settlements created by the settlor, whenever created.
- Introducing a standard 6% rate.

(ii) Accumulations:

- Giving statute recognition to capital status of accumulated income not distributed by the end of the second year in which the income arises.

(iii) Compliance alignment:

- Aligning with the self-assessment framework for filing and payment dates.

On 10 December 2013 HMRC formally advised that following representations made by the key interest groups which participated in the consultation process, changes had been made to the original proposals namely:

(a) to introduce a new rule providing for recognition of accumulated and undistributed income (not otherwise capitalised) which arose more than five years prior to the ten-year anniversary charge to be treated as trust capital for the purpose of calculating the ten-year anniversary charge only;

(b) to align filing and payment dates to six months after the end of the month in which the event occurred;

(c) to consult further on alternative proposals to split the nil rate band that will meet trustees' concerns whilst maintaining tax revenues and as a result:

    (i) put the simplification of the calculations on a slightly slower track so that any new legislation is introduced in the Finance Bill 2015; and

    (ii) defer the proposal to require trustees to 'self-assess' IHT due until Finance Bill 2015.

Draft legislation for (a) and (b) is included in *FA 2014* effective from 6 April 2014.

On 6 June 2014, HMRC issued an updated consultative document (the third) entitled 'Inheritance tax: a fairer way of calculating trust charges'. Its prime focus was on 'simplification' of the way in which the ten-year and exit charges are calculated and set out proposals for the treatment of the nil rate band where the settlor makes multiple settlements. HMRC proposed the introduction of a simple 6% rate to replace the current variable range of 0 – 6% but this had been mentioned in the earlier consultative documents and continued to be ill received from the professional community given its harsh impact on the majority of settlements where the effective rate is much lower if not standing at 0%. However, whilst the introduction of a single settlement nil rate band had been previously mentioned, unusually that document went much further by announcing that HMRC would push ahead with the reforms by introducing legislation in *FA 2015* effective from and applicable to all settlements created on or after the date of the document, namely 6 June 2014. It would seem that the use of the term 'directive' rather than 'consultative' might be perhaps more appropriate.

The December 2014 Autumn Budget announced that the earlier announced proposals relating to the settlement nil rate band were to be scrapped. In their place the *Finance Bill 2015* contained measures to remove the need to recognise the value of non-relevant property when calculating the ten-year charge/exit charge and introduce rules dealing with the same day addition of later added property/added value to multiple trusts. That same Bill introduced measures intended to provide more certainty and to ease the effect/complexity of the legislation applicable to the relevant property trust regime – in particular it was proposed that *IHTA 1984, s 144* which relied on the provisions of *IHTA 1984, s 65(4)* which prevent an IHT exit charge arising in the first three months after the will trust commenced would not apply to appointments so made, thereby allowing the appointment to be read back into the will and claim the benefit of the spousal exemption where appropriate. To block any pre-emptive steps, it was also intended that such measures as contained in the FB 2015 would apply to such trusts created before 10 December 2014.

In the haste to enact *FA 2015* prior to closure of the parliamentary session in advance of the May 2015 general election, none of these proposed measures passed into law. However, this was later partially addressed by the *F(No 2) A 2015*, which now provides for the following:

(i) Exclusion of non-relevant property

The calculation of the periodic and exit charges is simplified by removing the need to include the (historic) value of non-relevant property (namely that property not subject to the IHT system of ten-year and exit charges) within the notional transfer total. This applies to all chargeable events arising on or after 18 November 2015 (date of Royal Assent).

(ii) Same day additions

Aimed at negating the benefit of multiple trusts (pilot trusts) use, the rule operates to ensure that where property is added to more than one relevant property trust on the same day (on or after commencement of those trusts) that added value together with the original value of that trust when first settled (to the extent not already recognised as a related settlement) is brought into account in calculating the rate of tax for the purpose of the ten year and exit charges. There is a de miminis exemption where the same-day addition is £5,000 or less (*IHTA 1984, s 62(2)–(4)*). The new provision does not apply to a will executed before 10 December 2014 where that death occurred before 6 April 2017. This applies to all chargeable events arising on or after 18 November 2015 (date of Royal Assent).

The above anti-avoidance legislation does not apply if either (or both) trust A and trust B is a 'protected settlement' (*IHTA 1984, s 62C*) namely a trust which commenced before 10 December 2014 and either of two conditions (A or B) is satisfied:

- Condition A is broadly that the settlor has not added value to the settlement since 10 December 2014.
- Alternatively, Condition B is that the settlor makes a transfer on or after 10 December 2014 resulting in the value of the property being increased, where the transfer arises (under *s 4*) on the settlor's death before 6 April 2017 by reason of a 'protected testamentary disposition' (ie under the settlor's will, where its provisions are substantially the same as they were immediately before 10 December 2014).

It should be noted that it still remains possible for the settlor to create a new relevant property trust every seven years, each with its own nil rate band (assuming that no other chargeable transfers or potentially exempt transfers have been made in the intervening periods). Furthermore, consideration could be given to adding business property to an existing trust, although as indicated such additions should generally be made on different days.

(iii) The 'Frankland' trap

The three-month waiting period for an absolute appointment out of a will trust (in which no qualifying interest in possession exists) to the surviving spouse or civil partner is withdrawn, paving the way for full spousal relief. This action reflects the treatment already afforded to the carve-out of an interest in possession in favour of the surviving spouse or civil partner. The rule applies to the testators' death on or after 10 December 2014.

(iv) Section 80 rejigged

The wording of *IHTA 1984, s 80* is amended to correct an unintended effect which permitted a successive spousal non qualifying interest in possession to potentially escape IHT charge because the trust assets were neither part of the successor's estate nor comprised within a relevant property trust. The term 'interest in possession' is replaced with the term 'qualifying interest in possession' – the latter referring to an interest that is either a pre 22 March 2006 established interest, an IPDI, transitional serial interest (TSI) or disabled person's interest as set out in *IHTA 1984, s 59*. Accordingly, where one party to a couple succeeds to a life interest to which their spouse or civil partner was previously entitled during their life time, *IHTA 1984, s 80* continues to apply at that time.

Prior to 6 April 2017 a relevant property trust which comprised excluded property (see **6.10**) was outside the scope of IHT and thus did not attract either exit of or ten-year anniversary charges. This was also the case if the trust was settlor interested since the excluded property rules were considered to take precedence over the gift with reservation rules. *IHTA 1984, s 48(3)* defines excluded property as property situated outside the UK where '… the property itself, but not a reversionary interest in it, is excluded provided that the settlor was not domiciled in the UK when the settlement was made'.

However, *F(No 2)A 2017* included measures which provide that from 6 April 2017 IHT is payable on all UK residential property owned directly or indirectly by non-UK domiciliaries. This has a direct impact on the traditional non-resident relevant property trust structure which owns shares in an underlying offshore company that in turn owns UK residential property – the value of the shares attributable to that UK property asset will now fall within the scope of IHT and will potentially thereafter attract ten-year anniversary charges/exit charges. Furthermore, the measures will also impact on the trust's indirect ownership of the UK residential property by denying the latter's access to excluded property status thus, should the settlor be a potential beneficiary of the trust, the protection previously afforded from attack under the gift with reservation rule (see above) will be withdrawn albeit some relief can be gained if the 'protected' status rules apply (see **6.10**).

F(No 2)A 2017 addresses the position of mixed use property providing that the element subject to IHT be determined on a pro rata basis; however, in a move intended to block repositioning to avoid the charge, the legislation also contains an avoidance measure. This is intended to apply where that use subsequently changes from residential to non-residential (or vice versa) and that property had been a residential property at any time within the two years immediately preceding the chargeable event.

A fresh consultation on trust taxation was issued by HMRC in November 2018 with responses invited by 28 February 2019. HMRC will publish the outcome of that consultation in Summer 2019.

Date of charge

6.33 The first ten-year charge arises on the tenth anniversary of the date when the settlement began, which is the date on which the property first became settled (*IHTA 1984, s 61*). Therefore, if the settlement was established with £10 and then, six months later, the substantive funding is advanced, it is the date on which the £10 went into the trust that fixes the date for future ten-year anniversary charges.

Where property is left under a will on discretionary trusts or a trust arises out of a valid deed of variation, the date of death is the commencement of the settlement (regardless of how long it takes to administer the estate or the date of the deed of variation).

Two elements

6.34 It should be stressed at the very outset that the calculation of the ten-year charge (as the exit charge) contains a number of 'bear traps' which must be recognised if the calculation is to be mastered:

- The chargeable amount (*IHTA 1984, s 64*): This is the value of all 'relevant property' (see **6.39**) contained in the settlement immediately before the ten-year anniversary reduced by applicable APR/BPR (but with the relief adjusted for the measures contained in the *FA 2013* which with effect from 6 April 2013 now reposition new liabilities incurred in the direct purchase of a qualifying APR/BPR but secured on non APR/BPR assets in order to secure full APR/BPR relief – for more detail see *Inheritance Tax 2019/20* (Bloomsbury Professional) and subject to adjustment where property has changed its character during the ten years (see **6.44**). 'Relevant property' for this purpose will include the capital and accumulated income and, as provided for in the *FA 2014* (see **6.32** above) effective from 6 April 2014, does include undistributed un-accumulated income which arose more than five years immediately prior to the date of the ten-year charge – see **6.33** above. Neither income tax (borne out of income) or contingent CGT is a valid deduction, although liabilities secured on the property would be. BPR and APR where applicable are available to reduce the amount chargeable to tax.
- The rate of tax (*IHTA 1984, s 66*): This is 30% of the 'effective rate' applicable to a lifetime charge made by a hypothetical transferor with a gifts history equal to that of the settlor in the seven years before he made the settlement (unless recalculated under *s 67* – see **6.43**), but excluding the date of settlement, plus any amounts on which an exit charge have been imposed in the last ten years.

Importantly, this means that the seven-year chargeable gifts history of the settlor will persist in being relevant to the calculation of each ten-year anniversary charge within the settlement, irrespective of the passage of time.

Taking the hypothetical transferor, the settlor's gifts history is assumed to be the aggregate of gifts made by him in the seven years before the settlement plus any amount on which exit charges were imposed in the ten years before the particular ten-year anniversary (*IHTA 1984, s 66(5)*) but also see **6.43**.

Calculating the IHT payable

6.35 Having calculated the deemed chargeable transfer and the deemed cumulative total, the lifetime rate, ie 20%, is used to discover the tax figure. This figure, when divided by the deemed chargeable transfer, gives an effective rate, which is multiplied by 30% to discover the rate payable and then applied to the chargeable property to discover the tax payable. An example is given below.

However, it is important to note that measures contained in the *FA 2013* now prevent the ability to reposition liabilities incurred in the direct purchase of a qualifying APR/BPR asset in order to secure full APR/BPR thereon.

Example 6.6—Monty's Settlement (2): ten-year charge illustration

Continuing to build on Example 6.5, the Monty Trust was subject to a ten-year charge on 1 January 2016.

The value of the trust fund at that date, after an advance of capital of £50,000 made on 1 January 2015, was £800,000 – that is called the 'relevant property'.

The rate of tax is 30% of the 'effective rate' applied to a lifetime gift made by a hypothetical transferor with a gifts history equal to that of Monty in the seven years before he made the settlement, plus the capital advance made to the beneficiary in 2015. Monty, being well advised, had a nil chargeable transfer history during that seven-year period. However, the deemed cumulative total of the hypothetical transferor includes any amounts on which exit charges were imposed (even if at the nil rate) in the previous ten years (*IHTA 1984, s 66(5)(b)*) and this brings into account the £50,000 capital advance made in January 2015.

The ten-year charge is calculated as follows:

'Relevant property'		£800,000
Nil rate band (at ten-year charge date)	£325,000	
Less capital advance (2015)	(£50,000)	
		(£275,000)
		£525,000
Tax @ 20% (lifetime rate)		£105,000

The 'effective rate' is £105,000 divided by £800,000 = 13.125%

The ten-year anniversary rate is 30% of the 'effective rate' = 3.937% (rounded to three decimal places).

The tax on the ten-year anniversary, is therefore:

£800,000 @ 3.937% = £31,496.

EXIT CHARGE

6.36 The exit charge arises when property leaves the relevant property regime, by way of (non-exempt) gift (*IHTA 1984, s 65*), between ten-year anniversaries. Therefore, it would not apply to the sale or purchase by the trustees of trust property nor, indeed, to the payment of professional costs or other expenses, and neither would it apply if the property was paid to a charity or other tax relieved body, eg the National Trust.

Importantly, there is no exit charge if the event happens in the first quarter (three months) following either creation of the settlement or the last ten-year anniversary (*IHTA 1984, s 65(4)*). In addition, if a discretionary trust (as opposed to an IPDI) was created by will, there is no exit charge if the event happens at least three months (but see **6.32**) after but within two years after the death (see **13.17**) as the appointment is automatically read back to date of the testator's death under *IHTA 1984, s 144*. The absence of a chargeable IHT event will operate to deny access to general CGT holdover under *TCGA 1992, s 260*.

The exit charge taxes the fall in value of the relevant property (the 'estate before less estate after' principle). If the resultant IHT is paid out of the residual trust fund rather than by the recipient of the property, the IHT must be grossed up in the normal manner.

A distinction should be drawn between the exit charge in the first ten-year period and the exit charge following the first or subsequent ten-year anniversaries.

Exit in the first ten years

6.37 Like the ten-year charge, the exit charge in the first ten years (*IHTA 1984, s 66*) requires a deemed cumulative total of the hypothetical transferor, which is that of the settlor in the seven years before the settlement began. This is applied to the value of the settled property at commencement (not at exit), taking into account the initial value of related settlements and added property as discussed in **6.41–6.43**.

The lifetime rates are then applied to the deemed chargeable transfer on the basis of the deemed cumulative total, with 30% applied, ie just like the ten-year charge. However, there is then a reduction to take account of the number of completed quarters that have elapsed since commencement.

If, however, the rate is nil (even if a day before the ten-year anniversary), then whatever the value of the trust fund at exit, no IHT is charged.

An often overlooked 'bear trap' operates where, in calculating the chargeable value on initial creation of the trust, APR/BPR has been given for qualifying agricultural and/or business property. This latter APR/BPR is ignored when working out the exit charge in the first ten years (*IHTA 1984, s 68(5)(a)*). Accordingly, unless the gross value of the trust fund (and later additions) is within the nil rate band (post settlor seven-year gifts) on exit, *or* the property subject to the exit charge itself attracts APR or BPR in its own right, there could conceivably be a positive charge on exit, even though the existence of APR or BPR would have led to a nil charge on entry.

Exit after the first ten years

6.38 The exit charge between ten-year anniversaries adopts the rate established on the last ten-year anniversary, scaled down by reference to the number of complete quarters that have elapsed since then. If, since that ten-year anniversary, the nil rate band has increased, the ten-year anniversary rate is recalculated substituting the increased nil rate band, in effect to give a lower rate of exit charge (*IHTA 1984, Sch 2, para 3*).

Example 6.7—Monty's Settlement (3): exit charge

On 1 June 2018, the trustees of Monty's settlement decide to appoint capital of £100,000 equally between the four grandchildren – Katie, Tom, Cerys and Oscar. This will attract an exit charge, which will be borne out of the appointed capital, calculated as follows:

Step 1:
The exit charge is initially based on the rate established at the last ten-year anniversary on 1 January 2016, thus 3.937% – the rate does not need to be recalculated since the nil rate band in 2018/19 (the year of the exit charge event) has remained at the level of £325,000.

Step 2:
The rate of 3.937% is reduced by the fraction representing the number of complete quarters elapsed since the date of the last ten-year charge over the total of 40 quarters in the ten-year period. In this case only nine quarters have expired since the last ten-yearly charge thus the fraction is 9/40.

The exit charge rate is:

3.937% × 9/40 = 0.886%

Step 3:
The exit charge rate is applied to the value of the capital appointment thus:

£100,000 @ 0.886% = £886

The tax is payable out of the appointed funds: thus, each of the four grandchildren will receive £24,778 ((£100,000 – £886)/4). *Note:*

If the trustees agree to pay the exit charge the value attracting the exit charge would need to be grossed in the normal manner.

RELEVANT AND NON-RELEVANT PROPERTY

6.39 The legislation uses the expression 'relevant property' generally to mean property subject to the IHT relevant property trust regime of ten-year/exit charges. Importantly, where the relevant property regime applies, such title does not alter the nature of the trust itself which may for example still operate for income tax as an interest on possession. The expression is defined in *IHTA 1984, s 58* as settled property in which there is no qualifying (pre-March 2006) interest in possession. However, there are further exceptions, which are the standard favoured trusts, viz in particular:

- charities;
- pre-22 March 2006 A&M trusts (which, post 5 April 2008, provide for capital vesting at age 18);
- disabled person's trusts;
- qualifying employee trusts, maintenance funds for historic buildings, pension funds, etc; and
- excluded property trusts (see **6.10**).

Mixed property settlements

Focus

The initial value of excluded property, itself outside the relevant property regime, can still be brought into account in fixing the ten-year charge.

6.40 Prior to 18 November 2015, there was a further 'bear trap' which applied where a non-UK domiciliary set up a relevant property trust containing both UK and non-UK property. The non-UK property is clearly excluded property (namely, foreign *situs* property held within a settlement created at a time when the settlor was non-UK domiciled) and hence outside the scope of IHT. However, the existence of the non-UK (excluded) property (and, specifically, its value after commencement of the settlement) was until 18 November 2015 still taken into account as part of the settled property in computing the rate of IHT either on exit or at each ten-year anniversary.

The above principle applied in any case where, within the one settlement, there was both relevant and non-relevant property. The legislation operated to bring the non-relevant property into the deemed chargeable transfer to fix the rate, even though that non-relevant property did not itself attract tax.

This aggregation has now been removed for events taking place after 17 November 2015 (*Finance (No 2) Act 2015, s 11* and *Sch 1*).

There could be a situation where a discretionary settlement initially comprised 100% relevant property, but during the ten-year period a qualifying (pre-March 2006) interest in possession arose in part of the trust fund. For example, if trustees of a discretionary trust allow a beneficiary to occupy a residential property on terms and in circumstances which to all intents and purpose makes clear it is the beneficiary's permanent home, HMRC consider that exercise of power converts the settlement from discretionary into interest in possession (Statement of Practice SP 10/79 – although this has not yet been tested in the courts) and if, subsequently, the beneficiary leaves the residential property, the property reverts to being relevant property. The matter is handled by adjusting the rate on the ten-year anniversary and not the deemed chargeable transfer. If, by contrast, all the trust fund is appointed out of the settlement, there will have been an exit charge and no relevant property left to be taxed at the next ten-year anniversary.

With the 'alignment' of IHT for trusts on 22 March 2006, this rule ceases to have such an impact in calculating IHT. This is because (subject to the rules for 'transitional serial interests' – see **6.60**) an interest in possession created since 22 March 2006 out of a discretionary trust in circumstances described in the previous paragraph will be a non-qualifying interest in possession and so the capital concerned will still remain within the relevant property regime. If the property concerned is income-producing, there might be an income tax impact, since the special trust rates described at **4.32** would be dis-applied if there were an interest in possession, albeit non-qualifying for IHT purposes.

RELATED SETTLEMENTS

6.41 The concept of 'related settlement' is very pertinent to the 'relevant property' regime (*IHTA 1984, s 62*).

On commencement, a 'relevant property' settlement has a settlement related to it if the settlor is the same and the two settlements (with an exception for an exclusively charitable settlement or spousal IPDI) commence on the same day. However, where that related settlement is not itself a relevant property settlement its value will be disregarded for chargeable events taking place on or after 18 November 2015 (*F(No 2 A 2015, s 11* and *Sch 1*).

This is because, in calculating the settlor's cumulative total, transfers made on the day on which the 'relevant property' settlement commences are disregarded, and a related settlement could therefore be an avoidance device if not brought into account. Accordingly, the calculation of both the exit charge and the ten-year charge recognises related settlements, thereby negating the benefit that might be achieved should the settlor create a number of small settlements all on the same day to produce a lower overall rate of tax. Ten settlements each with £10,000 all sharing the same deemed cumulative total would obviously be preferable to one with £100,000, were it not for the aggregation of related settlements. To counter all this, the legislation requires the calculation of the chargeable value for both the ten-yearly and the exit charge to include related settlements made on the day of the 'relevant property' trust (see, for example, *IHTA 1984, s 66(4)(c)* for the ten-yearly charge).

In the past, a better alternative might have been to create a number of discretionary 'pilot' settlements all on consecutive days, and then on a single subsequent day to add the substantive trust property to each of the settlements. This, on the face of it, would avoid the rules; but, under the 'associated operations' provisions, it was always considered that there may be a risk that HMRC might treat a series of settlements made in such circumstances as a single transfer of value; however, HMRC were unsuccessful in the Court of Appeal in January 2003 in *IRC v Rysaffe Trustee Co (CI) Ltd* [2003] STC 536, where there was a series of five identical settlements made by each of two brothers on successive days with nominal initial trust funds, the substantive trust property being added to each of the settlements on a subsequent day. This landmark case decision provided good protection from HMRC attack but was further reinforced by inclusion of the same in an HMRC publication of illustrative situations not considered to be tax abusive and hence outside the reach of the general anti-abuse rule (GAAR). However, as stated in **6.31**, the effectiveness of the pilot trust route has been dented by anti-avoidance measures introduced by *F(No 2)A 2015* (see **6.31** above).

The disapplication of non-relevant property post 17 November 2015 will impact as follows:

Example 6.8—Comparison of position of non-relevant property exclusion pre/post *F(No 2)A 2015*

On 30 November 2005, Thomas, having made no previous chargeable lifetime transfers in the previous seven years, settled cash of £990,000 on A&M trust for his three grandchildren Albert, Betty and Carol which provided for income at age 25 and capital at trustee discretion. Under the pre-March 2006 rules that then prevailed this was a PET by Thomas hence no IHT fell due for payment and as he survived the PET by seven years the transfer achieved full exempt status.

On 1 March 2006, Albert became entitled to an interest in possession (IIP) in one-third of the fund. As that IIP was established before 22 March 2006 it is a qualifying IIP.

On 22 March 2006, neither Betty (aged 10) nor Carol (aged 12) had an established IIP and since the trust terms did not provide for capital entitlement at age 25, it did not qualify as an 18-25 trust under the *FA 2006* provisions.

On 6 April 2008, Betty and Carol's remaining two-thirds of the fund entered the relevant property regime.

On 30 November 2015, the trust reached its ten-year anniversary and Betty/Carol's two-third share was valued at £1.5 million.

(i) 30 November 2015 – ten-year charge pre-*F(No2)A 2015* enactment

	£
MV value of relevant property fund	1,500,000
Historic value of non-relevant property fund (Albert's one third IIP)	330,000
Hypothetical transfer	1,830,000
Nil rate band (2015/2016)	(325,000)
	1,505,000
£1,505,000 @ 20%	301,000
£301,000/£1,830,000 x100	16.448%
(16.448 × 30)%	4.934%
Ten-year charge:	
£1,500,000 @ 4.934% × (40 – 9*)/40	57,357

**Complete quarters before the trust became relevant property on 6 April 2008*

(ii) Ten-year charge post-enactment of *F(No 2)A 2015*

	£
MV value of relevant property fund	1,500,000
Nil rate band (2015/2016)	(325,000)
	1,175,000
£1,175,000 @ 20%	235,000
£235,000/£1,500,000 x100	15.667%
(15.667 × 30)%	4.700%
Ten-year charge:	
£1,500,000 @ 4.700% × (40 – 9*)/40	54, 637

**Complete quarters before the trust became relevant property on 6 April 2008*

Related settlement by will

> **Focus**
>
> An IPDI created in favour of a surviving spouse/civil partner, which converts to a relevant property trust on the latter's death, is treated as created by that spouse/civil partner and not the original spouse settlor – this can impact on the 'related property' settlement rule with potentially adverse effect (*IHTA 1984, s 80*).

6.42 Consider that a person under his will wishes to provide both a discretionary trust and some other settlement, eg a life interest trust which as an 'immediate post-death interest' (IPDI) falls outside the relevant property regime (*IHTA 1984, s 49A*): see **6.63**. As a will 'speaks from' death, the life interest trust would necessarily be related to the discretionary trust as both would be deemed created on the same day. Prior to 18 November 2015, a common practice to avoid the related settlement issue in such circumstances was as follows: on the day he makes his will the settlor makes a £10 'pilot' discretionary settlement and makes provision under his will that, on his death, funds (the substantive trust fund) will be added into that pre-existing settlement. As a settlement commences when property is first included in it, the discretionary trust will have commenced on the day it was made, ie on the day of making the will, not on the date of death when further funds are added to it, thereby avoiding the related settlement problem.

IHTA 1984, s 80, as amended by *FA 2006*, provides for an exception to the related settlement rules, where, as in this example, the other trust is an immediate post-death interest (or a disabled person's interest) for the settlor's surviving spouse. In other words, if, under his will, a husband leaves a nil rate band discretionary trust (A) and an IPDI of the residue to his wife (B), the related settlement provisions for recognition of the IPDI (prior to 18 November 2015) are disapplied in relation to that nil rate band discretionary trust (A). However, *s 80* goes on to provide that, if, on the later death of that surviving spouse, the IPDI converts to a discretionary trust (C), ie as directed under the husband's will, that follow-on trust (C) is treated as if made by that surviving spouse, ie the wife (the last life tenant of the IPDI). If, in this example, on the wife's death her will provides for a separate discretionary trust, that trust (at its initial value) will be regarded as related with that follow-on discretionary trust (B), which originally arose out of the husband's will: this will affect the computation of future ten-year anniversary and exit charges of that latter discretionary trust (C) but will still continue to have no impact on the initial nil rate band discretionary trust (A). All very confusing, but it is nonetheless critical that this outcome is fully understood.

FA 2015 amended the wording of *IHTA 1984, s 80,* replacing the term 'an interest in possession' with the term 'a qualifying interest in possession'. This slight tweaking ensures that where one party to a legally registered couple (spouse/civil partner) succeeds to a life interest to which their spouse/civil partner was previously entitled during the latter's lifetime, *IHTA 1984, s 80* will come into play (unless that successive interest was a TSI) (see **6.31** above).

The moral, with regard to will planning, is always to consider the wills of two spouses taken together when exploring the possible application of the related settlement rules.

ADDITIONS OF PROPERTY

6.43 The general advice to a settlor proposing to add property to an existing relevant property settlement is '*Don't*'. The reason is that, except where a transfer is exempt, eg within the annual £3,000 exemption or covered by the gifts out of income rule, there is a recalculation of the settlor's deemed cumulative total in any case where the addition by the settlor increases the settled capital (*IHTA 1984, s 67*). This recalculation means that, if the settlor's cumulative seven-year chargeable gifts total counting back from the period immediately before the addition is greater than his seven-year total immediately before creation of the settlement, the former (greater) figure is used in subsequent calculations of the ten-year charge.

For example, if a settlor takes out a life policy on his own life, settles the benefit on discretionary trusts and continues to pay the premiums, the payment of each premium will be an addition to the settlement unless the premiums fall within say the normal expenditure out of income exemption or the annual £3,000 exemption.

It should be noted that:

- There is a *de minimis* rule for transfers that are not primarily intended to increase the value of the settled property and do not in fact increase it by more than 5%.
- If on a person's death, his will adds property to an existing discretionary settlement, the addition is treated as having been made on the date of the death.

As in life, so in death, the advice must be generally not to add property to an existing discretionary settlement unless it is absolutely clear that there are no adverse effects, viz because the settlor's cumulative total before the addition is no greater than it was before the date of the original settlement.

Example 6.9—Monty's Settlement (3): effect of addition of property on ten-year charge

Referring once again to Monty's A&M settlement (No 1) (see Example 6.6 at **6.34**), consider that rather than making the £50,000 capital distribution on 1 January 2015, Monty had instead added another £50,000 to the trust two years earlier on 1 January 2013 and this same amount was reflected in the trust value of £800,000 as at the ten-year anniversary on 1 January 2016.

On 15 February 2006, Monty had made a second A&M settlement (No 2) for his nephews in the sum of £100,000 (having already used his annual exemptions for both 2005/06 and 2004/05). This was a PET (as made before the 22 March 2006 watershed). Monty died on 31 January 2013 – this was more than seven years after the creation of the No 1 A&M settlement but within seven years of the No 2 A&M settlement. That caused the PET to the A&M trust (No 2) on 15 February 2006 to fail (albeit covered by the nil rate band).

The later addition to the No. 1 A&M settlement made on 1 January 2013 is the trigger that causes the gifting history for seven-year period prior to creation to be compared to the gifting history in the seven years prior to the addition. The reclassification of the former PET made to the No 2 A&M settlement in February 2006 into a chargeable transfer means that the revised gifting history is now higher and must be substituted for the original gifting history. This means that the first ten-year charge for Monty's No 1 A&M settlement on 1 January 2016, must be recalculated.

Noting that the tax attributable to the addition of £50,000 is reduced by 28/40ths, as having been comprised in the settlement for only three years (*IHTA 1984, s 66(2)*), the ten-year charge due on 1 January 2016 is recalculated as follows:

No 1 A&M settlement	£	£
Trust fund (at January 2016)		800,000
Nil rate band (at event date) settlor's gift history (February 2006) Balance nil rate band	325,000 (100,000)	 (225,000)
		575,000
Tax at 20% lifetime rate		115,000
Effective rate (£115,000/£800,000 × 100)		14.375%
Ten-year rate (14.375 × 30)%		4.312%
Ten-yearly charge (£800,000 × 4.312%)		34,496
Less: £50,000 × 4.312% × 28/40		(1,509)
IHT payable		32,987

Furthermore, this rate of 4.312% will be the starting point for exit charges within the following ten years (subject to the increased nil rate band substitution mentioned at **6.38**). Indeed, on any future calculation of tax within the trust, it will always be Monty's cumulative total before he made the addition which will be taken into account.

PROPERTY CHANGING CHARACTER

6.44 The possibility that relevant property in the settlement at a ten-year anniversary might not have been relevant property throughout the preceding ten years is taken into account in reducing the rate of tax (see **6.39**).

In the past, this often gave rise to double counting because any value subject to an exit charge is also added into the deemed cumulative total. This would typically happen if there had been a life interest (which was not relevant property, ie pre March 2006) in part of the property for part of the ten-year period. This would have triggered an exit charge and, yet, if the property was still in the settlement and had become relevant property at the ten-year anniversary, it would form part of the deemed chargeable transfer.

To meet this problem, the deemed cumulative total is reduced by the lesser of two figures:

- the amount subject to the exit charge; and
- the value included for that property for the deemed chargeable transfer (ie the value immediately before the ten-year anniversary of the property which for a time had been subject to a life interest).

Example 6.10— The Harris discretionary trust: property changing character

On 1 January 2006, the Harris Discretionary Trust was created with initial capital of £200,000 – the settlor had made £20,000 cumulative lifetime transfers in the previous seven years.

On 15 March 2006, certain funds were appointed to Charles for life, with reversion to the main trusts of the settlement, valued at £100,000.

On 1 January 2012, Charles died and the property reverted back to discretionary trust.

On 1 January 2016, the Trust property is valued as follows:

The previously appointed funds	£240,000
Other assets	£150,000
Total	£390,000

The deemed chargeable transfer in calculating the ten-year charge is calculated as follows:

	£	£
Trust value (January 2016)		390,000
Amount subject to exit charge	100,000	
Adjustment: the lesser of £100,000 (amount subject to exit charge) and £240,000 (value of appointed fund)	(100,000)	
Deemed cumulative total		Nil
Total		390,000

PROPERTY MOVING BETWEEN SETTLEMENTS

6.45 It might be considered that moving property between settlements could:

- avoid or defer a ten-year anniversary; or
- benefit from a lower rate applying to one settlement rather than another,

The ten-year/exit rate calculation includes all relevant property (and non-relevant property prior to 18 November 2015) within a particular settlement (see **6.39** and **6.40**), thus no protection is needed for HMRC if the movement is within the settlement, eg an appointment to a sub-trust. The problem occurs when property leaves one settlement and enters another, and there could be CGT to consider at that point (see **9.5**), although there would not be a problem with sterling cash.

Although the tax at stake is unlikely to be substantial, the legislation contained in *IHTA 1984, s 81* does provide some protection for HMRC since, for purposes of the ten-year charge, the property that has moved is nonetheless treated as remaining within the first settlement.

Example 6.11—Mike's will trusts: property moving between settlements

Mike died on 1 January 2011. He left an amount equal to the nil rate band to be shared equally by his two adult children, with the remainder of his estate left on IPDI trust terms to his wife June, passing on her death to the two adult children (the remaindermen) absolutely.

The latter anticipate receiving £300,000 each on their mother's death and re-settle their reversionary interests (excluded property) on (settlor and spouse excluded) discretionary trusts while their mother, June, is still alive. They incorrectly assume that this would create a nil rate band settlement made by each of them. However, the effect of *s 81* is to treat the settled property of the new 'trusts' (£600,000) as remaining within the original settlement (and not two fresh settlements) for purposes of the relevant property regime whilst future ten year anniversary charges will be by reference to Mike's date of death.

The *s 81* rule would not have applied had the children waited for June's death and settled their inheritances at that point (outside a deed of variation), since the property concerned would have belonged to each of them outright and would not have been subject to trust.

RELEVANT PROPERTY TRUST PLANNING POINTS

6.46 The moral in advising on making a lifetime relevant property settlement is to ensure that the settlor always has as 'clean' a chargeable gifts history as possible.

Further, before 22 March 2006, if a settlor was minded to make both a PET (eg creation of an A&M settlement) and a chargeable transfer (eg creation of a discretionary settlement) at the same time, the traditional advice given was to make the chargeable transfer first. This was to protect against the possibility that he might die within seven years thereof, thus making the PET chargeable, which would therefore form part of his gifts history.

There is a subsidiary point in relation to allocation of the annual exemption: the annual £3,000 exemption is given against the gifts according to the order in which they are made during the tax year (see **3.18**). Thus, the £3,000 annual exemption could be 'wasted' if a PET were made before a chargeable transfer and the PET subsequently became exempt through the settlor's survival for seven years.

Example 6.12— George's trusts: order of gifts (pre 22 March 2006)

In December 2005, George, being well off and generously disposed towards his family, wanted to make both an A&M Trust for his grandchildren and a discretionary Trust for a wider class of beneficiaries – gifting £500,000 to each Trust.

He was advised to make the discretionary settlement at least one day before the A&M settlement:

- to get the benefit of the current year's and the previous year's annual £3,000 exemptions; and
- so that, if he died within seven years, the consequential chargeable transfer on making the A&M trust does not have to be taken into account in calculating the tax both on making and within the discretionary settlement.

A&M TRUSTS (MADE BEFORE 22 MARCH 2006)

Maintaining the s 71 conditions

The s 71 conditions

6.47 It has already been noted (see **2.7**) that an A&M trust was a 'privileged' type of discretionary trust introduced in 1976, albeit its favoured tax status was brought to an end on 22 March 2006 (subject to transitional rules for such trusts in being at that date). Whilst a *lifetime* trust incorporating the old-style A&M hallmark can still be made post 21 March 2006, it will simply be regarded as a 'relevant property' trust going forward. The aim behind this original A&M trust category was to give preferential tax treatment where the beneficiaries were all children or grandchildren of a particular family, ie with no possibility of benefiting anyone outside those categories so long as the A&M regime lasted. Hence, it is better to think in terms of A&M trusts as being not so much a type of settlement but more a particular IHT favoured regime. This is because, when or to the extent that the regime ends, if the settlement continues, it will then become some other type of settlement, typically an interest in possession trust.

The conditions that had to be satisfied were set out in *IHTA 1984, s 71* and fell into two parts. The first set of conditions was:

- at any time, that is when the settlement was tested, eg when there would otherwise be an exit charge, there was no interest in possession;
- the income from the settlement was to be accumulated, insofar as not paid out for the maintenance, education or benefit of the beneficiary; and
- one or more beneficiaries *must* become entitled to the trust fund, or to an interest in possession in it before attaining a specified age which must not exceed 25 years.

The second set of conditions was, *either*:

- not more than 25 years have passed since the settlement was created or, if it has been some other kind of settlement and has been converted into an A&M, not more than 25 years have passed since it became such a settlement (see **6.48–6.50** for the fixed charge trap following 15 April 2001); *or*

- rather more commonly, all the persons who are or have been beneficiaries are, or were, grandchildren of a common grandparent (note that for this purpose children includes step-children and adopted children). Where a grandchild has died before attaining an interest in income or capital then his children, widows or widowers may take his place as beneficiaries.

If there was any possibility of either set of conditions being breached, the settlement would not have A&M status and would therefore be treated as an ordinary discretionary trust within the relevant property regime of exit and ten-yearly charges. The important point, obviously, was to ensure that the *s 71* conditions were maintained.

Example 6.13—The Murray A&M Trust (2): later beneficiaries

Looking back to **Example 6.2** at **6.3**, when Adrian and Belinda made their A&M trust (the Murray Trust) for their children on 1 January 2001, they had just two children, Cerys, then aged five and Tom, aged two. Edward was born on 1 January 2005.

For the first five years of the settlement, there were two beneficiaries and therefore two prospective shares in capital (and income). The word 'prospective' is used because those shares could be defeated by subsequent appointment of the trustees.

Insofar as income is not paid out, it must be accumulated, that is, added to capital. However, it would be helpful for the accumulations to be shown separately in the accounts as, in particular, the trust deed gives power to the trustees to pay out accumulations of a previous year as if they were income of a current year.

The income for each of the first three years was £6,000 and, in the absence of any payments of income (given the parental settlement rules: see **4.30–4.31**), each of Cerys and Tom had an accumulations account of £3,000 per annum.

Once Edward was born, there were three prospective shares and, therefore, income from that moment on must be divided into three, ie £2,000 per annum. However, this will not defeat the existing shares in the accumulations already built up for Cerys and Tom.

(see Example 2.2 at **2.12** which summarises the options for A&M trustees on or before 5 April 2008).

The 25-year trap

6.48 Most settlements will satisfy the *s 71* conditions by having all the beneficiaries restricted to children of a common parent or a common grandparent. However, as explained in **6.47**, there is an alternative, viz that no more than 25 years have elapsed since the commencement of the settlement. The '25-year trap' is that, if an A&M settlement qualifies as such through the 25-year condition, but no action has been taken before those 25 years expire to remove the settlement from the A&M regime by awarding an interest in possession, an automatic charge to IHT arises. The first date on which such a charge could arise would have been 15 April 2001 (being 25 years on from 15 April 1976, the earliest date on which an A&M could have been created). It is quite clear that, although comparatively rare, there are or have been in existence a number of settlements which owe their qualifying status to the 25-year condition. The trap could arise even after 5 April 2008, with property within an A&M trust which has 18 as the age of absolute entitlement, which was made at least 25 years before but where there is no common parent or grandparent for the beneficiaries.

The tax charge

6.49 If a settlement is caught by the 25-year rule, tax is charged at rates that depend upon the number of quarters for which the settlement has lasted (ignoring periods before 13 March 1975) the rates are:

- 0.25% for each of the first 40 quarters, plus
- 0.20% for each of the next 40 quarters, plus
- 0.15% for each of the next 40 quarters, plus
- 0.10% for each of the next 40 quarters, plus
- 0.05% for each of the next 40 quarters.

A settlement that has lasted five years, has a tax rate of 5%. After ten years, it rises to 10%, after 20 years 18% and after 25 years 21%. The particular harshness of this rule is that, unlike the calculation of the exit charge for discretionary trusts, no allowance is made for the nil rate band.

The solution to the trap

6.50 The automatic IHT charge referred to above may be avoided if an interest is given to qualifying beneficiaries before the end of the 25-year period. This interest may be an interest in possession or an absolute interest. There would, of course, be no difficulty if all the beneficiaries had already received a right to income, eg on attaining the age of 18, because the settlement would then have ceased to qualify as an A&M settlement. Equally, there would be no problem if the permitted accumulation period had expired and therefore all the beneficiaries had obtained a right to receive all the income.

Provided the problem is spotted in advance, there is unlikely to be a difficulty as there will be powers in the settlement to end or vary it before the 25-year limit expires. In the absence of such a power, it may be necessary to consider an application to the court to vary the trust. If the amount of the IHT charge does not justify such an application it would be sensible to consult adult beneficiaries and carefully minute the decision of the trustees to show that the issue had been considered.

Example 6.14— Elsie's A&M Trust: the 25-year trap illustrated

On 30 January 1994, Elsie made an A&M settlement for the benefit of a nephew and unborn grandchildren on attaining the age of 25. Grandchildren were born in 1997, 2000 and 2001.

On 30 January 2019, the 25-year limit expired before any of the grandchildren had become entitled to the income. The settlement property was then worth £500,000 and the tax due as at 30 January 2019 is calculated as follows:

£500,000 × 21% = £105,000.

Had all of the beneficiaries become entitled to all the income before 30 January 2019, eg by reason of Elsie's death more than 21 years ago thereby capping the accumulation period, there would not have been a problem.

Transitional provisions from 22 March 2006

6.51 The effect of the trust reforms announced on 22 March 2006 on the 'inheritance tax alignment for trusts' is that no fresh A&M settlements qualifying for the favoured tax treatment can be created after 21 March 2006.

The regime for A&M trusts in being at 22 March 2006

Periods from 22 March 2006 to 5 April 2008

Focus

For the 'age 18-to-25' trust, the exit charge is calculated in the same manner as an exit charge occurring within the first ten years of the trust life, but with a simple age adjustment.

6.52 The ongoing treatment of the A&M is dependent on its terms and the entitlement of the beneficiaries as at 22 March 2006.

If an interest in possession arose post 21 March 2006 but before 6 April 2008, the 'relevant property' regime will apply only to the extent of the underlying capital of that share. Under the transitional provisions, if the terms of the A&M trust were changed (if necessary) before 6 April 2008 to provide that capital vests outright at or before age 18, the A&M regime will continue to apply throughout since the trust will be treated as if a BMT. Alternatively, if before 6 April 2008 the trust terms were changed so that capital arises at some point between 18 and 25, the A&M regime will not cease to apply in respect of a presumptive share of capital until the beneficiary attains 18, but there will then be an exit charge on vesting (calculated as illustrated in Example 6.15) – the trust will be treated as an 18-25 trust.

Example 6.15— Donald's A&M Settlement: exit from an age 18-to-25 trust

Donald made an A&M settlement for his grandchildren on 1 January 1995. Under the terms of the settlement there was a direction to accumulate income for 21 years (now therefore expired) with the children becoming entitled to income at age 18 and capital deferred broadly until they attained age 40, with wide powers of advancement of capital before that age. Before 6 April 2008, the terms of the trust were changed to become compliant with *IHTA 1984*, *s 71D* such that it fell within the category of an 18-to-25 trust.

Donald has three grandchildren: Alice, Betsy and Charles. Each of Alice and Betsy is in line for substantial inheritances from their godparents, and so before either attained an interest in possession under the settlement they were effectively excluded, leaving Charles as the sole prospective beneficiary. Charles became 18 on 1 January 2013 and acquired a (non-qualifying) interest on possession on that date.

In the seven years before he made the settlement, Donald had cumulative chargeable transfers of £100,000 and there were no related settlements. The initial value of the settlement was £200,000, its value at 6 April 2008 was £500,000 and its value when Charles becomes 25 on 1 January 2020 is estimated at £1 million.

The exit charge calculation on Charles's 25th birthday is as follows:

- The tax is calculated as: chargeable amount × relevant fraction × settlement rate (*s 71F(3)*).
- The 'chargeable amount' is £1 million (assuming that any tax is paid out of it and not out of any property remaining subject to *s 71D* trusts, in which case there would be grossing up (*s 71F(4)*)).

- Although the 'chargeable amount' is expressed as a bare value, HMRC have indicated that any available agricultural or business property relief will go to reduce the amount, the charge falling within *IHTA 1984, Pt III, Ch III*.
- The 'relevant fraction' is 30% × 28/40 (the number of complete successive quarters in the period and thus 0.21, expressed as a decimal (*s 71F(5)*).
- The 'settlement rate' is the effective rate found under *s 71F(7)–(9)* as follows:

	£	£
Deemed chargeable transfer (*s 71F(9)*)		£200,000
Nil rate band (at event date January 2020)	325,000	
Settlor's chargeable transfer total (*s 71F(8)(b)*)	(100,000)	
Balance of nil rate band		(225,000)
Deemed taxable amount		0
Settlement rate – 0/200,000		0

The exit charge is:

£1 million × 0.21 × 0% = £Nil

The regime on or after 6 April 2008

6.53 Subject to taking advantage of the two transitional rules mentioned at **6.52**, any property left within what was the A&M regime (thus providing for an interest in possession on or before age 25 but with capital at trustee discretion or at a date post age 25) now falls within the relevant property regime, that is with the system of ten-yearly and exit charges as described in **6.32–6.38**. As a consequence it will be necessary to ascertain the date on which the settlement originally commenced so as to identify the first ten-year anniversary which falls after 6 April 2008 and indeed to confirm the seven-year chargeable gifts history of the settlor up to the date of commencement, plus the existence of any related settlements on that day (but restricted to relevant property only post-17 November 2015) and any additional property since. This information may be hard to obtain in certain cases.

The regime introduced by *FA 2006* is applied below to Examples 6.16, 6.17 and 6.18.

Example 6.16—The Murray A&M Trust (3): the relevant property regime

(See **Example 6.13** at **6.47**) Given that no action was taken by the trustees before 6 April 2008, the Murray A&M trust made on 1 January 2001 entered the relevant property regime on that former date. The first ten-year anniversary arose on 1 January 2011 and a charge was levied on the value of the property comprised in the settlement at that date with the rate of tax calculated as stated in **6.32–6.35**. However, although one Trust was created, for IHT purposes each of Adrian and Belinda would have been deemed to create a settlement of their settled share and thus their respective seven-year cumulative total up to 31 December 2000 would need to have been ascertained.

It should be noted that the trust fund only entered the relevant property regime on 6 April 2008 and thus the ten-year charge would have been scaled back by 29/40 to exclude complete quarters when the property was not relevant property (ie 1 January 2001 to 31 March 2008 = 29).

Example 6.17—John's A&M Settlement: flexibility lost by the *FA 2006* regime

Hubert died in 1982, leaving his estate on IIP terms for wife Iris for life. On her death on 1 February 2006, the capital was divided equally between their children John and Anne, then aged 40 and 35 respectively. Anne was married, with two daughters; John was not then married though he anticipated he would do so and wished to provide for his future children.

John created an A&M settlement on 1 February 2006 for his nieces (Anne's children) and his future children, settling the assets which fell to him on his mother's death. John considered that because of the class gift, his later born children would automatically be added as beneficiaries. Assuming that none of the shares of his nieces had by then vested, the shares in the capital could be varied in favour entirely of John's own children. Even if this were to happen after an interest in possession had arisen to his nieces before 22 March 2006, there could be power in the settlement to take it away from them, thus causing them to make a PET of an absolute gift.

All this, of course, now operates subject to the *FA 2006* regime, described above.

Example 6.18— The Murray A&M Trust (4): business property relief to the rescue

(See Example 6.13 and Example 6.16 above) It can be seen that the fiscal luxury that Adrian and Belinda thought they had when making their A&M trust in 2001 was taken away from them on 6 April 2008.

Given the circumstances, namely the age of the children and the prospective inheritance of shares in the family company, Adrian and Belinda were unlikely to 'accept the carrot' of advancing the age of entitlement to capital at age 25; although it does at least seem that, had they done this and thus preserved freedom from the 'relevant property' regime, they could still have 'chopped and changed' prospective shares among their children up to 6 April 2008. It is more likely they considered it was simply too early to make a decision – and even age 25 is still perhaps too young to vest valuable assets. Happily in this case, they have the advantage of potential BPR at 100% which removes any IHT burden of the regime. It would of course be otherwise if the trust fund were comprised of quoted stocks and shares.

Wills and intestacies: bereaved minor trusts and 'age 18-to-25' trusts

6.54 If, at any time, the trust qualifies as a 'bereaved minor trust' under *IHTA 1984, s 71A*, it will remain outside the relevant property regime. In broad terms, the *s 71A* regime applies to property left under the will of a parent, step-parent or person with parental responsibility for a child who will become absolutely entitled by the age of 18, with any income or capital applied under that age only for the benefit of that child (though see the next paragraph). Under the 'age 18-to-25' regime introduced by *IHTA 1984, s 71D*, capital to which a person is presumptively entitled must vest on or before the age of 25 and the relevant property rules will apply to the capital in the trust between age 18 and the age of absolute entitlement will suffer an exit charge on that entitlement (see **6.51** and Example 6.15 for an illustration of how the rules work).

HMRC do allow some latitude in applying the strict statutory conditions for both bereaved minor trusts and 'age 18-to-25' trusts. In particular, a prospective share can be varied while the beneficiary is under the age of 18 or (with 'age 18-to- 25' trusts) 25, but the class of beneficiaries must be closed when the relevant trust comes into being. A power of advancement may be exercised to keep the property in trust beyond age 18 or 25, as appropriate, at which point the trust property will enter the relevant property regime.

INTEREST IN POSSESSION TRUSTS

The s 49 fiction for pre-22 March 2006 trusts and transitionally protected trusts

6.55 A person entitled to an interest in possession on (or before) 21 March 2006 is treated as beneficially entitled to the underlying property in the trust fund (*IHTA 1984, s 49(1)*). This is referred to as a 'qualifying' interest.

Therefore, for so long as a life tenant remains alive, and the interest in possession continues for their benefit, there is no chargeable event for IHT purposes. On the death of the life tenant, however, there will be a deemed transfer of value, which will be chargeable, subject to the spouse and charities exemptions. The value in the life interest trust is aggregated with the life tenant's free estate, and the combined total is subjected to IHT at the appropriate rate (the 'estate rate'). The trustees are liable for the IHT in respect of the trust fund and the executors for the tax on the free estate. Importantly, where the trust comprises a qualifying residential interest and that property is closely inherited on the death of the life tenant who last held the qualifying interest, the residence nil rate band is potentially in point – see *Inheritance Tax 2019/20* (Bloomsbury Professional) for more detail.

If the interest comes to an end during the lifetime of the life tenant (other than by outright advance to him), he will be treated as having made a transfer of value. This will be either:

- a PET if the capital is advanced to an individual or to trustees for a disabled person or (before 22 March 2006) passes on life interest or A&M trusts – and will become exempt if the life tenant survives for seven years; or
- a chargeable transfer by the life tenant if the capital becomes subject to discretionary trusts or (on or after 22 March 2006) is held on any form of continuing non-charitable trust (which is not a disabled trust and subject to the rules for transitionally protected trusts set out at **6.5896.62**).

Example 6.19—Victor: IHT due where both settled and free estate

Victor died on 1 January 2020 when the value of his qualifying interest in the family trust fund was £1.8 million – under the terms of the trust, the fund passed to Victor's children in equal shares. Victor's free estate (which does not include a qualifying residential interest for RNRB purposes) is £600,000 – there are no APR or BPR qualifying assets and the full nil rate band is available. Victor's will leaves two-thirds of his estate to his wife and one-third to his children.

The chargeable transfer on death, therefore, is:

	£
Free estate: one-third of £600,000 (two-thirds being spouse exempt)	200,000
Settled estate	1,800,000
Gross estate	2,000,000

Calculation of IHT:

Gross estate	2,000,000
Nil rate band	(325,000)
Chargeable estate	1,675,000
£1,675,000 @ 40%	670,000
Estate rate (£670,000/£2,000,000 × 100)	33.50%

IHT payable by the executors is therefore £200,000 × 33.50% = £67,000.

IHT payable by the trustees is £1,800,000 × 33.50% = £603,000.

Note: There is no RNRB as Victor did not have a qualifying residential interest.

Lifetime termination

6.56 There will be no positive IHT liability (although the first situation below may carry a reporting obligation) to the extent that:

- the trust fund consists of assets attracting APR or BPR at 100%;
- there is a capital advance by the trustees to the life tenant (ie technically from the deemed owner to himself) – *IHTA 1984, s 53(3)*;
- the termination is a PET, ie there is an advance of capital to one or more of the remaindermen and the life tenant survives for seven years post advance (*IHTA 1984, s 3A*);
- there is a transfer, whether during lifetime or on death, by the life tenant to his spouse – *IHTA 1984, s 53(4)*; or
- the life interest derives from an old estate where the trustees are entitled to the estate duty surviving spouse exemption and there is an advance of capital to the surviving spouse or life tenant. This assumes that under estate duty a person died before 13 November 1974 leaving a life interest in his will to his surviving spouse. Under estate duty, tax was paid on the first death with the spouse exemption

given on the death of the second provided that a life interest had come into being under the will of the first spouse to die. Both CTT and IHT have continued, on a transitional basis, this old estate duty relief (*IHTA 1984, Sch 6, para 2*).

Valuation

6.57 Where there is a notional chargeable transfer within a qualifying interest in possession trust on the death of the life tenant, the rule is quite straightforward (see **6.55**), in that IHT is calculated on the aggregated value of the settled property and the free estate.

What happens, however, where the qualifying interest in possession comes to an end during the life tenant's lifetime, but is a chargeable transfer, either because a discretionary trust (or, following 21 March 2006, other 'relevant property' trust) arises or the trust come to an end and the trust fund passes to someone other than the life tenant (ie remainderman) and the life tenant dies with seven years of that cessation?

The general IHT rule for valuing a transfer of value made during lifetime is on an 'estate before, less estate after' basis. That is, the value is taken of the individual's estate before the transfer and then again after the transfer – the difference is the amount of the transfer of value. Note that this is not necessarily the same as the value of that received by the donee.

For example, consider shares in an investment company (such that BPR is not in point) where the value of the shareholding depends upon the size of the shareholding and thus the extent to which they can carry votes. The critical threshold will be the 51% threshold carrying voting control, although there will be other significant thresholds of 90% and 75%, 25% and 10%, all based on company law principles. A gift of 2% out of a 51% shareholding will put the recipient in possession of a relatively small 2% holding, though its significance on the estate of the donor may be very great, depending on the circumstances.

Originally, HMRC took the view that this 'estate before, less estate after' principle applied in relation to qualifying life interest trusts where the interest came to an end during the lifetime of the beneficiary. HMRC changed their view in March 1990 and agreed that the settled property could be valued in isolation, subject always to the application of the associated operations provisions of *IHTA 1984, s 268*.

More recently, however, it appears that HMRC may have reverted to their pre-1990 stance, given the following sentence from HMRC Inheritance Tax Manual at IHTM16063: 'The effect of IHTA 84/S49 is that for all practical IHT purposes – and especially on valuation matters – the person having the interest in possession is treated as the absolute owner of the property'.

Planning points

Uses of life interest trusts

6.58 The *FA 2006* 'alignment of IHT for trusts' substantially put paid to planning advantages of lifetime interest in possession trusts: see, for example, **6.57** of the 2008/09 edition of this book which summarises six possibilities for trusts made before 22 March 2006, albeit subject to the TSI regime (see **6.60**).

For the future, however, there are distinct advantages of an 'immediate post-death interest' (IPDI) structure as against outright gifts (rather than relevant property trusts) in wills, which is the subject of Example 6.21.

Example 6.20—Peter's estate: pre-22 March 2006 position

Peter and Polly own Grey Gables (their matrimonial home) in equal shares. Grey Gables is worth £450,000 at the time of Peter's death in January 2006. In that pre-transferable nil rate band era, it was IHT effective for Peter to utilise his nil rate band, but he had no suitable assets other than his share in Grey Gables. He also wanted to ensure Polly's security of tenure and that seems to call for a trust, rather than an outright gift to the children.

If Peter were to make a gift to the children on interest in possession trusts, that would give them a right to live in Grey Gables, which is fine as the family get on and each of the children has a home elsewhere. However, if the trustees and Polly were to sell Grey Gables at a gain, the trustees' share would be subject to CGT without the benefit of principal private residence relief which would be afforded to Polly on her owned 50% share. The gain could be made free of tax if a beneficiary entitled under the settlement occupied the property but, realistically, this is unlikely to happen.

Peter made chargeable transfers of £235,000 in the seven years before he died. What he might have been recommended to do, therefore, is under his will create a life interest trust of his 50% share in Grey Gables, with 90% going to Polly (£202,500) and 10% to his two children (£22,500): the value of the chargeable transfers made in the seven years before death of £235,000, plus £22,500 representing the 10% life interest to the children, is still within the 2005/06 nil rate band of £275,000. After six months, the trustees could use their powers under the trust to reduce Polly's share to 10%, increasing the children's share to 90%. For CGT purposes, the situation would still be protected by principal private residence relief, as the actual share of the occupying beneficiary is immaterial. Polly continues to live in the house without paying any compensation, and the children will become entitled to capital on her ultimate death.

However, assuming that Polly survives the percentage change in shares by at least seven years, the value of 80% of a half share in the house will have left her estate without any IHT implications. There will be no reservation of benefit, as the PET was not caused by a disposition made by her.

Example 6.21—Peter's estate: post-21 March 2006 position

Assume the same facts of Example 6.20 above, except that all transactions take place on or after 22 March 2006.

The tax effect is different in one major respect: the analysis in the final paragraph no longer holds good as, under *FA 2006, s 102ZA*, the exercise by the trustees of their power of appointment is treated as a gift by the widow and, as she continues to occupy Grey Gables, a gift with reservation of benefit chargeable on her death assuming that she continues to occupy the property. The interest to Polly under the will must be treated as an 'immediate post-death interest' (see **6.62**) treated under *IHTA 1984, s 49A* as if Polly were entitled to the underlying capital; no change there, therefore.

To avoid the problem presented by *FA 1986, s 102ZA*, Peter's will trust should be a discretionary structure. Even so, it is essential that Polly does not acquire an interest in possession in that discretionary will trust within two years after the death. This is because an immediate post-death interest will then be 'read back' into the will under *IHTA 1984, s 144(3)*, so destroying the planning. If, therefore, it is possible to ensure a genuinely discretionary trust established by Peter's will, the *s 102ZA* point will not cause a problem, even if a right to income constituting an interest in possession were to arise more than 24 months after Peter's death.

Transitional rules for trusts in being at 22 March 2006

6.59 The *s 49(1)* 'fiction', whereby the underlying trust capital is treated as beneficially owned by the life tenant, is preserved for established qualifying interests in possession as at 22 March 2006, so long as that interest is not a 'bereaved minors trust' under *IHTA 1984, s 71A* (see **6.54**). But what happens when that interest comes to an end in favour of another?

If this occurs during the life tenant's lifetime, it will be treated as a PET by the life tenant (and hence subject to the seven-year survival rule) but only if:

- the capital passes to an individual outright;
- it is a gift to a disabled person's trust (*IHTA 1984, s 3A(1A)*); or it is followed by a transitional serial interest (TSI) – see **6.60**.

Otherwise, it will be treated as a chargeable transfer made by the life tenant, ie creating a 'relevant property' trust (see **3.17**), and the regime of ten-year and exit charges (see **6.32–6.38**) will apply.

If the qualifying interest comes to an end on the life tenant's death, there will be a transfer of value aggregated with the life tenant's free estate (see Example 6.19) and it will be exempt only if the capital passes absolutely to a surviving spouse or to a charitable trust. That is, subject to the next sentence, there will be a chargeable transfer (as indeed before 22 March 2006) if the interest passes to any other beneficiary absolutely or to a continuing trust (except for a disabled person). While, generally, the 'relevant property' provisions (see **6.32–6.38**) apply to a continuing trust, there is a special rule for TSIs (see **6.60**).

Transitional serial interests ('TSIs')

6.60 There are three types of category of trusts where the *IHTA 1984, s 49(1)* 'fiction' continues to apply. These require a 'prior interest in possession' to exist at 22 March 2006 and:

- *First*, for that interest to come to an end (whether by lifetime termination or in death) before 6 October 2008 and to be replaced by a 'current interest'. *IHTA 1984, s 49C* treats that current interest as if in being at 22 March 2006.
- *Secondly*, if the prior interest comes to an end on the death of a spouse after 5 October 2008 and is replaced by an interest in possession for the surviving spouse, that also is a TSI (*IHTA 1984, s 49D*). This rule does not apply either to a bereaved minor's trust or to a disabled person's trust (see **2.10**).
- *Thirdly*, contracts of life insurance written under life interest trusts before 22 March 2006 also have their own TSI regime in *IHTA 1984, s 49E*. The creation of a TSI is a PET under *IHTA 1984, s 3A*. The end of the transitional period for the first TSIs described above was originally 5 April 2008, though *FA 2008* extended it by six months to 5 October 2008.

In applying the TSI regime, it is critical to know what an interest in possession is and when a new one arises (even if for the same beneficiary). In broad terms, HMRC accept that where a beneficiary's interest arises under the terms of the settlement (and not from the exercise of the trustees' powers), the same interest in possession continues, even though it might arise under a different provision. For example, at 22 March 2006, X had an interest in possession by reason of *Trustee Act 1925, s 31* (having attained age 18) and then becomes entitled to an express interest in possession on attaining the age of 25. This is the same interest, relevant to two issues: first, whether a TSI can be created before 6 April 2008 once X becomes 25 before that date and, secondly, where X reaches 25 after 5 April 2008, whether the *IHTA 1984, s 49(1)* fiction continues to apply at that point and the trust property will not enter the relevant property regime. The answer to both is affirmative. For various different scenarios on this theme and HMRC's answers to certain other questions (released on 29 May 2007.

The fourth exchange of correspondence between STEP/CIOT and HMRC was released in late November 2007 and still constitutes good practice today. This concerned the application to the TSI regime of the principle under HMRC's Statement of Practice SP10/79, under which the exercise of a power by trustees of a discretionary settlement in relation to a dwelling house can give rise to an interest in possession.

Example 6.22— Edwin's IIP: TSI illustration

Edwin was the life tenant of an interest in possession trust made by his father in 1998. On 31 March 2008, the trustees used the wide powers of appointment to replace Edwin's qualifying interest in possession with a successive interest in favour of Edwin's daughter Frieda, aged 13.

On exercise of the power of appointment, Edwin ceased to be treated under *s 49(1)* as beneficially owning the trust fund. Under *FA 2006, Sch 20, para 9*, amending *IHTA 1984, s 3A*, Edwin was treated as having made a PET which became fully exempt on his survival by seven years.

Frieda's interest is a TSI within *IHTA 1984, s 49C* and she is treated as entitled to the underlying capital for IHT purposes. The IHT implications on termination of that interest are set out at **6.62**.

For CGT purposes, there is no disposal.

For income tax purposes, the income arising to Frieda does not come from a 'parental settlement' (namely one created by a parent) as such for purposes of the anti-avoidance income tax rule (see **4.30–4.31**) and so the income is assessed on Frieda alone for tax purposes.

Post-21 March 2006 interests

6.61 Apart from the continuing special treatment given to TSIs (see **6.60**), gifts to interest in possession trusts arising on or after 22 March 2006 (being 'non estate' interests in possession – IPDIs) no longer qualify as PETs. This means that, on creation, there will be a chargeable transfer (see **3.17–3.20**) whatever the type of trust (except for a disabled person – see **2.10**), including one where the settlor creates a life interest for himself or his spouse or indeed where, following a life interest, there is a successive life interest for the beneficiary's spouse.

Termination of life interest following 21 March 2006 in favour of continuing non-TSI trusts

6.62 The life tenant will be treated as making a chargeable transfer. If the value is within his nil rate band (£325,000 for 2019/20 and fixed at that level until 5 April 2021), there will be no IHT to pay, although form IHT 100 should be submitted by the beneficiary (see **3.20**). To the extent that the transfer of value exceeds his nil rate band, IHT will be payable at the lifetime rate of 20%, subject to a top up charge to 40% in the event of his death within seven years.

Should the trust already be within the chargeable transfer regime prior to the new life interest (as either a discretionary trust or a life interest created on or after 22 March 2006, which is not a TSI or a disabled trust), the trust will already be within the 'relevant property' regime and there will be no immediate IHT implications, given that no new trust is created for IHT purposes (see **6.45**).

Will trusts

6.63 An interest in possession may be created under a will and, if it meets the criteria of an 'immediate post-death interest' (IPDI) within *IHTA 1984, s 49A* (as almost every interest in possession created on death will be), the underlying capital will be treated as part of the life tenant's estate under *IHTA 1984, s 49* so long as it is neither a bereaved minor's trust (see **6.54**) nor a disabled person's interest (see **2.10**). If the IPDI comes to an end during the lifetime of the beneficiary in favour of another, tax is charged as if he had made a transfer of value, which will be a PET only if it passes to an individual outright or creates a disabled person's interest or (given a termination before 6 April 2008) a TSI (see **6.60**). Otherwise, if successive trusts arise, the life tenant will be treated as making a chargeable transfer, even if the transferee is the life tenant's spouse or civil partner.

Uses of IPDIs

6.64 In drafting wills, especially in the context of the transferable nil rate band under *IHTA 1984, s 8A*, a gift to a surviving spouse/civil partner by way of IPDI has the same IHT impact as an outright gift, thus it will attract the spousal exemption. Of course, it is important to note that an IPDI is not restricted to the spouse/civil partner but can also be for the benefit of any other beneficiary, perhaps in place of an outright gift, though this will be a chargeable transfer. An outright gift structure has the obvious advantages of simplicity. However, among some advantages of an IPDI, apart obviously from providing some form of security for the capital, are the following:

(1) The most obvious use is in the case of a second (or subsequent) marriage where the first to die wishes for the capital to pass to the children of the first marriage following the death of the surviving spouse life tenant. If the trustees terminate the IPDI during the surviving spouse's lifetime, with a view to creating a deemed PET intended to achieve exemption on the latter's survival for seven years but which condition is not met (so making the gift chargeable), the survivor's stepchildren will have first call on her nil rate band at the expense perhaps of her own children by her first marriage. The point needs to be appreciated and covered perhaps by a discretionary legacy to make adjustments as between the two sets of stepchildren/children in terms of the burden of IHT.

(2) If, following the first death, the survivor is no longer in a position (eg through age) to decide on making an absolute gift by way of a PET, it might be prudent to give the discretion to the trustees by way of termination of an IPDI, no doubt in conjunction with a letter of wishes.

(3) In the context of the transferable nil rate band, an IPDI structure avoids the risk of the surviving spouse distributing chattels (and perhaps other property) within two years after the death in pursuance of a letter of wishes, so triggering a chargeable transfer by the deceased, following *IHTA 1984, s 143*. The trustees of an IPDI can transfer the chattels, etc to the intended individuals, so terminating the IPDI and constituting a PET by the surviving spouse to that extent.

(4) With an IPDI, it is much easier to control the level of income for the purposes of means-tested benefits, and with protection in the context of care home fees.

(5) An IPDI might afford protection for the survivor from coercion or emotional pressure by the children, in appropriate circumstances.

(6) At least to the extent of the trust fund, an IPDI avoids the need for a lasting power of attorney for free assets or, indeed, issues (notoriously complex and time-consuming and delaying) over application to the Court of Protection, in appropriate circumstances.

(7) An IPDI might be preferable where there is a real risk of the survivor's insolvency.

Chapter 7

Trusts for disabled persons and vulnerable beneficiaries

SIGNPOSTS

- **IHT treatment of disabled person's interest trusts ('DPIs')** – Including *FA 2006* changes which added a further three types of trust which qualify as DPIs (see **7.2–7.6**).
- **IHT treatment of bereaved minor trusts ('BMTs')** – BMTs were introduced by *FA 2006* to replace A&M settlements (see **7.7**).
- **IHT treatment of 18-to-25 trusts** – This type of trust suffers IHT exit charges but is not subject to IHT ten-year charges (see **7.8**).
- **Income and capital requirements for trusts with vulnerable beneficiaries** – *Finance Act 2013* restricts how much income and capital can be advanced to beneficiaries other than the vulnerable beneficiary (see **7.9**).
- **Income tax and capital gains tax** – Special tax treatment for trusts for vulnerable beneficiaries (see **7.10**).
- **Calculating the relief** – A worked example (**7.11**).

BACKGROUND

7.1 Following a series of changes in *Finance Act 2006*, *Finance Act 2013* and *Finance Act 2014*, the tax treatment of disabled person's interest trusts ('DPIs') and vulnerable beneficiaries' trusts, which include bereaved minor trusts ('BMTs') and 18-to-25 trusts, is confusing and complex.

Finance Act 2005 introduced a special income tax and CGT regime for trusts for vulnerable beneficiaries. For income tax and capital gains tax, the definition of a 'vulnerable beneficiary' includes BMTs and DPIs; 18-to-25 trusts are treated differently.

The IHT treatment for DPIs, BMTs and 18-to-25 trusts is found in different parts of *IHTA 1984*:

- *IHTA 1984, ss 89, 89A* and *89B* determine the inheritance tax treatment of DPIs (see **7.2** to **7.6**);
- *IHTA 1984, ss 71A, 71B* and *71C* deal with BMTs (see **7.7**); and
- *IHTA 1984, s 71D* applies to 18-to-25 trusts (see **7.8**).

Finance Act 2013 made amendments to the various pieces of legislation to harmonise the IHT, income tax and CGT treatment of trusts for vulnerable beneficiaries.

Finance Act 2014 introduced capital gains tax-free uplift on death to all DPIs with underlying interests in possession under *TCGA 1992, s 72* for deaths on or after 5 December 2013.

INHERITANCE TAX

Original disabled person's interest (IHTA 1984, s 89)

7.2 The DPI is defined in *IHTA 1984, s 89*, which applies to settled property transferred into a settlement after 9 March 1981 and held on trusts under which, during the life of a disabled person, no interest in possession in the settled property subsists.

> For IHT purposes the disabled beneficiary is treated as beneficially entitled to an interest in possession in the settled property, which means that the value of the disabled trust will be aggregated with his estate on death.
>
> Until 6 April 2013 a disabled person was defined as someone who was–
>
> (a) incapable, by reason of mental disorder within the meaning of the Mental Health Act 1983, of administering his property or managing his affairs, or
>
> (b) in receipt of an attendance allowance, or
>
> (c) in receipt of a disability living allowance.
>
> This definition was amended by *Finance Act 2013* – see **7.6** below.

Until 22 March 2006, only discretionary trusts qualified as DPIs. Such trusts can be created by will or during the settlor's lifetime. Following *Finance Act 2006* there are now four types of DPIs under *s 89*.

Finance Act 2006 changes

7.3 *Finance Act 2006* introduced three further types of DPIs:

- *IHTA 1984, s 89A* – Self-settlement on discretionary trust on or after 22 March 2006 by person with a condition expected to lead to a disability;

- *IHTA 1984, s 89B(1)(c)* – DPI on interest in possession trust created by anyone during the lifetime of a settlor on or after 22 March 2006 for the benefit of a disabled person; and
- *IHTA 1984, s 89B(1)(d)* – Self-settlement on interest in possession trust on or after 22 March 2006 by person with a condition expected to lead to a disability.

Therefore, following *FA 2006*, there are four different DPIs. Transfers into pre-22 March 2006 trusts and *s 89B(1)(c)* trusts are treated as potentially exempt transfers (PET) for IHT purposes rather than chargeable transfers. Self-settlements into the other two trusts are not chargeable transfers for IHT purposes, as the trust property remains within the settlor's estate. These four types of trusts therefore are not relevant property trusts and do not suffer ten-yearly charges or exit charges for IHT.

Following *IHTA 1984, s 49(1)* the disabled person will be deemed to be the beneficial owner of the trust fund, with the result that the trust fund will be aggregated with the disabled person's other assets on death.

Following changes introduced by *FA 2014*, the capital gains tax-free uplift on death applies to DPIs with underlying interests in possession under *TCGA 1992, s 72* for deaths on or after 5 December 2013.

Self-settlement by person with a condition expected to lead to a disability (IHTA 1984, s 89A)

7.4 This type of trust was introduced to permit persons to provide for themselves in anticipation of a future disability. This type of trust is useful when someone suffers from a degenerative illness.

The legislation (in *s 89A*) defines this type of DPI as follows:

> '(1) This section applies to property transferred by a person ("A") into settlement on or after 22 March 2006 if–
>
> (a) A was beneficially entitled to the property immediately before transferring it into settlement,
>
> (b) A satisfies the Commissioners for Her Majesty's Revenue and Customs that, when the property was transferred into settlement, A had a condition that it was at that time reasonable to expect would have such effects on A as to lead to A becoming–
>
> (i) a person falling within section 89(4)(a) above,
>
> (ii) in receipt of an attendance allowance mentioned in section 89(4)(b) above, or
>
> (iii) in receipt of a disability living allowance mentioned in section 89(4)(c) above by virtue of entitlement to the care component at the highest or middle rate, and

(c) the property is held on trusts–

(i) under which, during the life of A, no interest in possession in the settled property subsists, and

(ii) which secure that Conditions 1 and 2 are met.

(2) Condition 1 is that if any of the settled property is applied during A's life for the benefit of a beneficiary, it is applied for the benefit of A.

(3) Condition 2 is that any power to bring the trusts mentioned in subsection (1)(c) above to an end during A's life is such that, in the event of the power being exercised during A's life, either–

(a) A or another person will, on the trusts being brought to an end, be absolutely entitled to the settled property, or

(b) on the trusts being brought to an end, a disabled person's interest within section 89B(1)(a) or (c) below will subsist in the settled property.

(4) If this section applies to settled property transferred into settlement by a person, the person shall be treated as beneficially entitled to an interest in possession in the settled property.'

This type of DPI has to be a lifetime discretionary trust in expectation of the settlor's disability and be for his/her own benefit, provided certain conditions are complied with:

- if any capital is distributed during the settlor's lifetime, it will be distributed for the settlor's benefit, or
- if the trust is brought to an end during the settlor's lifetime, the settlor is entitled to the trust fund, or someone else is entitled to the trust fund, so that it will form their estate for IHT purposes.

Alternatively, the settlement can be brought to an end in favour of another DPI's interest.

Extension of DPIs (IHTA 1984, s 89B)

7.5 *IHTA 1984, s 89B* extends *ss 89* and *89A* to include interest in possessions to qualify as DPIs, as follows:

'(1) In this Act "disabled person's interest" means–

(a) an interest in possession to which a person is under section 89(2) above treated as beneficially entitled,

(b) an interest in possession to which a person is under section 89A(4) above treated as beneficially entitled,

(c) an interest in possession in settled property (other than an interest within paragraph (a) or (b) above) to which a disabled person becomes beneficially entitled on or after 22 March 2006, or

(d) an interest in possession in settled property (other than an interest within paragraph (a) or (b) above) to which a person ("A") is beneficially entitled if–

(i) A is the settlor,

(ii) A was beneficially entitled to the property immediately before transferring it into settlement,

(iii) A satisfies Her Majesty's Commissioners for Revenue and Customs as mentioned in section 89A(1)(b) above,

(iv) the settled property was transferred into settlement on or after 22 March 2006, and

(v) the trusts on which the settled property is held secure that, if any of the settled property is applied during A's life for the benefit of a beneficiary, it is applied for the benefit of A.'

Section 89B(1)(c) applies to interest in possession trusts created during the settlor's lifetime for the benefit of a disabled person. However, this type of trust cannot be created on death, as the provisions in *IHTA 1984, s 49A*, which create immediate post-death interests, take priority.

Section 89B(1)(d) is similar to s *89A*, in that it allows for self-settlement in expectation of a disability, but on interest in possession trusts rather than on discretionary trusts. Again, this type of trust will be outside the relevant property regime for IHT.

DPIs created on or in addition to existing DPIs after 8 April 2013

7.6 *Finance Act 2013, s 216* and *Sch 44* made the following main amendments to the existing regime:

- alignment of income and capital requirements imposed by the income tax, capital gains tax and IHT treatment for vulnerable beneficiaries (see **7.9**); and
- inclusion in the definition of a DPI of persons who are in receipt of the new personal independence payment (PIP).

A statutory meaning of 'disabled person' was amended by *FA 2013* with effect from 6 April 2013 (*FA 2005, Sch 1A*). A disabled person is therefore someone who falls into one or more of the following categories:

(a) incapable of administering his property or managing his affairs by reason of mental disorder within the meaning of the *Mental Health Act 1983*;

(b) receiving attendance allowance;

(c) receiving a disability living allowance by virtue of entitlement to the care component at the highest or middle rate;

(d) receiving personal independence payment by virtue of entitlement to the daily living component;

(e) receiving an increased disablement pension;

(f) receiving constant attendance allowance; or

(g) receiving armed forces independence payment.

The requirements as to the allowances and payments etc in (b) to (g) above are set out in the legislation (*Sch 1A, paras 2–7*).

The legislation is confusing, as the 'new' definition of disabled person applies from 6 April 2013, and not 8 April 2013 when the *Welfare Reform Act 2013* was enacted. The new rules relating to income and capital requirements only came into force on 17 July 2013. This means that DPIs created between 6 April 2013 and 17 July 2013 will have the new definition of disabled person but the old rules as to income and capital conditions.

Bereaved minor trusts

7.7 Bereaved minor trusts ('BMTs') were introduced by *FA 2006* to replace A&M settlements. The provisions governing the trusts can be found in *IHTA 1984, s 71A*. The main conditions are:

- BMTs can only arise on the death of a parent;
- BMTs can be established under the terms of the will of a deceased parent or on intestacy, under the Criminal Injuries Compensation Scheme, or under the Victims of Overseas Terrorism Compensation Scheme;
- a bereaved minor must become entitled to the trust property at age 18;
- for so long as the bereaved minor is under the age of 18, any of the settled property is applied for the bereaved minor; and
- the bereaved minor is entitled to all of the income (if any) arising from any of the settled property, or no such income may be applied for the benefit of another person (although this is subject to the *FA 2013* changes – see **7.9**).

IHTA 1984, s 71B provides that BMTs are not subject to exit charges or ten-year anniversary charges for IHT, provided that the conditions of *IHTA 1984, s 71A* are complied with.

The capital and income requirements introduced in *FA 2013* (see **7.9**) also apply to BMTs. However, in practice, such distributions are rare, but they may arise by paying the guardian of a child some kind of retainer for looking after the child.

18-to-25 trusts

7.8 The provisions governing these trusts can be found in *IHTA 1984, s 71D*. The main conditions are:

- An 18-to-25 trust can only arise on the death of a parent or legal guardian (see *IHTA 1984, s 71D*).
- It can only be created either under the will of a deceased parent or under the Criminal Injuries Compensation Scheme. In addition, such trust must satisfy the following conditions:
  - a beneficiary must become absolutely entitled to the trust property, its income and any accumulated income on or before the age of 25;
  - for as long as the beneficiary is under the age of 25, the settled property must be applied for his benefit; and
  - he must be entitled to all the income arising on the settled property, or no such income may be applied for the benefit of another person.

For income tax (where an interest in possession does not exist) and capital gains tax, 18-to-25 trusts are taxed like discretionary trusts. *IHTA 1984, s 71F* provides that 18-to-25 trusts are not, as such, within the relevant property regime, but they are nonetheless subject to an exit charge which only runs from the beneficiary's eighteenth birthday (or 6 April 2008, if later). This has the effect that the maximum rate of an exit charge will be 4.2% when a beneficiary becomes absolutely entitled to trust property at the age of 25.

The capital and income requirements introduced in *FA 2013* (see **7.9**) also apply to 18-to-25 trusts.

Income and capital requirements for DPIs and trusts for vulnerable beneficiaries

7.9 For lifetime DPIs created prior to 8 April 2013, only 50% of capital had to be applied for the benefit of the disabled person during the disabled person's lifetime. This meant that, prior to *FA 2013*, DPIs could be set up for a disabled person but with a wide class of beneficiaries – for example, to include siblings, spouses, widows/widowers and children, with the benefit that the trust did not qualify as a relevant property trust. As distributions now are limited to the 'annual limit' (see below), families will have to think carefully whether to opt for DPIs.

For DPIs created between 22 March 2006 and 7 April 2013, distributions to beneficiaries other than the disabled beneficiary which exceed the 50% capital rule and were made during the lifetime of the disabled person are deemed to be potentially exempt transfers by the disabled beneficiary.

Finance Act 2013 amended the income and 50% capital rules in that, for trusts created from 8 April 2013, all the capital must be applied for the disabled person, subject to the exception of the 'annual limit' which is the lesser of £3,000 or 3% of the settled property applied for the benefit of another person during each tax year.

Distributions to beneficiaries other than the disabled beneficiary or vulnerable beneficiary in excess of the 'annual limit' on or after 8 April 2013 will be subject to IHT exit charges on the excess above the annual limit.

For DPIs arising under wills drafted prior to 17 July 2013 (when *FA 2013* was enacted) or new wills executed or confirmed after 17 July 2013, where the trusts' wording remains unaltered, the old rules apply. DPIs arising under wills drafted after 17 July 2013 will be subject to the new capital and income rules introduced in *FA 2013*.

INCOME AND CAPITAL GAINS TAX

Special income tax and capital gains tax treatment

7.10 Although 18-to-25 trusts qualify for privileged status for IHT, they are not within the special income tax and capital gains tax treatment for vulnerable beneficiaries. They are treated like discretionary trusts (or interest in possession trusts if an earlier income entitlement arises), and the trustees will have to report any income and gains accordingly.

The special income and capital gains tax regime for vulnerable beneficiaries introduced in *FA 2005, ss 23–45* applies to all four types of DPI (see **7.2** to **7.5** above) and BMTs. Care needs to be taken that the capital and income requirements post 8 April 2013 are not breached; otherwise, the special treatment does not apply.

DPIs qualify for special treatment for income tax and capital gains tax purposes, if a vulnerable person election has been made and is effective for the tax year in question (*FA 2005, s 34(2)*). The election has to be made on Form VPE1 and signed jointly by the trustees and the beneficiary. The election is irrevocable, although the benefit can be opted into/out of on an annual basis and will continue until one of the following events occurs:

- the vulnerable beneficiary ceases to be a vulnerable person;
- the trusts in relation to which the election is made cease to qualify; or
- the trusts are terminated.

On the occurrence of any of the above events, the trustees are required to give notice to HMRC within 90 days of the event.

In the case of BMTs, such trusts qualify for the special treatment, if the conditions outlined in **7.7** are met and the income and capital requirements post 8 April 2013 are not breached.

Where a claim for special treatment has been made, the regime provides that no more tax is paid in respect of the relevant income and gains of the trust for the tax year in question than would be paid had the income and gains accrued directly to the beneficiary.

For the special capital gains tax treatment to apply, the following conditions must be satisfied:

- Chargeable gains arise in the tax year to the trustees on the disposal of trust property held on qualifying trusts for the benefit of a vulnerable person.
- The trustees would be chargeable to CGT in respect of those gains were it not for the application of *FA 2005, Chapter 4*.
- The trustees are resident in the UK during any part of the tax year.
- The trustees make a claim for special treatment in the tax year.

If these conditions are fulfilled, the trustees and beneficiary are treated as if the chargeable gains had arisen to the latter, and he self-assesses accordingly. Thus, assuming the beneficiary had no other capital gains, the trustees would receive the benefit of the full capital gains tax exemption (for 2018/19, £11,700) rather than the maximum reduced allowance for trusts (for 2018/19, £5,850); if a beneficiary has capital gains tax losses, these would also be taken into account to reduce the tax charge on the trust. Any income tax (excluding notional dividend tax credit) paid by the trustees will still enter the tax pool and, on later discretionary income distribution, the beneficiary can then reclaim the tax back from the trustees (see HMRC's Trusts, Settlements and Estates Manual at TSEM3415) in the normal manner.

The special treatment does not apply in the tax year when the beneficiary dies.

Calculating the relief

7.11 The income tax liability of the trust is reduced to the actual income tax liability that the beneficiary would pay if the income had been received directly in his own right. However, the liability remains the liability of the relevant trust; it is merely the calculation of the liability that is affected.

HMRC express the relief as a formula which deducts the difference between the trust's liability and the beneficiary's liability as a credit. The credit is the difference between:

- TQTI (trust's original liability); and
- VQTI (the additional tax to which the beneficiary would be liable if the trust income were his).

However, the VQTI credit for the trust is calculated on a top-slicing basis, being the difference between the beneficiary's income tax liability before and after including the trust income. Thus, the beneficiary's tax liability is calculated, firstly, on the basis that no trust income has been received and, secondly, on the basis the trust income has been received, and the VQTI credit is the difference.

The relief for income tax requires a number of consecutive calculations to be made:

(i) Work out the tax that the trust would pay but for the election (A).

(ii) Work out the tax that the beneficiary would pay with the trust income treated as their income (B).

(iii) Work out the tax that the beneficiary would pay with the trust income NOT treated as their income (C).

(iv) Calculate the difference between (B) and (C) to arrive at the extra tax that the beneficiary will pay (D).

(v) The trust then deducts (D) from its liability to arrive at the credit (E).

(vi) The tax the trust actually pays is (A) – (E).

Example 7.1— BMT vulnerable beneficiary illustration (2018/19)

Both William's parents were killed in a car crash in 2013, neither having made a will. Under the intestacy rules, a trust has been established for William, now aged 14, which for 2019/20 received gross dividend income of £20,000, and gross interest income of £15,000; it made chargeable gains on the sale of shares of £12,000. William has no personal income.

Assuming that the trustees and William (or rather his guardian) make the necessary election on or before 31 January 2021, the effect of the regime is as follows:

Income tax

2019/20

TLV1 (see below) = £2,650

TLV2 (see below) = £0 (William's other income)

TQT1 (see below) = £17,570

VQT1 (see below) = £14,920

VQT1: Reduction in the trustees' tax liability on a claim is £14,920 (£17,570 – £2,650).

	William's assumed tax liability	*Trustees' actual tax liability*
	£	£
Dividend income	20,000	20,000
Interest income	20,000	20,000
	40,000	40,000
Personal allowance	(12,500)	
Savings allowance	(1,000)	
Dividend allowance	(2,000)	
Taxable	24,500	35,000
£6,500 (interest at 20%)	1,300	
£18,000 (dividends at 7.5%)	1,350	
	2,650	
First slice (£1,000 @ 20%)		200
Next £19,000 (interest at 45%)		8,550
Dividends at 38.1%		7,620
		16,370
Income tax payable	2,650	16,370

Capital gains tax

	William's assumed tax liability	*Trustees' actual tax liability*
	£	£
Gains arising	12,000	12,000
Less annual exemption	(12,000)	(6,000)
	0	6,000
Gains charged at 10%/20%		
Tax payable	0	1,200

Summary

	William's assumed tax liability	*Trustees' actual tax liability*
	£	£
Income tax payable	2,650	16,370
Plus capital gains tax	0	1,200
	2,650	17,570
	(TLV1)	(TQT1)

Chapter 8

Ending a trust

SIGNPOSTS

- **Basics** – Understand the manner in which a trust may come to an end and the principal tax charge (see **8.3** and **8.19–8.21**).
- **Tax treatment** – Review the differing tax treatment applied pre/post the *FA 2006* trust reforms (see **8.5** and **8.12–8.17**).
- **Health warning** – Consider the impact of the anti-avoidance measures, particularly in relation to clawback, principal private residence relief, and assets transferred at a loss.

THE PERPETUITY PERIOD

Capital distribution compared with termination

Focus

A fixed 125-year perpetuity period now exists for all post-5 April 2010 trusts, and a fixed 100-year trust period may be substituted for pre-6 April 2010 trusts, but not as of right.

8.1 Under English law, at least, a non-charitable trust cannot continue indefinitely. There is a 'rule against perpetuities' and the most common so-called 'perpetuity period' was 80 years from the date of the settlement, although there were other possible periods. A well-drafted trust document will prescribe what happens to any property left in the trust at the end of the perpetuity period (commonly called the 'vesting date'). Under the *Perpetuities and Accumulations Act 2009*, there is now a single perpetuity period of 125 years which applies to trusts created post 5 April 2010. However, where there is doubt or ambiguity over the length of a pre-6 April 2010 trust, the trustees are able by deed to opt for a defined period of 100 years (note that the 125-year rule is not substituted in full).

It is not uncommon to come across a trust deed that has not been drafted so completely, which leaves it open as to what happens should all the beneficiaries 'die out' and typically, there will be a 'resulting trust' to the settlor or to his estate. This carries the adverse effect of bringing into play the anti-avoidance rules for income tax (see **4.26–4.29**) and for IHT (see **6.18–6.23**). In any case, it is possible for the future, though not for the past, to remedy this situation by having the settlor or spouse as the case may be, irrevocably assigning any rights under the settlement to, for example, their named children.

Trustee responsibilities

8.2 For so long as the trust continues, the legal, though not the beneficial, ownership of the trust fund remains vested in the trustees. They have the responsibility for managing the property and they must deal with any income tax, CGT or IHT compliance duties. Once property leaves the trust, either through exercise of trustees' discretion, or because that is what the trust deed provides (eg on the 25th birthday of beneficiary X), the capital concerned is freed from the trust subject only to any necessary 'lien' for expenses or perhaps tax (in other words, the trustees may resort to that capital for paying such expenses or tax). Whether there is such a lien or not will depend on the terms of the trust deed. Once that capital belongs absolutely to a particular beneficiary, it will be his responsibility for dealing with compliance going forward as well as deciding what to do with the capital.

Capital distribution

8.3 There may be a distribution of capital out of the settlement, in which case the remaining trust fund continues subject to the trusts of the settlement. In either case, the trustees need to have regard to any compliance aspects, as well as to the possibility that even if future tax implications are down to the beneficiary, there could be some recourse against them if he defaults; typically, if any gain on leaving the settlement is held over – see **8.6–8.7**.

Example 8.1—Katie and Harry trust: the different stages

In June 2006, Katie and Harry created a discretionary trust in favour of their minor children, Lucy and Will, together with any future children. The children become entitled to their pro rata income share at age 25, but the capital is to be held for the grandchildren on attaining the age of 25.

The trust may perhaps be regarded as having five beneficial stages:

1. A discretionary trust for their children, Lucy, Will and any future children, which will come to an end in each presumptive share as the child reaches the 'specified age' of 25;

2. A life interest for Lucy, Will (and any future children) at age 25;

3. A successive discretionary settlement for the grandchildren of Katie and Harry, which again may translate into a life interest settlement insofar as the specified age for any of the grandchildren is lower than 25;

4. A life interest for the grandchildren between the specified age, typically 18, and age 25, followed by;

5. Absolute entitlement to capital on the part of the grandchildren at age 25.

On the assumption that the respective shares are not varied and that there are nine grandchildren in total, as each reaches the age of 25 they will become absolutely entitled to the income and capital underlying their share (if *per capita* see below). When the youngest of the grandchildren reaches the age of 25, the settlement will come to an end. This event is likely to occur within the perpetuity period of 80 years after the settlement commenced but it is only necessary to ensure that there is at least a vesting 'in interest' not necessarily in possession, ie it does not matter if there are still some grandchildren under the age of 25 on the vesting date. There is then simply an ongoing life interest in that share of capital until the age of 25 is reached.

It is likely that the trust deed will contain a default trust in favour of Lucy and Will and their respective legal personal representatives. If the share of any child or grandchild fails, the settlement will probably provide that this be added pro rata to the other shares.

There is an important distinction, at grandchild level, between *per capita* and *per stirpes*: the former means that the capital is divided between the grandchildren according to their number, regardless of how many children, Lucy, Will and any other children of Katie and Harry may have. *Per stirpes* means that the shares are to be divided according to each branch of the family. Thus, if Katie and Harry have four children, Lucy, Will, Chris and Monty, and Lucy has one child, Will two, Chris three and Monty none, Lucy's child will be entitled to one-third of the capital, each of Will's children to one-sixth of the capital, and each of Chris's children to one-ninth of the capital, all at age 25.

Note: The *FA 2006* rules for A&M settlements made before 22 March 2006 will generally mean that, from 6 April 2008, the trust fund entered the 'relevant property' regime unless and to the extent that an interest in possession had arisen by that date or advantage taken of the transitional rules else the trust terms already fall within the rules applying to a Bereaved Minor's trust or 18-to-25 trust. See **6.51-6.53**, and specifically **Example 6.15** at **6.53**, addressing the impact for the Murray A&M Settlement.

INCOME TAX

8.4 This section concerns capital, but not income, leaving a trust and, importantly, the commentary here only relates to the income tax (and thus not IHT or CGT) treatment of that capital.

- Question 13 of the 2018/19 trust and estate tax return (see **4.60**) seeks to establish what part of the trust income is subject to the trustees' discretion and what part is not, whether in each case charged at 7.5% (dividends) or 20% (all else).
- Question 14 goes on to ask whether any discretionary payments of income have been made to beneficiaries.
- Question 15 asks whether the trustees have made any capital payments to, or for the benefit of, 'relevant' (ie minor unmarried and not in a civil partnership) children of the settlor during his lifetime; this is because such payments could have income tax consequences (see **4.26–4.29**).
- Question 15A asks whether there were capital transactions between the trustees and the settlors; this is intended to seek out situations covered by *ITTOIA 2005, ss 633–645* where, for example, a settlor has made a loan to the trustees which is repaid in whole or in part and, to the extent of any undistributed income in the trust, that income is assessed on the recipient settlor at higher rates for up to a maximum of ten years; see **4.28**.
- Question 16 asks for details of capital payments or any benefits provided to the beneficiaries, this is only in a case where the settlement has been non-UK resident or has received any capital from another trust which has been non-UK resident; see **5.59**.

In other words, for income tax purposes there is no general obligation on the trustees' part to notify HMRC of capital distributions made to the beneficiaries. The only requirement, if the trust comes to an end during the tax year, is that the date of termination must be given in Box 21.4. This will (or should) ensure that no further self-assessment returns are generated by HMRC in subsequent years. It is, coincidentally, important to ensure that if a self-assessment return is generated, it is returned, even on a nil basis, to avoid the automatic penalty of £100 if not delivered on or before 31 January following the end of the tax year (it is hard to see that such a penalty would be levied if the trust had come to an end and HMRC had been told as much, but the point is made).

In other words, all that will happen for income tax purposes as a result of the capital leaving the trust is that any income generated in future by that capital will cease to be income of the trust. There is no obligation either on the trustees or on the recipient of the capital to notify HMRC. What the absolute beneficiary must of course do for the future is to ensure that he duly returns on his self-assessment return the income that is generated by the capital.

Example 8.2—Jack Daniel Settlement: tax liability for income

Following the resolution by the trustees of the Jack Daniel settlement to appoint £20,000 to Angus (a higher rate taxpayer) in May 2019, the income of the trustees for that 2019/20 year will, of course, reduce. Angus invests the capital for his own benefit and receives dividends of £500 per annum. He must ensure that he records this income on his 2019/20 self-assessment return.

CAPITAL GAINS TAX

8.5 As mentioned above, there are no particular obligations to notify, at least for income tax purposes, the event of capital leaving a trust (see **8.4**), but the same is not true for CGT.

When chargeable capital assets (thus excluding cash) leave a trust, whether or not the trust is terminated, the trustees are treated as having made a notional disposal and reacquisition of that capital at market value (*TCGA 1992, s 71(1)*). This means that if, over the trustees' period of ownership, there has been an increase in value, there will be a capital gain on the capital leaving the trust. To the extent that the gain (taken with other gains and losses during the year) exceeds the annual exemption (£6,000 for 2019/20), there will be a trust tax liability of 28% for gains attributable to residential property, else 20% for all other gains. If the trust is either within the relevant property regime or an 18-to-25 trust, such that the capital advance is an IHT event not otherwise qualifying for business/agricultural property relief or alternatively is a bereaved minor's trust where there is no IHT event then, subject to residence qualification, the trustees can, jointly with the beneficiary, make a hold-over election whereby the beneficiary effectively 'inherits' the in-built gain by acquiring the asset as its original cost to the trustees (or March 1982 value where appropriate) (see **3.5–3.7**).

Hold-over relief

8.6 If the asset advanced is sterling cash or other non-chargeable asset, there will be no CGT implications but in all other cases where a gain does arise, it must be reported as such on the capital gains supplemental pages SA 905 and again on the main SA 900, with the tax paid by 31 January following the end of the tax year. However, the trustees may decide to hold over the gain. This could be advantageous in a case where, for example, the trust had already used its annual exemption, or the gain far exceeded its annual exemption and the inherent gain in the hands of the beneficiary or beneficiaries could be realised over one or two tax years and perhaps at the lower 10% rate. A word of warning: given anti-avoidance principles, it would be sensible not to be too 'blatant', ie if, on day one, trustees of a relevant property trust appointed shares carrying gains of £30,000 to three beneficiaries equally, and on day two, those beneficiaries each sold the shares within their annual exemptions of £12,000 (for 2019/20), the circumstances may lead HMRC to argue that, in reality, the disposals had been made by the trustees. In such circumstances, no particular guidance can be given as to how long a period should safely be allowed to elapse. It is a good idea, for example, to have some income arising to the beneficiaries through dividends, for the beneficiaries to take independent advice and perhaps not all to act together. Having said that, it would be unlikely that an interval of a week or two could realistically be challenged, especially if the amounts of tax at stake are relatively small.

Clawback on emigration of beneficiary

> **Focus**
>
> Beware the CGT exposure to the trustees by reason of a beneficiary emigrating within six years of asset appointment.

8.7 There is a clawback provision for holdover relief, which must be considered with care. If, within six years after the end of the tax year in which the capital appointment is made, the beneficiary becomes non-UK resident, the held-over gain attributable to all but UK residential property (which since 6 April 2015 now falls within the scope of NRCGT as a non-resident gain) immediately crystallises (*TCGA 1992, s 168*). If the beneficiary fails to pay the tax within 12 months after the due date, HMRC have the right to pursue the trustees for the tax now recalculated at the trustee rate of 20% (for non UK residential property). Accordingly, it is very important for trustees to protect themselves in such cases, and they may consider that indemnities from the beneficiary (or where appropriate, the beneficiary's parents) are sufficient. However, the only safe way would be for them to retain the legal ownership of the assets concerned, or at least sufficient of the assets concerned to cover the tax until the danger period had expired.

Losses

8.8 If the deemed disposal of the asset(s) leaving the trust produces a loss, it must be first set against other trust gains of the same year. However, to the extent that a loss remains unused in the trust, it may be 'inherited' by the beneficiary recipient of that asset. Until June 1999, that loss could be used by the beneficiary against his general gains. Now, however, it can be offset *only* against a gain arising on disposal of the asset advanced to him out of trust or, if the asset was land, against some other interest in land deriving its value from that land (*TCGA 1992, s 71(2)–(2D)*).

Private residences: anti-avoidance rule

8.9 The rules effective from 10 December 2003 on transferring a property into a relevant property trust and electing to hold over the gain with a view to sheltering the later accrued gain by reason of principal private residence relief on later sale by the trustees, apply equally to restrict the relief on property coming out of trust: see **5.27 and Example 5.9**. There are various permutations. Broadly speaking, however, if the trustees and beneficiary jointly elect to hold over a gain on property leaving the trust (whether or not it has been occupied by a beneficiary at that time), the beneficiary receiving the property which he then occupies as his main home, cannot later make use of principal private residence relief himself to shelter the gain on ultimate disposal (*TCGA 1992, s 225A*). Problems may arise because the beneficiary and the trustees will have to join together in the hold-over election in these circumstances and it may not be in the beneficiary's interests, with anticipated long-term appreciation in property values, to take a proportionately larger CGT 'hit' in the future than the trustees, but the balance of advantage will depend on the specific circumstances.

Death of the life tenant

8.10 The general rule is that there is no CGT charge on the increased value at date of death and that the beneficiary under the will is treated as acquiring that asset at its market value (probate value) at the date of death. That is, any inherent gain in the assets is 'washed' out; by token any inherent loss simply disappears. A similar rule operates within qualifying (pre-March 2006, TSI or disabled trust) interest in possession trusts so that whether the trust continues or comes to an end on the life tenant's death, there is a deemed uplift to market value of the assets within the trust but with no CGT charge. There are, however, two exceptions to this rule:

(1) The capital on the life tenant's death 'reverts' to the settlor absolutely: In this case there is no uplift to market value and the assets are inherited at their original cost (*TCGA 1992, s 73(1)(b)*);

(2) Property was transferred into the trust with the benefit of a hold-over election: In this case, the held-over gain is crystallised (*TCGA 1992, s 74(2)*). It may, however, be held over again, either as a chargeable transfer under *TCGA 1992, s 260*, eg the assets passed to the life tenant's children on ongoing trust terms or under *TCGA 1992, s 165* where the

assets concerned are qualifying business/agricultural assets. A CGT charge will have to be paid therefore only where a surviving spouse inherits non-business/agricultural assets.

Note that, under the IHT regime for trusts introduced by *FA 2006* from 22 March 2006, the above treatment will apply on the death of the life tenant only where the trust (and by *FA 2014* now extended to include trusts for the vulnerable with effect from 6 April 2014) is not within the 'relevant property' regime (see **6.58**).

Revocable appointments

8.11 There will be CGT implications of property coming out of trust if some other person becomes 'absolutely entitled' as against the trustees (*TCGA 1992, s 71*). It may be that the property passes not to a beneficiary outright, but to the trustees of some other settlement. If the trustees of the second settlement are 'absolutely entitled' as against the trustees of the first, there will be a CGT charge in the usual way but as by virtue of *IHTA 1984, s 80* this is not a chargeable event for IHT, *CGTA 1992, s 260* holdover relief is denied. It may be possible, however, for the appointment of capital to be made in such a way that it is revocable, or that reference has to be made back to the original settlement for some administrative or beneficial powers, or, eg for the default trust (see HMRC Statement of Practice 7/84). In this case, it cannot be said that the trustees of the second settlement have become absolutely entitled and there will be no CGT event. It will mean, however, that any inherent gains in the assets concerned will be taken on board by the trustees of the second settlement, which they should bear in mind.

INHERITANCE TAX

Relevant property trust: the exit charge

8.12 The mechanics of the exit charge were explained in **6.36–6.38**. The thinking behind the IHT regime for relevant property trusts (which has been in place since 1975), is that such trusts should be treated as a separate taxpayer. Therefore, when capital leaves the trust and enters the estate of, say, a beneficiary, there is an 'exit charge', the calculation of which varies according to whether it occurs during the first ten years of the trust's life, or after the first or subsequent ten-year anniversary.

Even if there is no charge to IHT (perhaps because the value concerned is within the available trust nil rate band) and subject only to the *de minimis* provisions (as revised from 2007/08: *Inheritance Tax (Delivery of Accounts) (Excepted Settlements) Regulations 2008, SI 2008/ 606*), the trustees still have an obligation to report the event to HMRC on form IHT100 within six months after the end of the month in which the exit occurs (12 months for events prior to 6 April 2014 – see **3.19**). Note that for events occurring prior to 6 April 2014 the liability to pay any tax due falls six months after the end of the month in which the chargeable transfer was made, except in the case of one made after 5 April and before 1 October (otherwise than on death), when the tax falls due on 30 April in the following year (*IHTA 1984, s 226(1)*).

Example 8.3— Flossie Brownlow Discretionary Settlement: IHT on appointments out of trust

The trustees of the Flossie Brownlow Discretionary Settlement (created on 1 January 2003) have made the following appointments of capital:

- 1 June 2013: £20,000 cash to Crispin.
- 1 June 2018: £25,000 of shares to Debbie.

The trustees were aware of the first ten-year anniversary on 1 January 2013, and had submitted form IHT100 and paid the tax due. Thinking that they could now 'rest on their laurels', and need not do anything more on the compliance front until 1 January 2023, they were rather taken by surprise when the family's new solicitor did a 'financial health check' and advised them of the following:

- In respect of the distribution of capital to Crispin, form IHT100 should have been submitted on or before 30 June 2014 whilst the tax fell due on 30 April 2014.
- In respect of the distribution of shares to Debbie, both form IHT100 and the tax were due by 31 December 2018.

A&M trusts

8.13 Although in the heading to this section (and elsewhere in this book), the expression 'A&M' trusts is used, it is preferable, for reasons already given (see **6.47**), to refer to 'the A&M regime'.

The position before 6 April 2008

8.14 This commentary presupposes that capital leaving the trust, whether as a partial distribution or as a termination of the whole trust, does so at a time when it is subject to the A&M regime. However, a distinction should be drawn between the A&M regime coming to an end:

- but the trust continues, with an ongoing life interest (this would be the case for a standard A&M which provides for an income entitlement only at age 25); and
- but capital is advanced outright to any of the beneficiaries, whether this is at a particular age prescribed in the trust deed (ie age 25), or because the trustees exercise their discretion to advance capital earlier.

In the former case, there will be no IHT (or indeed CGT) implications of the A&M regime turning into an interest in possession regime. The trust simply continues. The difference for IHT will be that capital that was not hitherto treated as part of anyone's estate will now be treated as if it belonged to the relevant beneficiaries.

The same is of course true of the second eventuality, though in addition there would be a CGT event because someone, viz the beneficiaries, would be treated as absolutely entitled to the capital as against the trustees.

The position after 5 April 2008

8.15 If, following the *FA 2006* changes (see **6.51–6.53**), a pre-22 March 2006 A&M trust had amended its terms so that capital should vest absolutely at age 18, the above treatment would continue to apply.

If, before 6 April 2008, the trust terms had been changed (if necessary) to provide that capital entitlement should arise after age 18 but on or before age 25, there would be an exit charge (of no more than 4.2% but likely to be less in practice) on that entitlement, based on the number of completed quarters during which the property has remained in the trust since the beneficiary attained age 18 or, if later, 6 April 2008.

In any other case, the trust would enter the 'relevant property' regime on 6 April 2008 and would be subject to the system of ten-year and exit charges (see **6.32–6.38**).

CGT on advance of capital

> **Focus**
>
> General hold-over relief is denied in the absence of an IHT event in the first quarter post-trust creation or the first quarter after a ten-year anniversary.

8.16 One advantage of a pre-22 March 2006 A&M trust which, as at 6 April 2008, fell into the 'relevant property' regime is that, where capital vests outright following (and not at the same time as) an entitlement to income, hold-over relief is generally available to shelter gains on non-business assets under *TCGA 1992, s 260* – under the old rules, this beneficial treatment was denied unless appointment of income and capital occurred simultaneously. The only exception is the case where capital leaves the trust during a quarter beginning with the date of commencement of the settlement or with a ten-year anniversary (*IHTA 1984, s 65(4)*).

Example 8.4—The Murray A&M Settlement: decisions on trust capital

Consider the Murray A&M Settlement (see **Chapter 6**, **Example 6.2** at **6.3**) created on 1 January 2001 for children Cerys (born December 1996) and Tom (born December 1999) joined by Edward (born in March 2003) and Fiona (born in May 2005).

It is now November 2021 and the general tax regime has remained the same, apart from the *FA 2006* changes. The settlement has become very valuable, largely through expert and perhaps fortunate investment in some high performing stock exchange securities. None of the children have yet become entitled to income, though Cerys will soon do so on reaching the age of 25. Tom is 22, Edward is 18 and Fiona is 16. The 21-year accumulation period has not yet ended and as the terms of the settlement were not changed before 6 April 2008, the trust fund entered the 'relevant property' regime on that date and the first ten-year anniversary charge arose on 1 January 2011.

It would be open to the trustees to exercise powers in the settlement to advance to each of the four children the capital of their respective presumptive shares. In addition, the Trustees have the power to vary the shares, but they have agreed not to do so.

Each of the four children, therefore, ends up owning a considerable value of shares with large inherent gains. Those held-over gains attributable to non UK residential property would 'come home to roost' in respect of each share, if the relevant child were to become non-UK resident within six years after the end of the relevant tax year (*TCGA 1992, s 168*). That is the gains cannot be 'washed' simply by the children emigrating and becoming genuinely non-UK resident (which they now have to do for a period of at least five consecutive tax years), except after the six-year risk period has expired.

What Adrian and Belinda might have in mind is that, to protect the underlying capital, each of the children might resettle at least some of the capital. The basic trust issue is that, of course, this should not happen simply because 'Mum and Dad wanted me to' as there would be issues of undue influence, ie each of the children should get their own independent professional advice. The other problem is that such a settlement would trigger a disposal for CGT purposes. Any such settlement would be within the 'relevant property' regime, therefore attracting hold-over relief for CGT. However, to the extent that the value should exceed the nil rate band there would be an automatic charge to IHT at 20%.

It is unlikely that any of Cerys, Tom, Edward or Fiona would really want to make carve out from their entitlement a fresh trust from which they could not benefit. Cerys, though not her siblings, has married. Subject to general anti-avoidance principles, it might be open to her to give to her husband, say, £325,000 of investments, and for him, having retained the investments for a period of time and perhaps with independent advice, to make his own discretionary settlement. The wife to husband transfer would be 'no gain, no loss' so that the gain would be inherited by the husband, who would therefore be able to make his own nil rate band discretionary settlement.

Interest in possession trusts in (or deemed as in) being at 22 March 2006

8.17 This paragraph sets out the rules only for those interests in possession trusts, which were in being at 22 March 2006 or, which by virtue of being a TSI were treated as such (see **6.60**). These are qualifying interests.

An interest in possession trust may come to an end before the death of the life tenant in circumstances where:

- The capital has been advanced to the life tenant, in whole or in part – to that extent, he is treated as receiving capital that he is already treated as owning, and this is a 'non-event' for IHT purposes (*IHTA 1984, s 53(3)*).
- An advance of capital pursuant to powers in the deed to the spouse of the life tenant – this will be spouse exempt and therefore not a chargeable transfer for IHT purposes. The only qualification here is if the life tenant has a UK domicile, a deemed or elective UK domicile for IHT purposes and the spouse is none of the above but has a non-UK domicile. Here, the unlimited spouse exemption does not apply and from 6 April 2013, the exemption is limited to the level of the nil rate band, thus currently £325,000 (£55,000 for periods prior to 6 April 2013) on a cumulative lifetime basis, ie with no seven-year limitation (*IHTA 1984, s 18(2)*).
- An advance of capital to someone other than the life tenant or his spouse – this constitutes a PET by the life tenant, ie assumed to be exempt except and unless the life tenant dies within seven years. In the latter case, the gift will have 'first call' on the life tenant's nil rate band, subject to any chargeable transfers he might have made in the seven years before the capital left the trust (and therefore may attract tax at the nil rate, even

though it would have the effect of denying the nil rate band to that extent to the deceased estate).

Similarly, if the life interest continues until the death of the life tenant, it will be aggregated with his personal estate. The trustees will have to complete Inheritance Tax Account form IHT100 and they will be liable for their share of the tax at the estate rate on the trust assets (see **3.20** and Example 6.18 at **6.55**). If, however, under the trust terms the surviving spouse becomes absolutely entitled on the life tenant's death, there will be no liability to tax because of the spouse exemption.

There is one rather curious type of life interest settlement called an interest '*pur autre vie*'. There is a life interest insofar as the beneficiary is entitled to income from the trust property. However, the person by whose life the interest is measured is not the original beneficiary but someone else – that is the '*autre vie*'. Typically, when the *autre vie* dies, the interest will come to an end and the beneficiary will cease to be entitled to the income but what happens as a matter of trust law will depend on the terms of the trust. An interest '*pur autre vie'* may for IHT purposes either be a qualifying interest in possession or fall within the relevant property regime. The former is assumed here. Consider that the children of the *autre vie* then become entitled: so long as the life tenant survives the death of the *autre vie* for at least seven years, he will be treated as having made a PET, which becomes exempt and there will be no implications. If not, he will be treated as having made a chargeable transfer on the death of the *autre vie*.

Example 8.5—Toby's Settlement: capital leaving a qualifying interest in possession trust

The terms of the Toby settlement (created in March 2002) provide for a qualifying life interest to his son Stephen and on his death passing to Stephen's children absolutely at age 25.

The trustees decide to advance cash of £100,000 to Stephen. This has no IHT implications as for IHT purposes, Stephen is already treated as if entitled to the underlying capital. There will be no IHT compliance obligations either then, or indeed if Stephen were to die within seven years of that advance. In the latter event, the trustees will complete form IHT100, recording the assets then in the trust.

Insofar as they are chargeable assets (ie not business or agricultural property), the value of the trust fund on Stephen's death will be aggregated with his free estate. The IHT due thereon must be met from the trust fund and will fall due six months after the end of the month in which Stephen died.

Assuming that, at his death, all of Stephen's children have attained the age of 25, the trustees would want to ensure that:

- they have paid the IHT due;
- the executors have obtained a clearance certificate in the estate from HMRC Inheritance Tax (so that the trustees know that there are no further IHT liabilities in the estate that might impact on the estate rate for the settlement); and
- all costs and other liabilities of the trust are paid before capital is advanced to Stephen's children.

Lifetime termination: use of annual (or marriage/civil partnership) exemption

8.18 If, while the life tenant is alive, there is an exit of capital to someone other than the life tenant or his spouse, and the life tenant has not otherwise used his annual exemption for the tax year in question (and perhaps the previous tax year, which can be carried forward for one year only), the annual exemption of £3,000 (or total of £6,000 if also available for the prior year), or part, may be set against the transfer of value on exit. However, this is subject to notice being given by the life tenant to the trustees within six months of the exit (*IHTA 1984, s 57*) – despite HMRC comment to the contrary, there is no prescribed format for such notice and a simple written direction will suffice. Once the six-month period has passed, no relief can be given.

The same point applies to the use by the life tenant of his gifts on marriage/civil partnership exemption.

TAX PLANNING POINTS

Termination under the trust deed

8.19 This could be because:

- with an A&M settlement, capital vests outright, say, at age 18; or
- with an interest in possession trust, the life tenant has died and the trust deed provides that the children of the life tenant become absolutely entitled in equal shares, whether or not on attaining a particular age.

Under an A&M settlement where there is no prior interest in possession established as at 22 March 2006 or the capital has not vested absolutely by 6 April 2008 and the vesting age is over 18, the 'relevant property' regime will apply until it does vest (or, where there is an 18-to-25 trust, which strictly speaking does not fall within the relevant property regime, an exit charge will accrue from age 18). The same point will apply to an interest in possession arising on or after 22 March 2006 which is not a 'transitional serial interest' (see **6.60**).

On the face of it, there is not much that can be done about either eventuality, except that in the A&M case 'one can see the event coming'. The usual tax which comes to mind on the ending of a trust is CGT (rather than IHT). However, if, as in the qualifying life interest case, the trust comes to an end on death, there will not be a CGT issue (because of the tax-free uplift to market value on death). Nonetheless, remember that in that situation any gain previously held over on transfer to the trustees may crystallise (see **8.10**). By contrast, there will be an IHT cost, except to the extent that any value falls within the nil rate band or where the value is protected by reliefs for agricultural or business property.

In the A&M case which provides for capital at age 18 there will be no IHT to pay. Equally, post 5 April 2008, there should be no immediate CGT issue given the facility to hold over any gains because, under *TCGA 1992, s 260*, capital vests at age 18 without an intervening right to income. One advantage of a pre-22 March 2006 A&M trust which as at 6 April 2008 falls into the 'relevant property' regime is that, where capital vests outright following (and not at the same time as) the date of an entitlement to income, hold-over relief will now generally be available under *TCGA 1992, s 260*, whereas it would not have been before. However, see the last sentence of **8.16** for the one qualification to this principle.

For the case where capital under an A&M settlement is vested before 6 April 2008, reference should be made to the final paragraph of **8.19** in the 2008/09 edition of this book.

Trustees exercise discretion to pay out capital

8.20 Here the assumption is that the trustees are exercising powers in the settlement to advance capital. Well-advised trustees will always take into account the possible tax implications. For example:

- IHT with a relevant property trust: What are the exit implications? The trustees of every relevant property trust should carefully review the situation, say, nine years after commencement. This is because, if there has been rapid growth in the settlement, it may be possible to exit the funds, perhaps into some other type of trust. Remember, if an exit is made out of the trust within the first ten years, there will be no IHT to pay if, on entering the trust, the property was within the nil rate band, there are no related settlements and/or settlor's cumulative transfer history (subject to a caveat with agricultural or business property; see **6.37**) or later additions.
- For CGT, it may be possible to hold over any gain out of a relevant property trust (though bear in mind the danger of the beneficiary

emigrating within six years and subject to what is written elsewhere about private residences occupied by beneficiaries – see **8.7** and **8.9**). By contrast, with qualifying interest in possession trusts not brought within the relevant property regime, there may be a CGT problem unless the assets concerned are qualifying business assets and attract hold-over relief under *TCGA 1992, s 165*.

In every case, it is important to review the tax implications and ensure that all necessary returns are made to HMRC.

However the termination occurs

8.21 If capital leaves a qualifying interest in possession trust not brought within the relevant property regime by appointment to a person other than the life tenant or spouse, bear in mind the possibility of using the life tenant's annual exemption for the current tax year, and perhaps the previous tax year, or his exemption for gifts on marriage/civil partnership. However, this requires notice by the life tenant to the trustees within six months – see **8.18**.

STAMP DUTIES

8.22 Shares or land may cease to be owned by trustees, whether because they are sold and the proceeds of sale are held as part of the trust fund instead or where they are advanced out to a beneficiary, (either because he becomes absolutely entitled under the terms of the trust or because the trustees exercise a discretion whereby he becomes so entitled).

In the former case of sale, any stamp duty or SDLT is payable by the purchaser.

In the latter case of distribution to a beneficiary, there will be an exemption from either stamp duty or SDLT:

- In the case of shares, the transfer document escapes the normal £5 charge by being certified by Category J of the *Stamp Duty (Exempt Instruments) Regulations 1987*. The £5 charge was removed by *FA 2008, s 99* and *Sch 22* from instruments transferring stocks and shares on or after 13 March 2008 which were previously chargeable with that amount of stamp duty, whether fixed or *ad valorem*.
- In the case of land, the transfer to the beneficiary is self-certified under *FA 2003, Sch 3, para 1*. For land transactions made before 12 March 2008, this self-certificate (form SDLT 60) was then delivered to one of HM Land Registries in support of an application for re-registration of the beneficiary as the registered owner. The requirement to complete form SDLT 60 was removed from 12 March 2008 by *FA 2008, s 94* and *Sch 30*: the re-registration is now secured by delivery of Land Registry Transfer TP1.

Note a trap in particular in the latter case: if the land is subject to a mortgage and the beneficiary takes over the liability for the mortgage, the amount of the liability counts as chargeable consideration. In the case of residential land, the SDLT charge will be at 0% if the amount does not exceed £125,000 (£175,000 for transfers after 2 September 2008 and before 1 January 2010) or, in the case of non-residential land, £150,000. Otherwise, SDLT will be charged at 2% if the consideration does not exceed £250,000, 5% if the consideration does not exceed £925,000, 10% if the consideration does not exceed £1.5 million, and otherwise 12%. However, if there is consideration payable of £40,000 or more, the transaction cannot be self-certified and must be the subject of a land transaction return, which should be submitted to HMRC Stamp Taxes at Netherton within 30 days (see the last sentence of Example 8.6).

Example 8.6—Family Settlement: Appointments of shares and land to beneficiaries

On 1 January 2019, the trustees of a family settlement resolve to appoint £100,000 worth of shares and £300,000 of land to beneficiaries, Jack and Jill.

The transfer documents of the shares delivered by the trustees to Jack each carry the certification Category J under the *1987 Regulations*. Jack produces the transfers to the registrars of the relevant companies so that he may be registered as the new owner.

The land is subject to a mortgage of £50,000 for which Jill agrees to assume future responsibility. This land transaction cannot be self-certified and must be the subject of a land transaction return delivered by the trustees to the HMRC Stamp Taxes within 30 days after their appointment. HMRC Stamp Taxes will deliver certificate SDLT 5 to Jill with which she may procure registration of the land. Being within the £125,000 threshold for residential property, no SDLT is payable. (Had the mortgage been less than £40,000, no land transaction return would have been necessary, following an extension to the *de minimis* regime by *FA 2008, s 94(1), (2)* with effect from 12 March 2008: see *FA 2003, s 77A*).

Chapter 9

Deceased estates: introduction

SIGNPOSTS

- **Duties of personal representatives** – The duty of PRs is to gather in the assets of the estate, comply with any reporting requirements, pay off liabilities, and distribute the estate according to the provisions of the will of the deceased or the rules of intestacy (see **9.1–9.3**).
- **Compliance for IHT** – PRs need to complete the relevant IHT forms. Particular care needs to be taken with the valuation of assets, an area which HMRC are 'targeting' (see **9.4–9.17**).
- **Excepted estates** – There are three categories of excepted estates, where either simplified forms can be filed or the filing of forms is dispensed with altogether (see **9.18–9.23**).
- **Payment of IHT** – The PRs are liable to pay any IHT liability. In certain circumstances, it may be possible to offer heritage property in lieu of any IHT due (see **9.24–9.29**).
- **Interest and penalty regime** – The penalty regime introduced by *Finance Act 2007* identifies three categories of behaviour: the highest category, 'deliberate and concealed', carries a penalty of 100% (see **9.30–9.35**).

DUTIES OF PERSONAL REPRESENTATIVES

9.1 The expression 'personal representatives' (PRs) comprises both executors (in the event of a will) and administrators (in the event of an intestacy). The duty of the PRs is to gather in the assets of the estate, to pay off liabilities (including personal debts of the deceased, and IHT) and to distribute those assets, or their proceeds of sale, among the beneficiaries, according to the provisions of the will or intestacy.

In doing so, for example exercising any discretions or deciding whether to sell, when and at what price, the PRs should take into account, though they will not be bound by, the wishes of the beneficiaries.

It is surprising how many people die without having made a will. In this case, rules are found in the *Administration of Estates Act 1925* (with different provisions applying to Scotland), which lay down who is entitled to what. The rules are set out below.

The case of *Whittaker v Hancock* (2018) EWHC 3478 Ch confirmed that a personal representative who lost mental capacity can be replaced by their attorney for the purposes of administering the estate. However, in this case the donor of the power of attorney was also the sole beneficiary of the estate and this was likely to be material to the decision.

Intestacy rules – a summary (under English and Scottish law)

9.2 The Law Commission in its consultation paper 'Intestacy and Family Provision Claims on Death' examined options for reform of the current law.

The consultation closed on 28 February 2010 and, on 21 March 2013, the government announced acceptance of some of the recommendations in the *Inheritance and Trustees' Powers Act 2014,* which came into effect on 1 October 2014.

The *Inheritance and Trustees' Powers Act 2014* includes the following reforms:

- where a couple are married or in a civil partnership, assets pass on intestacy to the surviving spouse/civil partner in all cases where there are no children or other descendants;
- the sharing of assets on intestacy where the deceased was survived by a spouse and children or other descendants, in that after the statutory legacy of £250,000 is deducted, the residual estate is split equally between the surviving spouse/civil partner and issue;
- protects children, who suffer the death of a parent, from the risk of losing an inheritance from that parent in the event that they are adopted after the death;
- amends the legal rules which currently disadvantage unmarried fathers when a child dies intestate;
- removes arbitrary obstacles to family provision claims by dependants of the deceased and anyone treated by the deceased as a child of his or her family outside the context of marriage or civil partnership;
- permits a claim for family provision in certain circumstances where the deceased died 'domiciled' but was 'habitually resident' in the UK, outside England and Wales but left property and family members or dependants in England and Wales; and
- reforms trustees' statutory powers to use income under *Trustee Act 1925, s 31* and capital under *Trustee Act 1925, s 32* for the benefit of trust beneficiaries (subject to any express provisions in the trust instrument).

In essence the rules are as follows:

- A surviving spouse will take the whole estate if they survive for 28 days and the deceased left no issue, parents or siblings.
- If the intestate leaves issue, the spouse inherits the personal chattels, the statutory legacy of £250,000 (increased from £125,000 on 1 February 2009) and half the remainder absolutely. The other half of the residue goes to the children on 'statutory trust' (see bereaved minor trusts in **2.9**), which means that they become absolutely entitled in equal shares at age 18.
- If the deceased leaves no spouse and no issue, the estate passes first to the parents in equal shares, but if there are no parents, it passes to the siblings equally, then siblings of the half blood then grandparents. Then it passes to aunts and uncles, with cousins entitled if their parents have predeceased them.

The government has also announced that further recommendations, which would be given effect by the draft *Inheritance (Cohabitants) Bill* annexed to the Report, but which were rejected by the government. This Bill contained controversial provisions that would give certain unmarried partners who have lived together for five years the right to inherit on each other's death under the intestacy rules. Where the couple have a child together, this entitlement would accrue after two years' cohabitation, provided the child was living with the couple when the deceased died.

The *Estates of Deceased Persons (Forfeiture Rule and Law of Succession) Act 2011* took effect in England and Wales on 1 February 2012. The Act permits the children of disqualified or disclaiming adult heirs to inherit from an estate as if the *per stirpes* rules applied.

For Scottish intestacy cases, proposals were made by the Scottish Law Commission to make significant reforms of the laws of Scotland governing inheritance, wills and intestacy, some of which were enacted in the *Succession (Scotland) Act 2016*.

In Scotland, the intestacy rules are as set out in the *Succession (Scotland) Act 1964*, which was amended by the *Prior Rights of Surviving Spouse and Civil Partner (Scotland) Order 2011*. According to this Order, for deaths on or after 1 February 2012 the prior rights of the surviving spouse or civil partner are as follows.

If there are children, the spouse/civil partner inherits:

- the interest in the house up to £473,000 (subject to any mortgage liability);
- furniture and household items up to £29,000 (heirlooms are not included); and

- £50,000 of the balance,
- If there is movable estate left, one third of the movable estate passes to the spouse/civil partner, with one third being split equally between the children.

The remaining estate is shared equally between the children.

If there are no children, the spouse/civil partner inherits:

- the interest in the house up to £473,000 (subject to any mortgage liability);
- furniture and household items up to £29,000; and
- £89,000 of the balance.

The remaining estate (also called the free estate) passes as follows:

- If there are parents and brothers and sisters, half goes to the parents equally and half goes to the brothers and sisters equally.
- If there are no parents but brothers and sisters, the remaining estate is split equally between them.
- If there are only parents, but no siblings, it is split equally between the parents.
- If there are no parents or siblings, the spouse will get the remainder.

If the Deceased was not married or in a civil partnership and there are no children, the estate passes in the following order:

- parents, if there are no siblings;
- if there are parents and siblings, a third of the estate will pass to the parents with the remainder split equally between the siblings;
- aunts and uncles and their issue;
- grandparents and their issue;
- great-aunts and great-uncles and their issue; or
- other relatives.

The Inheritance (Provision for Family and Dependants) Act 1975

9.3 Generally speaking, a person can leave his assets to whomsoever he wishes (unlike the rules in most other European countries – the so-called 'community of property' regime – see **10.24**). That said, there is the ability under the *Inheritance (Provision for Family and Dependants) Act 1975 (I(PFD) A 1975)* for certain individuals, who feel that the terms of a will or the intestacy rules do not make reasonable financial provision for them, to apply to the court for such provision. Typically, these will be a surviving spouse, who can apply for what provision it would be reasonable in all the circumstances of the case for them to receive, whether this is capital or income. Other beneficiaries, such as an ex-spouse who has not remarried, a child, or anyone else treated as a child of the deceased, or someone being maintained by the deceased, may receive what it is reasonable for them to get by way of maintenance.

Applications have to be made within six months of the grant of probate. In the case of *Berger v Berger* [2013] EWCA Civ 1305 the Court of Appeal refused permission to bring a claim under the *Inheritance (Provision for Family Dependants) Act 1975,* as the application was made six-and-a-half years after the expiry of the time limit. In contrast in the case of *Beckett v McMillan* [2015] NICh 8, Mrs Beckett was allowed to continue her claim against the estate of her late husband, although more than 16 years had lapsed since grant of probate. However, the facts of this case are unusual and exceptional, and it therefore cannot be taken as an extension of the six-month time limit for bringing a claim under the *I(PFD)A 1975*.

It is possible for one or more beneficiaries to vary their entitlement within two years after the death. This variation can be done in an intestacy, just as much as with a will. This is discussed in more detail in **Chapter 12**.

COMPLIANCE OBLIGATIONS

Inheritance tax

Liability and incidence of tax

9.4 The difference between 'liability' and 'incidence' is similar to the difference between legal and equitable interests: liability is the duty to pay the tax from the assets of the estate, and concerns the relationship between HMRC and personal representatives; incidence is the allocation of the burden of the tax between beneficiaries. A personal representative will be concerned with the rules as to incidence when administering an estate where, for example, the residue passes partly to children and partly to charity. He is liable for the tax, but must apply the rules of incidence to ensure that, subject to the terms of the will and to the rules in *Re Benham's Will Trust* [1995] STC 210 and *Re Ratcliffe* [1999] STC 262, the tax is actually suffered by the children.

Accounts and returns

9.5 PRs must deliver 'an account' of the assets of the deceased (*IHTA 1984, s 216*). The time limit is the expiry of 12 months after the end of the month in which death occurred. Any IHT must be paid on or before delivery of the account (not including instalment property or cases where PRs are not primarily liable, eg failed PETs). Typically, a provisional account may be delivered to the extent that property cannot yet be properly valued.

If no UK grant has been taken up within the time limit, there is a duty on certain other people to deliver an account.

There is a *de minimis* provision in the case of 'excepted estates', where no account need be delivered (see **9.20–9.24**).

In the case of a PET that has become chargeable, or a gift with reservation, there is an obligation to report on the part of the transferee.

PRs also have a statutory obligation to report chargeable transfers made by the deceased within seven years before his death (see **9.10**).

The main form IHT400 and the supplementary forms constituting the inheritance tax account are discussed in detail; see **Chapter 10**. The forms are updated regularly.

Focus

- The simplest, free, version of Adobe Acrobat has been improved and it is now possible to save the forms mid-way through completing them and to return to the task later.
- There are a number of commercial providers whose software simplifies the probate process, as information is carried forward during the completion process.

The IHT400 series takes account of common practices such as the gift of personal effects to charity (dealt with in form IHT408), which is actually a 'one-off' variation of the dispositions of the estate and, as such, should be read in conjunction with any other variation contemplated by the personal representatives. Extra information, which was hitherto set out in a supplemental sheet, can now fit into page 16 of form IHT400.

Form IHT407, formerly IHT409, Household and personal goods, looks more user friendly than its predecessor, but its proper completion will be much more demanding than most families will expect or enjoy.

Following the *Inheritance Tax (Electronic Communications) Regulations 2015*, which came into force on 6 July 2015 it was announced that it would soon be possible to file IHT400 electronically; however, as of April 2019 it was not fully launched yet. The IHT online services are supposed to become available over the course of a number of phases. The first phase, dealing with sub-threshold cases for personal applicants, was made available in autumn 2017, if they are personal representatives of the person who has died, and they are applying for a grant of representation in England and Wales.

Professional agents need to continue using the existing paper process.

HMRC has introduced a new online trusts registration service in July 2017. The register will also provide a single point of access for PRs and their agents to register complex estates. An estate is considered complex, if:

- the value of the estate exceeds £2.5m;
- income tax due for the whole of the administration period exceeds £10,000; or
- the value of assets sold in any tax year for date of deaths up to April 2016 exceeds £250,000 or £500,000 for date of deaths after April 2016.

PRs will have to register estates that have already registered with HMRC, but are still being administered.

COMPLIANCE

9.6 Legislation was introduced in *Finance Act 2008, Pt 7* ('Administration') and *Schs 36, 37, 39* and *40* (dealing with inspection powers, record keeping, time limits for assessments, claims etc and amendments to the rules on penalties for errors etc). *Finance Act 2009, s 96* and *Sch 48* extended the rules as to information and inspection powers to IHT. By the *Finance Act 2009, Section 96 and Schedule 48 (Appointed Day, Savings and Consequential Amendments) Order 2009, SI 2009/3054*, this applies from 1 April 2010: see HMRC's Compliance Handbook at CH20150 and, for a useful summary of commencement dates, see the links there set out.

The general scope of the legislation is to amend the rules on record keeping and the information and inspection powers. The general thrust of the compliance checks is to reassure the majority who do comply that the system is fair and to ensure that taxpayers know what their obligations are in relation to registration for tax.

> **Focus**
>
> Personal representatives need to understand what records are required in order to calculate the tax due; and, in the context of the administration of estates, the preparation of proper executorship accounts must come high on the list.

The checks are also intended to expose deliberate understatement of tax. The whole approach is informed by what HMRC perceive to be the risk involved. On the one hand, as for example with valuation of chattels, the risk may only involve a small amount of tax each time, but errors may be widespread. Alternatively, there may be segmental risk where, for example, taxpayers in a particular category or holding a particular type of asset may exhibit behaviour leading to risk which can be addressed through work with representative bodies or trade organisations.

To some extent, none of this is all that new. The 'old' rules have not lacked teeth, as the following (non-IHT) cases show.

The First-tier Tribunal can take a robust and practical line, as it did in *Cairns v Revenue & Customs* [2009] UKFTT 67 (TC), an investigation into the estate of a former Chief Examiner with the Estate Duty Office. The deceased's house was in extremely poor condition and had been valued shortly before death at about £400,000. The personal representative adopted that figure in the IHT account (form IHT200, as it then was), not considering it necessary to revalue, since on sale the price achieved would very likely be substituted anyway. Following sale for £600,000, which was then agreed to be the value at date of death, HMRC pressed for penalties for delivery of an incorrect account. Fraud was not alleged; instead, HMRC alleged negligence on the basis that the personal representative should have obtained another valuation.

Not so, held the Tribunal. The account was not negligently delivered. The value specified should have been shown as provisional, but that was a mere technical error which had no consequence whatsoever. There was no loss to the public purse because, in fact, IHT had been overpaid and was later repaid. Any finding of negligence would have been the merest technicality. A proportionate approach would have been a nominal penalty.

A detailed consideration of the legislation, which appears at *Finance Act 2008, ss 113, 115-117* and *Schs 36–37* is beyond the scope of this book but is included in Chapter 1 of *Capital Gains Tax 2019/20* (Bloomsbury Professional). In practical terms, help is being rolled out to practitioners by HMRC in the form of 'checklists' for various taxes.

HMRC have published an 'Inheritance Tax Toolkit', which is aimed at 'helping and supporting tax agents and advisers in completing Inheritance Tax account form IHT400, although it may be of use to anyone, including trustees and personal representatives, in completing this form'.

The Toolkit states that it does not need to be used in order to demonstrate that 'reasonable care' has been taken, if the matter of penalties arises due to an error in the IHT400 account. However, HMRC's website states: 'They can also be used to help demonstrate that "reasonable care" has been taken'.

HMRC announced changes to their compliance checks in their December 2013 Trust and Estates Newsletter. If a case has been selected for a compliance check, an initial letter will be sent to the practitioner explaining that a case has been selected. HMRC stated that they will aim to complete the check within eight to ten weeks of receipt of the IHT account. The investigator will make contact with the practitioner by phone with the aim to agree a case plan to resolve the matter more quickly.

The UK government intended to introduce a banded system of probate fees from May 2017. Following representations by professional bodies that the fee constituted a form of taxation, the Ministry of Justice announced in April 2017 that the fee increase was on hold, but the government reinstated the probate fee increase in a revised form in the 2018 Autumn Budget, to be effective from 1 April 2019. However, at the time of writing this book, the necessary legislation had not yet been laid before Parliament and the introduction of the new fee scale (see below) has been delayed. As an interim measure, personal representatives have been told that they can submit probate applications before they receive IHT clearance.

Value of net estate	*Fee (£)*
Up to £50,000	0
Between £50,000 and £300,000	250
Between £300,000 and £500,000	750
Between £500,000 and £1m	2,500
Between £1m and £1.6m	4,000
Between £1.6m and £2m	5,000
Exceeds £2m	6,000

PARTICULAR COMPLIANCE ISSUES

Personal effects

9.7 An area of difficulty is personal effects, where HMRC consider that there may previously have been insufficient disclosure. The true value to be shown is governed by the market value rule in *s 160*. There is no such thing as 'probate value': the value to be disclosed is 'the price which the property might reasonably be expected to fetch if sold in the open market' at the date of death. That is the gross selling price, not the net. Here, in particular, Form IHT407 asks much more searching questions than the forms that accompanied the 'old' IHT account form IHT200, including: the registration number of the deceased's car; whether chattels that have been sold were purchased by relatives; and how the value of other chattels was arrived at.

Focus

- It is important to obtain professional valuation of chattels from appropriate experts, whether they might be auction houses or car dealerships: for example in relation to cars web-based valuations are likely to be insufficient. A value 'for insurance' may be higher than an open market value.

- Professional advisers may be negligent if they rely on estimates, rather than proper market valuations.
- Previous guidance stated that you did not have to get a professional valuation for items which have a value of less than £500. In the August 2018 HMRC Trust and Estates Newsletter this was increased to £1,500, unless an item cannot reasonably be estimated.

Estimates

9.8 There is statutory authority in *s 216(3A)* for the use of estimates. The personal representatives must make very full enquiries but, if unable to arrive at the exact value, must:

- say that they have made full enquiries;
- supply a provisional estimate of the value; and
- undertake to deliver a further account as soon as the value is ascertained.

For an example of litigation on these issues and on the costs of the litigation itself, see *Robertson v CIR* [2002] STC (SCD) 182 and *Robertson v CIR (No 2)* [2002] SSCD 242. For a case that highlighted the duty, see *Cairns v Revenue & Customs* [2009] UKFTT 67 (TC), noted at **9.6** above.

A 'Red Book' valuation from a qualified independent surveyor which meets the standards of the Royal Institute of Chartered Surveyors is essential for property valuations.

Focus

- HMRC are taking a much more aggressive stance against estimates.
- Good practice is to obtain valuations from a professionally qualified valuer rather than estimates. One paragraph valuations from a local estate agent are unlikely to convince HMRC.
- In relation to land, 'development value', 'hope value' and the state of repair of a property need to be addressed. Carefully document the state of the property (via photos etc) immediately after death and certainly before any work is done to prepare the property for sale or to improve it in any way.
- Following the introduction of the new penalty regime, these considerations are even more important.

Development value of land

9.9 Cases such as *Prosser v IRC* ([2001] RVR 170) have shown that the value of land for IHT must take some, but not full, account of 'hope' value. In that particular case, a plot of garden ground, in respect of which planning permission was eventually obtained, was held to be worth 25% of its ultimate value for probate purposes. The IHT Newsletter of 28 April 2006 stressed that development value must be accounted for, and that the value of a house should reflect any feature that makes it attractive to a builder or developer. If new information comes to light that enhances the value, the personal representatives should declare it, on pain of penalties for failure to do so.

Note that HMRC do now take the point that, if an asset is sold relatively soon after the death for substantially more than probate value, the personal representatives may have failed in their duty of disclosure, and penalties may result.

HMRC's approach to 'hope value' is reflected in the recent case of *Palliser v Revenue and Customs* [2018] UKUT 71 (TC). Here an individual's interest in a property was originally valued on his death in June 2012 without reflecting any 'hope value' for future development of the property or change of use. HMRC served a notice of determination on the PRs, valuing the property interest at £1,829,880. The PRs appealed, stating that the correct valuation was £1,113,840. The property was eventually sold for £2.525 million in March 2014. The Upper Tribunal concluded that 'hope value' rather than development value needs to be included, where planning permission had not yet been obtained. It arrived at a value of £1,603,930 for IHT purposes, which represented 50% of the difference between the net value of the property with and without the later extension.

Focus

- HMRC are now asking PRs how much care they took when getting an independent valuation.
- HMRC now consider that PRs have a duty to draw the valuer's attention to specific features of the property that may affect its price.

Discounts for co-ownership in property

9.10 HMRC seems to take a hard line approach in relation to discounts for property held jointly or as tenants in common.

Property owned as joint tenants passes to the survivor by the *ius accrescendi*, without the need for a grant of representation. That does not mean, however, that no IHT is due. If the surviving joint owner is neither the spouse nor the civil partner, the value may be taxable. Form IHT400 will be appropriate, with form IHT404 annexed.

Following the case of *Wight v IRC* (1982) EG 935; [1984] RVR 163 it is generally accepted that a discount of 15% applies to jointly owned property where the surviving joint owner has a right of occupation. The case of *Price (Executor of Price, Deceased) v HMRC* [2010] UK FTT 474 confirms that such discount however does not apply to joint ownership between spouses.

In *St Clair Ford v Ryder* [2006] WTLR 1647 the taxpayer argued for a 15% discount in the case of a commercial building. The Lands Tribunal allowed only 10% discount, but it stated that a higher discount may be accepted in cases where there are minority interests or other complicating factors.

Rather worryingly there is anecdotal evidence that HMRC now re-interpret the *Wight* case insisting that a 15% discount only applies to residential properties which are occupied by the co-owners as their main residence.

Joint bank accounts

9.11 The deceased may have opened an account jointly with a child, perhaps for convenience through frailty or failing intellect. Payment of money into such an account is not necessarily a gift of half to the child; but the withdrawal of funds by the child for her own purposes will usually be a transfer for IHT and should be brought into account. HMRC explained, in IHT Newsletter for December 2006, that they look critically at accounts opened shortly before death. See also *Taylor v HMRC* [2008] SpC 704.

Care needs to be taken when money was gifted into a joint bank account for the donor and donee. Even if there was an intention to make the gift, but the account was operated so that the donor potentially was able to withdraw the full amount, there might be a reservation of benefit and the whole account is likely to remain within the donor's estate for IHT purposes (see *Sillars v IRC* (2004) STC (SCD) 180 and *Matthews v Revenue and Customs Commissioners* [2012] UKFTT 658 (TC)).

Form IHT 404 includes a question about who provided the funds for assets owned jointly. If the deceased provided all the funds, it is likely that HMRC will argue that the whole value of the asset rather than a share should be included in the deceased's estate.

Inherited ISAs

9.12 The *Individual Savings Account (Amendment No 2) Regulations, SI 2015/869* took effect on 6 April 2015, which provides that the spouse or civil partner of a saver who died on or after 3 December 2014 can benefit from an additional ISA allowance equal to the value of the ISA at the holder's date of death. This is in addition to the surviving spouse's or civil partner's own ISA allowance and can be used within three years from the date of death or (if later) 180 days after the administration period has ended. One of the conditions is that the surviving spouse lived with the deceased at the time of their death. If so, the deceased's ISA can be transferred to the surviving spouse/civil partner.

Lifetime gifts

9.13 The case of *Timothy Clayton Hutchings v HMRC* [2015] UK FTT 009 highlights the importance of ascertaining all lifetime gifts made by the deceased and recording them fully on Form IHT 403. The facts of this case were that Robert Hutchings made a gift of an offshore bank account containing £443,669 to his son Timothy seven months before he died. The professional executors wrote to the family and the potential beneficiaries including Timothy asking about details of all life-time gifts. Timothy did not declare the gift, and said that he thought offshore accounts did not come within the scope of UK tax. The First-tier Tribunal determined that the penalty should be assessed on the beneficiary Timothy Huchings. The professional executors were exonerated, as they could prove that they made full enquiries by writing to the family and the beneficiaries.

Focus

- Following the *Hutchings* case professional advisers have to make detailed enquiries about lifetime gifts.
- Letters to family members and potential beneficiaries enquiring about lifetime gifts are advisable.
- PRs need to fully document their enquiries.

Annuities

9.14 There will seldom be any residual value of an annuity but, where payments do continue after death, as where the annuitant dies before the end of the guaranteed period, the right to the income stream must be valued. Whilst personal representatives may value as they think fit, many will want to make use of the HMRC calculator on their website, giving a reasonable estimate of the value under *s 160*; see www.gov.uk/government/publications/inheritance-tax-guaranteed-annuity-calculator.

Compensation payments

9.15 The treatment of compensation payments can cause difficulties for PRs. The right to pursue a claim for compensation is an asset of the estate, but it often is difficult to ascertain the market value of the right at date of death. The value of a claim will depend on a number of factors:

- the amount of compensation that might be reasonably anticipated;
- the likelihood of the claim being successful;
- the likely cost that would be expected to be incurred in obtaining a successful outcome; and
- the time delay between the date of death and the date when the compensation might reasonably be expected.

Where PRs are aware of a potential claim at the date of death, full disclosure and a reasoned estimate of the open market value of the right to pursue the compensation should be included in Form IHT400.

Care needs to be taken, as some compensation payments may be viewed as income rather than capital – see the recent case of *Gadhavi v HMRC [2018] UKFTT 0600 (TC).*

Nil rate band discretionary trusts – treatment of interest

9.16 Many wills were created with nil rate band discretionary trusts providing a debt and charge scheme with index-linking. On the death of the second spouse, PRs together with the trustees of the nil rate band discretionary trust now may have to consider how to treat the interest on the debt.

Interest may, but need not, be charged on the debt. In many instances the charging of interest will be tax neutral. Receipt of interest by the trustees of the nil rate band will attract income tax at 45%, whilst reducing the estate of the surviving spouse and thus saving IHT at 40%. At that point, therefore, the exercise seems not to be worthwhile. If, however, there are beneficiaries of the nil rate band who, perhaps because they are young, do not pay income tax, there will be a saving because after expenses the trustees can make distributions of income to the non-taxpaying beneficiaries who will recover some or all of the tax thus paid.

Occasionally, the nil rate band is index linked. On final resolution of matters it is certainly arguable that the extra money so received is essentially payment, by reference to time, for the use of money and is therefore interest receivable at the time of repayment of the loan, even though it is calculated by reference to inflation or a house price index. Others argue to the contrary, but there are no decided cases directly in point. HMRC have litigated arguing that the extra money received represents interest which is subject to income tax. The case settled and uncertainty therefore remains. Well-drawn wills allow the trustees to waive their rights as to index-linking or the charging of interest.

However, if the debt together with any interest is discharged on second death, the full sum can be deducted as a liability from the estate. HMRC state that the interest received will have to be taxed by the trustees as income at the rate of 45%. HMRC have stated in their April 2017 *Trusts and Estates Newsletter* that they will continue to challenge arrangements where interest was received by the trustees. HMRC have issued a number of closure notices and they intend to defend any resulting appeals.

If the interest is waived, there is not likely to be an income tax liability on the waived sum. HMRC state that there is unlikely to be any commercial purpose to the interest not being repaid, as, had the creditor been at arm's length, they would have wanted the interest repaid as well. The waived interest therefore does not represent a deductible liability on the estate.

IHTA 1984, s 175A (discharge of liabilities after death) will apply to old debt and charge schemes where the second spouse dies on or after 17 July 2013. The effect of the new provisions is that liabilities are only deductible in determining the value of an estate, if they are actually repaid out of an estate on or after death unless there is a real commercial reason for the liability to remain outstanding.

Digital assets

9.17 Digital assets are any assets that are accrued or held online, and range from online gaming accounts to photos, music, clients lists, bank accounts etc. There is no legislation dealing with the rights of PRs over digital assets, and owners of these assets often do not consider what should happen with these assets when they die. Many online providers have end user licence agreements which restrict access to the named individual, and expressly or implicitly exclude PRs.

Some domain names will have a financial value, so have balances in PayPal accounts or bitcoins.

This represents a challenge for PR who have to deal with digital assets of a deceased. Practitioners will have to consider the following steps:

- Making an inventory of the person's known digital estate. This may require contacting friends or family, or accessing a digital device that reveals the existence of various digital assets or digital accounts.
- If necessary, finding people who have the appropriate technical and legal knowledge to access the digital estate.
- Taking steps to manage any financial arrangements that are solely conducted through the digital estate.

- Paying any liabilities relating to digital accounts.
- If it is necessary to change passwords, changing them as soon as possible.
- Considering, in the case of death, in what form the digital devices should be given to beneficiaries.
- Considering whether it is prudent to buy an external hard drive and copy all data, and store it in a secure place.
- Obtaining the details of contact lists, email accounts and social media accounts so appropriate people can be notified.
- Considering who owns the digital accounts, whether access is regulated and the consequences of that regulation.
- Considering who should be given access to the digital accounts and, if possible, granting them access.
- Considering what needs to be done with the digital accounts – that is, whether they should be deleted, transferred, sold, cashed-out or, if an option, memorialised.
- Taking steps to protect the privacy of the person who has lost capacity or died.
- Informing the online service provider that the account user has died.

EXCEPTED ESTATES

Bare trusts

9.18 Following *FA 2006*, there was a resurgence in the popularity of bare trusts, since these were outside the scope of the relevant property regime. As usual, some advisers went to the limit of what might be considered to be a bare trust. Perhaps in response to this, HMRC revealed that they were considering one analysis of such trusts where there was, either expressly or by implication, a duty on the trustees to accumulate the income. Such arrangements might be substantive trusts and caught by *FA 2006*. A second issue was whether the power of advancement under *Trustee Act 1925, s 32* might be used to make settled advances, which would again allow ongoing trusts of precisely the kind eschewed by *FA 2006*.

This suggestion provoked uproar among professional advisers, who considered it to be wrong in law. If such trusts are substantive trusts, their creation is a chargeable transfer and much else follows. Some of the argument turns on the effect of *IHTA 1984, s 43(2)(b)* and its reference to accumulations. There is perceived to be inconsistency between the established treatment of bare trusts for income tax (see, for example, HMRC Trusts, Settlements and Estates Manual at TSEM1031) and as proposed for IHT. Cautious advisers will therefore exclude *TA 1925, s 31* to weaken the suggestion that there is a substantive trust. The argument that, where trustees have active duties, there is a substantive trust sits ill with, for example, the position of unit trusts, where the trustees are active and which are nevertheless bare trusts.

The issue now seems to have been resolved. A bare trust of capital for a minor beneficiary is not settled property and thus cannot be relevant property. HMRC have commented:

> 'We confirm that our view is that where assets are held on an absolute trust (ie a bare trust) for a minor the assets so held will not be settled property within the meaning of section 43 IHTA 1984 and that this will be the case whether or not the provisions of section 31 Trustee Act 1925 have been excluded.'

Transfers on death

9.19 There are now three categories of excepted estate; see *Inheritance Tax (Delivery of Accounts) (Excepted Estates) Regulations 2004 (SI 2004/2543)*. Many practitioners fail to take advantage of the regulations, using form IHT400 where it is not needed. This is not encouraged by HMRC, because it just makes for unnecessary work that yields no tax. The reporting levels were increased by *Inheritance Tax (Delivery of Accounts) (Excepted Estates) (Amendment) Regulations 2006 (SI 2006/2141)* with effect from 1 September 2006 and *Inheritance Tax (Delivery of Accounts) (Excepted Estates) (Amendment) Regulations 2011 (SI 2011/214)* with effect from 1 March 2011.

The *Inheritance Tax (Delivery of Accounts) (Excepted Estates) (Amendment) (No 2) Regulations 2011 (SI 2011/214)* were published in July 2011 and amend *SI 2004/2543* to remedy two defects. A further amendment was made by the *Inheritance Tax (Delivery of Accounts) (Excepted Estates) Regulations 2011 (SI 2011/2226)*.

HMRC confirmed in their December 2012 Newsletter that it will not be necessary to report any adjustments to the value of an excepted estate, unless the estate will no longer qualify as an excepted estate.

Category One: small estates: the traditional form

9.20 The conditions are:

(1) The deceased, UK domiciled, died on or after 1 September 2006.

(2) The estate relates to property in the following categories:

- it passes under the will of the deceased or on his intestacy;

- it passes under nomination taking effect on death;
- it is contained in one settlement only in which the deceased had an interest in possession; or
- it was joint property and passes by survivorship (or, in Scotland, by survivorship in a special destination).

(3) Of the property passing on death:

- no more than £100,000 was situated overseas; and
- no more than £150,000 was trust property.

(4) In the seven years before death, the deceased made transfers which, before deduction of business or agricultural relief, did not exceed £150,000.

Note: for deaths on or after 1 March 2011, gifts under *IHTA 1984, s 21* (normal expenditure out of income) in excess of £3,000 in any one tax year will be treated as chargeable gifts for reporting purposes.

(5) The whole estate, including certain categories of transfer, did not exceed the IHT threshold. Note that, for this purpose, the relevant threshold is the 'old' one in the period from 6 April to 6 August.

The categories of transfer referred to in this last condition are two. 'Specified transfers' are defined in *SI 2004/2543, reg 4(6)* to mean chargeable transfers in the seven years up to death consisting only of:

- cash;
- personal chattels or moveable property;
- quoted shares or securities; or
- interest in land (with qualifications).

The same regulations define 'specified exempt transfers' as those made in the seven years up to death which are exempt under one of the following headings:

- transfers between spouses;
- charities;
- political parties;
- gifts to housing association;
- gifts to maintenance funds for historic buildings; and
- employee trusts.

(6) The deceased had not made a gift with reservation of benefit or an IHT charge arises on an alternatively secured pension.

Category Two: estates: spouse/charity exemption

9.21 *SI 2004/2543* created a new category of excepted estate of a gross value of up to £1 million where, after spouse or charity exemption, the estate was still within the IHT threshold. To comply with this category, the following conditions must be satisfied:

(1) UK domicile, death on or after 6 April 2004.

(2) The estate to include only property passing:

- by will or on intestacy;
- under a nomination taking effect on death;
- under a single settlement of which the deceased was tenant for life; or
- joint property passing by survivorship or, in Scotland, by survivorship in a special destination.

(3) The estate included:

- not more than £100,000 foreign property;
- not more than £150,000 of settled property, but ignoring settled property that on death passes to a spouse or to charity; and
- that, in the seven years leading up to death, the deceased did not make chargeable transfers other than specified transfers (for a definition of 'specified transfer' see **10.18**) not exceeding £150,000 before deduction of business or agricultural relief.

(4) The estate did not exceed £1 million, including within that figure:

- the gross value of the estate;
- the value transferred by specified transfers; and
- the value transferred by specified exempt transfers.

(5) Applying the formula A – (B + C), the total does not exceed the IHT threshold. For this purpose:

- A is the aggregate of the estate, specified transfers and the specified exempt transfers;
- B is the total value transferred on death that qualifies for exemption as passing to a spouse or charity, but subject to qualification of that rule in relation to Scotland; and
- C is the total liabilities of the estate.

(6) The deceased had not made a gift with reservation of benefit or an IHT charge arises on an alternatively secured pension.

HMRC will not accept the shorter IHT205, if the deceased made a pension transfer within two years of date of death and IHT400 will have to be completed, unless the deceased was in normal health for their age, when the transfer was made.

IHT threshold: transferable nil rate band

9.22 *SI 2011/214* allows personal representatives to claim the benefit of the transferable nil rate band (TNRB) and apply for a grant as an excepted estate, provided that a number of conditions are met. The claim for TNRB in an excepted estate must be made on form IHT217. The conditions that must be met are:

- the deceased survived the earlier death of their spouse or civil partner and was married to, or in a civil partnership with, them at the earlier death;
- none of the nil rate band was used by the earlier death, so that 100% is available for transfer;
- a valid claim is made and is in respect of one earlier death only; and
- the first deceased person died on or after 13 November 1974, where the deceased was the spouse of the first deceased, or on or after 5 December 2005, where the deceased was the civil partner of the first deceased person.

The estate of the first deceased person must also meet the following conditions:

- the first deceased person died domiciled in the UK;
- their estate consisted only of property passing under their will or intestacy and jointly owned assets;
- if their estate included foreign assets, their gross value did not exceed £100,000; and
- agricultural and business property relief did not apply.

Where an estate meets the above conditions and a valid claim is made:

- in a 'standard' excepted estate, the gross value of the estate must not exceed double the applicable nil rate band, or
- if the estate is an exempt excepted estate, the gross value of the estate must not exceed £1 million and the net chargeable value of the estate (after deduction of liabilities and spouse or civil partner exemption and/or charity exemption) must not exceed double the applicable nil rate band.

Category Three: small foreign estates

9.23 This category of estate is one where the deceased was never domiciled or deemed to be domiciled in the UK, and the estate in the UK comprises only cash or quoted shares or securities with a total value not exceeding £150,000. Remember to state the value of worldwide estate. If below the IHT threshold, domicile is less likely to be examined in detail; there is no point.

The personal representatives of an excepted estate are not entirely excused from supplying information. In all such cases, they must complete the short form IHT205. This may, in any event, serve a separate function, by offering some protection to beneficiaries, especially charities, because without IHT205 there might actually be no formal inventory of the estate.

Payment of IHT

9.24 The personal representatives are liable and the tax is treated as part of the administration expenses of the estate. The *Administration of Estates Act 1925* sets out the order in which the tax is charged against the assets in the estate. That rule is limited by *IHTA 1984, s 211* to the value of property in the UK that vests in the personal representatives of the deceased and was not comprised in a settlement immediately before the death. There are rules for recovery of tax where property is vested in another person.

This was confirmed in the recent case of *Harris v HMRC* [2018] UKFTT 204. Glyne Harris was the personal representative and he distributed the estate to the deceased's brother on the understanding that the beneficiary would pay the inheritance tax due. However, he moved abroad and the personal representative was unable to contact him. The judge of the First-tier Tribunal determined that *IHTA 1984, s 200* was clear: the personal representatives were responsible for the inheritance tax arising on the deemed transfer on death.

IHT direct payment scheme

9.25 Since 31 March 2003 and by arrangement between HMRC and certain financial institutions, it has been possible for personal representatives to access funds in the name of the deceased before the grant of representation issues. This is a great help because tax must be paid 'up front' on all property except where it qualifies for the instalment option. Where, for example, a dispute about the will prevents the issue of a grant of representation, this facility still allows the tax to be paid, stopping interest from running.

The scheme is voluntary, so check with the financial institution whether they participate. Sadly, not all banks do. It applies only to accounts in the sole name of the deceased and, if the deceased has several accounts, the institution will not release more than the net value (ie after setting off overdrafts or credit card liabilities). The number of the account must be nominated on the form. Use form IHT423 for each financial institution from which the personal representatives wish to take money to pay the tax.

In some situations, especially where banks are unwilling to lend, it is possible to obtain the grant on credit. See HMRC Inheritance Tax Manual at IHTM05071 for an explanation of when HMRC may consider credit.

Acceptance of property in lieu of tax

9.26 This is a specialist topic but, in outline, it is possible to offer heritage property in satisfaction of tax liabilities. It must be of outstanding quality. The procedure is protracted, but it does secure for the nation valuable objects that might otherwise have been sold to overseas buyers to pay tax. As an incentive, the taxpayer receives a credit that slightly exceeds the net of tax commercial value of the item. This is known somewhat archaically as the 'douceur' (under a tax law rewrite, it would perhaps become 'cashback').

Payment of IHT by Instalments

9.27 *IHTA 1984, s 227* provides that IHT due in respect of specific assets may be paid by instalments, To claim such relief, an appropriate election must be filed with HMRC.

The instalment basis is available where:

- IHT is payable on the value transferred by a chargeable transfer that is attributable to the value of 'qualifying property'; and
- appropriate conditions are satisfied.

For this purpose 'qualifying property' is defined as:

- land (to include building thereon), irrespective of situs;
- '*s 228*' shares or securities (the meaning of which is described below); and
- a business or an interest in a business.

The 'appropriate conditions' for eligibility are that:

- the transfer is made on death; or
- the IHT is being paid by the person who benefits from the transfer; or
- the transfer comes within the settled property regime and either the IHT is borne by the beneficiary or the property remains within the settlement.

Importantly, the instalment option is not available for IHT payable in respect of a failed PET, nor on the IHT top-up charge of a CLT, unless the property concerned satisfies one of two conditions set out in *s 227(1C)*:

- the property was owned by the transferee throughout the period beginning with the date of the chargeable transfer and ending with the death of the transferor (or, if earlier, the death of the transferee); or
- for the purposes of determining IHT or top-up tax arising from the death of the transferor, the property qualifies for APR or BPR – in other words, the clawback charge.

Where the property consists of unquoted shares or unquoted securities, *IHTA 1984, s 228(3A)* sets out further conditions requiring the shares or securities to remain unquoted throughout the period beginning with the date of the transfer and ending with the death of the transferor (or the earlier death of the transferee).

IHTA 1984, s 228 applies to four categories of shares or securities of a company, as follows:

(1) quoted or unquoted shares or securities that, immediately before the chargeable transfer, gave the control of the company to the deceased, the transferor, or, within the trust regime, the trustees.

(2) unquoted shares, where the chargeable transfer is made on death and attracts not less than 20% of the total tax payable by that person in the same capacity (*IHTA 1984, s 228(2)*);

(3) unquoted shares, where HMRC is satisfied that the IHT attributable to their value cannot be paid in one sum without undue hardship. For this test to apply it is assumed (in the case of a chargeable transfer not made on death) that the shares will be retained by the person liable to pay the IHT; and

(4) unquoted shares not falling within (1) above (ie not controlling holdings), where conditions of s *228(3)* are satisfied, namely:

    (a) the value of the transfer is over £20,000; and

    (b) the nominal value of the shares is at least 10% of the nominal value of all the shares of the company at the time of transfer; or

    (c) the shares are ordinary shares and their nominal value is at least 10% of the nominal value of all the ordinary shares of the company at that time.

For this purpose 'ordinary shares' are defined as those carrying a right to dividends not restricted to those at a fixed rate, or those with a right to conversion to shares carrying such a right, and thus, preference shares fall outside this definition (*IHTA 1984, s 228(4)*).

Clearance application

9.28 It is customary, once the estate administration has run its course, for the PRs to submit a clearance application to HMRC Inheritance Tax (*IHTA 1984, s 239*) using Form IHT30. Generally speaking, this will confirm that the PRs have satisfied their liabilities in respect of the assets disclosed. The PRs may have some concern that, having completed the estate, a PET made within seven years before the death may subsequently come to light. HMRC Inheritance Tax have said that, provided the PRs have made the fullest enquiries as are reasonably practicable to discover the existence of such PETs, and have done all in their power to make disclosure to HMRC Inheritance Tax, HMRC will not hold them liable if they have obtained a certificate of discharge and distributed the estate before a chargeable lifetime transfer comes to light (IHTM30044).

IHTA 1984, s 239(2) states that it is appropriate to apply for clearance once two years have passed since date of death. HMRC stated that they will consider earlier applications, if the practitioner is certain that there will be no more changes to the estate reported.

The above said, HMRC announced in their IHT Newsletter of December 2012 that formal clearance certificates will not be issued in excepted estates. Instead, agents and taxpayers will have to rely on the assurance provided by HMRC's closure letter. In practice, solicitors and others dealing with deceased estates will continue to apply for a clearance certificate, given the measure of protection that it affords the personal representatives.

HMRC in their Trust and Estates Newsletter: Special Edition April 2018 stated that they will not issue standard clearance letters, when they have finished their checks. Practitioners will have to apply for a clearance certificate using Form IHT30.

Further HMRC Trusts and Estates have announced that they will not be issuing receipts for IHT paid.

Following complaints by practitioners of the delays within HMRC in dealing with the Form IHT400, HMRC stated that they will inform the personal representatives within 12 weeks of their initial calculation, if they are going to look at the estate in more detail.

Income tax and capital gains tax

9.29 The income and gains of the estate must be distinguished from those of the deceased. The tax liabilities of the deceased must be computed and paid by the PRs, and these will rank as a deduction in calculating his estate for inheritance tax purposes. The income and gains of the estate must be returned in form SA900 and supplementary pages. These are discussed in more detail in **Chapter 11**.

THE INTEREST AND PENALTY REGIME

Interest

9.30 Tax on death is due six months after the end of the month in which the death occurred. It is not uncommon for IHT to be paid later than that and this will trigger a liability to interest.

Finance Act 2014 addressed the issue that the time limits for reporting IHT periodic and exit charges differed from the time limits for paying any IHT due. Therefore, for chargeable events on or after 6 April 2014 the time limit for filing the return and paying any IHT due will be the end of the sixth month after the event.

Recent rates of interest on unpaid IHT are set out in **6.16**.

Penalties

9.31 A new penalty regime is in place for deaths occurring on or after 1 April 2009: see **6.15** and **4.13–4.15**. For deaths occurring before that date, see **10.24** of the 2008/09 edition of this book. Statute sets out various penalty regimes for failure to deliver accounts (*IHTA 1984, s 245*), failure to provide information, etc (*IHTA 1984, s 245A*) and provision of incorrect information (*IHTA 1984, s 247*). For example, under *s 247*, the delivery of incorrect accounts by the person liable for the IHT carries a maximum penalty of 100% of the additional tax liability. Delivery by a person not liable for the tax carries a maximum penalty of £3,000. For the statutory reductions of the maximum penalties, see **4.15**. Two Special Commissioner's cases (*Robertson v IRC* [2002] STC (SCD) 182 and *Cairns (personal representatives of Webb deceased) v R & C Commissioners* [2009] UKFTT 67 (TC), [2009] STI 1801) illustrate how HMRC Inheritance Tax are keen to apply penalties where they consider that a PR has not been sufficiently careful to ascertain market values at death, even where an urgent grant of probate is required and where reasonable care was taken. Happily, both cases found for the PR and overturned the penalty.

Degrees of culpability

9.32 *Finance Act 2007, Sch 24* had already set out the classifications, but the wording is tidied up by the amendments in *FA 2008, Sch 40*.

Penalties may arise if 'reasonable care' has not been taken in preparing an IHT account or excepted estate return, or if any inaccuracy is discovered but reasonable steps are not taken to inform HMRC about it. HMRC consider that personal representatives will have taken reasonable care in the following circumstances (see HMRC Inheritance Tax and Trusts Newsletter, April 2009):

- The PRs follow the guidance provided about filling in forms such as the IHT400 and IHT205/207/C5.
- They make suitable enquiries of asset holders and other people (as suggested in the guidance) to establish the extent of the deceased's estate.
- They ensure correct instructions are given to valuers when valuing assets.
- They seek advice about anything of which they are unsure.
- They follow up inconsistencies in information they receive from asset holders, valuers and other people.
- They identify any estimated values included on the form.

If the PRs leave the account or return to an agent, they are nevertheless required to check the entries carefully. Merely signing a form completed by an agent is not reasonable care.

The penalty regime identifies three categories of behaviour that can give rise to penalties for an inaccuracy in an account or return:

- The lowest level of culpability, described as 'careless', is where the taxpayer fails to take reasonable care in completing the return.
- The 'middle' level of culpability is 'deliberate but not concealed', where the return is wrong and it results from the deliberate action of the taxpayer, but the taxpayer makes no arrangements to conceal the inaccuracy.
- Finally, the most serious level of wrongdoing is that which is 'deliberate and concealed', where the taxpayer has deliberately sent in a wrong return and deliberately tries to conceal the parts of the return that are wrong, for example by submitting false evidence in support of false figures.

When it turns out that a return was inaccurate, the taxpayer will be treated as careless, even though he may not have been at the time of the return, if he discovers the inaccuracy some time later and does not take reasonable steps to inform HMRC.

In this summary of the law, the word 'return' has been used, but the rules apply in the much wider context of documents that, whether or not returns, fix the liability to tax.

The level of penalties

9.33 These maximum levels were established by *FA 2007, Sch 24*, but their scope was extended by *FA 2008*:

- The 30% rate: a penalty of 30% of the potential lost revenue applies where the taxpayer was careless.

- The 70% rate: a penalty of 70% applies where the action of the taxpayer was deliberate but not concealed.
- The 100% rate: a penalty of 100% applies where the action of the taxpayer was deliberate and concealed. This can apply in two circumstances. Under *FA 2007, Sch 24, para 4(C)*, the full penalty could apply to 'deliberate and concealed action'. That penalty still stands, but is extended to cover 'third party' acts. The collection of tax lost through third-party inaccuracy was extended by *FA 2008*, so that it includes any inaccuracy that results from the supply of false information or the withholding of information.

The penalty regime in *FA 2007, Sch 24* did not previously apply to IHT, so specialists in that area of practice may not have become familiar with the scheme of that schedule. In a situation where there are various errors, such as could easily apply in the administration of an estate, careless inaccuracies are corrected before deliberate inaccuracies; and deliberate but not concealed inaccuracies are corrected before deliberate and concealed inaccuracies. In calculating the lost tax, account is taken of any overstatement in any document given by the taxpayer that relates to the same tax period.

The level of the penalty, as shown in the table below, is also determined by the circumstances of each case.

Factor	*Disclosure*	*Minimum Penalty*	*Maximum Penalty*
Careless	Unprompted	0%	30%
Careless	Prompted	15%	30%
Deliberate	Unprompted	20%	70%
Deliberate	Prompted	35%	70%
Deliberate and Concealed	Unprompted	30%	100%
Deliberate and Concealed	Prompted	50%	100%

Practitioners also need to be aware of the offshore penalty regime, which strengthens existing penalties for:

- failure to notify;
- inaccuracy on a return; and
- failure to file a return in time.

There are three penalty levels, which depend on the territory in which the income, gain or disposition arises:

- Where the offshore matter or offshore transfer arises in a territory in 'Category 1' (which includes most of Europe and the United States), the penalty regime will be the same as under the existing legislation and the maximum penalty is 100% of the tax.

- Where the offshore matter or offshore transfer arises in a territory in 'Category 2', the penalty rate will be 1.5 times that in the existing legislation, up to 150% of tax.
- Where the offshore matter or offshore transfer in a territory in 'Category 3', the penalty rate will be double that in the existing legislation, up to 200% of tax.

There are no penalties for those who have taken reasonable care or have a reasonable excuse for the failure to notify taxable income and gains.

The case of *Timothy Clayton Hutchings v HMRC* [2015] UKFTT 9 (TC) highlights HMRC's tougher approach where the taxpayer deliberately withheld information relating to a gift of an offshore bank account. As the disclosure was prompted, a penalty of 50% was imposed on the taxpayer.

In the 2014 Autumn Statement it was announced that the offshore penalty regime will be extended to:

- include IHT;
- apply to domestic offences where the proceeds of UK non-compliance are hidden offshore;
- update the territorial classification system; and
- introduce a new aggravated penalty, up to a further 50% of tax lost, for moving hidden funds to circumvent international tax transparency agreements.

These changes came into force on 26 March 2015. Finance Act 2015 also increased the level of penalties for offshore tax avoidance from 30% to 37.5%, 70% to 87.5% and 100% to 125% respectively.

Penalties for late filing

9.34 *Finance Act 2009, s 106, Sch 55* applies penalties simply for late filing, something that has hitherto been almost routine in probate work.

Following *IHTA 1984, s 245,* the following penalty regime applies to late filing of an IHT account.

Where the due date for delivery of the account expires after 22 January 2005 and the account is filed between 6 months and 12 months late, the penalties are as follows:

- an initial penalty of £100 for late delivery; and
- a further penalty of £100 if the account is delivered between six months and twelve months after the time limit for delivery.

However, if the actual tax liability is less than the penalty chargeable under the above provisions then the maximum penalty is limited to the amount of the tax that is due, see *IHTA 1984, s 245(5)*. This also means that if, subsequent to the account being delivered, the tax that is due is reduced to nil, any late account penalty that has been paid under *IHTA 1984, ss 245(2)(a)* and *(3)* should be repaid.

The further penalty for accounts that are at least six months late will not apply if, during the six months following the time limit for delivering an account, HMRC have begun proceedings to have the failure to deliver an account declared (see IHTM36081).

Where the accountable person's failure to deliver an account continues beyond the period of 12 months after the due date for delivery specified in *IHTA 1984 s 216*, and where there would have been a liability to tax shown in the account, *Finance Act 2004* introduced a new penalty of up to £3,000: see *IHTA 1984, s 245(4A)*. This applies where the due date for delivery expires after 22 July 2004 and is in addition to the penalties in *IHTA 1984, s 245 (2)(a)* and *(3)*, which are as follows.

Where the account is submitted voluntarily the amount of the penalty relates only to the degree of lateness and the amount of tax involved:

•	for tax less than £100,000	the penalty is £200 (under *IHTA 1984, s 245(2)(a)* and *(3)*)
		plus £100 for each month (or part month) beyond the period of 12 months after the due date for delivery, up to a maximum of £3,000 (under *IHTA 1984, s 245(4A)*).
•	for tax between £100,000 and £1m	the penalty is £200 (under *IHTA 1984, s 245(2)(a)* and *(3)*)
		plus £200 for each month (or part month) beyond the period of 12 months after the due date for delivery, up to a maximum of £3,000 (under *s 245(4A)*).
		For tax over £1m, the penalty is £200 (under *s 245(2)(a)* and *(3)*)
		plus £400 for each month (or part month) beyond the period of 12 months after the due date for delivery, up to a maximum of £3,000 (under *s 245(4A)*)

These penalties are in addition to the interest that will be charged on all outstanding amounts, including unpaid penalties, until payment is received.

In the recent case of *Tager v HMRC* [2017] UKUT 161 the Upper Tribunal ruled that Romie Tager QC had to pay £1.25m of accumulated daily penalties imposed on him. The case is the first in which penalties were confirmed as punitive rather than restitutionary. The case ought to serve as a reminder to PRs not to ignore HMRC notices.

HMRC has issued information about the late filing penalties for the trusts registration service. HMRC stated that they will take a pragmatic approach, particularly where it is clear, that the trustees and PRs have made every reasonable effort to meet their obligation. The penalties will be as follows:

- For registration made up to three months from the due date, the penalty will be £100.
- For registration made three to six months after the due date, it will be £200.
- For registration more than six months late, it will either be 5% of the tax liability or £300, whoever is the greater.

TIME LIMITS FOR HMRC ASSESSMENTS

9.35 *Finance Act 2009, s 99* and *Sch 51* introduced extended powers for HMRC to issue assessment notices in relation to IHT matters.

They are as follows:

	IHT (account and payment submitted)	*IHT (no account and payment submitted)*
Careless loss of tax	6 years	20 years
Deliberate loss of tax	20 years	No limit
Other reason	4 years	20 years

If there is deliberate loss of tax and no account and payment has been submitted the legislation is silent on time limits for an assessment notice. It therefore is implied that there is no time limit.

Chapter 10

Deceased estates: practical IHT considerations

SIGNPOSTS

- **Probate process and 'excepted estates'** – In some circumstances, it may not be necessary to file a full IHT return IHT400 (see **10.1–10.5**).
- **Form IHT400 and its supplementary forms** – If the estate is not an 'excepted estate', the PRs need to complete the IHT400 and its supplementary forms (see **10.6–10.81**).
- **Corrective accounts** – Where estimated values are used, or where errors or omissions are discovered, a corrective account C4 may need to be filed (see **10.82**).
- **Relief for loss on sale of land** – A repayment of IHT can be achieved if the PRs sell land for less than valued at date of death. IHT38 is used for such claim (see **10.83–10.85**).
- **Relief for loss on shares** – If shares are sold within 12 months of date of death for less than market value at date of death, an IHT repayment claim can be made using IHT35 (see **10.86**).
- **Quick succession relief** – Where, within a period of five years, there are two chargeable transfers, relief is available against the IHT liability on second death (see **10.87–10.90**).
- **Estate duty surviving spouse exemption** – Where the first spouse died before 13 November 1974 and tax was paid, and the surviving spouse was left a life interest under the will, that life interest will not be aggregated with her 'free estate' for IHT purposes (see **10.91–10.93**).
- **Instalment option** – Where the assets of an estate concern land, a business or private company shares, PRs are entitled to pay any IHT due on these assets by instalments (see **10.94–10.97**).
- **Death of emergency service personnel or constables, or death arising from active military service** – The estate of a person who

died from injuries sustained or disease contracted during his line of duty is exempt from IHT (see **10.99–10.100**)

- **Grossing up rules** – Single and double grossing up (see **10.101–10.104**).

PROBATE PROCESS AND EXCEPTED ESTATES

Procedure

10.1

- The PRs first need to obtain probate from the court. Probate is the authority of the court for the PRs to deal with the assets of the deceased. Use form PA1 and associated leaflets (PA1A, PA2, PA3, PA4) to apply for probate if the deceased lived in England, Wales or Northern Ireland. Use form C1 and its continuation form C2 if the deceased lived in Scotland. Probate depends upon prior submission of the appropriate inheritance tax account and payment of IHT, if due.
- There then follows the period of administration of the estate, during which the PRs gather in the assets, pay off any debts, taxes or other liabilities and establish the entitlements of the beneficiaries. This would include paying off any legacies, leaving the PRs with something to pass on to those entitled to 'the residue'.
- It is not always easy to determine when the administration comes to an end, although this will be once the residue has been 'ascertained', and typically the estate accounts are signed by the residuary beneficiaries. It might also follow the submission of a final corrective account to HMRC Inheritance Tax and the issue of a clearance certificate by HMRC although, in any particular case, not all of these things may happen.
- Once the estate administration has come to an end, the PRs are relieved of their duties as such. If the will, or the intestacy rules, prescribe a continuing trust, eg for the children of the deceased, and the same persons are to be trustees, their 'hats' change and different tax rules apply to trustees from those that apply to PRs. The distinction is important, and it is vital in any case to know at what stage the administration comes to an end and in what capacity the individuals are acting, ie whether as executors or as trustees (see **2.16–2.18**).
- There can be interim distributions of assets from an estate, ie once the PRs are satisfied that those assets are not required to pay debts or other liabilities, they may be released to the beneficiaries.

Excepted estates – full IHT account is not required

10.2 Form IHT400 is the 'control' document for dealing with a person's inheritance tax liability following death. Replacing the IHT200, use of the IHT400 has been obligatory since 9 June 2009. Where the 'excepted estate' rules apply, it will not be necessary to complete IHT400.

For deaths after 1 September 2006, the estate is an 'excepted estate' if one of the following applies (see IHTM06001 and **9.19–9.23**):

- low value 'excepted estates', where there is no liability to IHT (see **9.20** and HMRC Inheritance Tax Manual at IHTM06012);
- exempt 'excepted estates', where the spouse or civil partnership exemption and/or charity exemption applies (see **9.21** and IHTM06013); or
- the deceased was a 'foreign domiciliary' – he lived permanently abroad and died abroad and the value of the UK assets is under £150,000 (see **9.23** and IHTM06021).

For death on or after 6 April 2010, an estate will also be an 'excepted estate' if both of the following apply:

- the value of the estate is less than twice the IHT threshold; and
- 100% of the unused IHT threshold from a late spouse or civil partner can be transferred to the deceased.

If you are dealing with an 'excepted estate', the following forms may need completing:

- IHT205 if the deceased's estate is an 'excepted estate' and the person died on or after 1 September 2006 as a permanent resident of England, Wales or Northern Ireland.
- C5 (2006) if the deceased's estate is an 'excepted estate' and the person died on or after 1 September 2006 with their permanent home in Scotland.
- C5 (SE) (2006) if the deceased's estate is a small estate (ie under £36,000), is likely to be an 'excepted estate' and the person died on or after 1 September 2006 as a permanent resident of Scotland.
- IHT207 if the deceased's estate is an 'excepted estate' and the person died on or after 1 September 2006 with their permanent home abroad and limited assets in England, Wales or Northern Ireland.
- C5 (OUK) if the deceased's estate is an 'excepted estate' and the person died on or after 1 September 2006 with their permanent home abroad and limited assets in Scotland.
- IHT217 Claim to transfer unused nil rate band for excepted estates. This form needs to be filed with either IHT205 or C5 (2006).

Focus

The gross value of an asset is the value before deducting liabilities, reliefs or exemptions.

10.3

Example 10.1—Qualification for reduced estate procedure

Gabriel died on 1 May 2019, domiciled in England and Wales. His estate consisted of:

- a half-share in a house, which he held as tenant in common in equal shares with his wife, Harriet. The gross value of their house is £400,000, subject to a mortgage of £150,000;
- a sole proprietor business, £150,000;
- stocks and shares worth £75,000;
- cash at bank, £10,000; and
- personal chattels, £5,000.

Three years before he died, Gabriel had made gifts of £20,000 to each of his three children. His will leaves legacies to the children of £50,000 in total.

He also leaves the business (attracting 100% business property relief) to his eldest son. Apart from the gifts to the children, Gabriel's will leaves all his property absolutely to Harriet.

The gross value of property passing under the will to chargeable beneficiaries, together with chargeable lifetime transfers, is as follows:

Lifetime gifts (net of two £3,000 annual exemptions)	£54,000
Gross value of business	£150,000
Legacies under will	£50,000
	£254,000

As the value of these assets does not exceed the IHT threshold of £325,000 (for 2019/20); the balance of his property passing to his wife is spouse exempt. The reduced account procedure may be followed.

Valuations

10.4 Where property goes to an exempt beneficiary, the PRs may estimate the open market value of the property without the need for a 'red book' valuation by a chartered surveyor for as long as the valuation is reasonable and proportionate in the circumstances. It may be that an open market value at the date of death is required for capital gains tax purposes.

> **Focus**
>
> - Property valuations are one of the areas HMRC views as high-risk.
> - As 'quick-fix' valuations may expose PRs to penalties, it is advisable to use a professionally qualified valuer to obtain a 'red book' valuation.

Corrective accounts

10.5 It may be that, after submitting a reduced account, it is found that the estate does not meet the conditions, or perhaps, as a result of a post-death deed of variation, exempt assets become chargeable. In such a case, a corrective account is required in the usual way. It may then be appropriate to obtain professional valuations.

INHERITANCE TAX ACCOUNT FORM IHT400 AND THE SCHEDULES

Inheritance Tax Toolkit

10.6 HMRC published a revised version of the Inheritance Tax Toolkit in July 2018 (see https://tinyurl.com/ycpzkyqr). This toolkit is not intended to replace the 'Guidance for Completion of IHT400', but it rather focuses on common errors, mistakes and omissions made by professional advisers.

> **Focus**
>
> The IHT Toolkit does not cover the more uncommon aspects of IHT such as APR, BPR and heritage relief.

IHT400

10.7 An IHT reference and a payslip must be obtained, using form IHT422, before form IHT400 can be submitted. When there is no IHT to pay on an estate, it is not necessary to apply for a reference number. This includes an estate where there is no IHT to pay due to the availability of a transferable nil rate band on second death.

Payment with the payslip is sent to HMRC's office in Cumbernauld, and the form IHT400 is sent to HM Revenue and Customs, BX9 1HT.

Form IHT400 is divided into the following parts:

- Deceased's details, including a question whether the deceased was resident in Scotland.
- Contact details of the person dealing with the estate.
- Deceased's will.
- Items referred to in the will but not included in the estate.
- What makes up the Inheritance Tax account – Schedules.
- Estate in the UK.
- Deductions from the estate in the UK incurred up to the date of death.
- Exemptions and reliefs.
- Other assets taken into account to calculate the tax.
- Working out the Inheritance Tax.
- Simple Inheritance Tax calculation.
- Direct Payment Scheme.
- Declaration.
- Checklist.
- Additional information.

The pack also includes: the IHT400 calculation, nil rate bands, limits and rates and the help sheet.

10.8 Within the pack, the most commonly used schedules are provided as follows:

- IHT401 Domicile outside the UK.
- IHT402 Claim to transfer unused Inheritance Tax nil rate band.

- IHT403 Gifts and other transfers of value.
- IHT404 Jointly owned assets.
- IHT405 Houses, land, buildings and interests in land.
- IHT406 Bank and building society accounts.
- IHT407 Household and personal goods.
- IHT408 Household and personal goods given to charity.
- IHT409 Pensions.
- IHT410 Life assurance and annuities.
- IHT411 Listed stocks and shares.
- IHT412 Unlisted stocks and shares, and control holdings.
- IHT413 Business and partnership interests and assets.
- IHT414 Agricultural relief.
- IHT415 Interest in another estate.
- IHT416 Debts to the estate.
- IHT417 Foreign assets.
- IHT418 Assets held in trust.
- IHT419 Debts owed by the deceased.
- IHT420 National Heritage assets: Conditional exemption and maintenance funds.
- IHT421 Probate summary.
- IHT422 Application for an Inheritance Tax reference.
- IHT423 Direct payment scheme, bank or building society account.
- IHT430 Reduced rate of Inheritance Tax.
- New form IHT435 Residence nil rate band.
- New Form IHT436 Transfer of unused residence nil rate band.

Finally, there are the IHT400 Notes 'Guide to completing your Inheritance Tax Account'.

The various schedules are referred to at Boxes 29 to 48 of the IHT400, with the instruction (familiar from self-assessment for income tax) to fill in any applicable schedules before proceeding to Box 49.

UK-domiciled deceased

10.9

> **Focus**
>
> If there is no IHT payable, it is not necessary to send form IHT422 (Application for an IHT reference) to HMRC. Instead, HMRC will allocate a reference number when they receive the forms and paperwork as part of the probate process.

In circumstances where the estate is taxable, form IHT400 and any supplementary pages, a copy of the will and form IHT421 (the probate summary) should be sent to HMRC Inheritance Tax, in a single envelope. In the absence of any complications, HMRC Inheritance Tax will endorse form IHT421 and return it to the sender to enable an application to be made to the Probate Registry for the grant of probate. It is this grant which authorises the executors to deal with the assets of the deceased.

Even if there is no tax payable, form IHT421 requires endorsement and therefore needs to be sent to HMRC Inheritance Tax (having completed Box 6 with 'nil' before signing the form) together with the inheritance tax account, supporting papers and a copy of the will.

Non-UK domiciliaries

10.10 If it is claimed the deceased was neither actually, nor deemed domiciled in the UK, the inheritance tax account, supporting papers, a copy of the will and form IHT421 needs to be sent to HMRC in the normal way. The estate is assessed and HMRC Inheritance Tax send out a calculation showing the tax due. Once the tax is paid, form IHT421 is endorsed and returned.

INHERITANCE TAX ACCOUNT FORM IHT400: DETAILS

10.11 The various parts of the form are scheduled at **10.8** above. Much of this is fairly routine detail, although this section of the book picks up one or two particular questions. The first point to note is that, whereas under IHT200 there was a separate supplementary form D1 governing the will, questions 24 to 28 of the IHT400 now cover this ground.

Deceased's address

10.12 Question 25 asks whether the address for the deceased shown in the will is the same as the one shown at Box 11 of form IHT400. Very often, a person will have moved house after executing his last will and testament. All that HMRC Inheritance Tax need to know is that the property mentioned in the will has been replaced by that shown on the form IHT400.

If, by contrast, no residential property is included as part of the estate, HMRC Inheritance Tax will want to know what happened to the property mentioned in the will and, if sold, whether the sale proceeds are included as part of the estate (Box 26). It might happen, for example, that where a will made by one spouse shows them as resident at an address, that spouse does not in fact have a beneficial interest in the property, which belongs in entirety to the other – this would have to be explained.

Specific gifts in the will

10.13 Question 27 seeks to ensure that any particular items, eg personal possessions, stocks and shares, etc which are referred to as given in the will are included in form IHT400. The point might extend to the writing-off of a loan still outstanding at death, or there might be reference in the will to gifts made during the deceased's lifetime, but within seven years before death. Alternatively, the asset concerned might have been sold, in which case, again, HMRC Inheritance Tax need to know which assets on form IHT400 represent the sale proceeds (assuming that they have not been spent). If the answers to these questions are not clearly positive, HMRC Inheritance Tax need to know why any items are not included in IHT400.

Example 10.2—Where the will mentions assets not owned at death

Joe died on 1 May 2019, having made his last will on 1 January 1984 'in contemplation' of his forthcoming marriage. Marriage normally revokes the will unless it is expressed to be in contemplation of a particular marriage. He was then living at 'Hollyhocks', which was sold after the marriage, the proceeds being reinvested in 'Town End House', which at the date of his death he owned as joint tenant with his wife.

Among the specific gifts mentioned in the will are three watercolours by a minor Norwich School artist, one left to each or his three children. In the year before he died, one of the pictures was stolen and a second was sold to meet grandchildren's school fees.

Joe's half-share in the house is left to his wife, with the residue of the estate (within the nil rate band) passing to the three children in equal shares.

Boxes 25 to 27 are answered as follows:

- The address shown in the will is not the same as the address on page 2 of form IHT400. This is because 'Hollyhocks' shown in the will was sold and the proceeds were reinvested in 'Town End House', which at the date of his death was owned jointly by the deceased and his wife.

- Two of the items mentioned in the will, viz two watercolours, are not included in form IHT400. One because it was stolen in the year before the deceased died and the insurance proceeds were included in the figure for cash. The second was sold (in order to meet grandchildren's school fees). The legacies to two of the three children therefore fail.

The chargeable estate

10.14 Pages 6 and 7 of the IHT400 (Boxes 49 to 79) detail the component parts of the estate in the UK. This is followed on pages 8, 9 and 10 by deductions from the estate (eg mortgages) in Boxes 80 to 91. Exemptions and reliefs form Boxes 92 to 96 (including the spouse and charities exemption), before Boxes 97 to 108 on page 10 require details of other assets taken into account to compute the tax, eg foreign assets and gifts with reservation of benefit. Page 11 (Boxes 109 to 117) deal with the calculation of inheritance tax, the option to pay by instalments and a simple calculation in an appropriate case. The top of page 12 (Box 118) asks whether the direct payment scheme is to be used under which participating banks and building societies will release funds from the deceased's accounts directly to HMRC to pay inheritance tax. And the form concludes at pages 12 and 13 with the declaration at Box 119 before a final checklist on page 14 and the white space on pages 15 and 16.

The treatment of liabilities

10.15 *Finance Act 2013* tightened up *IHTA 1984, s 162* and introduced conditions and restrictions in the way liabilities are treated for IHT purposes.

- A deduction is generally not taken into account for a liability that has been incurred directly or indirectly to acquire 'excluded property' for IHT purposes (new *IHTA 1984, s 162A*).
- Foreign currency accounts owned by non-UK domiciled individuals are 'excluded property' following *IHTA 1984, s 157.* Such accounts were used to sidestep restrictions for the deductibility of liabilities introduced by *FA 2013,* which disallow a deduction of liabilities used for acquiring 'excluded property'. For deaths occurring on or after 17 July 2014, *FA 2014* provides that no deduction will be allowed for liabilities incurred to fund foreign currency bank accounts.
- If the liability was incurred to acquire assets which qualify for IHT relief (ie business property relief or agricultural property relief or woodland

relief), the liability reduces the value of the asset. The deduction of the liability is matched against the asset acquired, and relief is restricted to their net value.

IHTA 1984, s 175A(1) states that a liability can only be taken into account if discharged on or after death.

Following representations by professional bodies, HMRC have issued the following statement:

> 'The starting assumption will be that liabilities on death will be repaid so that all liabilities can be deducted for the purposes of calculating the IHT due. After probate has been obtained, the expectation is that the liability will be repaid from the released funds. If a liability is not repaid later, HMRC will expect personal representatives to amend the IHT return accordingly.'

The amended HMRC Manual makes the following additional points:

- If PRs are aware that a liability is not being repaid, they should not deduct it.
- No enquiries are going to be made into liabilities which are clearly commercial and at arm's length, for example utility bills, credit card bills and outstanding tax liabilities.
- If liabilities have been incurred with family members, HMRC will ask for evidence that the money has been repaid.
- It appears that a liability which is not contractually due for repayment until a later day is not within *IHTA 1984, s 175A*.
- If there is a real commercial reason for the liability not being repaid, it will be taken into account when calculating any IHT due.

Most importantly the liability must be repaid out of the estate. This will affect cases where an individual takes out life insurance which will enable the mortgage to be repaid after his death and the policy is settled on trust for his family. If the trustees, after the individual's death, pay off the mortgage, for the purposes of *IHTA 1984, s 175A* the liability cannot be deducted because it has not been discharged out of the estate. A loan from the beneficiary from proceeds of a life insurance policy held in trust to the estate will qualify as a deduction.

See **10.76** to **10.78** in relation to completion of Schedule IHT419.

SCHEDULE IHT401: DOMICILE OUTSIDE THE UNITED KINGDOM

10.16 A person who has his domicile outside the UK is liable to IHT on, broadly, only property situated within the UK at death. There are further possible benefits for income tax and CGT during his lifetime, known as the 'remittance basis', but this is outside the scope of this publication. The domicile rules are complex, as both 'deemed domicile' under *IHTA 1984, s 267* and the domicile rules under the general law may need to be considered.

Information required

10.17

- Deceased's domicile: has it been agreed for other HMRC purposes?
- Deceased's residency for tax purposes: was the deceased UK resident for income tax purposes during the four years up to the date of death? If so, dates of UK residence are required for the 20 years before death.
- Deceased's history: to get a full picture of the deceased's life, specific information is required under various questions.
- Deceased's estate: who will benefit from the deceased's estate under the law or will that applies in the claimed country of domicile. Are you deducting surviving spouse/civil partner exemption? If 'Yes', brief details of property that the surviving spouse will receive are required. Did the deceased leave assets outside the UK? If so, give their approximate value. (Answering this question should be resisted, although HMRC Inheritance Tax have affirmed its importance. The intention is obviously to enable HMRC Inheritance Tax to see the advantage of claiming non-UK domicile, though the values should not be relevant to the issue of principle.) Does a double tax treaty apply to any of the foreign assets owned by the deceased? Is any foreign tax to be paid on UK-situated assets following the deceased's death?

Establishing domicile

10.18 Questions 7 to 18 ask for specific information to provide a full picture of the life of the deceased. This will help to establish the validity of a claim to a non-UK domicile. There was a particular complication for a woman married before 1 January 1974, in which case she automatically acquired the domicile of her husband. Since then, however, a wife has been able to establish her own independent domicile.

Importantly for IHT, there is a special deemed domicile rule under which a person is treated as being domiciled in the UK (*IHTA 1984, s 257*) if either:

- he has been domiciled in the UK during the previous three calendar years (not tax years), ie it takes at least three years effectively to 'shake off' a UK domicile; or

- he was resident in the UK for income tax purposes for at least 15 out of the last 20 tax years (not calendar years), remembering to include part years (ie under this rule, a person may become deemed UK domiciled at the beginning of the 15th calendar year of residence, starting with 6 April). Note: the deemed domicile rules were 17 out of the last 20 tax years for deaths prior to 6 April 2017.
- *Finance (No 2) Act 2017* introduced 'formerly domiciled resident' rule in that a person who was born in the UK, whose domicile of origin was in the UK and who again became resident in the UK, will be deemed domiciled in the UK, irrespective of the domicile status under general law.

A person who was not actually, but was deemed, domiciled in the UK is subject to IHT on worldwide assets, subject only to any relief under a double tax treaty.

Finance Act 2013 has introduced legislation to increase the spouse exemption for the non-UK domiciled spouse from £55,000 to the level of the nil rate band for IHT (£325,000 in 2016/17).

Finance Act 2013, s 177 inserted *ss 267A* and *268A* which amend these provisions for transfers from 6 April 2013 as follows:

- the non-UK domiciled spouse or civil partner can elect to be treated as UK domiciled, if one of two conditions is met:
  - condition A ('the lifetime exemption'): the person's spouse or civil partner must be UK domiciled at the time of the election and the person must not be UK domiciled; or
  - condition B ('the death exemption'): the person's spouse or civil partner died UK domiciled on or after 6 April 2013 and the person was not UK domiciled at that time and the election is made within two years of the UK domiciled spouse's date of death,
- if these conditions are met the restricted spouse or civil partner exemption is removed and it puts the non-domiciled spouse into the same position as a UK domiciled spouse ; and
- the election can be backdated for a period up to seven years but not a date before 6 April 2013.

The election is irrevocable and brings the person's worldwide assets into the UK IHT net. Although the election cannot be revoked, if the person making the election is not UK resident for the purposes of income tax for the whole of any 'period specified', the election ceases to take effect. The 'period specified' is any period of four successive tax years beginning:

- in the case of a lifetime election, at any time after it takes effect; or
- in the case of the death exemption, at any time after the election is treated as having effect.

Finance (No 2) Act 2017 included amendments to *IHTA 1984, s 267* in that from 6 April 2017 the qualifying period for a person resident in the UK to become deemed domicile is reduced from 17 out of 20 years to 15 out of 20 years. This extends the 'period specified' mentioned above from four years to now five years. The practical effect of this is that a person who elected to be treated as domiciled in the UK remains domiciled for a five-year period on ceasing to be UK resident. Additionally individuals who were born in the UK and who have a UK domicile of origin will revert to their UK domiciled tax status while resident in the UK.

The First-tier Tribunal case of *Gulliver v Revenue and Customs Commissioners [2017] UKFTT 222 (TC)* showed that a previous domicile decision by HMRC cannot be relied on later. In this case the First-tier Tribunal held that written confirmation of a non-UK domicile by HMRC in 2003 did not create a binding contract and that HMRC was therefore not prevented from reviewing the matter of a taxpayer's domicile at a later stage.

Care needs to be taken on lifetime gifts, as the election must state the date from which it is supposed to take effect to ensure that any gift benefits from the full spouse exemption.

SCHEDULE IHT402: CLAIM TO TRANSFER UNUSED NIL RATE BAND

The principle

10.19 Where the death occurred on or after 9 October 2007 and follows the prior death of a former spouse/civil partner, it is possible to enhance the nil rate band on the second death by the proportion of any unused nil rate band on the first death (*IHTA 1984, s 8A*). A claim is required. Schedule IHT402 seeks to ascertain the extent to which the nil rate band available on the first death was not used and therefore the percentage by which the nil rate band on the present death may be enhanced.

IHTA 1984, s 8A will apply where the IHT nil rate band of the first deceased spouse or civil partner was not fully used in calculating the IHT liability of their estate, whenever the first death occurred. When the surviving spouse or civil partner dies, the unused amount may be added to their own nil rate band.

Where a person dies having survived more than one spouse or civil partner (or dies having been married to, or the registered civil partner of, someone who had themselves survived one or more spouses or civil partners), the amount of additional nil rate band which can be accumulated by any one survivor will be limited to the nil rate band in force at the second death.

The claim mechanism operates at the second death only, to be made by (usually) the PRs of the second spouse or civil partner to die. But of course evidence will be required of the unused nil rate band on the first death, which could have been very many years before – and may present difficulties in digging out the paperwork.

The balance of advantage

10.20 On the assumption that the nil rate band will generally increase over time (though note that it has been frozen for the time being), it should prove sensible to minimise chargeable transfers on the first death, so maximising the nil rate band on the second. It is important to remember that chargeable gifts made in the seven years before death or caught by the reservation of benefit regime will in effect eat into the nil rate band on the first death.

The spouse/civil partner exemption under *IHTA 1984, s 18* can be achieved by an IPDI as much as by an outright gift. As soon as reasonably possible after the first death, the survivor should make such gifts as he/she can reasonably afford to do without, keeping outside the gifts with reservation of benefit regime; however, gifts which exceed the survivor's nil rate band will need to be absolute rather than in trust, to avoid an immediate 20% IHT charge. Under an IPDI the trustees would terminate the life interest to that extent (and, being an IPDI, there would be no reading back into the will under *IHTA 1984, s 144*). CGT should be considered, but should not be a problem insofar as no growth in value since death.

Clearly, an outright gift or IPDI to the surviving spouse should not be regarded as providing the best structure in all circumstances. A nil rate band will trust may still be advantageous in the following circumstances:

- protection of the home from liability for care fees;
- cases where the capital appreciation in the nil rate band will trust is anticipated to outstrip future increases in the nil rate band; and
- cases where it is desired, perhaps for non-tax reasons, to have two relevant property nil rate band trusts for children/grandchildren going forward, the one established under the will of the first to die and the other set up *inter vivos* by the survivor.

Some practical points

10.21 As well as generally maximising the benefit of the zero rate of IHT in the two estates, the regime will prove especially beneficial in dealing with the family home, not having to worry about the debt/charge scheme etc or nil rate band discretionary trusts (viz, do they in substance give an interest in possession to the survivor, and what about CGT main residence relief in the light of *TLATA 1996, s 12* etc)?

Where, on the first death, there is property which clearly attracts APR or BPR at 100%, advantage should be taken of this, perhaps by a gift into a discretionary trust, or by gift to non-exempt beneficiaries.

Beware the scope of *IHTA 1984, s 143* with chattels or other property. For example, a gift by the surviving spouse of a painting to a child within two years after the death (even if the wish of the deceased was expressed informally) will take effect as a chargeable transfer by the deceased.

In applying the *IHTA 1984, s 8A* rule, it matters not that the estate of the first to die was below the nil rate band threshold.

How does IHTA 1984, s 8A work if the first death occurred during capital transfer tax or estate duty? HMRC advice

10.22 The same basic principles apply, subject, however, to some modifications to reflect the differences between inheritance tax and capital transfer tax/estate duty. Inheritance tax was introduced on 18 March 1986, so points to bear in mind for deaths before that date are:

- Where the first spouse died between 13 March 1975 and 18 March 1986, the estate would have been subject to capital transfer tax. Any transfers to the spouse would have been exempt from tax in the same way as for inheritance tax and the transfer of nil rate band provisions will operate in exactly the same way as it works for inheritance tax.
- Before 13 March 1975, estate duty applied. Under estate duty there was no tax-free transfer permitted between spouses until 21 March 1972 when a tax-free transfer between spouses of up to £15,000 was introduced. This limit was removed for deaths after 12 November 1974.
- Where the first spouse died between 21 March 1972 and 13 March 1975, a claim to transfer the nil rate band to the surviving spouse will be based on the proportion of the tax-free band that was unused on the death of the first spouse. For example, if a husband died in 1973 and left an estate valued at £10,000 that was all transferred to his wife, then, as this is all within the spouse's exemption, the husband's tax-free band is unused. So, if his widow dies in December 2011, her nil rate band can be increased by 100% to £650,000. Where any part of the first spouse's individual tax-free band was used, there will be a proportionate reduction in the amount by which the surviving spouse's IHT nil rate band may be increased.
- Before 21 March 1972, there was no relief from estate duty for transfers between spouses, so the amount by which the surviving spouse's IHT nil rate band may be increased will be based on the proportion of the individual tax-free band that was unused on the death of the first spouse.

The above adopts an HMRC publication from November 2007. Of course, in practice, where the first death occurred under estate duty and certainly before 21 March 1972, it is going to be only in the comparatively rare case that the gross estate was below the threshold that any benefit is going to be obtained from *IHTA 1984, s 8A* – except in the situation where there was complete exemption under the so-called 'killed in war' provisions of what is now *IHTA 1984, s 154* (see **11.98–11.99**).

Example 10.3—Transferable nil rate band

(i) On first death, none of the then nil rate band was used because the entire estate was left to the surviving spouse. If the nil rate band on the second death is £325,000, that would be increased by 100% to £650,000.

(ii) If, on first death, the chargeable estate is £150,000 and the nil rate band £300,000, 50% of the original nil rate band would be unused. If the nil rate band on the second death is £325,000, that would be increased by 50% to £487,500.

SCHEDULE IHT435 AND IHT436: RESIDENCE NIL RATE BAND AND TRANSFER OF UNUSED RESIDENCE NIL RATE BAND

Residence Nil Rate Band (RNRB)

10.23 An increased nil rate band (or 'residence nil rate band') is available on death from 6 April 2017, where a residence is passed on death to a lineal descendant of the deceased (see *IHTA 1984, ss 8D–8M*). The residence nil rate band, if available, is in addition to the IHT threshold (or main nil rate band).

The RNRB will be phased in over a period of four years:

- For deaths in 2017/18 the RNRB will be £100,000.
- For deaths in 2018/19 the RNRB will be £125,000.
- For deaths in 2019/20 the RNRB will be £150,000.
- For deaths in 2020/21 and thereafter, the RNRB will rise to £175,000.

The residence nil rate band applies if a person's estate includes a 'qualifying residential interest', and all or part of that interest is left to one or more lineal descendants, that is, it is 'closely inherited'.

A residential property interest is broadly an interest in a dwelling-house that was the deceased's residence when it was part of their estate. Where the person's death estate includes only one residence, that residence will be the qualifying residential interest. If the person's estate includes more than one residence, the deceased's personal representatives may nominate one of them, and that residence will be treated as the qualifying residential interest.

A property is 'closely inherited' for the above purposes if it is inherited by the person's child, grandchild or other lineal descendant. The meaning of closely inherited has been extended to include stepchildren. Furthermore, an adopted person may be treated as a child of a natural parent or an adoptive parent. A person who was fostered at any time is treated (at that and all subsequent times) as the foster parent's child. Where a guardian or special guardian (both as defined) has been appointed for a person under 18 years old, that person is subsequently treated as a child of the guardian or special guardian. The direct descendants of someone treated as a child of another person for these purposes are also to be treated as direct descendants of that other person (*IHTA 1984, s 8K*).

The legislation provides that a beneficiary inherits a property if it is transferred to him under the deceased's will, or under the intestacy rules or otherwise as a result of the deceased's death. This does not generally apply to settled property, unless a beneficiary becomes entitled to an immediate post-death interest or disabled person's interest, or unless the property becomes settled on trusts to which *IHTA 1984, s 71A* (ie trusts for bereaved minors) or *IHTA 1984, s 71D* (ie age 18 to 25 trusts) applies and is for the beneficiary's benefit.

Importantly the RNRB does not apply if residential property is left on a discretionary trust.

Where the property is treated as forming part of the deceased's estate immediately before death as a result of the gifts with reservation provisions (*FA 1986, s 102(3)*) applying following the gift, a lineal descendant inherits the property if he or she was the recipient of the deceased's gift (*IHTA 1984, s 8J(4)*).

If the deceased's estate does not include a qualifying residential interest, or if it does include such an interest but none of it is inherited by lineal descendants, the deceased's residence nil rate band is nil. However, the residence nil rate band that has not been used is available for transfer to a spouse (or civil partner) (*IHTA 1984, s 8F*). Therefore a surviving spouse who is the sole owner of the matrimonial home may still be able to claim the deceased spouse's unused residence nil rate band. The transferable amount is expressed as a percentage, which is subject to an overriding maximum of 100%, or one additional residence nil rate band.

The value attributable to the qualifying residential interest is after deduction of any agricultural property relief and business property relief.

The residence nil rate band also applies to disposals of residential property on or after 8 July 2015 where the taxpayer has downsized, or where the property is sold or given away and the taxpayer for example moves into residential care.

The residence nil rate band is subject to a taper threshold, which reduces the nil rate band available according to the value of the deceased's estate. This taper threshold is set at £2 million for 2017/18 and subsequent tax years. It is subject to indexation increases (to be specified in regulations) by reference to the CPI unless Parliament determines otherwise, but is fixed at £2 million until 2021/22 at the earliest.

The person's residence nil rate band allowance is adjusted using a formula set out in the legislation (*IHTA 1984, s 8D(5)*), which withdraws the 'default allowance' (see below) by £1 for every £2 that the value of the estate exceeds the threshold:

$$\text{Default allowance} - \left(\frac{E - TT}{2}\right)$$

where:

- 'default allowance' is the total of the residence nil rate band at the person's death, plus any 'brought forward allowance' (ie unused residence nil rate band transferred on an earlier death of a spouse or civil partner);
- E is the value of the person's estate immediately before death (ie before any reliefs and exemptions); and
- TT is the taper threshold.

Therefore for 2020/21, the residence nil rate band of £175,000 will be reduced to nil if the person's estate value is £2,350,000 or higher. This assumes that no residence nil rate band has been brought forward (ie transferred) following the earlier death of a spouse or civil partner.

The transferable residence nil rate band must be claimed (*IHTA 1984, s 8L*). The claim should generally be made by the deceased's personal representatives within a permitted period. Alternatively, a claim may be made by any other person liable to IHT on the person's death within such later period as HMRC may allow. The 'permitted period' is two years from the end of the month in which the deceased died, or three months from the date the PRs started to act.

'Community of property'

10.24 If the surviving spouse/civil partner exemption is claimed, it must be confirmed whether or not, in the country of domicile, there was a 'community of property' and whether that jurisdiction recognised civil partnerships or something equivalent. This might have arisen simply because of the deceased's marriage, or because he signed a marriage contract. The rules vary from country to country, but broadly speaking fetter the ability of a party to the community to dispose of his property (and of course this is especially relevant to any property under the community that might have been situated in the UK at the date of death). For example, the rules might provide that the estate should be divided into three parts, one of which must go to the spouse (or civil partner), one to the children and the third of which the deceased would have a discretion.

SCHEDULE IHT403: GIFTS AND OTHER TRANSFERS OF VALUE

10.25 IHT works by adding to the total chargeable estate on death, the chargeable value (ie after any exemptions) of all gifts made in the seven years before death. It has always been necessary for PRs to know the total of such gifts, because in particular, they would not otherwise be able to confirm the amount of the nil rate band left unused (if any) at the date of death – lifetime gifts have first call on the nil rate band according to the order in which they are made. However, *FA 1999* imposed a statutory obligation on PRs to give this information to the best of their knowledge and belief. Ascertaining the existence of such transfers can be quite an onerous task.

It is not necessary to complete Schedule IHT403 if the only gifts made by the deceased were:

- to the spouse or civil partner and the spouse or civil partner exemption applies;
- outright gifts to any individual which do not exceed £250;
- outright gifts to any individual of money or listed stocks and shares that are wholly covered by the annual and/or gifts out of income exemption; or
- outright gifts made regularly from income that did not exceed £3,000 in total each year.

Schedule IHT403 is divided into four parts.

Gifts made within the seven years before death

10.26 The question is whether the deceased in that period:

- made any gift or transferred assets to or for the benefit of another person;
- created any trust or settlement;
- transferred additional assets into an existing trust or settlement;

- paid any premium on a life policy for someone other than his spouse/civil partner;
- ceased to benefit from any assets held in trust; or
- made any gifts claimed to be exempt as regular gifts out of income.

In the event that the answer to any of these questions is affirmative, full details are requested.

Each of these events would be a transfer of value, which, subject to an exemption, would be a chargeable transfer. The exemptions, of which details are requested by the schedule, are set out below. Only outright gifts between individuals that are covered by an exemption need not be listed.

Gifts with reservation

10.27 If, on or after 18 March 1986, the deceased made a gift from which he enjoyed some benefit (other than a minimal one), and he enjoyed that benefit at his death, he is treated for IHT purposes as still being entitled to the property given away, ie at its value at date of death. If the benefits ceased in the preceding seven years, he is treated as having made a potentially exempt transfer of the asset at the value at the date of cessation of benefit (see **6.18–6.23**). Details must be given at Boxes 8 to 12. The rules also apply if the recipient of the gift failed to enter into 'possession and enjoyment' of it.

Pre-owned assets

10.28 Questions 13 to 16 ask for details of any gifts made where the pre-owned assets regime (see **4.44–4.53**) would apply but for an election out of that regime into the gifts with reservation of benefit regime, so obviating the income tax charge but treating the assets concerned as continuing to be owned by the donor for IHT purposes.

Earlier transfers

10.29 The normal 'danger period' for recapture of gifts for IHT is seven years. However, there is a trap, which can make gifts within 14 years before death relevant. This is where there was a gift in the seven years before death, and within seven years before that gift, there had been a chargeable transfer (or itself made more than seven years before death). That earlier transfer can have an effect on the IHT implications of the later gift. This is the point behind questions 18 and 19.

The lifetime exemptions

10.30

- The spouse/civil partner exemption (*IHTA 1984, s 18*). This is unlimited, except where the transferor is actually or deemed UK domiciled and the transferee is not, in which case the exemption is limited to £325,000.
- The annual exemption of £3,000 per donor per tax year. Where in any tax year more than £3,000 is given, any unused balance of the £3,000 annual exemption of the previous year may be carried forward (though for one year only): *IHTA 1984, s 19*.
- The small gifts exemption of £250 per donee (*IHTA 1984, s 20*).
- The 'normal expenditure out of income' exemption. A transfer is exempt to the extent that it is made out of the income of the year, having taken account of all normal 'revenue' type expenditure. A pattern of giving must be established over at least three years, or it must be shown that the deceased had made a commitment to a series of gifts (*IHTA 1984, s 21*). Information on such gifts is provided on Schedule IHT403 at Boxes 20 to 22.
- The marriage exemption, which is £5,000 for a gift to a child, £2,500 to a grandchild or £1,000 to anyone else (*IHTA 1984, s 22*).

Note that the above prevent a transfer of value from being a chargeable transfer. There is a rule in *IHTA 1984, s 11* which prevents a lifetime disposition from being a transfer of value at all (dispositions for maintenance of family). This is one made by one spouse or civil partner for the maintenance of the other or for the maintenance, education or training of a child while under the age of 18 or in full-time education or training. *IHTA 1984, ss 10* and *12–17* list other types of disposition which are not transfers of value.

HMRC expects detailed information about the deceased's income and expenditure if the 'normal expenditure out of income' exemption is claimed. To pre-empt lengthy queries many practitioners supply HMRC with relevant documents. The 5% tax-free withdrawal on investment bonds does not count as income for the purposes of this exemption.

Example 10.4—Implications of lifetime gifts

Charles died on 1 May 2019. He had made the following gifts in the seven years before he died:

- On 1 January 2016, £50,000 to his son.
- On 1 January 2017, £50,000 to his daughter.
- On 1 January 2018, a gift of £10,000 to his grandson on his marriage.

- On 1 January 2018 and 1 January 2019, premiums of £5,000 on a new life insurance policy written on the joint lives of his wife and himself, written on wide discretionary trusts (excluding settlor and spouse).

The IHT implications are as follows:

Date	*Transfer of value*	*Exemption*	*Chargeable transfer*
1.1.16	£50,000	Two annual exemptions	£44,000
1.1.17	£50,000	One annual exemption	£47,000
1.1.18	£10,000	£3,000 annual + £2,500 marriage	£4,500
1.1.18	£5,000	? normal expenditure	? Nil
1.1.19	£5,000	? normal expenditure	? Nil
Total	£120,000		£95,500

Accordingly, as at his death in 2019/20, when the nil rate band was £325,000, Charles had used £95,500 (probably) of his nil rate band, leaving £229,500 available for use against chargeable gifts under the will.

Where market conditions have changed following a PET or a chargeable transfer and the value of the property transferred is less at the time of the transferor's death (or on a prior sale by the transferee or his spouse) than at the time of his gift, relief is available in certain circumstances when computing the IHT or additional IHT, so that the tax or additional tax is charged on the reduced value (*IHTA 1984, s 131*).

The relief is available in the following circumstances:

- tax or additional tax is chargeable on the value transferred by a chargeable transfer or a potentially exempt transfer because of the transferor's death within seven years of the transfer; and
- all or part of the value transferred is attributable to the value of property which, at the date of the death, remains the property of the transferee or of his spouse, or has before the date of the death been sold by the transferee or his spouse by a qualifying sale.

For the purposes of the relief, it is important that:

- any transaction was an arm's length transaction for a price freely negotiable at the time of the sale; and
- the vendor (or any person having an interest in the proceeds of the sale) is not the same as or connected with the purchaser (or any person having an interest in the purchase); and

- no provision is made, in or in connection with the agreement for the sale, that the vendor (or any person having an interest in the proceeds of sale) is to have any right to acquire some or all of the property sold or some interest in or created out of it.

In order to avoid giving too much relief, there is a special rule for calculating the relief where the property also qualifies for business or agricultural relief. In this case the market values of the transferred property on the two dates that are compared to establish the reduction in value must be taken as reduced by the percentage appropriate to any available business or agricultural relief.

SCHEDULE IHT404: JOINTLY OWNED ASSETS

The law

10.31 English law distinguishes between a joint tenancy and a tenancy in common. An interest under a joint tenancy passes on death of one joint tenant automatically by operation of law (or 'survivorship') to the surviving joint tenant(s), *pro rata* if more than one. By contrast, an interest under a tenancy in common is an asset of which the owner can dispose, whether by his will or otherwise, and will be in a particular percentage or proportion of the asset, ie not necessarily 50/50 where there are two tenants in common. The law presumes joint ownership to be a joint tenancy, unless there is evidence to the contrary, in particular where one joint tenant has served notice on the other(s) of the intention to 'sever' the joint tenancy.

For IHT purposes, each type of interest must be valued and, subject to the spouse exemption, will be charged to tax on death according to the share in the asset owned by the deceased. If the other joint owner was the surviving spouse, the percentage taken is simply the proportion owned. For example, where the matrimonial home was owned as tenants in common in equal shares, the deceased's share will be one half of the whole. To the extent that the joint owners are not husband and wife, a discount of certainly 10% and arguably up to 15% (or even more) may be applied from the proportionate share of the deceased. This discount is intended to reflect the difficulty in realising a part share in property. In appropriate cases it may be as well to take specialist valuation advice. This discount is not applicable to cash.

The required information

10.32 Schedule IHT404 deals separately with joint interests in houses, buildings and land and a controlling holding of shares and securities (Box 1) on the one hand and other jointly owned assets (eg bank accounts, household and personal goods) at Box 6 on the other. For each category of jointly owned assets values must be shown, with applicable liabilities and exemptions and reliefs.

Survivorship assets

10.33 Applying the principle set out at **10.32**, Box 11 requires details of assets which pass by survivorship and hence while included in the deceased's estate for IHT purposes, are not included in the value of the estate for probate or (in Scotland) confirmation purposes. Brief explanations are given of the position under English and Scottish law respectively.

Example 10.5—'Things may not always be what they seem'

This example is based on a Special Commissioner's case in 1998 (*O'Neill v IRC* [1998] STC (SCD) 110). Father opened a bank account in the Isle of Man in his sole name. Later in 1980, the balance was transferred to a new account in the joint name of the father and daughter. Father added to the account. Interest was rolled up until June 1992. Thereafter, interest was paid to an account in father's name.

In 1984, father opened a second account in his name jointly with daughter, and added to it. Interest was rolled up. Daughter did not know of the accounts during father's lifetime. She received from him an envelope just before his death to take to the bank manager. This disclosed the existence of the accounts. HMRC determined that all of the money formed part of father's estate.

Daughter and father's executors appealed, arguing that only half of each account belonged to father, and that IHT should, therefore, be charged, only on half of each account.

The Special Commissioner asked whether daughter had a present interest in the accounts during father's lifetime. HMRC had argued that a gift of a joint bank account might be an immediate gift of a fluctuating and defeasible asset, and that daughter's interest was defeasible by father's. The Commissioner agreed that father had a general power over the whole account, which meant that he should be treated as beneficially entitled to all of it. Father's motives looked obvious. He took the money offshore, which was suspicious. The interest was never returned for tax purposes, which turned the suspicion into a virtual certainty. But for daughter's honesty, HMRC might never have known of the account. Father had been estranged from his wife and in matrimonial proceedings he had denied the existence of the fund. It was not until the divorce was over that any interest came back to father. Father intended some benefit to daughter, but that was not his only motive.

Daughter was of full age seven years before father died, yet daughter was not informed of the account. Only father could operate the accounts because daughter was never asked to sign. Father had made provision for daughter in his will, which suggested that he had intended the earlier provision by way of joint accounts to operate as a 'legacy only', through survivorship. The normal presumption of 'advancement' whereby daughter would be treated as entitled to a half share in each account, was rebutted by all these factors.

The Commissioner concluded that father enjoyed the entire beneficial interest in the accounts during his lifetime and the appeal was dismissed.

See **9.11** on problems arising out of joint bank accounts and the recent cases of *Sillars* and *Matthews*.

SCHEDULE IHT405: HOUSES, LAND, BUILDINGS AND INTERESTS IN LAND

10.34 In many cases, this schedule will be completed simply to reflect an interest in the family home. There may of course be other buildings or interests in land to include on this form. It is a good idea in every case to get a professional valuation as at the date of death and enclose it with Schedule IHT405. It is permissible to use estimates but full enquiries need to be made. The two cases of *Linda Frances Chadwick and another (Hobart's executors) v CRC*, Lands Chamber, 25 March 2010 and *Revenue & Customs Comrs v Cairns (PR of Webb Deceased)* [2009] STC (SCD) 479 highlight the sometimes unreasonable approach that HMRC may take if they feel that valuations are too low.

Such land or buildings may be:

- the main family home;
- a second family home (whether or not in the UK);
- a house or flat owned for investment purposes;
- an interest in land owned for a business; or
- farmland or buildings.

The two latter categories may attract business property relief or agricultural property relief (see **10.51–10.64**).

IHT405 is divided into five sections:

- Details of the person HMRC should contact about the valuation of houses or land: the name and address of the valuation adviser to be contacted by the Valuation Office is to be given, along with reference and telephone number. Where the client's valuers have not already been instructed, this section need not be completed and HMRC will refer to the practitioner, with whom any minor problems can be sorted out without reference to a specialist valuer.

- Deceased's residence: this asks for the full address or description, the tenure (ie freehold or leasehold), details of any leases, the element of agricultural, timber or heritage value, and the open market value.
- Other land, buildings and rights over land: this asks for similar details as for the deceased's residence, in relation to such as fishing or mineral rights.
- Special factors that may affect the value: any of the properties listed might have been subject to major damage, which would affect their value; this must be detailed. If the damage is covered by buildings insurance, HMRC Inheritance Tax need to know details of the policy. For example, a loss in value of £75,000, of which £60,000 will be covered by insurance, should result in a deduction of only £15,000 from the open market value of the property, although this is likely to be reflected in the open market value given at G in Box 7 or 8.
- Property sale within 12 months after death: the sale price received on sale within 12 months after death will usually be a good indication of value at the date of death, though not conclusively, ie circumstances, namely the market, or perhaps planning considerations, might have changed since death. It is the value at the date of death that is required for IHT purposes. Note that selling costs may not be deducted. If the sale was for a preferential price to a relative, arm's-length value will have to be substituted. Any apportionment of value to fixtures and fittings, carpets, curtains etc must be given. You are given the option of using the sale price as the value at the date of death.

Finance (No 2) Act 2017, Sch 10 includes new rules which bring all UK residential property held indirectly through an offshore structure or trust within the UK IHT net from 6 April 2017.

SCHEDULE IHT406: BANK AND BUILDING SOCIETY ACCOUNTS AND NATIONAL SAVINGS AND INVESTMENTS

10.35 The five boxes on this schedule ask for:

- details of bank and building society accounts in the deceased's sole name;
- National Savings accounts, including the account numbers;
- Premium Bonds, including the bond numbers and the value of any unclaimed or uncashed prizes;

- other National Savings and Investment products; and
- total of National Savings and Investments.

SCHEDULE IHT407: HOUSEHOLD AND PERSONAL GOODS

10.36 This schedule asks about what are formally known as 'personal chattels'. It is important not to be too cavalier, ie simply to put in a 'broad-brush figure' of, say, £1,000. Clearly, things like clothes are likely to be of no realistic value, except in particular circumstances. However, it may be rather different with household furniture, especially anything which ranks as antiques, paintings, silverware, etc and indeed personal possessions of any particular value.

Note that a half share as joint tenants of property owned by the deceased with his spouse (albeit such value will be subject to the spouse exemption) now has to be recorded both on IHT407 and on Schedule IHT404 'Jointly owned assets'.

'Personal chattels': the statutory definition

10.37

> 'Carriages, horses, stable furniture and effects (not used for business purposes), motor cars and accessories (not used for business purposes), garden effects, domestic animals, plate, plated articles, linen, china, glass, books, pictures, prints, furniture, jewellery, articles of household or personal use or ornament, musical and scientific instruments and apparatus, wines, liqueurs and consumable stores, but do not include any chattels used at the death of the intestate for business purposes, no money or securities for money.'

The definition is found in *Administration of Estates Act 1925, s 55(1)(x)*. The fact that this Act was passed over 80 years ago might explain some of the terminology in the definition. The definition is expressly to be used in the case of intestacies, although it is of general application.

The *Inheritance and Trustees' Powers Act 2014* amends the definition of personal chattels in the *Administration of Estates Act 1925, s 55(1)(x)* which becomes:

> 'Tangible moveable property, other than such property which:
>
> - consists of money or securities for money;
> - was used at the death of the intestate solely or mainly for business purposes; or
> - was held at the death of the intestate solely as an investment.'

Various categories of goods

10.38 The four sections of IHT407 deal separately with: (a) jewellery; (b) vehicles, boats and aircraft; (c) antiques, works of art or collections; and (d) other household and personal goods, in each case distinguishing between goods which have been sold (in which case, the relationship between the purchaser and the deceased must be stated) and goods which have not. Individual items of jewellery valued at £500 or more must be detailed, together with a professional valuation if obtained.

Sales

10.39 It may be that, at the time of completing the inheritance tax account, goods have already been sold, in which case the gross sale proceeds must be completed. The gross sale proceeds are presumed to be the value at death. Note that no deduction is allowed for professional costs of sale. It may be that a sale is intended but has not yet taken place. Generally speaking, a sale which takes place within a reasonable time after death will fix the value at death.

Basis of valuation

10.40 HMRC emphasise that the basis of valuation of all property owned at death, including household and personal goods, is open market on the basis of a hypothetical sale (*IHTA 1984, s 160*).

Note that insurance value is not market value. It has been traditionally thought that 'probate value' means a value (acceptable to HMRC) which represents a discount of up to one-third on market value. That is not the case. In the authors view, it is important not to use the expression 'probate value', as this might suggest to HMRC that a discounted value has been adopted. The legislation requires all the assets of the deceased to be valued on an open market basis, 'willing buyer, willing seller', and this extends to personal chattels. In the absence of a formal valuation, brief details of the items and their value must be given.

Where professional valuations are not obtained

10.41 The most straightforward method of dealing with this subject is to get a professional valuation of everything owned by the deceased.

The value of any items included in 'other household and personal goods' may have been individually listed on the deceased's household insurance policy; if so, a copy of the policy at schedule if appropriate should be supplied.

SCHEDULE IHT408: HOUSEHOLD AND PERSONAL GOODS DONATED TO CHARITY

10.42 This is used to record details of gifts to be made to charity by the original beneficiary, so enabling the application of the provisions of *IHTA 1984, s 142* (deeds of variation within two years after death) and therefore the charity exemption from IHT. For deaths on or after 6 April 2012, proof must be provided to show that the charity has received these gifts.

SCHEDULE IHT409: PENSIONS

10.43 Schedule IHT409 comprises seven parts:

- Part 1 – Did any pension payments continue after the deceased's death? If so, details must be given in part 2. The deceased may on retirement have taken out a pension with a minimum period guarantee. The value of future guaranteed instalments must be discounted back to the date of death.
- Part 2 – Details are requested of the pension scheme or policy, including the right to receive payments falling due after death.
- Part 3 – Was a lump sum payable as a result of death? Here, a distinction (drawn out by the various questions) should be drawn between:
  - cases where the lump sum is payable to the PRs, or where the deceased could have made a 'nomination', which bound the pension scheme trustees to make the payment to the deceased's nominee. In this case, the lump sum forms part of the deceased estate. The lump sum will be treated as forming part of the deceased's estate if the deceased could have bound the trustees of the pension scheme to make a particular payment. In other words, it is not enough simply to ascertain that the death benefit has been transferred into trust. The personal pension scheme rules of the pension provider must be reviewed to see what rules apply to the distribution of the lump sum death benefit and a copy of any letter of wishes, direction or nomination made by the deceased must be obtained.
  - cases where the death benefit was held under trust, whether or not made by the individual when he took out the policy. In this case, the lump sum does not form part of the taxable estate.

  However, HMRC like to know about both cases, with the production of evidence to substantiate the latter.
- Part 4 – Did the deceased, within two years of the death, dispose of any of the benefits payable, or make any changes to the benefit to which

he was entitled under a scheme? Here, HMRC Inheritance Tax want to know whether the deceased had within two years before death:

- nominated or appointed the death benefits to another person;
- assigned the death benefits into a trust; or
- made changes to the pension benefits intended to be taken when there may have been a liability to IHT.

- Part 5 – Did the deceased (or his/her employer) make any contributions to a pension scheme for the deceased, within two years of the death? Here, HMRC Inheritance Tax want to know whether the deceased or their employer make any contributions to a pension scheme within two years of the death. This could encompass payments made by the employer of the deceased, presumably which benefits another person (see **10.44**).
- Part 6 – Did the deceased benefit from an alternatively secured pension at the date of death and, if so, how did it arise? However this is only relevant for deaths prior to 5 April 2011.
- Part 7 - Was the deceased entitled (as a 'relevant dependant') to an unsecured benefit arising under a registered pension scheme established by a person who had died aged 75 or over? If so, various details are requested. Again this is only relevant for deaths prior to 5 April 2011.

Changes in benefit

10.44 Until the early 1990s, the then Inland Revenue argued that, if a person could take a pension but exercised his right not to do so, eg having attained the age of 50 under a personal pension scheme (and being under age 75 at death), he might be charged under rules which provide that a person makes a transfer of value if he omits to exercise a right (*IHTA 1984, s 3(3)*). Although strenuous opposition from the Association of British Insurers at the time led the Revenue to back down in 1991, the case of *Fryer & Ors v HMRC* [2010] UKFTT 87 (TC) has re-affirmed HMRC's standpoint. In this case, the deceased died aged 61 without having taken the retirement benefits under her pension plan. HMRC argued successfully that there was a disposition by the deceased at the time of her normal retirement age of 60, as stated in the plan.

Even prior to the *Fryer* case, HMRC said that, if the deceased was in very poor health and then took out a new policy and assigned the death benefit into trust, or assigned a death benefit of an existing policy into trust, or paid further contributions to a policy where the death benefit had previously been assigned into trust, or deferred the date for taking his retirement benefit, the point might apply unless, perhaps, the death benefit were paid to the spouse or dependants, or where the member survived two years or more after making such arrangements. This is partially the background to part 4 of Schedule IHT409.

Under the 'income drawdown' option, a person elects to convert part of the fund to provide an annuity, with the remaining fund left to build up in the normal tax preferred pension regime.

Two examples (among others) of change in benefit are given on page 28 of the Guide, viz:

- the deceased reaches pension age and decides not to take the payment of pension at the time, or chooses to take 'income drawdown'; and
- where the deceased, having got to pension age and having chosen to take 'income drawdown', decides at a later date (and whilst in ill-health) to reduce the level of income taken.

The case of *Fryer* was recently revisited in *HMRC v Staveley* [2017] UKUT 004 (TCC). The issue was whether Mrs Staveley's omission to exercise her right to take her pension should be treated as a transfer of value. The Upper Tribunal held that the proximate cause of the increase in value of the son's estate was the exercise of the discretion of the scheme administrator, not the omission by Mrs Staveley to take her pension benefits during her lifetime. The pension benefits therefore passed outside Mrs Staveley's estate and were not subject to IHT. HMRC took the case to the Court of Appeal who decided that the omission to take her pension was an 'operation' within *IHTA 1984, s 268* and one intended to confer a gratuitous benefit on the two sons. HMRC's appeal was allowed and the Mrs Staveley's omission to take her pension was held to be subject to IHT under *IHTA 1984, s 3(3)*: see *CRC v Parry & Ors* [2018] EWCA Civ 2266.

Pension regime changes 6 April 2006 and 6 April 2015

10.45 It is beyond the scope of this book to go into the regime in any detail. The existence of the regime is merely noted. The broad principles applying to pension benefit trusts up to 5 April 2006 continue thereafter, however, subject to some specific changes, and the concessionary practice noted at **10.44** now has legislative authority (*IHTA 1984, s 12*). Specifically, the last two questions noted at **10.43** have been introduced following the changes – the *Staveley* case predated the changes.

Fundamental changes to the pension regime were introduced on 6 April 2015. Specialist advice needs to be sought when dealing with pensions during the administration of an estate.

Pensions often are held in trust and therefore in most cases they will pass free of IHT.

SCHEDULE IHT410: LIFE INSURANCE AND ANNUITIES

10.46 This form is required if the deceased was paying regular monthly or lump sum premiums on any:

- life assurance policies, or if any sums are payable by insurance companies to the estate as a result of the deceased's death. (It does not matter if the policies were on the deceased's life or someone else's life or whether the policies were for the deceased's benefit);
- unit-linked investment bonds with insurance companies or other financial service providers that pay 101% of the value of the units to the estate;
- investment or reinvestment plans, bonds or contracts with financial service providers that pay out to the estate on death;
- insurance policies and unit-linked investment bonds that are payable to the beneficiaries under a trust and do not form part of the estate; or
- joint life assurance policies under which the deceased was one of the lives assured but which remain in force after the date of death.

Life assurance policies

10.47 Question 1 simply asks whether, as a result of the death, sums were payable by insurance companies to the estate. This would cover a case where the deceased had taken out a life policy, whether endowment or whole of life, and the proceeds had not been written under trust. Box 2 asks for details of sums paid.

Question 3 is aimed at continuing life policies, eg a joint lives and survivor policy where the other life assured has not died. Question 4 asks whether the deceased is a beneficiary of another life policy on the life of someone else who remains alive. Such a policy might have been purchased second-hand. The value of any such policy, as provided by the insurance company, should be included, together with a copy of the insurance policy. Box 5 requires details of all relevant life policies, with copies to be provided and the total value to be given at Box 6.

Other questions

10.48

- Was the deceased at his death receiving annuity payments, which are guaranteed to continue after his death (Boxes 7 and 8)? The right to receive the remaining payments will be an asset of the estate and must be discounted back to the date of death.

- Was a lump sum payable under a purchase life annuity as a result of the death (Boxes 10 and 11)?
- Was the deceased paying premiums on policies for someone else's benefit, other than a spouse/civil partner (Box 12)? The payment of such premiums will rank as a gift (subject to the lifetime exemptions).
- Did the deceased, within seven years of his death, pay any premium on a life insurance policy for the benefit of someone else, other than the deceased's spouse/civil partner? Was an annuity purchased at any time (Box 13)? If so please provide a copy of the policy schedule and provisions.
- Did the deceased have a right to benefit on a life policy written on another's life and held in trust for the benefit of the deceased – and others (Box 14)?

Example 10.6—Various life policies

George died unexpectedly aged 55. Some 20 years before, he had taken out a with-profits policy on his own life, which he had written in trust for his two children. In the seven years before he died, he was making premium payments of £3,000 per annum (and was not otherwise using his annual exemption). Question 12 must be answered affirmatively. These premium payments will constitute transfers of value, protected by the £3,000 annual exemption to be reported on IHT403.

George's wife had predeceased him. When George died, there were five years outstanding on an endowment policy, which he and his late wife had previously taken out on a joint lives and survivor basis to pay off the mortgage when George was age 60. The endowment policy proceeds fell into George's estate and must be reported in Box 1. The policy had not been written in trust for the lender under the mortgage, though the lender had retained possession of the policy document. The outstanding liability under the mortgage will be deductible in George's estate, with the policy proceeds chargeable as an asset.

Finally, George had been in partnership with two others in a business that made widgets. They had, some years ago, taken out cross life policies, written in trust for the surviving partners, with a view to enabling the survivors to buy out the estate of the deceased under options (not constituting 'binding contracts for sale', which would have denied the availability of business property relief). Annual premiums were charged against the partnership profits each year, though these were not deductible for income tax purposes. While the policy payable on George's death crystallised the benefit of his two surviving partners, he also had a right to benefit from their life policies. Accordingly, question 14 must be answered in the affirmative. Although the point must be put to HMRC Inheritance Tax, the argument would be that the value at George's death of his rights under the other policies should not have been brought into his estate because the arrangements were made as part of an arm's-length transaction, under which any rights he had were balanced by the rights of the others under the policy on George's life.

SCHEDULE IHT411: LISTED STOCKS AND SHARES

UK government and municipal securities

10.49 Included here are:

- any government securities; and
- any municipal securities, mortgages, debentures and stock held in countries, cities and towns, docks, harbours and water boards.

The basis of valuation is the CGT one, viz either:

- one-quarter up from the lower to the higher limit of the prices quoted; or
- halfway between the highest and lowest bargains recorded for the day, but excluding bargains at special prices (*TCGA 1992, s 272*).

Any dividend or interest due, but unpaid at the date of death, must also be valued as an asset (ie not included in the valuation).

Listed stocks, shares and investments that did not give the deceased control of the company

10.50 This will include:

- shares held in an Individual Savings Account (ISA), including a figure for any uninvested cash but not for any other cash or insurance policies;
- unit trusts (give the full name, for example, AXA Equity and Law Unit Trust Managers, Pacific Basin Trust Accumulation Units);
- investment trusts;
- holdings in open-ended investment companies (OEICs); and
- foreign shares, but only if they are listed on the London Stock Exchange.

Example 10.7—Share valuation: adapting a former HMRC example

Fred died on 1 August 2018, owning 1,250 10p Ordinary shares in XYZ plc. The Stock Exchange list provides that the closing quotation on the date of death was 'p1091-11 xd' and the dividend was 2.3p.

To calculate the value of the shares, the number of shares should be multiplied by the 'quarter-up' price. The 'quarter-up' price is the lower price (1091) plus one-quarter of the difference between the two prices (one-quarter of 10p = 2.5p). The 'quarter-up' price is, therefore, 1091 + 2.5 = 1093.5p. Therefore, the value of the shareholding will be 1,250 × 1093.5 = £13,668.75.

The shares are marked xd. Let us say that the dividend per share was 2.3p. The value of the dividend will then be 1,250 × 2.3p = £28.75.

Alternatively, the dividend may be given as a percentage, say, 2.6%. In such case, the amount of the dividend can be calculated by finding out the percentage of the nominal value of the stock. If the deceased had owned £400 of loan stock, the dividend would be 2.6% of £400 = £10.40.

If the death occurred when The Stock Exchange was closed, the price for either the following day or the last day when The Stock Exchange was open may be taken. Therefore, if the death occurred on a Sunday, the price for either the Monday after or the Friday before may be taken. Whichever day gives the lower valuation may be used.

SCHEDULE IHT412: UNLISTED STOCKS AND SHARES AND CONTROL HOLDINGS

10.51 IHT412 deals with stocks and shares:

- listed on the Alternative Investment Market (AIM) or traded on OFEX;
- held in a private limited company, Business Expansion Scheme (BES) or Business Start-up Scheme (BSS); or
- listed on a recognised stock exchange where the deceased had control of the company.

Five categories of stocks and shares are given as follows:

- traded unlisted stocks and shares that did *not* give the deceased control of the company;
- unlisted stocks, shares and investments that did not give the deceased control of the company;

- unlisted stocks, shares and investments that gave the deceased control of the company;
- traded unlisted stocks, shares and investments that gave the deceased control of the company; and
- listed stocks, shares and investments that gave the deceased control of the company.

In each case, the following information is required:

- name of the company and type of shares or stock;
- number of shares or amount of stock held;
- market price per share/stock at date of death;
- total value of shares/stock at date of death;
- dividend due to date of death;
- owned for two years (Yes or No);
- amount of business property relief (BPR) due; and
- rate of BPR, 100% or 50%.

The valuation, whether estimated or final proposed, will be referred by HMRC to their Shares and Assets Valuation (SAV) division.

SCHEDULE IHT413: BUSINESS AND PARTNERSHIP INTERESTS AND ASSETS

10.52 Again, this is a complex subject (*IHTA 1984, ss 103–114*) and professional advice may have to be sought. In outline, however, see below.

Relevant business property

10.53 'Relevant property' means (*IHTA 1984, s 105(1)*):

- a business, or an interest in a business, which must be carried on with a view to profit;
- unquoted shares or securities;
- a controlling holding of quoted shares;
- land or buildings, machinery or plant used in a business by a company controlled by the deceased, or by a partnership of which he was a partner; and
- land or buildings, machinery or plant owned by trustees and used in a business where the deceased had a life interest.

Period of ownership

10.54 The relevant business property must have been owned for at least two years by the deceased subject to provisions for replacement of property (*IHTA 1984, s 106*).

Rate of relief

10.55 100% relief will be given for the first two categories above, otherwise 50% (*IHTA 1984, s 104*). Shares in AIM companies are treated as unquoted companies for this purpose.

Type of business

10.56 The business must not be an investment or a dealing business. Generally speaking (*IHTA 1984, s 105(3)*), BPR is given only to trading businesses. Accordingly, a business of owning property that is let residentially or commercially will generally not attract BPR. Many businesses will be 'mixed', comprising of a number of different factors. Here, regard must be had to the whole, to see whether the trading or the investment side predominates. In cases where there may be an issue whether the business is one of wholly and mainly holding investments, the cases of *Farmer and anor (executors of Farmer Decd) v IRC* [1999] STC (SCD) 321 and *Executors of Piercy (deceased) v Revenue and Customs Commissioners* [2008] STC (SCD) 858 give an indication of how to approach such cases.

Excepted assets

10.57 Even if the business as a whole qualifies, there may be some assets in the business regarded as 'excepted assets' (*IHTA 1984, s 112*). These will be excluded from relief where broadly not used for the business for future business use; that is, a business cannot simply 'park' spare cash, surplus to business requirements, with the proprietors expecting to get BPR on all the cash.

It may also be necessary to exclude properties which are held for investment purposes rather than for the business. For example, a plot of land used as a car park by a neighbouring business may have to be excluded.

Details of IHT413

10.58 Here, there are four main parts, with the last one relating only to gifts made within seven years before death where BPR is claimed:

- Ownership, contract for sale and business interests. This seeks to ensure that the period of ownership condition is met (see **10.54**) and that relief is not prejudiced because the property was at the date of death subject to a binding contract for sale which denies BPR under *IHTA 1984, s 113*.
- Business or interest in a partnership. Boxes 7 to 17 request various details, including questions designed to clarify the proper valuation of the net value of the business on which relief is claimed. Box 8 asks for the main activity of the business or partnership, to ensure that it is not disqualified as wholly or mainly dealing or investment (see **10.56**).
- Asset(s) owned by the deceased and used by a company controlled by the deceased or a partnership of which they were a member. This asks for details of the assets listed at bullet point 4 of **10.58** which attract 50% relief.
- Business relief on lifetime gifts. This is the 'clawback' question, as with APR. If a lifetime gift of business property had been made within seven years before death, BPR will be denied retrospectively unless, broadly speaking:
  - the original donee had retained either the original asset given away or qualifying replacement property throughout the period from the date of the gift to the date of death; and
  - the original or qualifying replacement property continued to attract relief in the hands of the donee at the date of the donor's death.

SCHEDULE IHT414: AGRICULTURAL RELIEF

10.59 Agricultural relief (or, rather, agricultural property relief or APR), together with its sister relief, business property relief (BPR) (see **10.52–10.58**), are very complex (*IHTA 1984, ss 115–124C*). See further *Business and Agricultural Property Relief* (7th edn) (Bloomsbury Professional) by Chris Erwood. What follows is only a summary.

Agricultural property

10.60 This is defined as: (1) agricultural land or pasture; (2) woodland and buildings used for intensive rearing of livestock or fish, if the occupation of the woodland or building is ancillary to agricultural land or pasture; and (3) cottages, farm buildings and farm houses together with their land as are of a character appropriate to the property (*IHTA 1984, s 115(2)*). The agricultural property must be situated within the European Economic Area (or, in cases where inheritance tax was paid or was due before 23 April 2003, in the United Kingdom, the Channel Islands or the Isle of Man): *IHTA 1984, s 115(5)*, as amended by *FA 2009, s 122*. A controlling interest in a farming company will also attract APR (*IHTA 1984, s 122*).

The ownership or occupation test

10.61 The deceased must have occupied the agricultural property for agricultural purposes for at least two years, or must have owned the agricultural property for at least seven years with continuous occupation by someone for agriculture (*IHTA 1984, s 117*). There are reliefs for replacement of property (*IHTA 1984, s 118*).

Rate of relief

10.62 By virtue of *IHTA 1984, s 116*, the rate is 100% if:

- the deceased has vacant possession, or the right to obtain it within 12 months (or 24 months by concession F17) of his death;
- the deceased had owned his interest in the land since before 10 March 1981 and would have been entitled to the old 'working farmer' relief, with no right to vacant possession since then; and
- the deceased was the landlord of a tenancy commencing on or after 1 September 1995.

Otherwise, the PRs will get only 50% relief, typically where he is the landlord of property let under a tenancy under which he does not have the right to obtain possession within 24 months.

Agricultural value

10.63 APR is given not on the market value of the property (as with BPR), but on the 'agricultural value' only; this presumes that the property is subject to a perpetual covenant prohibiting non-agricultural use (*IHTA 1984, s 115(3)*). District valuers have been using this to argue for a discount of up to one-third on the market value of the farmhouse. This (or, rather, 30%) was the discount applied by the Lands Tribunal in the case of *Lloyds TSB Private Banking plc (Personal Representative of Antrobus (Deceased)) v Twiddy* [2006] 1 EGLR 157. Claims to APR on the farmhouse have been the subject of a number of recently decided cases. The property must be a farmhouse on the facts before any question of relief arises. Revised Chapter 24 in HMRC's Inheritance Tax Manual confirms that, contrary to the analysis of the Lands Tribunal in the so-called *Antrobus No 2* case, a farmhouse can be the place from which management operations are conducted (under for example a contract farming agreement) as well as the residence of the day-to-day farmer.

Details required by IHT414

10.64

The six parts of the schedule are broken down as follows:

- Agricultural property. The address and a full description of the holding must be given. In addition, Schedule IHT405 Houses, Land, Buildings and Interests in Land must be completed to give details of the property concerned.
- Use of agricultural land. Here a detailed description of the day-to-day farming activities carried out on the land throughout the seven years or two years in question must be given, together with details of the extent of the deceased's involvement in these activities. As an example, the actual tasks carried out by the deceased and the number of hours spent on those tasks should be given.
- Let land. Here the details of any lease, licence or tenancy to which the land was subject should be given.
- Farmhouses and cottages. This part of the schedule addresses limb 3 of the definition of 'agricultural property' in *IHTA 1984, s 115(2)*: see **10.60**. There is room for details of two properties, with further properties to be given on an additional sheet. Details are required of address, occupation, whether the deceased lived there (if not, the details of the occupant and the extent of their involvement in the farming activities) and details of any letting
- Farm buildings. Full details of use must be given, noting that phrases such as 'general storage' or 'agricultural purposes' are unacceptable.
- Agricultural relief and lifetime transfers. These questions are intended to address the matter of the clawback of relief in *IHTA 1984, ss 124A* and *124B* – and to confirm that the property was not subject to a binding contract for sale. Broadly, to retain APR, it must be shown that the donee of the property given away occupied it for agricultural purposes throughout the period from the gift to the date of death and that he continued to own that property at the donor's death, with provision for replacement.
- There is then the white space for 'any other information'

> **Focus**
>
> Care needs to be taken when completing IHT414. All too often, APR is initially denied because of insufficient information and inconsistencies on the form.
>
> It is advisable to visit the farm, to see and understand how the land and buildings are used.

SCHEDULE IHT415: INTEREST IN ANOTHER ESTATE

10.65 This form is for use where the deceased had a right to a legacy or share in an estate of someone who died before them but which they had not received before they died. A separate form should be completed for each estate in which the deceased had a right to a legacy or share. Clearly, if someone is entitled to a gift of, say, £50,000 under the unadministered estate and this has been paid over by the executors, and the beneficiary then dies, the £50,000 (or such of it as remains unspent), will be a chargeable asset in the beneficiary's estate, attracting IHT (subject to the rules for quick succession relief: see **10.87–10.90**). If, on the other hand, the executors have not yet paid out the legacy when the beneficiary dies, it cannot be said that the beneficiary has an entitlement to £50,000. For example, all or part of the money may be required to pay IHT on the earlier death or perhaps debts owed by the deceased or his estate. In other words, until such time as an entitlement is paid over, all that a beneficiary under an estate has is what is called a 'chose in action', that is a right to have the estate property administered and, in the course of time, his entitlement (whatever it may turn out to be) paid over to him by the executors. Even in a case where there is a legacy of a specific chattel, eg a grandfather clock, it may have to be sold, and the proceeds used to pay tax or other liabilities. All that said, the beneficiary does have a valuable right in the unadministered estate, which will be an asset of his. This is the purpose of IHT415.

Example 10.8—Interest in unadministered estates

Jim died on 1 January 2018, leaving half the residue of his estate to his brother, Kenneth. Kenneth died on 1 May 2019. Jim's estate was complex and is still in the course of administration.

In Kenneth's form IHT400, Schedule IHT415 must be completed, giving:

- Jim's name;
- the date of Jim's death;
- the HMRC Inheritance Tax reference of Jim's estate;
- Kenneth's entitlement from Jim's estate, viz a one-half share in residue;
- whether Kenneth had received any part of his entitlement before he died; answer 'No'; and
- details of the entitlement that Kenneth had still to receive.

This question may well be difficult, and indeed not possible, to answer when submitting the details of Kenneth's estate to HMRC. The solicitors acting in Jim's estate should be asked for an estimate, perhaps subsequently to be confirmed, of the extent of Kenneth's entitlement, subject obviously to any legacies, taxes or liabilities.

There will be an entitlement to quick succession relief, as Kenneth died at least three, but less than four, years after Jim. (see **11.87–11.90**).

SCHEDULE IHT416: DEBTS DUE TO THE ESTATE

10.66 The deceased might have had an involvement with a debt, not as a sum of money that he owed, but as a sum that was owed to him. This is an asset that forms part of his chargeable estate, except perhaps to the extent that it can be shown clearly that the debt was irrecoverable. A separate form should be used for each debt. Questions 1 to 5 ask various details of the debt, including the original value of the loan and the amount of the loan including interest outstanding at the date of death. Question 9 envisages that a figure for the loan might be different from the total amount outstanding at Box 3: if so, an explanation is required.

Alternatively, the debt might have been written off. This would take effect as a gift and, if written off within seven years before the date of death, should again be included in the list of chargeable lifetime transfers. In the normal case, a debt should be written off by deed, ie not orally or by a letter that is not executed as a deed. This is because those methods of writing off are not generally enforceable and, whatever the intention as between the parties, the creditor (who has now died) should have a legal claim for the debt against the debtor if a deduction is to be obtained. (However, note that there is an argument to the contrary, based on the *Bills of Exchange Act 1882*.) Hence, HMRC will need to be satisfied as to the circumstances of writing off.

Irrecoverable debts

10.67 Many of the debts due to the estate will have been between members of the family and it may not always be easy to determine the precise terms. A debt will be irrecoverable at law if it has become 'statute barred'. Where a loan is made orally, or under simple writing (ie not a deed) and the debt was not for a fixed term, the limitation period is normally six years. This means that, if no acknowledgement is made of the debt, eg by payment of interest, and a period of more than six years has run since the loan or the last acknowledgement was made, the debt becomes irrecoverable. If the loan was made by deed, the period becomes 12 years. This is one of the reasons why question 8 asks for evidence of the existence of a loan, question 6 for payment of interest and question 7 repayment of capital.

Insurance schemes

10.68 There is a further point on question 8. A number of insurance-based IHT mitigation products include a loan made by the taxpayer (in this case the deceased) to the trustees of a settlement or of a life policy. It may be that under the arrangement any outstanding part of the loan (that had not been repaid during the lifetime) must be repaid on the death of the taxpayer. The effectiveness of the scheme will often depend upon the independence of the loan from the policy and, therefore, HMRC will wish to have copies of all relevant documentation.

Example 10.9—Writing off loans

In 1997, Fred made a loan to his son of £100,000 interest-free to help the son meet some heavy trading losses. The loan was made by a simple letter, with no interest payable, expressed to be repayable on demand. Father and son had informally agreed between them that the son would repay 'as and when' he could.

As time went by, Fred realised that it would be more IHT efficient to turn the loan into a gift and, annually as from 2006/07, has purported to write off £3,000 of the loan within his annual exemption. This was done by simple letter. The letter serves as acknowledgement of the loan, ie it cannot be argued that it has become statute-barred. However, after Fred's death on 1 May 2019, a claim for use of his annual exemptions is likely to be resisted by HMRC because the annual writings off were not effected by deed. It could be worth challenging the refusal of the exemptions, on the grounds of the *Bills of Exchange Act 1882* argument (see **10.66** above).

SCHEDULE IHT417: FOREIGN ASSETS

10.69 Assuming that the deceased was domiciled or deemed domiciled in the UK at death, the worldwide estate will be subject to IHT. It may of course be that foreign tax is paid on the foreign assets, typically where these consist of real property. There may be a double tax treaty, which expressly gives relief for the foreign tax paid against the UK liability, eg Ireland, The Netherlands, South Africa, Sweden or the US. Otherwise, 'unilateral relief' may be given by deducting the foreign tax against the UK liability (*IHTA 1984, s 159*). In no circumstances will there be a repayment of the foreign tax; ie if the UK liability is 50 but the foreign tax 60, there will simply be no UK IHT to pay.

If, by contrast, the deceased was not actually domiciled outside the UK (nor deemed domiciled within the UK), IHT417 should not be used; instead, HMRC request an approximate value for all the non-UK assets owned by the deceased in answer to question 22 on Schedule IHT401 (though there is no obligation to provide this): see **10.17**.

The schedule asks first for details of houses, land and buildings; businesses or interest in businesses; and controlling holdings of shares and securities. In each case there must be given a description of the assets, the value in foreign currency at the date of death, the exchange rate at the date of death and the pounds sterling value of the assets at the date of death. There follow boxes for details of deductible liabilities and exemptions and reliefs in each case, concluding with a net total of those types of assets. Next, in Boxes 6 to 10, such details must be given of any other assets owned by the deceased outside the UK, eg bank accounts.

Foreign liabilities

10.70 Subject to satisfying the general rules about deductibility (viz in particular the deceased must have given value for the debt, see **10.76–10.77**), a foreign liability may be deducted for IHT purposes just as a UK liability. However, where the debt is to be discharged outside the UK and is not secured on UK property, it is, so far as possible, taken to reduce the value of the non-UK property (*IHTA 1984, s 162(5)*).

Expenses of administration

10.71 The legislation recognises that there may be extra expenses of administering foreign property. However, the executors are not given 'carte blanche' and there is a limitation to 5% of the value of the property at death (*IHTA 1984, s 173*). If, therefore, the expenses amount to 3%, it is those actual expenses that are deductible. If they amount to 6%, only 5/6ths of the expenses are deductible.

Example 10.10—Foreign assets

John died UK domiciled, owning the following non-UK assets:

- shares quoted on the New York Stock Exchange worth £5,000;
- a bank account in Greece, with a balance at date of death of £1,000; and
- a holiday home in Greece, worth £200,000.

His PRs will complete:

- The first part of the form deals with the holiday home. On such assets, tax may be paid by instalments; the family may want to keep the property and may wish to pay the tax by instalments; Greek death duties, if any, can be deducted. The resultant IHT will be payable by ten equal annual instalments, the first falling due six months after the end of the month in which death occurred and the remaining nine on the annual anniversaries. Any interest due will be added to the unpaid instalments. Here the value of the Greek property will be shown, less the costs of administering the property (interestingly, this would not be allowed on UK property) of, say, £10,000, net value £190,000.
- The second part of the form by listing the US shares and the Greek bank account, showing a total value of £6,000 from which there are no liabilities or exemptions and reliefs, other than the management costs of the Greek letting agents outstanding at date of death of £200, total net value £5,800.

SCHEDULE IHT418: ASSETS HELD IN TRUST

10.72 With trusts or settlements, the basic distinction has been explained (see **2.6–2.16**) between:

- a trust made before 22 March 2006 in which a person has a right to receive the income, or enjoy the trust fund (eg a right to occupy a property) – called a life interest or an interest in possession; and
- a trust where the trustees have a discretion over income, called a discretionary trust, or any other non-charitable trust (other than a qualifying disabled trust) made on or after 22 March 2006.

The rule with life interest trusts is that the income beneficiary is treated for IHT purposes as owning the assets that support his interest: if, for example, he has a right to half the income, then he is treated as owning half the capital.

The trustees of a life interest trust have a 'stand-alone' obligation to return the chargeable transfer, which occurs on the life tenant's death (subject, of course, to the spouse exemption). However, IHT418 exists to enable the personal representatives to return details of the trust in order that they can correctly compute the total tax payable. The notes emphasise that the primary compliance liability rests on the trustees and not on the PRs. The way in which IHT is calculated and shared between the trustees and the PRs is explained in **6.55** and Example 6.18.

What types of qualifying life interest trust are potentially subject to IHT?

10.73

- Settled property situated outside the UK, held by trustees of a settlement made by a settlor who was UK domiciled when the trust was made.
- Settled property in the UK held in a trust made by anyone, ie regardless of domicile when the trust was established.
- Settled property over which the deceased had a general power of appointment (ie he could determine who, including himself, would benefit from the property *and* the deceased exercised that power in the will).

What types of trust are not caught?

10.74 If the settled property was situated outside the UK, and the settlor was domiciled outside the UK when the trust was made, this is an 'excluded property settlement' and is outside the scope of IHT (*IHTA 1984, s 48(3)*). The reference to domicile includes the deemed domicile rule (see **6.7**). Even here, however, the notes say that the details of such a trust should be included in questions 2 to 5. This gives HMRC the opportunity to check the facts.

10.75 Schedule IHT418 is divided into six parts:

- Deceased's interest in possession. Here, there must be distinguished: an interest in possession which commenced before 22 March 2006 and remained in existence until death; an immediate post-death interest; a disabled person's interest; and a transitional serial interest. With all of these, the deceased will be treated as having owned the underlying capital, for which the details must be given in the remainder of the form.
- About the trust. Here details are required, including HMRC's unique taxpayer reference.
- Assets in the trust. Here are required details of houses land and buildings; businesses or interests in businesses; and controlling holdings of shares and securities. On these types of property instalment relief (see **10.94–10.97**) may be claimed.
- Other assets in the trust. This is non-instalment property, for example bank accounts and quoted shares.
- Future rights to assets in a trust. This series of questions is intended to seek out reversionary interests, that is at the date of death some person other than the deceased was entitled to income. While generally such a future reversionary right will not be taxable in the deceased's estate, it may be in some circumstances eg where the deceased or his spouse/civil partner was the settlor.
- There is then a white space box for 'any other information'.

SCHEDULE IHT419: DEBTS OWED BY THE DECEASED

10.76 The PRs will want to rank as a deduction any debts that were properly owed by the deceased, from the chargeable estate for IHT purposes. These will not extend to liabilities, eg money owed to local tradesmen or funeral expenses, but will rather cover debts which are claimed to be owed to members of the family, other more substantial loans, debts covered by a guarantee, and debts which may be subject to anti-avoidance rules.

10.77 The five sections on the form ask for the following details:

- Money spent on the deceased's behalf, eg the payment of domestic bills during the deceased's lifetime.
- Loans and liabilities. Details of the loans, including written evidence, must be provided whether they were from financial institutions or from close friends and relatives.
- Liabilities related to an insurance policy, whether a policy or an investment bond where the value of the policy or bond is not fully reflected elsewhere in the IHT400.
- Guaranteed debts. If the deceased had guaranteed to pay someone else's borrowing, the deceased would get a deduction only if the guarantee had been, or was likely to be, called. If there was only a contingent possibility of the guarantee being called, any deduction is likely to be merely nominal.
- Gifts to and loans from the same person. This is designed to catch situations where the deceased made a gift to someone before or after 18 March 1986 and, at any time after that gift, borrowed money from that same person. These represent complicated anti-avoidance rules, which are on the 'other side of the coin' of the reservation of benefit regime (*FA 1986, s 103*). It would be quite easy to get round the reservation of benefit rules; see, for example, the scenario described in Example 11.11 at **10.78**. Broadly, a deduction is denied (*IHTA 1984, s 103*) if:
  - the deceased had borrowed money from a person on or after 18 March 1986; and
  - if the deceased had at any time (whether or not after 18 March 1986 and whether or not connected with the loan) made a gift to the creditor; or
  - the liability is in any way related to a policy of life assurance and the sum assured is not fully reflected in the estate of the deceased.

If the creditor was a close friend or relative of the deceased, details of the loan may already have been given in Box 2.

Finance Act 2013 includes IHT provisions which amend *IHTA 1984, s 162(4)* and *(5)* and disallow a deduction from the value of an estate for liabilities owed by the deceased on death in the following circumstances:

- excluded property – no deduction will be allowed for a liability to the extent that it has been incurred directly or indirectly on or after 6 April 2013 to acquire property which is excluded from the charge to IHT. However, where the acquired property has been disposed of or where the liability is greater than the value of the excluded property, the deduction may be allowed providing certain conditions are met – see new *IHTA 1984, s 162A*; or

- where the liability has been incurred to acquire assets on or after 6 April 2013 on which a relief such as BPR, APR or woodlands relief is due, the liability will be taken to reduce the value of those assets that can qualify for relief. The deduction for the loan will be matched against the assets acquired and relief will be restricted to the net value of the assets. Any excess liability will be allowable as a deduction against the estate in general subject to the new rule about unpaid debts – see new *IHTA 1984, s 162B*;

- a deduction for a liability will be allowed only to the extent that it is repaid to the creditor, unless it is shown that there is a commercial reason for not repaying the liability and it is not left unpaid as part of arrangements to get a tax advantage – see new *IHTA 1984, s 175 A*; or

- for deaths occurring on or after 17 July 2014, *FA 2014* provides that no deduction will be allowed for liabilities incurred to fund foreign currency bank accounts and foreign bank accounts will be treated the same as excluded property.

The measure will have effect for transfers of value, including transfers arising on death, made on or before 17 July 2013 the date on which *FA 2013* received Royal Assent. The provisions in *IHTA 1984, s 162B* dealing with liabilities in relation to relievable property only applies to liabilities incurred on or after 6 April 2013.

A liability may be deducted against an estate only to the extent that it is discharged out of the estate.

Focus

Individuals who have assets qualifying for APR or BPR and also have debts are advised to take professional advice to check whether their estate might be affected.

10.78

Example 10.11—Anti-avoidance rules (*FA 1986, s 103*)

Without these rules, it might be quite easy to get around the reservation of benefit regime by using, for example, the following arrangement.

Father gives to his daughter shares worth £200,000. Daughter sells the shares and buys a house. Father then buys from the daughter the house for £225,000 (its market value), but cannot afford to pay for it, so leaves the purchase price outstanding as an interest-free, repayable on demand loan. Father dies five years later, when the house is worth £300,000. In the absence of these rules, father's IHT400 would show a house worth £300,000 less a liability owed to the daughter £225,000, net equity £75,000. However, these rules prevent a deduction and, therefore, the £300,000 is charged in father's estate in full.

The thinking behind the rules is that father has enjoyed a benefit from a gift that he made to the lender and therefore, to the extent of the gift, is denied a deduction. Interestingly, the rules would be applied even if father had paid interest at market rate on the loan. By contrast, if the money had been borrowed at interest from a clearing bank or building society, a deduction would have been applied.

In the authors view, the rules are applied by HMRC more widely than is justified by the legislation, which implies (by the use of the word 'consideration') some necessary connection between the gift and the loan.

There is no *de minimis* let-out. The only limitation afforded is that the rules cannot apply to a disposition which is not a transfer of value. Hence, if, at the outset, father had sold the shares to his daughter and later bought the house leaving the price outstanding, there would be a deduction for the debt.

Spouse/civil partner exempt gifts are not excluded from the operation of the rules. This was the basis of the decision of the Special Commissioner in the case of *Phizackerley v HMRC* [2007] STC (SCD) 328. Dr Phizackerley had given to his wife a half share in the house. On her death, her share in the house was assented to Dr Phizackerley on his giving an IOU for its then value to the trustees of her nil rate band trust. On Dr Phizackerley's death, a deduction for the IOU was denied because of the prior gift of the half share in the house.

SCHEDULE IHT420: NATIONAL HERITAGE ASSETS – CONDITIONAL EXEMPTION AND MAINTENANCE FUNDS

10.79 Conditional exemption from IHT is available for objects, land and buildings if they are important to the national heritage (*IHTA 1984, ss 30–35*). In return, new owners must agree to look after the assets and provide public access. This form is used:

- to claim conditional exemption for any assets in the estate;
- if heritage exemption was allowed on any of the assets in the estate in the past; or
- if the PRs wish to offer any assets in lieu of IHT.

HMRC published new guidance on the conditional exemption on 22 September 2011 – see www.hmrc.gov.uk/inheritancetax/conditionalexemption.pdf.

Legislation is included in *Finance Act 2016* to create a charge to IHT or estate duty on conditional objects which are subject to an estate duty exemption and which have been lost due to negligence. This will be with effect from the date of Royal Assent.

Finance Act 2016 revised the way estate duty and IHT interact, in that HMRC can elect which charge to raise in relation to chargeable events on or after 16 March 2016.

OTHER HMRC INHERITANCE TAX FORMS

Further schedules to account form IHT400

10.80 Schedules IHT401 to IHT420 have been discussed in **10.16–10.79**. There are four further schedules:

- IHT421 (or, in Scotland, C1) is the form which is sent to the Probate Registry (or, in Scotland, Sheriff Court), once endorsed by HMRC Inheritance Tax: see **10.9**.
- IHT422 is the application for an IHT reference (see **10.7**).
- IHT423 is an application to transfer funds from any of the deceased's bank or building society accounts to pay IHT (the direct payment scheme).
- IHT430 is used when at least 10% of a person's net estate is left to charity and an application is made to pay the reduced rate of 36%. This form is used:
  - where the deceased died on or after 6 April 2012;

- at least 10% of the deceased's net estate is left to a qualifying charity; and
- the PRs want to claim the reduced rate of IHT of 36%.

The PRs will have to establish the *general component*, the *survivorship component* and the *settled property component*. The net value of each component after the deduction of liabilities, reliefs and exemptions then benefit from the apportioned nil rate band for IHT – for a detailed description of the tax analysis see *Inheritance Tax 2018/19* (Bloomsbury Professional).

If components are merged this form must be signed by all appropriate persons for each component.

To check whether the estate qualifies for the reduced rate of IHT, HMRC published a calculator (see www.hmrc.gov.uk/tools/iht-reduced-rate/calculator.htm)

Other forms

10.81

- C4 Corrective Account/Inventory: see **10.82**.
- IHT38 (claim for relief: loss on sale of land): see **10.83–10.85**.
- IHT35 (claim for relief: loss on sale of shares): see **10.86**.

Corrective accounts

10.82 It would be unusual for PRs to 'get it right first time' when delivering the inheritance tax account. Provided that all proper care is taken, and reasonable estimates of valuations are made, the inheritance tax account will be accepted, so long as any estimated values are clearly marked as such. If revisions need to be made to the estimated accounts, or if further assets come to light, this is dealt with by means of a 'corrective' account.

There is no need to notify HMRC every time there is an amendment to the initial calculation, provided the changes do not:

- total, individually or collectively, more than £50,000;
- comprise items of land/realty or unquoted shares;
- comprise loss on sale of land or share claims; or
- relate to a case that is subject to compliance checks.

You will only need to tell HMRC 18 months from the date of death or at the point the estate is finalised, whichever is earlier, using form C4.

In cases where errors arise as a result of carelessness (previously, negligence) or fraud, penalties might apply, and HMRC Inheritance Tax expect to be told immediately when such errors are discovered (see **9.30**).

Relief for loss on sale of land within four years after death

10.83 If, having agreed a market value at death of, say, £200,000, the land is subsequently sold for £180,000, it is possible by election to have that lower value substituted, thus achieving any consequential repayment of IHT (*IHTA 1984, ss 190–198*). The claim is made on form IHT38.

For this to apply:

- the reduction in value must be greater than the lesser of £1,000 and 5% of the value at death;
- all sales must be aggregated for computing the relief, ie including sales at a gain within three years after death and sales at a loss within four years after death;
- the relief is restricted *pro rata* to the extent that the seller, viz typically the PRs (although it could be the beneficiary), reinvests in replacement land within four months after the last sale within three years after death;
- the relief will apply only if a value has to be 'ascertained' at death, ie it cannot apply if the land passes to a spouse, or is covered by 100% agricultural and business property relief, or is entirely within the nil rate band;
- the relief is given only if the sale is made by the 'appropriate person', viz the person who pays the tax. The person who pays the tax *must be* the person who makes the sale;
- the sale must be to a person *other than* the beneficiary, the spouse of the beneficiary, a direct descendant of the beneficiary or trustees of a settlement in which the beneficiary has a life interest. The beneficiary means the person to whom the property is bequeathed, either under the will, or to whom it passes under the intestacy, or (remember this trap) to whom the property is redirected under a post-death deed of variation or disclaimer (see **12.1–12.4**); and
- the revised IHT value at death will be used as the beneficiary's base cost in computing any gain on a future sale.

Focus

Care needs to be taken making a loss relief claim when a discount was claimed for joint ownership of property, as the discount formerly claimed will no longer apply.

It therefore may not be advantageous to make a loss relief claim, as it may increase the total IHT liability on the property sold.

10.84 HMRC have updated IHTM33026 to confirm that the IHT38 procedure cannot be made to substitute a higher sale value in disposals of land.

How soon can a claim be made after sale?

10.85 The rules for making a claim on form IHT38 provide that the claim cannot be submitted within four months after the date of sale. If all the qualifying property has not been sold, relief will not be final until four years from the date of death. Form IHT38 has been revised, allowing the claimant to say whether or not the relief claimed is final. If final, HMRC Inheritance Tax will be able to deal with the claim before the four-month period has elapsed (and will be able to issue clearance as soon as all other matters on the estate have been agreed).

Relief for loss on shares

10.86 The relief for sales of quoted shares or units or authorised unit trusts for a price less than their market value on death (*IHTA 1984, ss 178–189*) is similar to the relief for land (see **10.83–10.85**), except that:

- the shares must be sold, or become valueless, within 12 months after death;
- it does not matter to whom they are sold;
- the repurchase restriction applies if shares are bought within two months after the last sale in the 12-month period; and
- there is no *de minimis* restriction.

Example 10.12—Shares sold at a loss

Don's estate included four parcels of quoted shares each worth £5,000 at death. In the following 12 months, the PRs sold three parcels at £3,000, £4,000 and £6,000 respectively.

The aggregate loss on sale is: £15,000 – £13,000 = £2,000 and, on a claim on form IHT35, the chargeable value of the shares will be reduced to £18,000.

QUICK SUCCESSION RELIEF

10.87 Where, within a period of five years, there are two chargeable transfers of which the second is (if not both are) on death, relief is given against the

IHT liability on the second event (*IHTA 1984, s 141*). There is no requirement that the person given the asset under the first transfer retained the actual asset. What is required is that the value charged on the second transfer reflected the increase in value made by the first.

Measure of relief

10.88 The relief is a prescribed proportion of the tax charged on the value transferred by the previous transfer as is attributable to the donee's estate. The table is set out below.

Quick succession relief (QSR) is calculated using the following formula:

$$\text{QSR} = \text{Allowable percentage} \times \frac{\text{Net value received} \times \text{Tax paid}}{\text{Gross value received}}$$

Donee predeceasing donor

10.89 Suppose that, at the date of the donee's death, the donor is still alive, ie having made a PET. If the donor dies within seven years of the gift, the PET will become chargeable. Quick succession relief will become available on the donee's estate.

Rates of quick succession relief

10.90

Period between transfer and death	*Percentage relief*
Less than 1 year	100%
1–2 years	80%
2–3 years	60%
3–4 years	40%
4–5 years	20%

Example 10.13—QSR on failed PET

Dominic gave his nephew, Freddy, £50,000 in November 2016. Dominic was very generous and his nil rate band was used up by previous PETs to nephews and nieces. Dominic died in July 2017 and Freddy paid the IHT due of £20,000 on the failed PET.

Freddy died in January 2019 and his PRs therefore can claim QSR, which is calculated as follows:

$$QSR = 60\% \times \frac{£30,000 \times £20,000}{£50,000} = £7,200$$

Freddy's PRs, therefore, are able to obtain relief of £7,200 against any IHT payable on Freddy's estate.

THE ESTATE DUTY SURVIVING SPOUSE EXEMPTION

The estate duty regime

10.91 Tax was charged on the whole estate of the first spouse to die (subject to the threshold, to any spouse exemption and to reliefs for business property). Provided that, under the will of the first to die, the surviving spouse was left a life interest, under which there was no power to draw on capital, the value of the assets subject to the life interest on the second death were exempt from estate duty.

Transitional provisions

10.92 Transitional provisions under both CGT and IHT ensure that, where the first spouse died before 13 November 1974, ie under estate duty, and tax was paid, or would have been paid but for the threshold or any relief, the estate duty exemption that would have applied on the second death is carried over (*IHTA 1984, Sch 6, para 2*). Accordingly, this is known as an 'estate duty protected life interest'. Cases benefiting from this exemption still exist, although they will reduce in number as the years go by. This means in effect that the life interest is a capital tax-free fund, exempt on death from both CGT and IHT, and hence is hugely valuable.

Lifetime assignments

10.93 The life interest could come to an end during the lifetime of the surviving spouse, eg if she (let us assume it is the widow) assigns the right to receive income to say, her children, who will become entitled to capital on her death. This creates an 'interest *pur autre vie*'. On the face of it, that is bad news, in the sense that the usual CGT-free uplift to market value will not be available on the second death. However, in cases where CGT is not such an issue, such a course of action might be appropriate. This is because although the estate duty protected life interest does not itself come into charge on the second death, it is nonetheless taken into account in valuing other property in the surviving spouse's free estate. The legislation provides that in such a case if the surviving spouse dies within seven years after the assignment of the life interest, no IHT is payable, ie it is not treated as a PET that becomes chargeable.

Example 10.14—First spouse's death under estate duty

Leonard died on 1 October 1973 and estate duty was paid on his estate. His will left a life interest to his widow, Gladys. Gladys had a long widowhood and died only on 1 June 2019, having made no chargeable gifts in the seven years before she died. She had a free estate of £300,000 and an estate settled under the will of her late husband worth £1 million. No capital taxation (IHT or CGT) is payable on her death. Her own estate is covered by the nil rate band of £325,000, and the £1 million is covered by the 'estate duty protected life interest' exemption.

INSTALMENT PAYMENT

10.94 The legislation recognises that it might be unfair to require executors to pay tax within (broadly) six months after death if the property concerned is land or, perhaps, business or private company shares which are not going to or cannot easily be sold and there is no spare cash in the estate to pay the tax. Accordingly, under the instalment payment rules, provided that the property concerned falls within certain prescribed categories (whether the property is within or outside the UK), an election to pay the tax by instalments may be made (*IHTA 1984, s 227*): see **11.96** below.

The first instalment falls due on the date on which the tax would otherwise have to be paid and the remaining nine instalments on anniversaries of this date, so that, broadly speaking, the whole tax has been paid nine and a half years or so after death. If at any time during the instalment period, the property is sold, the whole of the outstanding instalments become immediately due and payable.

Qualifying property (IHTA 1984, ss 227(2) and 228)

10.95

- Land or buildings, wherever situated.
- Quoted or unquoted shares or securities, which gave control.

- Other unquoted shares or securities where:
  - there would be undue hardship if the tax were to be paid in one sum; or
  - the transfer was on death and at least 20% of the tax due is attributable to unquoted shares or securities, or to other property qualifying for instalment relief.
- Unquoted shares worth more than £20,000 where either:
  - the shares constitute at least 10% of the issued share capital of the company; or
  - the shares are ordinary shares, and their nominal value is at least 10% of all the ordinary shares in issue.
- The net value of the business or an interest in a business carried on for gain.
- Timber.

See pages 6 and 7 of form IHT400 and pages 53 and 54 of the Notes.

Interest

10.96 If the qualifying property is an interest in a business, shares or securities which attract BPR, land used in a business or timber, no interest is payable on outstanding instalments, providing that they are all paid on the due dates. Otherwise, for example, in the case of the main family home or a holiday home, any interest due is payable on outstanding instalments. In this case, an assessment made by HMRC Inheritance Tax for each instalment of the tax will have added to it a request for interest due.

Elect with care

10.97 There was an unfortunate Special Commissioner's case in 1997 called *Howarth's executors v IRC* [1997] STC (SCD) 162. The two executors were the son of the deceased, and a solicitor (not a partner) in the firm which acted in the estate. An election was made for instalment payment, following which the property was transferred into the name of the son as the residuary beneficiary. The son then became bankrupt and the instalment property was sold. The Special Commissioner upheld a determination made by HMRC against the solicitor who had retired on account of ill health: 'In trusting the beneficiary, he took a risk'.

This decision emphasises that IHT is a personal liability of each personal representative and is not a responsibility that can easily be shed. A personal representative in such a case needs to ensure, eg by retaining legal ownership of the assets concerned, that the instalments of tax can be met.

PAGE 11: CALCULATING THE TAX LIABILITY

10.98 HMRC expect a solicitor or other agent acting on behalf of the PRs to work out the tax due before submitting form IHT400. If lay PRs are applying for a grant without the help of a solicitor or other agent, there is a choice, either to work out the tax themselves or to let HMRC do the work.

The exercise may be quite straightforward, or (especially where grossing up applies – see **10.101–10.104**) it may be extremely complicated.

In any event, the figures shown on form IHT400, which brings in the amounts from the supplementary pages, are carried over onto the IHT worksheet.

There is also a checklist on page 14 of the IHT400 to ensure that all the appropriate forms are sent to HMRC Inheritance Tax. An example of how the tax calculation works is shown below.

Example 10.15—Tax on instalment and non-instalment property respectively

Alfred died on 1 May 2019, owning a UK estate worth £500,000, including his home worth £200,000. He had an interest in a trust fund set up by his late father, which passes on his death to his children, worth £150,000.

He had, in 2007, made a gift to his son of a cottage in Brighton, worth then £25,000 but worth at his death £175,000 in which his use had amounted to a reservation of benefit. In the seven years before he died, Alfred had made net chargeable gifts of £40,000. Just under a year before he died, he had received a net legacy from his brother's estate of £50,000 after tax of £30,000.

Tax on both the home and the Brighton cottage is payable by instalments.

Alfred was divorced. After charitable legacies of £5,000, he leaves his estate equally between his two adult children. The calculation works as follows:

Assets where tax may not be paid by instalments	
UK estate (less charities exemption)	£295,000
Settled property	£150,000
Assets where tax may be paid by instalments	
Home	£200,000

Other property taken into account to calculate the total tax	
Gifts with reservation	£175,000
Chargeable estate	£820,000
Cumulative total of lifetime transfers	£40,000
Aggregate chargeable transfer	£860,000
Working out the total tax that is payable	
Aggregate chargeable transfer	£860,000
Nil rate band	(£325,000)
Residence nil rate band	(£125,000)
Value chargeable to tax	£410,000
Tax due (at 40%)	£164,000
Tax on lifetime transfers	Nil
Relief for successive charges (see **10.87–10.90**)	(£18,750)
Tax payable on chargeable estate	£145,250
Tax which may not be paid by instalments (£445,000/£820,000) × £145,250	£78,825
Tax which may be paid by instalments (£375,000/£820,000) × £145,250	£66,425

DEATH OF EMERGENCY SERVICE PERSONNEL OR CONSTABLES, OR DEATH ARISING FROM ACTIVE MILITARY SERVICE

10.99 It has long been a very reasonable principle of the death duties regime that the estate of a person who gave their life for their country should be free from death duties (*IHTA 1984, s 154*).

The principle is subject to the condition that the death arose from:

- a wound inflicted, accident occurring or disease contracted at a time when he was a member of any of the Armed Forces of the Crown or, not being such a member, was subject to the law governing any of those forces (by reason of association, whether accompanying any body of those forces) and was either on active service against an enemy or on other service of a war-like nature, which in the opinion of the Treasury involved the same risks as service of a war-like nature; or

- a disease contracted at some previous time, the death being due to, or hastened by, the aggravation of the disease during a period when the above conditions were satisfied.

The main point is that the wound, accident or disease need not be the only or even the main cause of death, just 'a' cause of death. That is, it may well be possible, even now over 60 years later, to claim the exemption in respect of a wound inflicted, etc during the Second World War, not of course to mention conflicts since, most recently in Iraq and Afghanistan.

This exemption was invoked in *Executors of 4th Duke of Westminster (otherwise Barty-King) v Ministry of Defence* [1979] STC 218, QBD, where the 4th Duke of Westminster died many years after his war wound from cancer. Although there was no direct causal connection between the war wound and the cause of his death, the exemption was successfully invoked.

All that is required is to find a 'reasonable link' which may have caused the death. For example, a limp caused by a war injury may have caused a fall which resulted in death.

Finance Act 2015 included the following provisions to take effect on or after 19 March 2014:

- *IHTA 1984, s 153A* covers the death of emergency and humanitarian aid workers responding to emergency circumstances, or death hastened by a disease contracted during a period when the deceased was responding to an emergency in his capacity as emergency responder.
- *IHTA 1984, s 155A* extends the IHT exemption to constables and armed service personnel targeted because of their status. Again this relief is extended to cover death from disease contracted in their line of duty.
- *IHTA 1984, s 154* has been amended so that the treatment available to emergency service personnel also applies to members of the armed forces.
- *FA 2015, s 75* extends the death in service exemption to IHT payable on lifetime gifts that arise on death.

Procedure

10.100 The procedure is relatively straightforward. When form IHT400 is submitted, it should be accompanied by a letter or report by a physician who knew the deceased, in support of the application, the exemption being claimed by the person who sends in the account. HMRC will then pass the letter or report to the Ministry of Defence, who may ask further questions and then will simply respond affirmatively or negatively.

The exemption is a complete exemption, and therefore well worth having. Note, however, that it will be given only if the death actually resulted from the wound, accident or disease. That is, if a person who had been wounded in active conflict, and who would certainly have qualified for the exemption, is in fact killed in a car crash, no relief will of course, be due. In other words, it is only following the death that one can be sure that the exemption is given.

Example 10.16—The 'killed in war' exemption

Joe has recently died at the age of 45. He was a captain in the army and had been wounded in Iraq in 2003 and had been retired from the Army on medical grounds. He had never been able to hold down a job since, and had worked from time to time on his own account. The death certificate (helpfully) refers to the war wound as having been a contributing cause of death.

On application, subject to the appropriate medical evidence, the exemption should be given.

Joe's estate amounted to £800,000. Under his will he left the whole of this to his wife. It would be open to his wife, within two years after Joe's death, to vary his will (see **12.1–12.4**), whereby part of the estate is held on discretionary trust for the beneficiaries to include her and their children.

However, HMRC will not consider the exemption unless there is at least £10,000 of IHT at stake. It may, therefore, be necessary in the first place for the widow to vary Joe's will. For example, she could agree to transfer £355,000 on discretionary trust. This would have been a chargeable transfer of £30,000 with tax due of £12,000, if the exemption is not given. This, however, is thought to be a risk worth taking. Then, once the exemption is given, she could make a second deed, within the two-year period, varying a further part of the estate into the same discretionary trust.

THE GROSSING-UP RULES

10.101 Grossing up is an issue that can crop up, although (happily) not all that frequently. However, it is necessary to have some understanding of what grossing up is, and in what circumstances it might happen.

Taxable and/or exempt transfers

10.102 When someone dies, they are treated as making, for IHT purposes, a single gift of the whole estate, which may be:

- wholly taxable, eg passing just to the children;

- partly taxable and partly exempt, eg passing partly to a surviving spouse and partly to the children; or
- wholly exempt, eg passing entirely to the surviving spouse or to charity.

There are rules to ensure that, where there are both exempt and chargeable gifts, exemptions are properly attributed among the various gifts (*IHTA 1984, s 38*).

Residue and specific gifts

10.103 There is a distinction between:

- gifts of residue, which may or may not be exempt, but where they are chargeable always bear their own tax; and
- specific gifts, which may or may not be exempt and, where they are non-exempt, may or may not bear their own tax, depending on the terms of the will.

The main difficulty for IHT purposes lies in calculating the value of non-exempt specific gifts where there may or may not be the need to gross up and where any grossing up may be on a single or on a double basis. The situation in any particular case is dependent on:

- whether any non-exempt specific gift does, or does not, bear its own tax; and
- the nature of any gift or gifts, which there may be in addition to any specific non-exempt gift.

Although not described in any detail here, the purpose of the grossing-up rules is to ensure the proper attribution of, in particular, the nil rate band.

Example 10.17—No grossing up

Fred died on 1 April 2019, leaving an estate of £700,000, having made no lifetime chargeable transfers. His will gives a legacy to his son of £100,000, subject to tax, and divides residue between his widow and daughter equally. Residue is, therefore, £600,000 and a half share is £300,000. As £300,000 attracts the spouse exemption, the chargeable estate is £400,000 at death. Taking into account the nil rate band of £325,000, the IHT liability will be £30,000.

The son will pay:	(£100,000 ÷ £400,000) × £30,000	=	£7,500
The daughter will pay:	(£300,000 ÷ £400,000) × £30,000	=	£22,500
			£30,000

No grossing up is required, because the only non-exempt specific gifts bear their own tax. Where, on the other hand, the only non-exempt gifts are specific gifts not bearing their own tax, there must be grossing up (on a single basis). This has the result that the amount attributable to the specific gifts is the total of the sum of their value, and the amount of tax chargeable is the value transferred equal to that total.

Example 10.18—Single grossing up

Having made no prior lifetime chargeable transfers, Jim died on 1 April 2019 with an estate of £800,000. His will leaves a legacy of £425,000, free of tax to his son, with residue of £375,000 to his widow.

Jim is treated as having made a net transfer on death of £100,000 on top of the net nil rate band of £325,000. IHT on £100,000 net is £66,667 (ie £166,667 less tax @ 40% is £100,000). The grossed-up legacy is therefore £491,667 and the exempt residue is £308,333.

Double grossing up

10.104 This gets rather more complicated. It arises where there is both a specific gift, which is free of tax and residue, which is partly exempt and partly chargeable. In other words, in the above example, had residue been divided between Jim's widow and Jim's sister, there would have been the need to gross up on a double basis, to ensure that both the son and the sister have fair call on the nil rate band. Such an example is, however, not illustrated.

THE *BENHAM* ISSUE AND THE *RATCLIFFE* RATIO

10.105 The names '*Benham*' and '*Ratcliffe*' refer to two cases decided in the courts: *Re Benham's Will Trust* [1995] STC 210 and *Re Ratcliffe (deceased)* [1999] STC 262.

The decision in *Re Benham* rather 'put the cat among the pigeons' in apparently expressly disregarding a statutory rule. The statutory rule in question (*IHTA 1984, s 41(b)*) provides that a share in residue that is exempt (eg as passing to a surviving spouse) shall not bear the tax on a chargeable share of residue, eg as passing to the daughter.

The tax issues in *Re Benham* were rather complicated but may be illustrated simply as shown below.

The judge in *Re Benham* ruled that, because (in our example) the testator had indicated that he wanted the widow and the daughter to receive the same amount in terms of cash (notwithstanding the effect of the spouse exemption), the daughter's share of residue had to be grossed up so as to produce an amount which, after tax, would equal the same as the widow's share. This had the unfortunate result of increasing the amount of tax payable.

Re Benham caused some concern as, in a not atypical situation, one would always expect in a case where the chargeable gifts exceed the nil rate band, the widow to be better off than the daughter because of the spouse exemption. Happily, the decision was not generally applied by HMRC Inheritance Tax, and so, for most probate practitioners and indeed wills draftsmen, life continued as usual. *Re Benham* did, however, do everybody a service in focusing the mind on the problem as to whether or not, in making a will with residue divided between the surviving spouse and one or more children, the testator did in effect want the benefit of the spouse exemption to be shared among all members of the family. The presumption in *s 41(b)* is that it should not be.

Even more happily, four years later in 1999, the decision in *Re Ratcliffe* effectively overruled *Re Benham*, which by then had generally been written off by the experts as wrong (though being too polite to say so, they used the expression that it had been decided '*per incuriam*'). Because, like *Re Benham*, *Re Ratcliffe* was decided in the High Court and not in the Court of Appeal, the decision did not expressly overrule *Re Benham*, but nonetheless is generally thought to represent the law in upholding the effect of *s 41(b)*. The judge in *Re Ratcliffe* said, 'If I had thought that *Re Benham's Will Trust* laid down some principle, then, unless convinced that it was wrong, I would have felt bound that I should follow it. I am not able to find that it does and, accordingly, I do not feel bound to follow it'.

Example 10.19—The *Re Benham* effect

Suzy dies, leaving residue of £800,000 (having used her nil rate band in lifetime gifts). Under her will, residue is split equally between her husband and her son.

In the following two columns are set out, first, the solution normally expected applying *s 41(b)* where, albeit there is pre-tax equality, the non-exempt beneficiary bears the tax; and, second, the situation following *Re Benham* where HMRC receive more tax, but the exempt and non-exempt beneficiaries receive the same after tax. To achieve this result, the will would have to provide, for example, that 'the rule in *Re Benham* shall apply'.

	Section 41(b)	*Re Benham*
HMRC	£160,000	£200,000
Exempt beneficiary (husband)	£400,000	£300,000
Chargeable beneficiary (son)	£240,000	£300,000
	£800,000	£800,000

Chapter 11

Deceased estates: income tax and CGT

SIGNPOSTS

- **Income to date of death** – Any outstanding income tax liability to date of death is a debt of the estate which reduces the value of the estate for IHT purposes. PRs may not be able to discharge any income tax liabilities until they have obtained grant of probate. In such cases, HMRC will not charge interest until the later of the due date and 30 days after grant of probate (see **11.2–11.7**).
- **Administration period** – During the administration period, PRs are liable to income tax at the basic rate of 20% for all income, apart from dividend income which is charged at 7.5%. In most circumstances, the appropriate tax office is the one which dealt with the tax affairs of the deceased (see **11.8–11.11**).
- **General legatees** – A general legatee is normally not entitled to interest on his legacy unless the legacy remains unpaid at the end of the executor's year (a one-year period since date of death). Interest is paid gross by the PRs (see **11.12–11.13**).
- **Specific legatees** – A specific legatee is entitled to any net income arising on the asset since date of death. PRs will issue the specific legatee with an R185 (see **11.14**).
- **Annuitants** – An annuitant can insist on a capital sum to be set aside to provide for his annuity, thereby creating an interest in possession trust with the annuitant as life tenant (see **11.15–11.18**).
- **Residuary beneficiaries** – A residuary beneficiary may have a limited, absolute or discretionary interest in the estate. Any income paid to him is net of tax deducted by the PRs who will issue the residuary beneficiary with an R185. PRs ought to consider the income tax position of such beneficiary by planning distributions in the most tax-efficient manner for the beneficiary (see **11.19–11.24**).
- **CGT compliance** – PRs are treated as acquiring the deceased's assets at market value as of date of death. If these assets increase in value during the administration period, PRs ought to consider transferring assets to beneficiaries to take advantage of their annual exemptions (see **11.25–11.35**).

INCOME TAX COMPLIANCE

11.1 Personal representatives (PRs, meaning both executors and administrators) are under a duty to administer a deceased's estate. From the point of view of taxation, this involves:

(1) Settling the deceased's outstanding tax liabilities to the date of death. Although this chapter is concerned primarily with income tax, there may also be outstanding CGT liabilities, and the PRs cannot generally obtain a grant of probate until any IHT, payable on their application for a grant, has been accounted for.

The outstanding income tax liability of the deceased is worked out as usual, is paid by the PRs and ranks as a deduction for IHT purposes.

(2) Liability to income tax on any income produced during the administration period. In addition, the PRs may incur a CGT liability, and the original IHT bill may require adjustment as a result of events happening after the death.

PRs must pay income tax on the estate income during the period of administration. They are not entitled to personal reliefs and allowances, although the income they receive is taxed only at the 7.5% dividend or 20% basic rate (for 2018/19 and 2019/20).

Note: administration expenses, even if properly chargeable to income, are not tax deductible. The only deductible expense is interest on a first loan taken by the PRs, obtained before they acquire the grant of probate, to satisfy the IHT on personal property. Interest relief is given only for a period of one year from the making of the loan (*ITA 2007, ss 403–405*).

PRs will be treated as UK resident (and therefore liable to tax on worldwide income) unless (*ITA 2007, s 834*) the deceased was neither resident, ordinarily resident nor domiciled in the UK, and:

- the PRs are all resident and ordinarily resident outside the UK; or
- there is at least one PR who is, and at least one PR who is not, resident, and the deceased at his death was neither domiciled, resident nor ordinarily resident in the UK.

THE DECEASED'S INCOME

11.2 The PRs are accountable for any income tax owed by the deceased (*TMA 1970, s 74(1)*). They should report the death to the appropriate tax office and complete an ordinary income tax return on behalf of the deceased for the period from 6 April preceding his death to the date of death, and for earlier tax years (if necessary!). In computing the income tax of the deceased, normal principles operate and full personal allowances are available for the year of death.

From 13 October 2014, it is not necessary for the PRs to complete Form R27 (the form used to reclaim or pay tax when somebody died). Instead any outstanding income tax liabilities/repayments of the deceased will be dealt with automatically for PAYE cases with a more tailored service for self-assessment cases.

Any outstanding income tax is a debt of the estate, thereby reducing the value of that estate for IHT purposes. Conversely, any repayment of income tax will increase the assets of the estate and may increase the IHT liability on death. HMRC can assess the PRs, at any time within four years after 31 January following the year of assessment in which the death occurred, for any tax that is owing for a period ending within six years of the date of death (*TMA 1970, s 40*). An assessment is made for these purposes when the inspector authorised to make assessments signs the certificate contained in the assessment books kept at the relevant district (*Honig v Sarsfield* [1986] STC 246, 59 TC 337 CA). Following a review, it is now agreed by HMRC that, as a result of the *Human Rights Act 1998*, penalties are no longer collectable.

Focus

- PRs can use Form 64-8 when dealing with a deceased's PAYE, self-assessment and NI contributions.
- The completed form needs to be sent to HM Revenue & Customs, Central Agent Authorisation Team in Newcastle.

Dividends

11.3 Dividends received before the deceased's death form part of the deceased's income. For IHT purposes, the quoted securities in the deceased's estate must be valued at death; if that valuation was *ex div* (ie it did not include the value of a declared dividend), the outstanding dividend must be added to the value of the security. This problem does not arise when the shares were valued at death *cum div*, since the valuation includes any accruing dividend to date.

Prior to the enactment of the *Trusts (Capital and Income) Act 2013* on 1 October 2013 it may have been necessary to apportion (*Apportionment Act 1870, s 2*) dividends paid after death but which relate to a period partly before and partly after death. The portion which relates to the period prior to death may be chargeable to inheritance tax. The apportionment rules are cumbersome and expensive to administer, and most wills and trust documents therefore exclude them. For wills and trusts executed after 1 October 2013 there is no need to disapply the apportionment rules.

However, whether or not the dividend is apportioned for succession purposes, any dividend paid after the deceased's death is treated as the income of the estate and not of the deceased, and must not be included in the deceased's tax return (*IRC v Henderson's Executors* 1931 SC 681, 16 TC 282). This rule follows from the fact that, as the dividends were never owed to the deceased, they never became a part of his income.

Only in cases where a dividend is declared due before death, but paid after that death, will it be taxed as the deceased's income (see, for instance, *Re Sebright* [1944] Ch 287, and contrast *Potel v IRC* [1971] 2 All ER 504, 46 TC 658). Similarly, certain other investment income paid after death but relating to the period before death (eg bank deposit interest) should be apportioned for succession purposes, but included as estate income for tax purposes. This may lead to some double taxation, in that the income which is deemed for succession purposes to accrue before death is charged both to IHT (as part of the deceased's estate on death) and also to income tax in the hands of the PRs and beneficiaries. *ITTOIA 2005, s 669* affords some relief against such double taxation but only to an absolutely entitled residuary beneficiary who is a higher rate taxpayer.

Example 11.1—Treatment of dividends

Suzy died on 30 May 2019, leaving her residuary estate (including 5,000 shares in Lazy Suzy's Ltd) to her brother Barry absolutely. On 15 June 2019, Lazy Suzy's Ltd declared a dividend on those shares of £4,500 in respect of the year ending on 30 June 2019. The dividend was paid on 28 July 2019.

Of this dividend, 11/12ths (£4,125) is deemed to have accrued before Suzy's death and will be reflected in the value of the shares in Suzy's estate which will have been valued *cum div*. For inheritance tax, it will thus be taxed as part of the capital in Suzy's estate.

However, for income tax purposes the whole dividend is taxed as the income of the estate, albeit with some relief for double taxation against any higher rate liability of Barry under *ITTOIA 2005, s 669*.

Trust income

11.4 Where the deceased was a life tenant under a trust, any income that was received by the trustees before his death is treated as the deceased's income and must be included in the PRs' tax return to the date of death.

For trusts created prior to 1 October 2013, where *s 2* of the *Apportionment Act 1870* was not excluded, any income paid to the trustees after the death, but attributable in part to the period before death, the actual apportionment determines the tax payable. Any income that is apportioned to the deceased life tenant is taxed as the income of the estate – and not of the deceased (*Wood v Owen* [1941] 1 KB 92, 23 TC 541).

Income that is apportioned to the deceased life tenant forms an asset of his estate, thereby increasing his IHT liability. This could result in an element of double IHT, because the apportioned income will also affect the value of the trust assets on which the trustees pay IHT on the life tenant's death. This double taxation is avoided by deducting the apportioned income from the value of the settled assets.

For trusts created prior to 1 October 2013 where the *Apportionment Act 1870, s 2* is excluded so that all the income is paid to either a subsequent life tenant or a remainderman, income tax follows the actual payment made. Any income paid after the date of death of the life tenant, therefore, is not taxed as part of the deceased life tenant's estate, but taxed as income of either the subsequent life tenant or remainderman.

Trusts created after 1 October 2013 can rely on the Trusts (Capital and Income) Act 2013 which excludes the apportionment rules and provides that income tax follows the actual payment made.

Example 11.2—Trust interests

Suzy was also a life tenant of a trust which was established in 2004, where *Apportionment Act 1870, s 2* was not excluded. Included in the settled assets was debenture stock in Brother's Ltd. On 30 November 2019, Brother's Ltd paid the trustees the annual interest of £1,000 gross. This interest was apportioned by the trustees as to half (£500) to Suzy and half (£500) to the remainderman, Xanthe.

The £500 apportioned to Suzy is estate income. Notice, also, that the £500 increases the value of the trust fund on which the trustees may have to pay IHT at Suzy's rates, as the trust is a pre-22 March 2006 interest in possession settlement.

If the settlement was set up after 22 March 2006, and is therefore subject to the relevant property regime, the trustees may have to pay an exit charge for IHT on the apportioned income, on the death of a life tenant. To avoid the £500 being charged twice to IHT, it is deducted from the value of the settled assets. (If Suzy's free estate passed to a residuary beneficiary absolutely, the latter may be entitled to relief under *ITTOIA 2005, s 669*; see **11.3** above.)

Example 11.3—Trust interests post-1 October 2013

Joseph died on 30 June 2018. He was the life tenant of a trust which was set up on his uncle's death on 1 November 2015, which was after the *Trusts (Capital and Income) Act 2103* came into force. Again the settled fund included debenture stock in Brother's Ltd and on 31 October 2018 Z Ltd paid the trustees annual interest of £1,000 gross. The income tax follows the actual payment made and it is therefore taxed on the remainderman.

Sole traders and partners

11.5 A sole trader's business is discontinued as a result of death: tax for the year of death is based on profits for the previous basis period to the date of death, less any overlap profits. Unused losses or capital allowances are not available for use by the PRs but can be carried back as a terminal loss. If the business is carried on by the surviving spouse, capital allowances are given on the basis that the spouse acquired the assets at probate value. If the deceased had been a member of a partnership, his death is treated as the discontinuance of the separate trade carried on by him alone.

Life insurance policy or life annuity contracts

11.6 The chargeable event legislation is complex and any liability to income tax depends on a number of factors.

In most cases the insured person and the beneficial owner are the same individuals. In these circumstances, if any rights are extinguished by the death of the insured person and the policy is not held on trust, the chargeable event gain will be that of the deceased person in the period to date of death rather than that of the PRs (*ITTOIA 2005, s 465*).

PRs are only liable in cases where the insured person is different from the beneficial owner, or the policy is a capital redemption policy and the policy continues to run following the death of the beneficial owner and it passes into the estate of the deceased. Any chargeable event arising on the policy will be treated as estate income (*ITTOIA 2005, s 466*).

In cases where the policy is held on trust, which is a very common scenario, and a chargeable event gain arises on the death of the settlor, the settlor will be chargeable to income tax on the chargeable event gain. It is not the tax liability of the estate or the trustees.

If a policy is subject to a UK resident trust and continues after the death of the settlor, but the chargeable event gain occurs before the end of the tax year in which the settlor died, the gain will be chargeable as part of the total income of the deceased settlor for that tax year.

If a policy is held on a UK resident trust, a chargeable event gain will only be chargeable on the trustees, if the settlor is 'absent', for example where he is non-UK resident or has died and the chargeable event gain occurred after the end of the tax year in which the settlor died.

There are transitional provisions that apply where both the trust and the policy were in existence before 17 March 1998 and:

- at least one of its creators was an individual; and
- one of the creators died before 17 March 1998.

In such cases, provided the policy has not been varied on or after 17 March 1998 to increase benefits or extend its term, there is no chargeable event gain and proceeds therefore escape a charge to income tax in the hands of the trustees.

Special anti-avoidance provisions (see *ITA 2007, Ch 2, Pt 13*) are in force in relation to policies which are held on non-UK resident trusts, where:

- trustees would have been chargeable under the chargeable event regime had they been UK resident when the event took place; or
- in relation to certain rights under a policy or contract, where:
  - a foreign institution beneficially owns a share in those rights,
  - the rights are held for the purposes of a foreign institution; or
  - a share in the rights is held as security for a foreign institution's debt.

These provisions are designed to prevent avoidance of tax where an individual who is ordinarily UK resident benefits from a transfer of assets and provide that:

- in the case of non-UK resident trustees, to treat the gain as becoming payable to the trustees, as if income arose to the trustees in the tax year in which the gain arises; or
- in the case of a foreign institution, to treat the gain as becoming payable to the institution, and as if income arose to the institution in the tax year in which the gain arises.

Administrative issues

11.7 In cases where the PRs have to pay income tax for the period to the date of death, but they cannot pay until they have obtained grant of probate or letters of administration, HMRC, by concession, will not charge interest until the later of the normal due date and 30 days from the grant of probate or letters of administration (ESC A17 – now obsolete and replaced by *FA 2009, Sch 53, Pt 2*).

THE ADMINISTRATION PERIOD – INCOME TAX

Duration of administration

11.8 The administration period is the period from the date of death until the date when the residue is ascertained and ready for distribution. Until that time, no beneficiary is entitled to the income or to any property comprised in the estate and, accordingly, is generally not liable to income tax unless income is actually distributed to him. Identifying precisely when completion of the administration of the estate occurs can present problems. In respect of Scottish estates, the administration is considered complete when debts, specific legacies and liabilities of the estate have been discharged or provided for and the residuary estate can be ascertained (see *ITTOIA 2005, s 653(2)*). This also seems to be the position in England and Wales: see, for instance, *Commissioner of Inland Revenue v Sir Aubrey Smith* (1930) 15 TC 661, *IRC v Pilkington* (1941) 24 TC 160, CA and *Prest v Bettinson* (1980) STC 607, 53 TC 437 and HMRC's Capital Gains Manual at CG30700.

Taxing PRs during administration

11.9 During the administration period, the PRs are liable, in a representative capacity, to income tax on all the income of the estate computed in the usual way.

From 6 April 2008 to 5 April 2016 the basic rate of 20% applied to all income except for dividends, which were taxed at 10%. UK dividend income was paid with a 10% tax credit that covered the tax due.

Finance Act 2016 introduced changes to the way dividends and bank or building society interest is paid from 6 April 2016. It introduced a new tax rate of 7.5% on all dividends (the basic rate for all other income remained at 20%) and any interest and dividends paid on or after 6 April 2016 is paid gross of tax. The PRs will have to account for any income tax due in the usual way. However the result of these changes is that some estates that did not have to file tax returns may now have to report untaxed interest and dividends. HMRC announced transitional measures for the tax years 2016/17 and 2017/18 in that PRs will return any income, if the only source of income of the estate is interest income and the tax liability is less than £100. HMRC confirmed that these arrangements also continue to apply to 2018/19 and it is expected that they also apply to 2019/20.

Tax liabilities arise even when the beneficiaries are not liable to income tax, for example charities or non-tax paying beneficiaries. In such cases the tax paid (apart from any non-repayable tax credit on dividends) can be reclaimed by the beneficiaries.

Some income tax received by the PRs will already have borne tax: in those cases the PRs have no further tax to pay. Generally such income falls into two categories:

(1) bank/building society interest received prior to 6 April 2016 which has borne tax at the basic rate; and

(2) dividends received prior to 6 April 2016 which carried non-repayable 10% tax credits.

The main examples of income on which PRs directly are assessed are:

- gross interest from banks or building societies;
- UK dividends received after 6 April 2016;
- rents from property;
- foreign source income;
- interest (eg from National Savings) which is paid gross; and
- royalties.

Which tax office?

11.10 HMRC has introduced the Online Trusts Registration Service in July 2017. Only complex estates will need to be registered, which includes estates that have already registered with HMRC, but where the administration has not been finalised.

An estate is considered complex, if:

- the probate/confirmation value of the estate exceeds £2.5m; or
- the tax payable by the PRs in respect of the administration period exceeds £10,000; or
- the proceeds of assets sold in any one tax year for dates of deaths up to 6 April 2016 exceeds £250,000 or £500,000 for date of deaths on or after 6 April 2016.

If the estate is considered complex, PRs have to complete full self-assessment returns. If the estate is not considered complex but it cannot be dealt with under the informal payments procedure (see below), personal representatives are advised to contact HMRC Administration of Estates Cardiff.

If the estate is not complex, it is not necessary for the PRs to complete a formal tax return. It is sufficient to report the relevant details in a simple letter to HMRC using the informal procedure. HMRC will then provide a payment slip with a reference number and the personal representatives can then make a one-off payment. Informal payments are usually accepted by the tax office that dealt with the tax affairs of the deceased during his lifetime – see HMRC Manual TSEM7410.

However, HMRC will not accept the informal procedure, if a self-assessment return has been issued to the PRs – see the First-tier Tribunal case of *David Hogg v Revenue and Customs Commissioners* [2017] UKFTT 538 (TC).

If a trust arises under the terms of the will (or intestacy) the PRs should account to the relevant trust office which normally is HMRC Administration of Estates, Cardiff.

If the deceased was a Lloyd's underwriter, the PRs may need to account to the High Net Worth Unit Bradford West Yorkshire or Public Department 1.

If the estate does not fall into any of the above categories but it cannot easily be dealt with under the informal payments procedures, advice should be obtained from HMRC Administration of Estates Cardiff.

Interest relief

11.11 If PRs raised a loan for IHT payable on delivery of the PRs' account, tax relief is available for interest paid within one year from the making of the loan. Interest on loans to pay inheritance tax after the grant of representation does not qualify for relief. The tax for which the loan is required must be attributable to personal property owned beneficially by the deceased and which vests in his PRs, (see *ITA 2007, s 403*). Relief is given against the income of the estate for the year in which the interest is paid but, where that income is insufficient, relief may be given against income of the preceding year and then against the future income of the estate (*ITA 2007, s 403*). In practice, this is normally the only deduction that can be made against the estate income: expenses incurred by the PRs in administering the estate are not deductible, except for the purpose of determining residuary beneficiaries' shares of the income for their own tax purposes.

TAXATION OF DISTRIBUTIONS TO BENEFICIARIES

The basic principles

11.12 Income received by the PRs suffers the equivalent of basic rate tax, either by deduction at source (if received prior to 6 April 2016) or by direct assessment in their hands, with dividends being taxed at the rate of 7.5% on or after 6 April 2016 (10% prior to 6 April 2016). From this taxed income the PRs deduct administration expenses chargeable against income, leaving a net sum available for distribution to beneficiaries entitled to the income from the estate. These different types of income fall to be divided between beneficiaries as is just and reasonable having regard to their different interests (*ITTOIA 2005, ss 663* to *670*). The legislation does not specify against which types of income administration expenses are to be deducted. The best approach used to be to set expenses first against income carrying a non-reclaimable credit (ie dividend income received prior to 6 April 2016), then against income bearing tax at basic rate.

For income received on or after 6 April 2016 the position is more complex. If a beneficiary benefits from the savings allowance (£5,000, £1,000 or £500) or the dividend allowance of £2,000 from 2018/19 (was £5,000 in 2017/18) it may be more beneficial to use estate expenses against non-savings income first, then savings income followed by dividend income. The income tax position of the beneficiary will determine the most tax efficient use of administration expenses.

If the PRs have a discretion whether to deduct administration expenses from income or capital, they may consider the tax position of a beneficiary (if any) absolutely entitled to the residue of the estate. When that beneficiary has a large income, they may deduct their expenses from income so as to reduce the beneficiary's income and, therefore, the higher-rate tax bill. Conversely, if the beneficiary has only a small income or is a charity, they may deduct expenses from capital so as not to prejudice any claim that the beneficiary may have for a repayment of income tax.

The relevant provisions can be found in *ITTOIA 2005, ss 649–682*.

General legatees

11.13 A general legatee is a person who is entitled to a sum of money (a pecuniary legacy) not charged on any particular fund. This sum is capital and the legatee is generally not entitled to any interest unless:

(1) the will directs the PRs to pay him interest; or

(2) the legacy remains unpaid at the end of the executor's year, in which case he is entitled to interest at the rate payable on funds in court, in the absence of a contrary direction; or

(3) the legacy is a 'statutory legacy' arising on intestacy (eg to a surviving spouse), in which case he is similarly entitled to interest at the rate indicated above from the date of death to the date of payment.

Interest is paid gross by the PRs, and the legatee is assessed directly to tax under *ITTOIA 2005, s 369* on the interest (unless the interest is paid to a person whose usual place of abode is outside the UK, when basic rate tax must be deducted by the PRs: see *ITA 2007, s 874(1)*). If that interest is neither claimed nor paid, there is no income to be assessed in the beneficiary's hands (*Dewar v IRC* [1935] 2 KB 351). Once a sum has been set aside to pay the legacy it may, however, be too late to disclaim any income (*Spens v IRC* [1970] 3 All ER 295, 46 TC 276). For the PRs, interest is ignored in computing their tax liability and so does not appear on their tax returns: this follows from the basic principle that the payment of interest does not attract tax relief. Such interest may, however, be treated as an administration expense and properly be deducted from the net income that is available for allocation and vouching to the residuary beneficiaries (*ITTOIA 2005, s 666*).

Focus

PRs are meant (subject to anything in the will) to pay legacies within the 'executor's year', ie a year after death. Interest on a legacy paid thereafter is paid gross (subject to income tax for the beneficiary).

Specific legatees

11.14 A specific legatee is entitled to a particular item of property and to any income produced by it as from the date of death. Therefore, once the PRs vest the asset in the beneficiary, any income from it that arose during the administration period is related back and taxed as the legatee's income for the tax year(s) when it arose (*IRC v Hawley* [1928] 1 KB 578). It will have suffered tax either through deduction at source or as a result of direct assessment on the PRs. Accordingly, the net income will be passed to the beneficiary together with a tax deduction certificate, form R185, completed by the PRs.

Example 11.4—Rental income

Alfie died in September 2018, leaving one of his 'buy-to-let' properties to his nephew Terry. The PRs continue to collect the monthly rental on the property. The administration is completed and the property vests in Terry in May 2019 together with the rental income. Terry must include the net rental income (after expenses) in his income tax return for the tax years 2018/19 and 2019/20 as it arose, rather than all the income in 2019/20 when received.

Annuitants

Definition

11.15 An annuity is a pecuniary legacy payable by instalments. The payments are income from which the PRs must deduct basic rate income tax (see *ITTOIA 2005, s 426*). The net sum will be paid to the annuitant, who will be given a certificate of tax deducted.

Modern wills rarely provide for the payment of an annuity.

Use of formula

11.16 A testator may want the annuitant to receive a constant sum, despite fluctuations in the tax rates. The two methods most commonly employed are:

(1) The testator provides for the payment of 'such sum as will after deduction of income tax at the basic rate for the time being in force leave (say) £1,000 pa'.

The PRs must pay £1,000 grossed up at the current basic rate to give a gross equivalent of £1,250. They must pay basic rate tax on that grossed-up figure, but they are not liable to indemnify the annuitant against any higher rate income tax for which he may be liable. Conversely, if the annuitant can reclaim all or any of the basic rate tax paid, he need not account for it to the PRs.

(2) If the testator provides for the payment of '£1,000 pa free from income tax', this imposes an obligation on the PRs to pay such sum as, after deducting basic rate income tax, leaves £1,000. However, it also means that the annuitant can recover from the PRs any higher rate tax that he may have to pay on the annuity, and any basic rate tax that he reclaims must be repaid to the PRs. In effect, he will never be left with more or less than £1,000 (see *Re Pettit, Le Fevre v Pettit* [1922] 2 Ch 765, 127 LT 491).

Setting aside a capital sum and purchased life annuities

11.17 An annuitant can insist on a capital sum being set aside to provide for his annuity (thereby creating an interest in possession trust for IHT purposes). If the capital in the estate is insufficient, he can demand that the actuarial value of the annuity be paid to him, abated if necessary (*IRC v Lady Castlemaine* [1943] 2 All ER 471, 25 TC 408). This capitalised annuity is not subject to income tax, either in the PRs' or the annuitant's hands.

If the will directs the PRs to purchase an annuity for the beneficiary, he will be charged to income tax on the full amount of each annual payment and cannot claim relief under *ITTOIA 2005, s 717* which taxes only the income element. The beneficiary should, therefore, request that the PRs give him the appropriate capital sum so that he can buy the annuity himself and claim *s 717* relief.

Beware top-ups!

11.18 Where there is insufficient income in the estate to pay the annuity in full, the will may direct the PRs to make up the income from capital. If they do so, that capital is treated as income from which basic rate tax must be deducted (*Brodie's Will Trusts v IRC* (1933) 17 TC 432, 12 ATC 140). The unfortunate result of such 'top-up' provisions is to convert capital into income and it is, therefore, better to give the PRs a discretion to make good any shortfall in the annuity by capital advances.

Residuary beneficiaries

11.19 A beneficiary may have a limited interest, an absolute interest in residue or a discretionary interest in residue. A limited interest exists where he is entitled to income only; for example, if the will leaves residue to 'my wife for life, remainder to my children', the wife is entitled only to income from the estate. An absolute interest exists when the beneficiary is entitled to both the income and capital of the residue, as where the residue is left to 'my wife absolutely'. A discretionary interest exists where a discretion must be exercised in favour of a residuary beneficiary to pay any income to him.

Beneficiary with a limited interest in residue

11.20 Any income paid to the beneficiary during the administration period will be paid net of tax deducted by the PRs. The beneficiary must gross up these sums, at the tax rate applicable in the year of *receipt by him* to that category of income, as part of his total income in the year of receipt for the purposes of his excess liability or to obtain a repayment of tax (as appropriate). Where any sum remains payable on completion of administration, it is treated as being the income of the beneficiary in the tax year in which the administration ends (see *ITTOIA 2005, ss 654–655*).

Example 11.5—Life interest in residuary estate

Suzy died on 6 March 2018, leaving a life interest in her residuary estate to Frances and, after Frances's death, to her son Michael. The interest income of the estate was:

Tax year		*Amount before tax*	*Amount after tax*
		(£)	*(£)*
2017/18 (gross) *		6,000	4,800
2018/19 (gross)*		25,000	20,000
2019/20 (gross)*		2,000	1,600
	Total	33,000	26,400

* As the tax liability for 2017/18 to 2019/20 exceeds £100 in each tax year, the transitional measure announced by HMRC does not apply – see **11.9**. The PRs will have to pay income tax of £1,200 in 2017/18, £5,000 in 2018/19 and £400 in 2019/20

Payments made to Frances were:

Tax year		*Amount*
		(£)
2017/18		nil
2018/19		18,000
2019/20		8,400
	Total	26,400

Frances is taxed on the payments in the tax years of receipt, ie in 2018/19 and 2019/20.

Note: if, at the end of administration, there is an undistributed income balance, it is deemed to have been paid to the beneficiary in the tax year when the administration ended (this being the one exception to the receipts basis). For instance, if the administration of Suzy's estate had been completed on 4 April 2019, the undistributed income balance of £8,400 would be taxed on Frances in 2018/19, even though she did not receive it until the following tax year.

Beneficiary with an absolute interest in residue

11.21 Such a beneficiary is entitled to receive both income and capital from the estate. They can, of course, only be charged to income tax insofar as any payments that they receive represent income. The position is that:

(1) payments during administration are taxed as income up to the amount of the aggregate income entitlement of the beneficiary for the year of assessment in which the sum is paid (see *ITTOIA 2005, s 652*): ('aggregate income entitlement' means the net income to which the beneficiary is entitled);

(2) if, on completion of the administration, the beneficiary has not received his full aggregate entitlement to income, the shortfall is treated as having been paid to him immediately before the end of the administration period; and

(3) the beneficiary must gross up the sums treated as income, at the tax rate applicable in the year of receipt by him to that category of income, as part of his total income in the year of receipt for the purposes of his excess liability or to obtain a repayment of tax (as appropriate).

Focus

Payment of income to a residuary beneficiary will be made after deduction of basic rate tax. The beneficiary will be given form R185 (Estate Income), which takes into account dividend tax at 7.5% as well as income tax at 20% for 2019/20. The applicable tax rate is that in the year of distribution (and not in the year of receipt).

Example 11.6—Absolute interest in residuary estate

Serena died on 6 March 2018, leaving her entire estate to Garry. Savings income arising to the estate was as follows:

Tax year		*Net income (£)*
2017/18 (gross) *		11,250
2018/19 (gross)*		37,500
2019/20 (gross)*		3,750
	Total	52,500

* The transitional measure does not apply to the income of Serena's estate, as the tax liability exceeds £100 for 2017/18 to 2019/20 – see **11.9.** The PRs will have to pay £10,500 income tax on the interest received – the simplified procedure applies to Serena's estate.

(1) *Tax year 2017/18*: Assuming that no payment is made to Garry, £9,000 is carried forward to 2018/19. Therefore, as at 5 April 2018, Garry's aggregated income entitlement is £9,000.

(2) *Tax year 2018/19*: At 5 April 2019, Garry's aggregated income entitlement, assuming no payments in 2018/19, is £39,000 (£48,750 less tax at 20%). As a result, if a payment of £72,000 is made to him in this year, the first £39,000 is treated as income.

(3) *Tax year 2019/20*: Assuming the administration period has ended and the estate is distributed, Garry will be taxed on the remaining income of £3,000 (£3,750 received gross less tax due £750).

Focus

(a) The timing of the payment in the tax year is irrelevant: it could, for instance, occur on 6 April 2018 but nonetheless it is the beneficiary's aggregated income entitlement at 5 April 2018 that is crucial.

(b) The rules apply to the payment of 'any sum': it is not possible for the PRs to specify that the payment is 'of capital'. Furthermore, HMRC consider that, for these purposes, the payment of 'any sum' includes a transfer of assets or release of a debt. They will therefore treat the value of such assets as income up to the amount of the beneficiary's aggregated income entitlement (see *ITTOIA 2005, s 681*).

Relief against a double charge

11.22 Income which accrued before death, but is received by the PRs after death, is included in the value of the deceased's estate for IHT purposes and is also taxed as the income of the estate. Some relief against this double taxation is provided by *ITTOIA 2005, s 669* that allows a reduction in the residuary income for the purposes of any liability to higher rate tax of a residuary beneficiary absolutely entitled to residue. The reduction is of an amount equal to the IHT chargeable on that income at the estate rate, and the resultant sum is then grossed up at the basic rate of income tax or dividend ordinary rate for the tax year in which the charge to higher rate arises.

Example 11.7—Relief against double charge

Xavier died on 30 April 2019. He left his residuary estate including 1,000 debentures in B Ltd to his daughter Deborah. His PRs received interest of £200 from B Ltd in November 2018. (B Ltd's accounting year ended 31 October 2019). The whole interest is taxed as the income of the estate but, as half the interest accrued before death, that portion is included in Xavier's estate for IHT purposes. Under *ITTOIA 2005, s 669*, if Deborah is a higher rate taxpayer, one half of the interest is eligible for relief. Assume that the estate rate of IHT is 30%.

	£
Interest (gross)	200
Sum accrued before death	100
Less: income tax for year of death	20
	80
The relief is calculated as:	
£80 × 30% (IHT estate rate)	24
Grossed-up (at 20%) amount that can be deducted from the residuary income to reduce D's liability to higher rate income tax only	30

Beneficiary with a discretionary interest in residue

11.23 A beneficiary with a discretionary interest in residue is taxed on the amount paid to him in the tax year the discretion was exercised. The beneficiary is assessed on the basic amount grossed up at the applicable tax rate.

The 'bunching' effect

11.24 Under the receipts basis, all the income is taxed in the year of receipt. That could have the unfortunate consequence of pushing a beneficiary up from being a non-taxpayer to a basic rate taxpayer, if, for example, the income year by year would have been within the personal allowance or a basic rate taxpayer up to a higher rate taxpayer. It is always open to the PRs to avoid this result by distributing income as they go along, but to do so they need to have some awareness of the personal income tax circumstances of each of the beneficiaries and, except from within a closely knit family, this might be quite difficult.

There is a further problem: the payment of capital or the release of a debt although capital in nature, might trigger an income tax liability on the beneficiary to the extent that there is during that tax year, or a previous tax year of the estate, undistributed income (*ITTOIA 2005, s 681*). Accordingly, a distribution of chattels to beneficiaries may trigger income tax liabilities: beware. There is an example below. The effect of *ITTOIA 2005, ss 649, 652, 681, 665, 660* and *656* (most helpfully, in that order) is that, assuming no distribution of income, the value of the chattel is grossed up at 'the applicable rate' for the year, as defined in *ITTOIA 2005, s 663*, which varies according to the rate of income tax borne by the various elements of income of the estate and, therefore, in relation to a particular distribution of income, the income out of which the payment is made.

Example 11.8—A trap for the unwary

Susan's estate is worth £500,000. The residuary beneficiary is her daughter, Ursula. The residuary income for 2017/18 is £5,000, and for 2018/19 it is £6,000. In 2018/19, while the estate administration continues, the executors transfer to Ursula a collection of silver owned by her mother worth £15,000. No other distributions are made.

In 2018/19, Ursula is treated as having received income of £11,000 gross, subject to deduction of tax of £2,200 (at 20%), which she should therefore record in her self-assessment return. The executors are not paying out income and therefore need not deduct and account for it to HMRC. This is simply a consequence of the statutory rule. However, they should issue form R185 which shows the receipt of income of £8,800 net.

Assuming Ursula is a higher rate taxpayer who pays income tax at the rate of 40%, she may have to pay a further £2,200 (additional 20%) in income tax on transfer of the silver to her.

As and when, say, in 2019/20, the executors distribute income to Ursula, they will need to take into account, on form R185 (Estate Income), the fact that £11,000 of the estate income has already been treated for tax purposes as income arising in her hands.

CGT COMPLIANCE

11.25 The CGT affairs of the deceased, as with income tax, must be put into order. Any liability paid by the PRs will be a deductible liability in the estate.

The general rule is that the PRs are treated as acquiring the deceased's assets at their market value at death, but without involving a disposal by the deceased (*TCGA 1992, s 71(1)*). If a value is 'ascertained' for IHT purposes, that will be the base cost for future CGT purposes. If such a value is not ascertained (eg where covered by the spouse exemption or by 100% reliefs for agricultural or business property or within the nil rate band), it is a matter of agreeing with HMRC the value of the asset following the ultimate disposal, whether by the PRs or by the beneficiary – if, indeed, such disposal takes place. For example, the beneficiary could well retain the asset until his own death, when the same CGT-free uplift to market value would occur.

The First-tier Tribunal in *Executors for JJ Leadley (dec'd) v HMRC* [2014] UKFTT 892 (TC) confirmed that any losses made by a deceased can be offset against gains made to date of death. It also confirmed that losses made to date of death cannot be offset against gains made by the PRs during the administration period.

Finance Act 2014, s 60 amended *TCGA 1992, s 72* so that an interest which is a disabled persons interest under *IHTA 1984, s 89(1)(a)* or *(b)* is treated as an actual interest in possession in relation to deaths occurring on or after 5 December 2013. CGT uplift on death therefore will apply to such interests.

Transfers to legatees

11.26 Where PRs dispose of property to a legatee entitled under the will, no chargeable gain accrues. Rather the acquisition of the asset by the PRs is related to that of the legatee, ie he is treated as acquiring the asset at the date of death with a base cost equal to market value at that date (*TCGA 1992, s 62(4)*). Generally speaking, it does not matter when the transfer to the legatee takes place.

Effective dates for appropriation – CGT purposes

11.27 Sometimes, the PRs will have to appropriate assets between various beneficiaries. Suppose that there are two equal beneficiaries of residue. To achieve absolute equity, each asset in the estate, after legacies, taxes and other liabilities have been paid, would simply be divided down the middle. This may not be practical, however, and some assets might in entirety go to one beneficiary and other assets to the other. The date on which assets are valued for this appropriation purpose is the date of appropriation. However, the value date for CGT purposes is the date of death. There could, therefore, be a mismatch between appropriation values and base costs for CGT purposes (which relate back to the date of death).

Residence

11.28 The residence of PRs for CGT is different from the income tax rule (*FA 1989, s 111*). The residence of the PRs follows that of the deceased (*TCGA 1992, s 62(3)*). If the deceased was non-UK resident at his death, disposals by the PRs (even if themselves UK resident) will attract no CGT liability unless the disposal relates to UK situs residential property. By contrast, if the deceased was UK resident, disposals by the PRs will be subject to tax. If the deceased was UK resident but non-UK domiciled, no remittance basis is available to the PRs, as they are not individuals.

From April 2015, non-residents disposing of UK residential property are subject to CGT. This affects PRs of a non-resident deceased who owned property in the UK, or PRs who are disposing of property on behalf of beneficiaries who are not resident in the UK.

Example 11.9—Value for appropriation purposes

There are two residuary beneficiaries of the estate, one of them resident in the UK (ie personally subject to CGT) and the other resident in Switzerland (ie not personally subject to UK CGT).

The residue comprises shareholdings in four companies, A, B, C and D. Values at date of death and one year after death, when the PRs decide to appropriate the shares, are as follows:

Company	Value at death	Value at appropriation
A	£40,000	£50,000
B	£50,000	£60,000
C	£60,000	£50,000
D	£70,000	£60,000

As one beneficiary is non-UK resident, it would be helpful for him to have assets assented to him showing a gain since death, and for the UK resident beneficiary to have assets assented showing a loss. In order to achieve equity between them, the values at the date of appropriation are taken.

Accordingly, the PRs might appropriate shares in companies A and B to the Swiss resident beneficiary, and shares in companies C and D to the UK resident beneficiary (subject always to their respective wishes and, of course, to Swiss taxation).

THE RATE OF TAX AND THE ANNUAL EXEMPTION

Rate of tax

11.29 Any chargeable gains realised by PRs over and above the annual exemption were subject to CGT at 18% for gains realised prior to 23 June 2010. Following *F(No 2)A 2010*, gains realised on or after 23 June 2010 are taxed at 28%. *Finance Act 2016* reduced the CGT rate to 20% for disposals by PRs on or after 6 April 2016. However, there is an additional 8% surcharge on gains arising from residential property which does not benefit from private residence relief.

Annual exemption

11.30 For the year of death, the deceased is entitled to the whole of his annual exemption (£11,700 for 2018/19 rising to £12,000 for 2019/20). For the balance of the year of death, as well as for the following two years of assessment, the PRs are also entitled to full annual exemptions. If the estate administration continues beyond 5 April following two tax years after the end of the year in which death occurred, they receive no annual exemption.

So, assuming death occurs on 1 September 2017, the PRs have an annual exemption of £11,300 for 2017/18, £11,700 for 2018/19 and £12,000 for 2019/20. If the administration continues beyond 5 April 2020, no exemption is available to set off against gains made in 2020/21 or subsequent years. The PRs do not receive the trustees' exemption, because they are not trustees.

Computing the gain

11.31 Gains of the PRs are worked out in the normal way, ie deducting from the gross sale proceeds the base cost, which is the market value at date of death, less allowable expenses.

There is an alternative acquisition expenditure available to PRs intended to compensate them for the costs of acquiring title to the asset. As an alternative (not an addition) to the actual allowable expenditure incurred, they can claim the allowance set out in Statement of Practice 02/04, for expenses incurred by personal representatives and corporate trustees. The expense is greater for smaller disposals, less on larger estates. The scale is set out at **11.33** below.

Capacity at the date of any sale

11.32 Because the trigger date for CGT purposes is an unconditional contract under *TCGA 1992, s 28(1)* (rather than completion), one should think carefully about who owns the asset, ie whether it is an executor sale or whether the asset has been released from the estate and it is owned by one or more of the beneficiaries. This would be relevant to the availability of annual exemptions, especially as substantial CGT savings can be achieved if there are a number of beneficiaries who all have unused annual CGT exemptions. Where it is stocks and shares that are concerned, typically held in nominee names with the stockbrokers or investment managers, consideration should be given before the sale to the matter of what instructions have been given to them as to the nature of the beneficial ownership.

Example 11.10—Minimising CGT liabilities

Bobby died in May 2018, leaving his estate to his five children. His estate included shares in an AIM listed company, Beaver Ltd, which were valued at £100,000 at date of death. The shares have risen substantially in value since date of death and, in July 2019, they are valued at £150,000. The administration period has ended and Bobby's PRs are considering the distribution of the estate.

If the shares are sold by the executors in 2019/20, then, disregarding allowable expenditure, the tax would be as follows:

Sale proceeds	£150,000
Less cost	(£100,000)
Gain	£50,000
Less annual exemption	(£12,000)
Taxable gain	£38,000
Tax @ 20%	£7,600

If the shares are assigned to the five children and sold by them in 2019/20, the tax for each beneficiary would be as follows (assuming they all have full annual exemptions available):

Sale proceeds for each beneficiary	£30,000
Less cost	(£20,000)
Gain	£10,000
Less annual exemption	(£12,000)
Taxable gain	£0
Tax @ 20%	£0

A total tax saving of £7,600 can be achieved.

Statement of Practice 2/04

11.33 PRs can claim the actual cost of obtaining probate and other costs that relate specifically to gaining title to an asset. Generally PRs will rely on the standard scale set out in SP2/04. HMRC will accept computations based either on this scale or on the actual allowable expenditure incurred, but not both.

The allowable expenditure under SP 2/04 often is overlooked and depends on the gross value of the estate:

Gross value of estate	Allowable expenditure
A. Not exceeding £50,000	1.8% of the probate value of the assets sold by the PRs.
B. Over £50,000 but not exceeding £90,000.	A fixed amount of £900, to be divided between all the assets of the estate in proportion to the probate values and allowed in those proportions on assets sold by the PRs.
C. Over £90,000 but not exceeding £400,000.	1% of the probate value of the assets sold.
D. Over £400,000 but not exceeding £500,000.	A fixed amount of £4,000 to be divided as at B above.
E. Over £500,000 but not exceeding £1 million.	0.8% of the probate value of the assets sold.
F. Over £1 million but not exceeding £5 million.	A fixed amount of £8,000 to be divided as at B above.
G. Over £5 million.	0.16% of the probate value of the assets sold, subject to a maximum of £10,000.

CGT PRINCIPAL PRIVATE RESIDENCE RELIEF

Agreeing the gain

11.34 It may happen that property is sold during the administration of the estate but, say, within a year after death, at a price higher than that submitted for probate. Straightforwardly, the factual issue is simply whether the value of the property at the date of death was that submitted for probate or at the higher sale price: did indeed values move in the interim? At face value, if any additional amount would attract IHT in a fully taxable estate at 40%, whereas CGT for 2019/20 is charged at 20% (unless residential property which increases the rate to 28%), it might seem preferable to argue for a lower, rather than a higher, base cost at death and, ideally, one would like to be able to show changed market circumstances since death which would justify any increase in value.

However, remember that the two taxes 'do different things': CGT charges gains realised over the period of ownership, whereas IHT charges transfers of value. In particular (for 2019/20):

	CGT	IHT
Exempt band	£12,000	£325,000
Rate of tax	20% (on or after 6 April 2016), unless the disposal relates to residential property without the benefit of PPR relief when the rate remains at 28%	40%
Possible exemptions or reliefs	Principal private residence relief	Spouse exemption/ nil rate band/ agricultural property relief/ business property relief

What matters is the ability to establish a proper market value at death. If a market value has already been agreed with a district valuer, that will be the value, even if a higher value is achieved on a subsequent sale. If the value has not yet been agreed, the matter should be raised with HMRC with arguments as to why, if the lower value is maintained for market value at death, values have changed in the interim.

Principal private residence ('PPR') relief

11.35 PRs are not trustees, and therefore the extension of PPR relief to trustees (see **5.25–5.27**) will not apply where executors realise the family home at a gain.

There is a limited concession, now enacted by *FA 2004* in *TCGA 1992, s 225A*, where PRs dispose of a house that both immediately before and after the death was used as the main residence of beneficiaries entitled under the will or intestacy to all, or substantially all (ie 75% plus), of the net proceeds of sale, whether absolutely or for life. The PRs must make a claim to benefit from PPR relief under this concession.

Example 11.11—Achieving CGT efficiency on main residence sales

Bill died owning 'Blackacre'. His estate is split equally between his four adult children, who all are higher rate tax payers. Its market value at his death is thought to be around £200,000. About one year after death, a purchaser is prepared to pay £300,000 for the property. There are good arguments as to why the increase in value has occurred over this brief time. It is thought possible that a market value at death of £200,000 can be sustained.

If the house is sold by the executors in May 2019, then, disregarding allowable expenditure, the tax would be as follows:

Sale proceeds	£300,000
Less cost	(£200,000)
Gain	£100,000
Less annual exemption	(£12,000)
Taxable gain	£88,000
Tax @ 28%	£24,640

Vesting the property in the four adult beneficiaries before sale would have some beneficial effect, although, quite apart from the gain, their incomes make each of them a higher rate taxpayer.

The chargeable gain would be as above, though deductible from it would (if available) be four annual exemptions of £12,000, viz £48,000, reducing the taxable gain to £52,000, with tax payable @ 28% of £14,560, or £3,640 assessable on each beneficiary. The tax saving will be even larger, if one or more beneficiaries are basic rate tax payers. It is probably unrealistic to expect all four of the beneficiaries to occupy the property as their main residence, as each has their own home and family. Supposing, however, just one of them was prepared to do so. They could together vary the will to create a will trust of residue, perhaps discretionary or life interest under which the beneficiaries would be the four children and also spouses, their own children, etc (see **12.1-12.4**). The one child, call him Alan, who was prepared to go and live there, say, nine months after death, takes up residence for a decent period of at least six months and preferably more, perhaps letting his own property. A year and a half or so after death, the trustees of the will trust would sell the property at a gain of £100,000. However, since, during their period of ownership, in fact less than 18 months, the house has at some time been occupied by a beneficiary as his only or main residence, the whole of the gain is exempt, even though there are other beneficiaries who live elsewhere. There is a potential tax saving of around £25,000. Clearly, so as not to invoke anti-avoidance principles, the trust should not simply be wound up and the proceeds distributed to the four children following the sale of the house by the trustees. It would be useful if there could be established a continuing family reason for having an ongoing trust.

Chapter 12

Deceased estates: post-death re-arrangements

SIGNPOSTS

- **Variations and disclaimers** – Beneficiaries can rewrite the provisions in a will or intestacy, or disclaim an interest in an estate, within two years of death – *IHTA 1984, s 142* (see **12.1–12.5**).
- **Variations** – Variations can sever a joint tenancy in property or bank accounts. A disposition that has been varied once cannot be varied again (see **12.6–12.8**).
- **Variations and minor beneficiaries** – A deed of variation can be effective, even if there are minor beneficiaries, either with the approval of the courts or if it can be shown that the beneficiaries are better off following the variation (see **12.10**).
- **Income tax and CGT consequences** – For income tax and CGT, the beneficiary who varies the will is deemed to be the settlor (see **12.12**).
- **Disclaimers** – Disclaimers are much 'cruder' instruments, in that the interest in the estate cannot be re-directed. The disclaimed benefit is treated as if it had never been conferred (see **12.13–12.16**).
- **Discretionary will trusts** – Following *IHTA 1984, s 144*, appointments out of discretionary will trusts within two years of death are read back into the will (see **12.17–12.21**).
- **Limited relief under s 143** – By *IHTA 1984, s 143*, there is a limited relief, where the will sets out a wish that property is passed to someone else (see **12.22**).

VARIATIONS AND DISCLAIMERS

Beneficiaries and their personal representatives in an estate have a two-year window from the date of death to rewrite the provisions of the deceased's will or the passing of property on intestacy following *IHTA 1984, s 142*. This provision is extremely useful, but it needs approaching with care.

12.1 *IHTA 1984, s 142* operates where:

- within a period of two years after the individual's death;
- the destination of any of the assets of his estate (excluding assets charged under the reservation of benefit rules);
- passing by will, intestacy or 'otherwise';
- is varied/altered or the benefits disclaimed by an instrument in writing made by one or more of the original beneficiary(ies); and
- for variations (but not disclaimers) from 1 August 2002, the instrument of variation (IOV) contains a 'statement' that the IOV is to apply for IHT.

HMRC have no discretion to extend the two-year period. The section has effect, for IHT and for certain aspects of CGT, as if the variation had been effected by the deceased or, as the case may be, the disclaimed benefit had never been conferred.

The 'instrument' is usually effected by way of a deed. This is not essential, but it is helpful as it ensures that the variation is binding as between the original beneficiary and the donee. The IOV must clearly indicate the dispositions that are the subject of it, and vary their destination as laid down by the deceased's will, or under the law relating to intestate estates. Under *IHTA 1984, s 142(6)*, a variation can apply even though the administration of the estate has been completed and the assets advanced to the beneficiary in accordance with the original dispositions.

12.2 If the variation changes the amount of IHT payable, either in the estate of the deceased or in the estate of someone else, the beneficiaries making the variation should send a copy of the variation to HMRC. If the variation results in additional IHT being due, the executors or personal representatives must make the payment of additional IHT. They may decline to do so if there are insufficient assets in the estate to cover the extra IHT (*IHTA 1984, s 142(2A)*).

The personal representatives must, within six months, notify HMRC of the amount of any additional IHT payable and send a copy of the variation to them. Practitioners should refer to the useful HMRC Inheritance Tax Instrument of Variation Checklist (IOV2) If the variation results in property being diverted to a charity, and death occurred after 5 April 2012, HMRC need to be shown evidence that the charity has been notified of the existence of the variation. A letter to the charity is not sufficient, and an acknowledgement by the charity will be required.

12.3 The Conservative government tried to repeal this facility in 1989, although the offending Finance Bill clauses were withdrawn. Five years later, the Labour Party said that, when elected, they would reintroduce such a repeal. Subsequent governments left this facility unchanged.

The Chancellor announced a review of the use of deeds of variation as part of the government's clampdown on tax avoidance in his 2015 Budget speech. Following representations from professional bodies, it was announced in the 2015 Autumn Statement that the Government decided not to restrict the use of deeds of variations for the time being, but that they will closely monitor it closely.

Variation or disclaimer?

12.4 There are distinctions between variations and disclaimers:

- In a variation, the beneficiary redirects the asset as he chooses; whilst in a disclaimer he has no choice and his disclaimer merely accelerates the subsequent interest. Thus, a disclaimed legacy may fall into residue.
- HMRC appear to take the view that, as a matter of English law, a partial disclaimer is not possible and that the whole of the interest must be disclaimed (HMRC Inheritance Tax Manual at IHTM16180), but there has been some challenge to this. To try to avoid this, a suitable clause for inclusion in a will might be as follows:

  'I HEREBY DECLARE that any gift or other benefit made under or in pursuance of this my Will or any codicil thereto may be disclaimed as to any part of such gift or benefit or as to the whole thereof. I accordingly authorise:–

  (a) any person benefiting under this my Will or any codicil thereto; and

  (b) my executors and trustees and any person acting in pursuance of their authority, to deal with and administer my estate in respect of any such partial (or full) disclaimer as hereby authorised.

  In furtherance of this authorisation (but not otherwise) all gifts of money or share or shares of residue shall be deemed at any relevant time to be gifts of money in separate denominations of £1 each for the purpose of enabling any relevant beneficiary of this my Will or any codicil thereto to disclaim separate parts divisible in £1 units.'
- *Cook and anor (executors of Watkins dec'd) v IRC* [2002] STC (SCD) 318 illustrates the possibility of disclaimer by conduct. The deceased had left two flats by her will, one let and the other her residence. There was a trust of the residence for her husband for life. The issue was whether the husband had, by his conduct, disclaimed the gift. The evidence was finely balanced, but the Special Commissioner held that

it was not strong enough to displace the presumption that the legacy would be accepted.

- With a variation, it makes no difference that the beneficiary may earlier have received some benefit. In the case of a disclaimer, however, it is a condition that, before the disclaimer, he has received no benefit (see IHTM16180). The survivorship provisions in *IHTA 1984, s 92* would be relevant here. To enable a surviving spouse to disclaim his or her interest in a home effectively for IHT (ie not having received any interim benefit), the gift of the home could be conditional on surviving the testator for the maximum period of six months within the section.
- A variation can benefit anyone, not merely another beneficiary or a member of the family, but the interests of minor beneficiaries cannot be reduced without the court's consent. This gives rise to a fine point of will drafting. Where the testator gives a life interest (eg to spouse), the remaindermen should be restricted to the testator's children *per stirpes* living at the death of the testator, not at the death of the life tenant. The clause may include his issue if he dies before the life tenant, but if the class is left open until the second death a variation of a testator's will by the remaindermen would be extremely difficult because of the contingent entitlement of future born issue.

Written variations

12.5 A beneficiary (or, indeed, all the beneficiaries taken together) can rewrite the provisions of a will (or intestacy), as long as it is done in writing within two years after the death. For deeds made since 1 August 2002, the deed must simply contain a statement by all the parties that the IHT and/or CGT reliefs are intended to apply. Generally, the effect of such a variation is to regard for IHT purposes the terms of the variation as written into the will; see Example 13.1 (*IHTA 1984, s 142*).

Example 12.1—A simple variation illustrated

Under James' will, there is a nil rate band gift to a discretionary trust, with residue left to his wife. The trustees appoint, within two years after James' death, £50,000 to each of James' children, Bill and Ben. Bill wishes to benefit his own children, Thomas and Serena, and transfers the £50,000 to them within two years after his father's death. It is open to Bill to make a variation under *s 142*, within six months after the transfer to his own children. This will have the effect of avoiding a gift for IHT purposes by Bill and treating the gift to Thomas and Serena as made directly to them under their grandfather's will.

Severance of joint tenancy

12.6 *Section 142* permits a variation of the dispositions of the property comprised in the estate of the deceased 'whether affected by will, under the law relating to intestacy or otherwise'. The words 'or otherwise' have been taken to include dispositions that take effect by operation of law, such as survivorship to joint property. Accordingly, it is possible by deed of variation posthumously to sever the joint tenancy in any property (for IHT purposes, at least) so that the share belonging to the deceased can pass under the will as varied, rather than direct to the other joint owner. This was often essential where it was proposed to put in place the debt or charge scheme by deed of variation.

Some points to watch

12.7

- A disposition that has been varied by deed of variation may not be further varied (see **12.8**).
- There must be no consideration for entering into a deed of variation (see *IHTA 1984, s 142(3)*), other than consideration consisting of the making, in respect of another of the dispositions, of a variation or disclaimer to which that subsection applies.
- The deed of variation may not be effective if it purports to take away value from minors or unborn beneficiaries (but see **12.10**).
- The deed will be ineffective if made for consideration, ie there must be a genuine gift from the original beneficiary to the new beneficiary (*IHTA 1984, s 142(3)*).
- If the effect of the deed is to create a life interest trust, that trust must last for at least two years, unless terminated by death of the beneficiary (*IHTA 1984, s 142(4)*).

Multiple variations

12.8 There have been some cases in which a number of IOVs have been executed in relation to the same will or intestacy. HMRC emphasise that these cases must be considered on their precise facts, but in broad terms their view will be as follows:

- an election which is validly made is irrevocable;
- an instrument will not fall within *IHTA 1984, s 142* if it further redirects any item or any part of an item that has already been redirected under an earlier instrument; and

- to avoid any uncertainty, variations covering a number of items should ideally be made in one instrument.

12.9 However, a 'two bites of the cherry' situation in practice may be achieved as follows (see **12.19**):

- Execute an *IHTA 1984, s 142* variation of certain assets into a *s 144* two-year discretionary trust.
- The assets can then be redirected out of the discretionary trust without further IHT within the two-year period (or up to ten years if the assets are within the nil rate band).

Variations where there are minor beneficiaries

12.10 Generally, variations where there are minor beneficiaries are not effective.

Focus

- However, two courses of action are open.
- The first is to apply to the court for an order permitting the variation to take place on the ground that it is in the interests of the infant beneficiaries.
- The simpler course, which is not objected to by HMRC, is to frame any variation in such a way that it does clearly benefit younger members of the family.

Example 12.2—No need for an application to the court

William left his estate in four equal shares, one for each of his three sons and the last for his grandchildren in equal shares. One of the sons does not need his inheritance and wishes his share to pass immediately to his children. There is no need for any of the children to sign the resulting deed of variation. None of them gives anything up. There is no need for any application to the court.

Example 12.3—Avoiding an application to the court

Stuart, who was widowed and who remarried late in life, made a will which leaves the residue to his widow for life with remainder in four shares, one to each of his sons and the fourth to his grandchildren equally per capita. The widow is very frail and her life expectancy is short. The sons are financially secure and indicate that they do not need the inheritance.

The parties therefore wish to enter into a deed that will comply with *IHTA 1984, s 142*. They agree to vary the terms of the will. The gift of residue is changed so that each son receives 20% only and the grandchildren receive 40% between them.

Although there will be no benefit to the grandchildren during the lifetime of their grandmother, it is nevertheless clear from the face of the deed that the grandchildren, who are themselves too young to sign the deed, are better off by virtue of the deed than they would have been under the will. It is therefore not necessary to seek the approval of the court to the variation.

Passing on growth, tax free

12.11 The value of the whole estate, or perhaps that of one or two assets, may increase in the two years following death. Such value could be passed under a variation to chargeable beneficiaries; see Example 12.4.

An election made for IHT purposes will ensure that the value of the asset at the date of death is treated as passing under the will to the new chargeable beneficiary. That will also be the acquisition cost for CGT purposes.

Income tax and CGT

12.12 For CGT purposes, specific rules were introduced in *FA 2006* to identify the settlor following the variation of a will or intestacy, where an election is made under *TCGA 1992, s 62(6)* (see below) for the variation or intestacy to be effective for CGT purposes (*TCGA 1992, s 68C*). Previously, the House of Lords decided that it was the *beneficiary* (not the testator) who is treated as the settlor (CGT exemption therefore not applying to remitted gains, if the trustees were (or were treated as being) non-resident); see *Marshall v Kerr* [1994] STC 638, HL.

The Revenue subsequently confirmed the view that the decision in *Marshall v Kerr* has no application to IHT. This is still the case following the *FA 2006* changes. For income tax, there is no election: income is assessable on the UK beneficiary under *ITA 2007, s 720* in respect of overseas trusts or, in the case of a UK trust, under *ITTOIA 2005, s 624*.

The right to interest on a cash sum gifted by an instrument of variation is not clearly defined. Unless the variation defines otherwise, the original beneficiary retains the right to receive the income under the will up to the date of the variation, whether the gift is made out of a specific legacy or devise, or made out of residue.

Focus

Note the anti-avoidance provisions in *ITTOIA 2005, s 629* where the intended beneficiaries include the settlor's unmarried minor children.

(See **4.26–4.31** for the income tax implications.)

Example 12.4—Securing IHT freedom for post-death appreciation

Marcus died on 1 December 2018, with an estate of £1 million, all of which is left to Antonia, his wife, who survives him. Twelve months after his death, the value of the estate has increased to £1.5 million, the whole of this increase being attributable to quoted shares worth £325,000 at his death. Antonia could effect a deed of variation under which there is a specific gift of those shares, either to her children, or to a nil rate band discretionary trust.

Alternatively, if Marcus had made chargeable transfers of £325,000 in the seven years before he died, the deed of variation could have Antonia take a legacy of £1 million, with residue to the children. The effect of the IHT legislation would be to attribute the whole of the estate to the exempt specific gift to Antonia.

In either case, the result would be to have the uplift in value of £500,000 passing to the children free of tax.

DISCLAIMERS

12.13 A disclaimer is a slightly curious animal, which can apply to any property, but which is particularly apt to wills. It is not enough for a gift to be made, it has to be received. Suppose a will leaves Blackacre to X, and X turns round and says, 'I don't want it': there is no obligation on him to receive Blackacre, and the will is effectively read as if X had died before the testator. The effect is that Blackacre falls to be divided as part of the residue of the estate. If, instead, X had been entitled to part of residue and had disclaimed that, the disclaimed share of residue would fall into intestacy. If X had been entitled to receive income under a will trust and had disclaimed his right to income, the will trust would be read as if the next succeeding life interest (or an outright capital gift) came into being.

The *Estates of Deceased Persons (Forfeiture Rule and Law of Succession) Act 2011* took effect in England and Wales on 1 February 2012. The Act confirms that children of disclaiming adult heirs now inherit from the estate as if the *per stirpes* rules apply.

The IHT effect

12.14 Where the disclaimer is made within two years after the death, the property is treated as passing under the will as if the disclaimed benefit had never been conferred (*IHTA 1984, s 142*).

The no benefit rule

12.15 The important point with disclaimers is that an asset cannot be disclaimed if a benefit has already been taken from it. Further, there is no right to disclaim in part unless the will (or other instrument) gives power to do so.

Focus

- Disclaimers can be of use in simple cases.
- They came into their own in 1989 when everyone thought that the Finance Bill provisions outlawing deeds of variation (and, incidentally, appointments under two-year discretionary will trusts) would be enacted.
- When the threat passed, people got less excited about disclaimers.

Where more than two years have elapsed

12.16 Like a variation, a disclaimer, to be effective, must be made within two years. If more than two years have elapsed since the date of death, and no benefit has been taken from the asset concerned, there is a possible line of escape if it is desired to avoid a particular asset coming into a beneficiary's estate for IHT purposes. There is a separate provision (in *IHTA 1984, s 93*) that deals with settled property. Generally, a person given a right under a trust who has taken no benefit from it can disclaim that right whatever length of time has elapsed and the trust deed will be read as if he had never become entitled.

Example 12.5—Using a disclaimer

Anne's will gives to Benedict all the furniture in her house and a life interest in residue. The will provides that, subject to Benedict's life interest, the residue is to be divided equally between Benedict's two (adult) children. Benedict wants to take neither of the benefits under the will. He can, therefore, execute a disclaimer. The effect of the disclaimer will be:

- to pass the legacy of the furniture into residue, viz subject to the trust; and
- to treat the interest of Benedict's children as coming into effect immediately, ie to presume Benedict has died.

Accordingly, given notice of the disclaimer, the executors can simply distribute both the furniture and the residue of the estate direct to Benedict's two children.

DISCRETIONARY WILL TRUSTS

12.17 The provisions relating to deeds of variation and disclaimers are contained in *IHTA 1984, s 142*. There is a parallel, albeit different, provision in *IHTA 1984, s 144*. This provides that where a person has left all or part of his estate on discretionary will trusts, and the trustees make an appointment out of those trusts within two years after his death, the terms of the appointment are read back into the will with no exit charge under the discretionary trust regime (see **6.36–6.37**). This could apply where there was simply a nil rate band discretionary will trust or a discretionary will trust of residue. The terms of the appointment may be to give absolute interests, or they may create a life interest.

For deaths before 22 March 2006 it was vital that the trustees did not make their appointment within three months after the death; this was established by a Court of Appeal decision in a case called *Frankland v IRC* [1997] STC 1450. The appointment, therefore, must be made at least three months, but less than two years, after the death. For deaths on or after 22 March 2006, *IHTA 1984, s 144(3)* has generally cured the problem, with settled appointments, though not with outright gifts to a surviving spouse or to charity.

Legislation was included in *Finance (No 2) Act 2015* which in effect overrides *Frankland* in that, where an appointment is made within three months of date of death in favour of the deceased's surviving spouse or civil partner, it can be read back into the will and spouse exemption under *s 18* will be given.

This device is commonly used in circumstances where a testator does not know exactly what the circumstances as to assets and/or children are likely to be at the date of his death, but anticipates leaving a surviving spouse. He might choose to write the whole of his estate under a discretionary will trust giving power to the trustees to make an appointment before probate has been granted or residue ascertained. Given survivorship by his wife, the idea would be that, at the same time as putting in the inheritance tax account, the trustees would make and submit their appointment, which would set up either a nil rate band discretionary trust, or pass the to the surviving spouse, either for life or absolutely. In other words, there would be no IHT charge on the death because the will would be read as though the terms of the appointment were the provisions.

Capital gains tax

12.18 Note that, if the effect of the appointment is to create an absolute interest in residue on the part of the surviving spouse and there has been significant growth in the value of the assets since death, the whole of the growth will be assessed on the trustees at 20% from 6 April 2016, unless the disposal relates to residential property without the benefit of private residence relief, when the CGT rate remains at 28%. In other words, although assets are coming out of a discretionary trust, there can be no hold-over of the gain under *TCGA 1992, s 260* (see **8.6**) because *s 260* requires there to be a chargeable transfer and this is expressly precluded by *s 144*. By careful ordering of events, however, there may be a way round this problem: see the example below.

Example 12.6—Applying the '*chose* in action' principle

Suppose that Gerald dies on 1 June 2018 leaving an estate worth £600,000 at his death. His estate is left on a discretionary will trust. He is survived by his wife and three children. The trustees intend to make an appointment under *s 144*, creating a nil rate band discretionary trust of £325,000, the beneficiaries to include the widow, the three children and their future spouses and issue and to give residue to the widow absolutely. When they are considering this, a year or so after the death, the assets (all representing quoted shares) earmarked for the widow have appreciated by £100,000. If, therefore, they simply proceed with their plan, they will, on distributing the assets to her, make a gain of £100,000. Deducting the annual exemption of £5,850, this gives rise to a taxable gain of £94,150, which with tax @ 20% produces a tax bill of £18,830. The point is that, once the executors transfer Gerald's property to the trustees, the trustees' base cost and acquisition date are related back to the date of death. The CGT implications of any appointments by the trustees within two years after Gerald's death will follow normal principles (without any ability to hold over the gain, except where defined business assets); see the next paragraph.

We have said already that a beneficiary under a will has no right to specific assets, only the '*chose* in action' described at **2.19**. The beneficiary of the estate is the trustee, albeit to hold on the trusts provided in the will. The conventional order of things is that the PRs wind up the estate by distributing the £600,000 (now worth £700,000) to the trustees to use as they see fit. Suppose, on the other hand, that, before the distribution of the estate, the trustees make their appointment on the nil rate band trust and the gift of residue to the surviving spouse. HMRC helpfully take the view that, at that stage, nothing happens for CGT purposes. As and when the PRs appropriate the assets in the estate to the trustees and bring the administration to an end, the trustees are bound by their appointment. They hold assets worth £325,000 on the discretionary trusts, and the balance now worth £375,000 they hold for the widow as 'bare trustees'. Normally, it would be the acquisition date and acquisition cost of the trustees that would be related back to the date of death. In this case, however, it is the acquisition circumstances of the widow, who is the ultimate beneficiary, which are related back to the date of death. Accordingly, there is no chargeable gain, no tax to pay and she is simply treated as having inherited assets now worth £375,000, with a base cost of £275,000, ie an inherited gain of £100,000, but at least with time to plan the disposals in a tax-efficient manner.

IHTA 1984, SS 142 AND 144 INTERACTION

12.19 The decided case of *Russell v IRC* [1988] 1 WLR 834 established that you cannot vary the same property twice, ie you cannot have two bites at the same cherry. However, there is no reason in principle why, within the same estate, there should not be two or more variations.

Section 144 followed by s 142

12.20 An appointment by trustees under *IHTA 1984, s 144* can also, in principle, be the subject of a subsequent variation under *IHTA 1984, s 142* (see Example 12.7).

Example 12.7—Appointment followed by variation

Jeremy, a bachelor, left his entire estate subject to a discretionary trust. A year after Jeremy's death, the trustees make appointments within *s 144* passing the whole trust fund absolutely to Jeremy's three nieces. One of the nieces varies her entitlement, within two years after her uncle's death, into a discretionary trust for her own children. Subject to claiming the benefit of *s 142* in the deed of variation, the transfer into trust will not be a chargeable transfer made by the niece, but will be treated as a new will trust made by Jeremy. Hence, if the niece settlor were to die within seven years after the settlement was made, there would be no IHT implications of her death for the will trust. Note that, whilst the redirection is effective for IHT purposes, the niece will nonetheless be regarded as the settlor for income tax and CGT purposes. Accordingly, if the niece's children are minors, then any trust income arising during their minority will be assessable upon the parent settlor.

Section 142 followed by s 144

12.21 This situation envisages the original beneficiary, say the surviving spouse who is left the whole estate, varying her interest to create a nil rate band trust including herself as a beneficiary. If, subsequently, the assets concerned turn out to be worth rather more than originally envisaged, the trustees could, within two years of the death, appoint back to the widow the excess over the nil rate band reducing the chargeable value on death to nil (see Example 12.8).

Example 12.8—Variation followed by appointment

Malcolm dies in November 2018, leaving his estate worth £400,000 to his wife, Jill. Jill varies the will to put specific assets worth £325,000 into a nil rate band discretionary trust. It turns out six months later that the assets put into the trust are in fact worth £350,000. This produces an IHT liability in Malcolm's estate of £25,000 × 40% = £10,000. Given that Jill is a beneficiary under the trust, the trustees could, within two years after Malcolm's death, appoint £25,000 back to her to restore the *status quo* and to restrict the chargeable transfer on Malcolm's death to £325,000, viz the nil rate band.

IHTA 1984, S 143

12.22 By *IHTA 1984, s 143*, there is limited relief where the will sets out a wish that property be transferred by a legatee to other persons and the legatee does, within two years, carry out those wishes.

An attempt to push this rule to the limit was illustrated in the case of *Harding (executors of Loveday) v IRC* [1997] STC (SCD) 321. The will contained a discretionary trust for the widow and children. The executors appointed a fund to the widow. The Revenue argued that this was not an exempt transfer, being outside the terms of *IHTA 1984, s 144*. The executors appealed, wishing the appointment to be treated as a transfer under *IHTA 1984, s 143*. The Special Commissioner decided against the executors for three reasons:

(1) a legatee could include a trustee, but here the trustees were not legatees within *IHTA 1984, s 143*;

(2) an appointment of property was different from a transfer of it, so outside what *IHTA 1984, s 143* contemplated; and

(3) there was no evidence that the appointment was what the deceased had wanted, thus failing the requirement expressed in *IHTA 1984, s 143*.

In practice, a gift to a spouse that is quickly followed by an ongoing gift to a non-exempt beneficiary may well be challenged by HMRC.

Chapter 13

Stamp duties: trustees and personal representatives

SIGNPOSTS

- **Basics** – Stamp duties are charged on the acquisition of shares and marketable securities; stamp duty reserve tax is charged on agreements to acquire chargeable securities; and stamp duty land tax is charged on the acquisition of land (see **13.1**).
- **SDLT issues for trustees on transfers between funds** – Where there are two funds within the same settlement, an exchange of land between the funds, or the acquisition of land by one fund from another, will not trigger an SDLT charge (see **13.2**).
- **General SDLT issues for trustees** – On a purchase of land, the trustees are treated as any other purchaser and are responsible for any SDLT which may become payable (see **13.3–13.5**).
- **SDLT issues for personal representatives** – The transfer of shares or land to a beneficiary is exempt unless the beneficiary gives consideration (see **13.6–13.7**).

BUYING UK SHARES OR LAND – THE BASICS

13.1 Stamp duties have been with us since 1694. Following the introduction of stamp duty reserve tax (SDRT) in 1996, a major reform in 2003 means that stamp duties may be divided into three categories:

- stamp duty charged at 0.5% on the acquisition for value of shares and marketable securities (see Example 7.1);
- stamp duty reserve tax (SDRT) on agreements to acquire chargeable securities for value (largely through The Stock Exchange); and
- stamp duty land tax (SDLT) on the acquisition of UK land and buildings (see Example 13.2).

Trustees and personal representatives are purchasers of shares or land like anyone else, and must therefore understand both the liability to pay the tax and the compliance obligations necessary. Broadly speaking, stamp duty on shares at 0.5% and SDLT on land and buildings at rates in the range of 0%–15% must be paid within 30 days after the relevant transaction.

FA 2014, s 115 and *Sch 24* provide that purchases of shares admitted to trading in growth markets such as AIM will be exempt from stamp taxes as from 28 April 2014.

Purchases of land for values up to £125,000 escape a charge to SDLT, but this changed from 1 April 2016 in relation to purchases of 'additional property' – see below. A two-year temporary stamp duty relief period for first-time buyers, for purchases up to £250,000, was introduced from 25 March 2010, but this period expired on 25 March 2012. *Finance Act 2010, s 7* also introduced a rate of 5% for properties worth above £1 million as of 6 April 2011.

The *Finance Act 2012* introduced a new stamp duty rate of 7% for purchases of residential property where the consideration exceeds £2 million. The new rate applies on or after 22 March 2012, subject to a transitional rule to ensure that the new rate does not apply to contracts entered into before 22 March 2012 but completed on or after that date.

As a special anti-avoidance measure, where residential property is purchased by a non-natural person, an even higher rate of stamp duty of 15% was introduced as of 22 March 2012 for purchases of residential properties worth over £2 million. This was extended in *FA 2014* to all dwellings worth £500,000 or more from 6 April 2014. For this purpose, non-natural persons include companies, collective investment schemes and partnerships in which a non-natural person is a partner. This anti-avoidance measure is specifically targeted at the use of offshore structures. Exclusions apply to property developers and certain corporate trustees.

Finance Act 2013 included provisions which, in addition to the increase of SDLT to 15%, introduced an annual charge (called annual tax on enveloped dwellings or ATED) of a rate between £3,500 and £140,000 (rising to £218,000 from 1 April 2015) to apply to 'non-natural persons' owning high-value property from April 2013. These rates will increase by 50% above inflation – more detail about ATED can be found in *Capital Gains Tax 2018/19* (Bloomsbury Professional).

Contrary to announcements in the 2012 Budget, the draft legislation contained within *FA 2013* does not include non-UK resident trustees in the definition of a 'non-natural person', which directly own relevant UK properties. Classic trust/company structures, however, are caught.

FA 2014 changed SDLT rates on purchases of residential property with effect from 4 December 2014. SDLT now is payable at the rate listed below on the proportion of the purchase price that falls within each band rather than at a single rate on the whole transaction value.

The rate and thresholds were also amended as part of this reform and are:

Purchase price of property (£)	*Rate*
0–125,000	0%
125,001–250,000	2%
250,001–925,000	5%
925,001–1,500,000	10%
1,500,001 and over	12%

Finance Act 2016 provided that from 1 April 2016 an additional 3% is applied to the current SDLT rate for the purchase of additional residential properties above £40,000, such as buy to let properties and second homes. The result of this is that SDLT will be charged at 3% on the first £125,000, if the purchase price exceeds £40,000.

These rules also present problems for trusts and their beneficiaries. Beneficiaries who have a life interest or interest in possession in a property are liable to the surcharge if they purchase a property, for example a second home, a buy-to-let property or a holiday home. For trustees who are purchasing a new main residence for a beneficiary to occupy before having sold the old residence, the additional 3% rate will initially be payable, but can be reclaimed by the trustees if the old residence is sold within 36 months. Moreover, where there is no interest in possession in the property, purchases by trustees are liable to the higher rates, whatever the circumstances. This includes all discretionary trusts and accumulation and maintenance trusts, where a beneficiary has not yet acquired an interest in possession.

Finance Act 2016 introduced provisions which reformed the SDLT charging provisions for non-residential property. From 17 March 2016 SDLT for purchases of freehold, assignments of existing leases and upfront premium payments on new leaseholds, is charged at the rate on the portion of the purchase price which falls within each band.

Purchase price of property (£)	*Rate*
0–150,000	0%
150,001–250,000	2%
250,001 and over	5%

For leasehold transactions on or after 17 March 2016 a new 2% rate for rent paid under a non-residential lease will be introduced where the net present value of the rent is above £5 million. The new rate bands and thresholds for rent paid under a lease are:

Net present value of rent (£)	*Rate*
0–150,000	0%
150,001–5,000,000	1%
5,000,001 and over	2%

As announced at the Autumn Budget 2017, legislation in *Finance Act 2019* will reduce the time limit purchasers (including trustees) have to file a SDLT return and pay the tax due from 30 days to 14 days. The new time limit will apply to transactions with an effective date on or after 1 March 2019.

The government is currently consulting on the introduction of a 1% surcharge for non-UK residents who are purchasing property in the UK.

SDLT ISSUES FOR TRUSTEES

Transactions and transfers between funds

13.2 A point has been cleared up by *FA 2006* and by assurance from HMRC Stamp Taxes. This concerns the case where, say, within a settlement there are two funds and there is either an exchange of land as between funds or acquisition of land by one fund from another. While there is a land transaction, is there chargeable consideration? In the case where the beneficiary has to give consent, *FA 2006, s 165* confirms that there is no chargeable consideration, and HMRC have now said that in all other cases there never was chargeable consideration, going back to 1 December 2003.

Example 13.1—Share purchase

Caesar owns 100 shares in Brutus Ltd, which is a private company manufacturing knives. He is also a beneficiary of the Caesar Family Discretionary Settlement, which was set up by his grandfather in 1982.

The trustees decide to acquire Caesar's 100 shares in Brutus Ltd for full market value of £50,000. Stamp duty at 0.5% of £250 will be payable within 30 days. Note that there is no general market value rule. Prior to *FA 2008*, there was no *de minimis* provision either (as in SDLT). However, for transfers after 12 March 2008 (which are not stamped before 19 March 2008), there is no stamp duty on transfers of shares or marketable securities if the sale proceeds are £1,000 or less and the transfer document is certified at £1,000 or less (*FA 1999, Sch 13, para 3A*).

Example 13.2—Inter-fund exchange of land

Within the Caesar Family Discretionary Settlement there are two funds, 'Casius' and 'Decimus'. There is an exchange of real property within the funds (without any beneficiary involvement), with any balance of market value made up by cash. The exchange has no implications for either CGT or SDLT purposes.

SDLT issues for trustees on the purchase of land

13.3 On the sale of land to a trust, the trustees are treated as the purchaser of a chargeable interest in land (*FA 2003, s 47(4), (5)* and *Sch 16, para 4*). The 'responsible trustees' have all the responsibilities of a purchaser, viz for payment of any tax and submission of a land transaction return or self certificate.

Example 13.3—Land purchase

The trustees of the Caesar Family Interest in Possession Settlement decide to buy a flat in London for £600,000 for Caesar to occupy. They borrow £300,000 and pay the balance in cash. The existence of the mortgage does not affect the SDLT liability. The trustees calculated that SDLT will be £20,000 (0% on the first £125,000, 2% on the next £125,000 and 5% on the final £350,000). Unfortunately Caesar decides sometime between exchange and completion that he does not want to move from Leeds, where he currently lives, to London and he therefore continues to occupy the flat he owns personally. The trustees therefore will be liable to the additional 3% charge which will increase the SDLT charge from £20,000 to £38,000 (3% on the first £125,000, 5% on the next £125,000 and 8% on the remaining £350,000).

A transfer of land to a trust for no consideration in money or money's worth is exempt from SDLT (*Stamp Duty (Exempt Instruments) Regulations 1987*).

Focus

If the property transferred is subject to a mortgage, the value transferred represents the outstanding mortgage debt, and SDLT may become payable.

Example 13.4—Transfer of property subject to a mortgage (I)

Cornelia wishes to set up a discretionary settlement for her daughter Julia and Julia's children, and to transfer a buy-to-let a property to the trustees. The property's market value is £300,000, but is subject to a mortgage of £260,000.

Generally, a transfer to a trust for no money or money's worth is exempt from SDLT; however, here, as the property is subject to a mortgage, the value transferred represents the outstanding mortgage debt, and SDLT of £10,800 (3% on the first £125,000, 5% on the next £125,000 and 8% on the final £10,000) will become payable by the trustees. As the trust is a discretionary trust the additional 3% rate becomes payable.

Example 13.5—Transfer of property subject to a mortgage (II)

Julia does not own a property and she currently lives in rented accommodation. Cornelia therefore might want to consider setting up an interest in possession trust with Julia as the life tenant.

If Julia moves into the property, the higher SDLT rate will not apply. The SDLT charge therefore will be £3,000 (0% on the first £125,000, 2% on the next £125,000 and 8% on the final £10,000).

If Cornelia is not comfortable with giving Julia a right to occupy the property, she could still opt for a discretionary trust. The trustees will appoint Julia a revocable life interest in the trust fund immediately before the transfer. Once the property is transferred and all SDLT charges have been paid, the trustees could exercise their power to revoke the life interest.

Who are the 'responsible trustees'?

13.4 The 'responsible trustees' in relation to a land transaction are defined as the persons who are trustees at the effective date of the transaction and any person who subsequently becomes a trustee (*FA 2003, Sch 16, para 5*).

Where the trustees are liable to pay the tax, interest on unpaid tax, a penalty or interest on the penalty (or to make a payment because of an excessive repayment of tax) monies can be recovered from any one or more of the responsible trustees. No penalty or interest on the penalty can be recovered from a person who does not become a responsible trustee until after the date of the transaction.

Filling in the land transaction return: the 'relevant trustees'

13.5 A land transaction return may be delivered to the Land Registry by any one or more of the trustees who are 'responsible trustees' in relation to the transaction. The trustees who make the return are defined as the 'relevant trustees'. The declaration confirming that the land transaction return is complete and true must be signed by all the relevant trustees.

That is, the trustees between them can appoint one or more of their number to deal with the compliance aspects of the acquisition of land or buildings.

Example 13.6—Compliance

The trustees of the Joseph settlement buy Blackacre on 1 July 2019 for £500,000. The SDLT liability is £30,000. The trustees appoint two of their number to deal with compliance, ie submission of a land transaction return and payment of the tax within 30 days.

However, if those two trustees do not fulfil their obligations, the tax, interest on unpaid tax (currently running at 3.25%) and a penalty or interest on the penalty can be recovered from any one or more of the responsible trustees. If the return is less than 12 months late, the maximum penalty will be the *lower* of the amount of stamp duty due and £300. However, the maximum penalty increases to the *higher* of the amount of stamp duty due and £300 if the return is more than 12 months late. In some circumstances, the stamp duty penalty may be reduced.

Moreover, if, let us say, Raymond is appointed as a trustee of the settlement on 1 August 2019, Raymond is personally liable for the tax and interest on tax: only in respect of a penalty or interest on the penalty can HMRC Stamp Taxes not recover that from him. An incoming trustee needs to be aware of this.

Focus:

- A trustee of a discretionary trust purchasing a residential property will be subject to the higher rate of SDLT, even if a beneficiary occupies the property. The only way to avoid such charges is giving the beneficiary a revocable life interest in the property – this assumes he does not own another property which he claims as his private residence.
- A trustee of a life interest trust escapes the higher rate if the purchase is to provide a main residence for the beneficiary. The beneficiary will be treated as the purchaser.

- When the beneficiary is under the age of 18, the child's parent will be treated as the beneficiary.

SDLT ISSUES FOR PERSONAL REPRESENTATIVES

Share transactions

13.6 The transfer of shares by personal representatives to a beneficiary may be certified as exempt from stamp duty by certificating the relevant stock transfer form with the appropriate category under the *Stamp Duty (Exempt Instruments) Regulations 1987*:

- Specific Gifts: Category B;
- Specific Intestate Property: Category C;
- Satisfaction of General Legacies and Intestacies: Category D; or
- Transfers of Residue: Category E.

Land transactions

13.7 The transfer of land to a beneficiary entitled will be exempt from SDLT unless the beneficiary gives consideration (*FA 2003, Sch 3, para 3A*). Interestingly, in this case assumption of secured debt by the beneficiary does not constitute consideration (whereas it does in a trust case). For land transactions before 12 March 2008, a transfer document is self-certified with form SDLT60, which is provided by the beneficiary to the Land Registry to enable his re-registration as beneficial owner. Where the transfer takes place on or after 12 March 2008, *FA 2008* has dispensed with the need for form SDLT60; re-registration is procured by delivering to the Land Registry the assent by the personal representatives, together with Land Registry transfer form TR1.

The SDLT rules in *Finance Act 2016* also have an impact on beneficiaries of estates.

If a beneficiary inherits a major interest in a dwelling, that beneficiary is not treated as having a major interest in the inherited dwelling in the three-year period beginning with the date of inheritance, provided that the beneficiary's share in the interest does not exceed 50% (*Finance Act 2003, Sch 4ZA, para 15(1) and (2)*). If, at any time in that three-year period, the beneficiary's share in the interest exceeds 50%, the beneficiary is treated as having a major interest in the inherited dwelling from that date (*Finance Act 2003, Sch 4ZA, para 15(3)*).

A beneficiary's share in a major interest exceeds 50% if any of the following conditions are met:

- The beneficiary is beneficially entitled as a tenant in common to more than half the interest.
- The beneficiary and the beneficiary's spouse or civil partner taken together are beneficially entitled as tenants in common to more than half the interest.
- The beneficiary and the beneficiary's spouse or civil partner are beneficially entitled as joint tenants to the interest and there is no more than one other joint tenant who is so entitled. (*Finance Act 2003, Sch 4ZA, para 15(4)*).

Consequently, if a beneficiary does not dispose of his interest in an inherited property within three years of his inheritance, the higher rates will apply on the beneficiary's purchase of another dwelling, unless that purchase is to replace an existing only or main residence. This provision was added following consultation to give beneficiaries of estates a breathing space in which to sell inherited property.

For these purposes, 'inheritance' is defined as the acquisition of an interest in or towards satisfaction of an entitlement under or in relation to the will of a deceased person, or on intestacy (*Finance Act 2003, Sch 4ZA, para 15(5)*). HMRC accepts that an interest in an unadministered estate (which is generally considered to be a chose in action) is not a major interest in land. Therefore, it appears that the date a beneficiary acquires an interest in any land that comprises part of the estate will be the date on which that interest is transferred or appropriated to him or (if earlier) when the administration of the estate is completed (on the residue being ascertained) and the personal representatives hold the assets on bare trust for those entitled.

The definition of 'inheritance' uses the same wording as the exemption from SDLT for assents and appropriations by personal representatives where there is no consideration other than the assumption of a secured debt (*Finance Act 2003, Sch 3, para 3A*).

Example 13.7— Entitlements under a will: stamp duty compliance

Under the terms of her father's will, Fiona is entitled to shares worth £100,000. This is a specific testamentary gift, and the transfer forms are certified by the executors with Category B of the *1987 Regulations*, enabling Fiona to be re-registered in the books of the relevant companies.

Her brother Gerald is, as the residuary beneficiary, entitled to Black Horse Farm. The transfer will not be subject to SDLT under Category E of the Regulations.

Index

[All references are to paragraph number]